C. (Charles) Stedman

The History of the Origin, Progress, and Termination of the American War

Vol. II.

C. (Charles) Stedman

The History of the Origin, Progress, and Termination of the American War
Vol. II.

ISBN/EAN: 9783337010782

Printed in Europe, USA, Canada, Australia, Japan

Cover: Foto ©ninafisch / pixelio.de

More available books at **www.hansebooks.com**

HISTORY

OF THE

AMERICAN WAR.

VOLUME THE SECOND.

THE

HISTORY

OF THE

ORIGIN, PROGRESS, AND TERMINATION

OF THE

AMERICAN WAR.

By C. *STEDMAN*,

WHO SERVED UNDER SIR W. HOWE, SIR H. CLINTON, AND
THE MARQUIS CORNWALLIS.

IN TWO VOLUMES.

VOL. II.

LONDON:

PRINTED FOR THE AUTHOR;

AND SOLD BY J. MURRAY, FLEET-STREET; J. DEBRETT, PICCADILLY; AND
J. KERBY, CORNER OF WIGMORE-STREET, CAVENDISH-SQUARE.

1794.

CONTENTS.

CHAP. XXI.

Page

EFFECTS of the Surrender of Saratoga—Bills brought into Parliament for Reconciliation and Peace with the Americans—Treaties entered into between the French King and the Thirteen revolted Colonies—Commiſſioners appointed for ſettling the Differences between the Mother-country and her Colonies—Rupture between Great Britain and France—Fate of Burgoyne's Army—The Commiſſioners for Peace arrive in America, and enter on the Execution of their Office. — 1

CHAP. XXII.

The Evacuation of Philadelphia—General Waſhington prepares to impede and haraſs the Britiſh Troops in their Retreat—Sir H. Clinton purſues his March to New York by Sandy Hook—Diſpoſition of the American Army—And of the Britiſh—Battle of Freehold Court Houſe in the County of Monmouth—The Britiſh Army arrives at New York. — 14

CHAP. XXIII.

Page

The French Fleet sets sail from Toulon to North America—Thither also a British Fleet sets sail under Vice-Admiral Byron—The Count D'Estaing, missing the British Army in Philadelphia, comes to an Anchor off New York—The Harbour of this Place defended by a small Fleet, under Lord Howe—D'Estaing sets sail to the Southward—but changes his Course, and arrives at Rhode Island—American Preparations for an Attempt on Rhode Island—frustrated—Naval Operations—Lord Howe resigns the Command of the Fleet to Admiral Gambier. 25

CHAP. XXIV.

A particular Account of the Progress and Issue of the American Attempt on Rhode Island, already generally mentioned. 34

CHAP. XXV.

Discontents and Clamours in the American States—Riots between the American and French Seamen at Boston—and at Charlestown, South Carolina—Expedition to Buzzard's Bay—Expeditions against Little Egg Harbour, a noted Rendezvous for Privateers—The Weather this Summer uncommonly boisterous in the Atlantic Ocean—Dispersion and Fate of the Fleet under Admiral Byron—The Admiral struggles in vain against adverse Fortune—The Count D'Estaing sets sail to the West Indies. 38

CONTENTS.

CHAP. XXVI.

Page

Expedition to the West Indies under the Command of General Grant—The British Commissioners return to England—Review of their Proceedings—Expedition against Georgia—Reduction of Savannah. — — — 48

CHAP. XXVII.

War between the Americans and Indians—War between France and England—Channel Fleet commanded by Admiral Keppel—Engagement between the French and English Fleets—Irreconcileable Difference between the Admirals Keppel and Palliser—Inflamed by the Zeal of their respective Partizans—War in the East Indies. — — — 73

CHAP. XXVIII.

General Alarm throughout the British West India Islands—Quieted by the Departure of Count d'Estaing to Hispaniola—Reduction of Sunbury in Georgia—Colonel Campbell's Expedition to Augusta—Circuit for the Encouragement of the Loyalists performed by Colonel Hamilton—Colonel Hamilton quits Augusta and returns to Savannah—Attempt of General Lincoln to straiten the British Quarters—Frustrated by Colonel Prevost—Unsuccessful Attempt of General Prevost on Charlestown—General Prevost retires from Charlestown, and takes post at John's Island. — — — — 102

CHAP.

CONTENTS.

CHAP. XXIX.

Page

General Prevoſt departs from John's Iſland to Savannah—Succeeded in the Command at John's Iſland by Lieutenant Colonel Maitland—Britiſh Troops under Colonel Maitland attacked by General Lincoln—The Americans repulſed—General Prevoſt having eſtabliſhed a Poſt in the Iſland of Port Royal, retires with the reſt of the Army to Georgia. — — 115

CHAP. XXX.

The Count d'Eſtaing ſets ſail for the American Continent—and arrives on the Coaſt of Georgia—Efforts Military and Naval for the Preſervation of Savannah—Count d'Eſtaing ſummons Savannah to ſurrender to the Arms of his Moſt Chriſtian Majeſty—General Prevoſt ſuccoured by Colonel Maitland—The combined Armies of France and America beſiege Savannah—attack the Britiſh Lines—repulſed with conſiderable Loſs—raiſe the Siege—The Campaign to the ſouthward of North America concluded—Campaign in other Parts of the American Continent ſpent in deſultory Operations—Naval Operations of Sir George Collier. — — — 121

CHAP. XXXI.

Reduction of two ſtrong Poſts on Hudſon's River—Expedition againſt Connecticut — Ravages—Murmurs in Connecticut—Fort Stoney Point ſurpriſed by General Wayne—Stoney Point evacuated by the Americans—Again poſſeſſed by the Britiſh—Britiſh Settlement in Penobſcot—attacked in vain by the Americans

Page

Americans—Reinforcement brought to the British Army by Admiral Arbuthnot, who succeeds Sir George Collier in the Command of the Navy—American Incursions into the Country of the Indians—Incursions of the Indians into the American Settlements. — — — — 140

CHAP. XXXII.

The Confederacy against Great Britain joined by Spain—French Attack on Jersey—repelled—Naval Transactions—The combined Fleets of France and Spain threaten an Invasion of Great Britain—Engagement between Captain Paul Jones and the Convoy of a British Fleet from the Baltic—Blockade of Gibraltar—Incursion of the Americans into West Florida—West Florida reduced by the Spaniards—The Spaniards attack the British Logwood-cutters in Honduras—Reduction of the Spanish Fort Omoa, the Key of the Bay of Honduras—Protection afforded to the British Commerce—General Retrospect of British Affairs at the Conclusion of 1779. — — 156

CHAP. XXXIII.

Expedition under Sir Henry Clinton to South Carolina—Fortifications of Charlestown described—Garrison of Charlestown—Siege and Reduction of Charlestown—Incursion of the Spaniards into West Florida—Consequences of the Fall of Charlestown—Three new Expeditions set on foot by the British Commander—His Address to the Inhabitants of South Carolina—Its Effect—Defeat of the American Colonel Burford—Disposition of the British Troops in South Carolina—Administration of

CONTENTS.

Page

Earl Cornwallis there—Counter-revolution among those who had submitted to the Power of Britain on the Fall of Charlestown—Detachment from Washington's Army sent into North Carolina—Movements of the American Colonel Sumpter—His Attempt on the British Post on Rocky Point. — 176

CHAP. XXXIV.

Earl Cornwallis sets out from Charlestown to Camden—Action between the Americans under General Gates, and the British under Earl Cornwallis, near Camden—The American Force under Colonel Sumpter surprised by Colonel Tarleton—Perfidy of the Americans—Restrained by Examples of Severity—Lord Cornwallis marches into North Carolina—Defeat and Fall of Major Ferguson. — — — 204

CHAP. XXXV.

The Americans under Colonel Clarke make an Attack on Augusta—Retreat of Clarke—The Detachment under Major Ferguson attacked and overpowered by American Mountaineers—Lord Cornwallis falls back to South Carolina—Colonel Tarleton checks the Inroads of the American Partizan Marion—Junction of the American Forces under Sumpter, Clarke, and Brannen—Action at Blackstock's Hill between Sumpter and Tarleton. — — — 219

CHAP. XXXVI.

Effects of the Defeat and Fall of Major Ferguson—General Gates resigns the Command of the Southern American Army

to

Page

to General Greene—Danger arising to the British Garrison in New York from the extreme Rigour of the Winter—Measures taken for the Defence of New York—Unsuccessful Attempt to establish the royal Standard in the Jerseys. — 232

CHAP. XXXVII.

The Americans dislodged from Springfield, and that Town destroyed—A French Armament arrives at Rhode Island—A Scheme formed by one of General Washington's Officers, Arnold, for delivering an important Post into the Hands of the British Army—Adventure and Fate of the British Adjutant-General Major André—A general Exchange of Prisoners—The Troops on both Sides retire into Winter Quarters. 243

CHAP. XXXVIII.

Transactions in Europe and the West Indies—Successes of the British Fleet under Admiral Rodney—Relief of Gibraltar—Growing Differences between Great Britain and Holland—Armed Neutrality, or Association among Neutral Maritime Powers, for the Purpose of establishing the Doctrine that Free Ships make Free Goods—Suspension of the Treaties between Great Britain and Holland—Naval Transactions—Commercial Treaty between America and Holland—War on the Part of Great Britain against the Dutch. — 255

CHAP. XXXIX.

French Attempt on the Island of Jersey—defeated—Naval Exertions of both France and Britain—Relief of Gibraltar—

 Capture

Page

Capture of the Dutch Island St. Eustatius—And of Demarary and Issequibo, Dutch Settlements on the Spanish Main—Fruitless Attempt of the French on St. Lucie—The Island of Tobago surrendered to the French. — — 274

CHAP. XL.

Reduction of Pensacola by the Spaniards—The combined Fleets of France and Spain, to the Amount of seventy Sail, threaten Destruction to the marine Force of England—The British Admiral, with twenty-one Ships of the Line, prudently retires into Torbay—where the Enemy do not think it advisable to attack him—Causes why the Combined Fleets enjoyed a temporary Superiority over that of Great Britain—Action between a British and a Dutch Fleet, near the Dogger Bank—British Armament sent against the Dutch Settlement at the Cape of Good Hope—attacked by the French Admiral Suffrein—The Dutch Garrison at the Cape reinforced by the French—Commodore Johnstone makes Prizes of four Dutch East Indiamen—The British Armament under General Meadows sails for the East Indies—Invasion of the Carnatic by Hyder Ally—Defeat and Disaster of a British Detachment under Colonel Baillie—Ravages committed in the Carnatic by Hyder Ally—The Command of the British Army in the Presidency of Madras committed to Sir Eyre Coote—Operations of the British Fleet in India. — — — 290

CHAP. XLI.

Disaffection to Great Britain of the Southern Colonies—The British Army under Lord Cornwallis joined by a large Reinforcement

Page

ment under General Leslie—Action at the Cowpens, between General Morgan and Colonel Tarleton—Colonel Tarleton defeated—Consequences of Colonel Tarleton's Defeat—The Army under Lord Cornwallis crosses the River Catawba—Lord Cornwallis, joined by the other Division of the Army under Colonel Webster, pursues General Morgan—A Junction formed between the two Divisions of the American Army—General Greene driven out of North Carolina—The Royal Standard erected at Hillsborough—General Greene, again crossing the Dan, re-enters North Carolina—Lord Cornwallis falls back from Hillsborough, and takes a new Position—Effects of this retrograde Movement—Action near Guildford between Lord Cornwallis and General Greene. — — 316

CHAP. XLII.

Proclamation by Lord Cornwallis—The British Army arrives in the Vicinity of Wilmington—General Greene marches against Lord Rawdon at Camden—Embarrassment of Lord Cornwallis—Lord Cornwallis determines to march through North Carolina into Virginia—Lord Rawdon resolves to attack the Camp of General Greene at Hobkirk's Hill—Fort Watson surrenders to the Americans—A Detachment under Colonel Watson joins Lord Rawdon at Camden—Lord Rawdon, after various Efforts to bring General Greene to an Engagement, retires from Camden—and proceeds to Monk's Corner—British Outposts reduced by the Americans—Augusta surrendered to the Americans. — — — 350

CHAP. XLIII.

Page

State of the British Army at Ninety-six—The Siege of Ninety-six raised—Lord Rawdon, having arrived at Ninety-six, pursues General Greene—Lord Rawdon, with Half his Force, marches to the Congaree—Retires to Orangeburgh—Hostilities suspended by the intense Heat of the Season—Lord Rawdon, on account of his Health, embarks for Europe —Action between Colonel Stuart and General Greene, near the Eutaw Springs—Victory in this Action claimed by both Parties. — — — 364

CHAP. XLIV.

Operations of the British Army in Virginia under the Command of General Philips—Destruction of American Stores—Death of General Philips—Junction between the Armies under Lord Cornwallis and General Arnold—Charlotteville surprised by Colonel Tarleton—Stratagem practised with Success by Colonel Simcoe on Baron Steuben—Unfavourable Aspect of American Affairs—Apprehension of Sir Henry Clinton for the Safety of New York—Lord Cornwallis crosses James River, and retires to Portsmouth—Evacuates Portsmouth, and concentrates his Force at York and Glocester—Junction of the Forces of Washington and Rochambeau—Naval Operations—The French Fleet under Count de Grasse arrives in the Chesapeak—Partial Action between the Count de Grasse and Admiral Graves—New London taken by General Arnold. — — — 382

CONTENTS.

CHAP. XLV.

Page

The Confederate Armies arrive at Williamsburgh in Virginia—Lord Cornwallis vindicated from the Charges of Colonel Tarleton—The Combined Armies encamp before York Town—York Town regularly invested—Surrendered to General Washington—Efforts of Sir H. Clinton for the Relief of Lord Cornwallis—Recapture of St. Eustatius—Successful Cruize of Admiral Kempenfeldt. — — 405

CHAP. XLVI.

Effects of the Capture of Lord Cornwallis's Army—Meeting of Parliament—Siege of Fort St. Philip's in the Island of Minorca—Capitulation of Fort St. Philip's—Reduction of the Island of St. Christopher's—General Carleton appointed Commander in Chief in America instead of Sir Henry Clinton—Naval Engagement between Admiral Rodney and the Count de Grasse—Prosperity of British Affairs in the East Indies—Conduct of the new Administration—Repulse and Discomfiture of the Spaniards and French before Gibraltar—Relief of Gibraltar. — — — 420

CONTENTS.

CHAP. XLV.

[illegible]

CHAP. XLVI.

[illegible] —Siege of Fort St. Philip's in the Island of Minorca— [illegible] of Fort St. Philip's— [illegible] Island of St. Christopher's— [illegible] Carleton appointed Commander in Chief in America instead of Sir Henry Clinton— [illegible] Admiral Rodney and the Count de Grasse— [illegible] Affairs in the East Indies— [illegible] of the Spaniards and French before Gibraltar—Relief of Gibraltar. [illegible]

HISTORY
OF THE
AMERICAN WAR.

CHAP. XXI.

Effects of the Surrender of Saratoga—Bills brought into Parliament for Reconciliation and Peace with the Americans—Treaties entered into between the French King and the Thirteen revolted Colonies—Commissioners appointed for settling the Differences between the Mother-country and her Colonies—Rupture between Great Britain and France—Fate of Burgoyne's Army—The Commissioners for Peace arrive in America, and enter on the Execution of their Office.

CHAP. XXI. 1778. Effects of the surrender of Saratoga.

THE surrender of Saratoga forms a memorable æra in the history of the American war. Although the success of the British arms had not been so brilliant, nor the progress made in repressing the spirit of revolt so considerable, as either the magnitude of the force employed under sir William Howe, or the military character of that general, gave reason to expect; still, upon the whole, until the unfortunate expedition from Canada, the advantages that had been gained were on the side of Great Britain.

 Whenever

CHAP. XXI. 1778.

Whenever the British and American armies had been opposed to each other in the field, the superiority of the former was conspicuous in every thing, and, in general, even in numbers. The Americans themselves, impressed with an opinion of their own inferiority, were dispirited; and it was with reluctance that they ever attempted to engage the British troops upon equal, or even nearly equal, terms. But so uncommon an event as the capture of a whole army of their enemies animated them with fresh ardour, invigorated the exertions of the congress, lessened in the mind of the American soldier the high opinion which he had entertained of British valour and discipline, and inspired him with a juster confidence in himself.

The consequences, however, which this event produced in Europe were of still greater moment. In Great Britain the most sanguine expectations had been raised from the Canada expedition, the rapid success of which, in its first stages, seemed to promise the most fortunate issue. A junction of the northern army with that at New York was confidently expected; and it was hoped that by this junction a decisive blow would be given to the rebellion, by cutting off the northern from the middle and southern colonies. The British nation, elevated with such hopes, and encouraged to cherish them by the first intelligence from Canada, which brought an account of the almost instantaneous reduction of Ticonderoga, and the destruction or capture of the provincial naval force in Lake Champlain, suffered proportionate disappointment upon hearing of the ultimate failure of the expedition and the total loss of the army. But if the disappointment of the nation was great, that of the ministry was still greater; and in a fit of despondency, it would seem, they determined, for the sake of peace, and of getting rid of a troublesome and expensive war, to give up every thing for which they had originally contended. To the surprise of all, and to the no small mortification of those who had hitherto zealously supported

the

CHAP. XXI.

1778.

Bills brought into parliament for reconciliation and peace with the Americans.

the meafures of adminiftration, the minifter in the month of February introduced two bills into the houfe of commons, which were paffed through both houfes of parliament with great difpatch, and received the royal affent on the eleventh of March. By the firft of thefe the duty payable on tea imported into America, which was the original caufe of difpute, was repealed, and a legiflative declaration was made, that the king and parliament of Great Britain would not in future impofe any tax or duty whatfoever payable in the colonies, except only fuch as fhould be neceffary for the regulation of trade, and in fuch cafe that the nett produce of the duty fo impofed fhould be applied to the particular ufe of that colony in which it fhould be collected, in the fame manner as other duties collected under the authority of the affemblies. By the other of thefe acts, authority was given to the king to appoint commiffioners with full powers to treat, confult, and agree, with any affemblies of men whatfoever in America, and even with individuals, concerning any grievances exifting in the government of any of the colonies, or in the laws of Great Britain extending to them, concerning any contributions to be furnifhed by the colonies, and concerning any other regulations which might be for the common good of both countries; with a provifo, however, that fuch agreement fhould not be binding until ratified by parliament. But in the following inftances the commiffioners were to be invefted with abfolute power, exercifeable however according to their difcretion, for proclaiming a ceffation of hoftilities by fea and land, for opening an intercourfe with the mother-country, for fufpending the operation of all acts of parliament relating to the North American colonies paffed fince the tenth of February 1763, and for granting pardons to all defcriptions of perfons.

Never perhaps was there a moment during the whole of the Britifh hiftory, in which the nation had greater caufe of mortification than at the time of paffing thefe acts: And it will be difficult to de-

 fend

CHAP. XXI. 1778.

fend the ministers of that day against the imputation of either want of wisdom or want of firmness. If what was now proposed was a right measure, it ought to have been adopted at first, and before the sword was drawn: On the other hand, if the claims of the mother-country over her colonies were originally worth contending for, the strength and resources of the nation were not yet so far exhausted as to justify ministers in relinquishing them without a further struggle. But such was the disappointment in consequence of the failure of the expedition from Canada, and so great an alteration had it produced in the opinions of those who directed the councils of the nation, that the concessions which had been repeatedly refused to the petitions of the colonists were now to be offered to them with arms in their hands; and they were even to be courted and intreated to accept of them.

This moment of despondence, humiliation, and debasement, was seized by the court of Versailles to give a fatal blow to the over-grown power of her rival. Ever since the commencement of the rebellion the American colonists had been encouraged in their revolt by secret assurances of assistance from the court of France, and by supplies of money, arms, and ammunition, clandestinely conveyed to them. The French were in the mean time making preparations; and their original design was, probably, to abstain from an open declaration, until Great Britain and her colonies had mutually weakened each other in their civil contention. But the disaster which happened to general Burgoyne's army, and the consequent conciliatory measures about to be adopted by the British cabinet, at last obliged them to throw off the masque. They knew that the Americans, notwithstanding their success at Saratoga, still laboured under very great difficulties; and that, for want of internal resources, whilst their foreign trade was almost annihilated by the British cruisers, it was impossible for them, without assistance, to keep a respectable army in the field for any length of time; and they dreaded, lest, under

such

ſuch unpromiſing circumſtances, they ſhould be induced to accept the very liberal terms which they knew were to be offered to them*. To prevent this, and to defeat the effect of the conciliatory meaſures about to be adopted by the Britiſh cabinet, two treaties were now entered into between the French king and the thirteen revolted colonies; one of commerce, and another of defenſive alliance; which were finally ſigned at Paris the ſixth of February in the preſent year, by the chevalier Gerard, in behalf of the French king, and by Dr. Franklin, Silas Deane, and Arthur Lee, in behalf of the American colonies. The firſt of theſe, as its title imports, was intended to regulate the commerce to be carried on between the countries of the contracting parties; and the principal object of the other was to ſecure the ſovereignty and independence of the revolted colonies; it being ſtipulated, that if a war in conſequence of this treaty ſhould break out between Great Britain and France, the two contracting parties ſhould mutually aſſiſt each other according to their power and ability, and that peace ſhould not be made without the conſent of both, nor until the ſovereignty and independence of the colonies, both in matters of government and commerce, ſhould be either expreſly or tacitly acknowledged by the king of Great Britain.

CHAP. XXI. 1778. Treaties entered into between the French king and the thirteen revolted colonies.

A meaſure of ſuch conſequence could not, even in France, eſcape the vigilance and penetration of the lord viſcount Stormont, the Britiſh ambaſſador at Paris, who, with the utmoſt purity of morals, and even in the midſt of literary purſuits, knew how to eſtimate the friendly profeſſions, and to penetrate the real views and deſigns, of ambitious courts. Intelligence of the engagements between France and America was quickly tranſmitted by the viſcount to the Britiſh ministry;

* Before the receſs of parliament for the Chriſtmas holidays it was known that new and very liberal terms of reconciliation were to be offered to the Americans. And on the 24th of December the treaties between France and the revolted colonies were firſt agreed upon, although they were not formally ſigned till the 6th of February following.

CHAP. XXI. 1778.

ministry; and this was the cause why the conciliatory bills were passed with so much dispatch through the two houses of parliament. It was, perhaps, hoped that they might reach America before the congress had received intelligence of what had been done in France, but certainly before they had ratified the new engagements entered into by their deputies; and, that they might be apprized of what was intended, even before it was completed, rough draughts of the bills, as soon as they were introduced into parliament, were immediately dispatched to the commander in chief in America, to be forwarded to the congress. The conciliatory acts of parliament being passed, and a commission made out under the great seal, the earl of Carlisle, William Eden, and George Johnstone, esquires (who, with the admiral and the general commanding in America, or, in case of the absence of the latter, sir Henry Clinton, were the persons named in the commission, and entrusted with the execution of the powers for settling the differences between the mother-country and her colonies), sailed for America on the twenty-second of April.

Commissioners appointed for settling the differences between the mother-country and her colonies.

Rupture between Great Britain and France.

Somewhat more than a month previous to the sailing of the commissioners, the French ambassador, by order of his court, formally notified to that of London the nature of the engagements entered into between his sovereign and the American colonies, and some days after quitted London and returned to France, about the same time that the British ambassador quitted Paris. This notification was considered as amounting to a declaration of war; and although war was not actually declared, both kingdoms vigorously prepared for open hostilities.

Fate of Burgoyne's army.

Such was the train of political consequences which, in succession, followed the capture of general Burgoyne's army. Here it may be proper to notice the subsequent fate of those brave but unfortunate men, whom the chance of war had thus subjected to the power of the Americans. By one of the articles of capitulation it was stipulated that the ſurrendering army ſhould be at liberty to tranſport itſelf to Great Britain, upon condition of not ſerving againſt America during the war. Boſton was fixed upon as the place from which it was to embark; and thither the Britiſh troops were marched to wait for tranſports. When the army had reached its aſſigned quarters, it was found that it would be much eaſier, and more expeditious, to march the troops acroſs the country to Rhode Iſland, to meet the tranſports, than at that ſeaſon of the year, it being the middle of winter, to bring the tranſports from thence round to Boſton. An application was accordingly made by general Burgoyne to the congreſs, for leave to change the place of embarkation from Boſton to Rhode Iſland, or ſome other port in its neighbourhood. But the congreſs, probably reflecting that the moment the convention troops landed in England, an equal number could be ſpared from thence to ſupply their place in America, determined, inſtead of complying with the general's requeſt, to prohibit the embarkation of the Saratoga troops from any port whatſoever, "until a diſtinct and explicit ratification of the convention at Saratoga ſhould be properly notified by the court of Great Britain to congreſs;" and entered upon their journals a reſolution to that effect. This reſolution was evidently a breach of the convention. It was admitted to be ſo by the congreſs themſelves; but as a kind of juſtification, they pretended to ſet forth ſome grounds of ſuſpicion that the Britiſh troops did not hold themſelves bound by the convention, and meant, if they were ſuffered to depart, inſtead of returning to Great Britain, to join the army at New York. They alſo attempted to ſpecify ſome inſtances in which, on the part of the Britiſh troops, the convention had already been broken; but the inſtances on which they relied were of a nature ſo frivolous and unimportant, that it was clear to all the world that the congreſs, by this proceeding, ſacrificed national faith and honour to preſent convenience.

CHAP. XXI. 1778.

It was in vain that general Burgoyne remonſtrated to the congreſs againſt the injuſtice of this reſolution, and proved, to a demonſtration, that there was no breach of the convention on the part of the Britiſh troops, even in thoſe inſtances, frivolous and futile as they were, on which that aſſembly relied. In order to remove every doubt, and ſilence every objection, he offered to enter into a new engagement, ſhould it be deſired, and to engage his officers to join in it, for fulfilling all the articles of the convention. But the congreſs determined not to be ſatisfied, and obſtinately perſiſted in the reſolution which they had taken. They gave the general leave to return to Great Britain upon his parole, to be forthcoming when called for, but they retained his army in captivity; which, after remaining more than a year in the province of Maſſachuſet's Bay, was marched from thence as far to the ſouthward as Virginia, in the interior parts of which new quarters were aſſigned to it; nor were any of the convention troops releaſed during the war, except ſuch as were exchanged for American priſoners; although repeated offers were made by ſir Henry Clinton, and by the American commiſſioners, to ratify or renew, on the part of Great Britain, all the articles of that convention.

We ſhould now return to the two armies, which we left towards the middle of the preſent year, the one in Philadelphia, and the other encamped in huts in the woods at Valley Forge, upon the Schuylkill, where general Waſhington had determined to remain, that he might be enabled to ſend out detachments during the winter to hover round the Britiſh quarters, for the purpoſe of preventing a communication between them and ſuch of the inhabitants in the country as were well affected to the Britiſh cauſe: An object, which, as we have ſeen, for ſome time, he in part accompliſhed. But before we reſume the narrative of military operations it will be proper to advert to certain political tranſactions and circumſtances by which these were immediately preceded, and, in some measure, affected.

CHAP. XXI. 1778.

The commissioners for peace arrive in America, and enter on the execution of their office.

Within less than a fortnight after sir William Howe's departure from Philadelphia, the British commissioners sent to offer peace to North America, arrived in the Delaware, and without delay entered on the execution of their office.

Here it may be proper, before we proceed, to relate the steps which they took to fulfil the purposes of their mission; to throw into one point of view some previous proceedings of the congress, by which it will appear that, even before the arrival of the commissioners, and without waiting to hear what they might have to urge, that assembly had determined not to accept the terms which they had to offer. In the month of November of the preceding year, the congress, with a view of removing the only obstacle or ground of apprehension which impeded the success of their application to the court of France, entered into a resolution, declaring that all proposals for a treaty with the king of Great Britain, inconsistent with the independence of the United States, or with such alliances as might be formed under their authority, would be rejected. And in the month of April of the present year, upon the arrival of the rough draughts of the conciliatory bills, they passed resolutions of such a contemptuous, insulting, and provoking nature, as left no hope that any reasonable terms of accommodation would be accepted *. In these resolutions they affected to consider those bills as the sequel of an insidious plan formed by the British government for enslaving America. The object of them, they maintained, was to disunite the colonies, create divisions, and prevent foreign powers from interfering in their behalf. They pretended to demonstrate

* See the Resolutions of Congress of the 22d of April 1778.

CHAP. XXI. 1778. that thoſe bills were an evidence either of the weakneſs or wickedneſs of the Britiſh government, or both; and, after various other ſarcaſtic ſtrictures, they finally reſolved, that any man, or body of men, who ſhould preſume to make a ſeparate agreement with the Britiſh commiſſioners, ought to be conſidered as open and avowed enemies; and that the United States neither could nor would hold any conference with theſe commiſſioners, unleſs they ſhould, as a preliminary thereto, either withdraw their fleets and armies, or elſe in poſitive and expreſs terms acknowledge the independence of the United States. It happened too, that the conciliatory bills, after they had been paſſed through both houſes of parliament, and received the royal aſſent, being immediately diſpatched to America, reached that country ſome days previous to the arrival of the commiſſioners. They were forthwith forwarded to congreſs; but that aſſembly returned no other anſwer* than to refer to the aforeſaid reſolutions, in which they alledged that they had already expreſſed their ſentiments upon bills not eſſentially different from thoſe which were now tranſmitted to them.

Although theſe previous proceedings afforded a very unfavourable proſpect of the ſucceſs of the negotiation, which was rendered ſtill more hopeleſs by the arrival of Silas Deane at York Town on the ſecond of May, with copies of the treaties, already mentioned, entered into between the French king and the American plenipotentiaries at Paris, the commiſſioners neverthele ſs entered upon the execution of their office with apparent alacrity. They diſpatched their ſecretary, doctor Adam Ferguſon, a name well known in the literary world, to proceed to York Town, and lay before the congreſs a copy of their commiſſion, with the concili-

* Reſolutions of Congreſs of the 6th of June 1778.

atory

atory acts of parliament upon which it was founded, and a letter explaining the extent of their powers, and setting forth in detail the nature of those terms which they were authorised to offer for settling the differences between the mother-country and her colonies; and proposing to the congress that they should appoint a place for the British commissioners to meet them, either collectively or by deputation, for the further discussion of every subject of difference. A previous application had been made to general Washington for a passport and safe-conduct for Dr. Ferguson, which it was not doubted would have been granted; but upon his arrival at the first out-post of the American army, he was not suffered to proceed any farther, general Washington having refused to grant a passport, until he should consult the congress, and have their permission. Thus a man, whose unstained integrity precluded suspicion, and the celebrity of whose writings, it might have been supposed, would have secured to him a favourable reception in any civilized country on the face of the earth, was refused permission even to pass through the American territory, although the messenger of peace and reconciliation. Such are ever the harsh and ungracious effects of stern republican policy. Dr. Ferguson, being thus denied a passport, returned to Philadelphia; and, that no delay might ensue, the papers of which he was intended to have been the bearer were now forwarded to congress by the ordinary military posts of their army, and reached York Town on the thirteenth of June. After deliberating for some days on the subject of these communications, the congress, through their president, returned for answer, that the acts of parliament, the commission and the commissioners letter, all of them supposed the people of the American States to be subjects of the king of Great Britain, and were founded on an idea of dependance which was utterly inadmissible: But that they were ready

CHAP. XXI. 1778.

to enter upon the confideration of a treaty of peace and commerce, not inconfiftent with treaties already fubfifting, whenever the king of Great Britain fhould demonftrate a fincere difpofition for that purpofe; the only proof of which would be an explicit acknowledgment of their independence, or the withdrawing his flects and armies; and they approved of general Wafhington's conduct in refufing a paffport to Dr. Fergufon. Such was the anfwer of congrefs to the Britifh commiffioners; an anfwer which fhewed that all negotiation, except upon the ground of acknowledging their independence, would be unavailing, and that nothing but conqueft could re-unite the colonies to the Britifh empire: And fuch the iffue of this fecond attempt to bring about a reconciliation; which, whatever might be the effect of it in Great Britain towards inducing a greater union of fentiment on the fubject of colonial affairs, produced in America no good confequence whatfoever. It flattered the pride of the American republicans, confirmed them in purfuing the meafures which they had adopted, and finally eftablifhed the authority of congrefs, which the commiffioners had in fact recognized by offering to treat with them. On the other hand, it had a moft unfavourable effect upon all the inhabitants of the colonies who were attached to the Britifh caufe: Thofe who had not yet openly declared their fentiments, were difcouraged and difheartened; whilft the active and perfecuted loyalift was plunged into the deepeft defpair. Even the officers of the army felt themfelves lowered in their own eftimation, when, without any apparent neceffity, they faw every thing for which they had been yet contending, in effect given up. To this order of men, therefore, as well as to the profcribed loyalifts, the contemptuous proceedings of congrefs, in confequence of an application which was confidered as the greateft act of condefcenfion on the part of the mother-country, was peculiarly offenfive, and gave

a new

CHAP. XXI. 1778.

a new edge to their resentment. They hoped, as all reasonable prospect of accommodation was at an end, that the most strenuous exertions would be made to take signal vengeance on the authors and abettors of the rebellion, whose guilt was now aggravated by their insolence; and they looked with impatience for the moment when they should be led out to assail the American camp at Valley Forge.

CHAP. XXII.

The Evacuation of Philadelphia—General Washington prepares to impede and harass the British Troops in their Retreat—Sir H. Clinton pursues his March to New York by Sandy Hook—Disposition of the American Army—And of the British—Battle of Freehold Court House in the County of Monmouth—The British Army arrives at New York.

CHAP. XXII. 1778.

BUT the firſt active meaſure of the campaign did not accord with ſuch expectations. This was no other than the evacuation of Philadelphia, and the retreat of the army to New York. Preparations for this purpoſe were making even while the commiſſioners were tranſmitting their diſpatches to congreſs; and before an anſwer was received the evacuation had actually taken place.

Through the interference of a hoſtile maritime power, the command of the ſea was about to be diſputed by the contending parties. Hence greater circumſpection became neceſſary in the choice of poſts for the Britiſh army. It was uncertain where the French might attempt to ſtrike a blow; whether upon the continent of America, or in the Weſt Indies. It was therefore proper that the army ſhould occupy a ſtation from which reinforcements might be moſt eaſily and expeditiouſly ſent wherever they ſhould be required. But of all the ſtations hitherto occupied by the ſouthern army, Philadelphia was the leaſt adapted to ſuch a purpoſe. It was diſtant from the ſea not leſs than a hundred miles, and communicated

3 with

with it only by a winding river. Thefe, or other more weighty confiderations, influenced the miniftry fo far, that orders were fent from England for the evacuation of Philadelphia; which was effected at three in the morning of the eighteenth of June, the army retiring to the point of land below the town formed by the confluence of the Delaware and the Schuylkill, where the boats and veffels belonging to the navy were ready to receive them. And fo judicious was the admiral's arrangement, on this occafion, that the whole army, with its baggage, was paffed over the Delaware, and encamped on the Jerfey fhore, by ten in the forenoon; meeting with little interruption from the enemy, though the Americans entered Philadelphia before the Britifh entirely left it. The fame fleet of tranfports that carried the foldiers, provifions, and ftores, carried alfo the property of the Philadelphian merchants attached to government. The great body of the loyalifts of Philadelphia went along with the army: Such of them as had the imprudence to remain behind were treated with great feverity. Some were banifhed. Several were thrown into prifon, and tried for their lives. Two of thefe, Roberts and Carlifle, very refpectable characters, of the fect of Quakers, fuffered death.

The country through which the Britifh army had to march being naturally ftrong, and abounding with difficult paffes, which, if occupied by the enemy, might greatly retard its progrefs, fir Henry Clinton thought it neceffary, in order to guard againft the confequences of fuch obftructions, to carry along with him a confiderable quantity of baggage and a large fupply of provifions. The progrefs of the army, thus heavily incumbered, was uncommonly flow.

The preparations and arrangements previous to the evacuation could not be made fo fecretly but that intelligence of them was conveyed to general Wafhington. From this intelligence he was enabled

CHAP. XXII. 1778.

abled to penetrate the design, and had detached general Maxwell with a brigade into New Jersey, with orders to assemble the militia, break down the bridges, and, by every means in his power, impede and harass the British troops in their retreat, until he, with the main army, should cross the Delaware and fall upon their rear. There are two roads leading from Philadelphia to New York; one along the western shore of the Delaware, as high as Trenton Ferry; the other, that which was taken by the British army, running parallel with the first, but on the eastern bank of the river. The route of the British army being along the eastern bank of the Delaware as high as Trenton, general Washington was obliged to make a considerable circuit to cross it higher up. But, even after he had effected his passage, he kept for some time a very cautious and respectful distance, sending forward detachments of his light troops to watch the motions of the British army, and hang on its flanks and rear. A little to the left of the most northerly road leading from Trenton to New York, the country of New Jersey becomes high and mountainous. This country general Washington entered when he passed the Delaware at Correll's Ferry, and he thought that the very slow movement of the British army indicated a design in sir Henry Clinton to draw him down from his advantageous situation, and either force an engagement in the level country, or, by a rapid movement, gain the high grounds which he had quitted. This idea alone can account for the extreme caution with which he approached a retreating enemy. The course of the British army now pointed from the Delaware; and the farther it advanced in this new direction, the more general Washington strengthened his detachments; all of which were composed of chosen men.

Sir Henry Clinton had hitherto met with very little molestation from the enemy. His light troops had been sufficient to drive the Americans from the passes which they occupied; and the greatest impedi-

impediments which he met with, arofe from the deftruction of the bridges. His courfe, fo far as he had yet gone, was the fame, whether he meant to proceed to New York by the way of Sandy Hook, or by South Amboy, oppofite to Staten Ifland, and the North River; but he had now arrived at that point where the highways diverge, and where it was neceffary for him to make an option which of thefe roads, during the remainder of his march, he would purfue. The roads which led to Staten Ifland and the North River on the left, were the fhorteft; but in that direction the river Rariton intervened, the paffing of which, in the face of an enemy fuperior in number, might be both difficult and dangerous; more efpecially as intelligence had been received that general Gates, with another army, was advancing from the northward to form a junction with general Wafhington, near that river. This confideration determined the Britifh general to take the road which led to Sandy Hook, as that which prefented the feweft impediments to obftruct his progrefs, and by inclining to the right carried him clear of the courfe of the Rariton altogether. Along this road, therefore, the Britifh army was ordered to march; and having proceeded fome miles, they encamped on the twenty-feventh of June on fome high grounds in the neighbourhood of Freehold Court-houfe, in the county of Monmouth.

Sir H. Clinton purfues his march to New York by Sandy Hook.

General Wafhington had from time to time fo powerfully reinforced his advanced detachments, that the marquis de la Fayette firft, and afterwards general Lee, were in fucceffion fent to take the command of them. They now amounted, according to general Wafhington's account, to more than five thoufand men, and had taken poft at Englifh Town, a few miles in the rear of the Britifh army. A corps of fix hundred men under colonel Morgan, hovered on the right flank of the Britifh, and eight hundred of the Jerfey militia, under general Dickenfon, were on the left; whilft

Difpofition of the American army,

CHAP. XXII. 1778.

general Waſhington, with the main body of the American army, encamped about three miles in the rear of his advanced corps.

Such was the diſpoſition of the two armies on the evening of the twenty-ſeventh of June; and as it was now obvious, from the courſe which the Britiſh army had lately taken, that their march was a real retreat, and not a feint; this diſcovery ſeems to have at laſt determined the American general to riſque an attack; which he reſolved to make the following morning, before the Britiſh troops ſhould reach an advantageous poſition, about twelve miles in their front. Orders were accordingly ſent to general Lee to begin the attack with the advanced corps as ſoon as the Britiſh army ſhould be in motion, with an intimation that general Waſhington, with the main body of the American army, would advance and ſupport him. Sir Henry Clinton was ſufficiently apprized that general Waſhington, with the American army, was near him, from the frequent appearance of his light troops during the preceding day; and judging that his deſign was rather to make an attempt upon the baggage, in which he thought himſelf vulnerable, than to riſque a general engagement, he made a new diſpoſition in order more effectually to protect it. and of the Britiſh. The army marched in two diviſions; the van commanded by general Knyphauſen, and the rear by lord Cornwallis; but the whole of the baggage was now put under the care of general Knyphauſen's diviſion, that the rear diviſion, under lord Cornwallis, which conſiſted of the flower of the Britiſh army, being diſincumbered, might be ready to act with vigour, as circumſtances ſhould require. This arrangement being made, general Knyphauſen's diviſion, conſiſting of the German troops, the yagers excepted, and the ſecond battalion of light infantry, with the baggage, marched in purſuance June 28. of orders at break of day on the twenty-eighth of June, whilſt the other diviſion, with which the commander in chief remained, did

not

not move till near eight, that it might not preſs too cloſe upon the baggage, which was ſo enormous as to occupy a line of march of near twelve miles in extent. But ſcarcely had the rear-guard of the Britiſh army deſcended from the heights of Freehold, into a plain of three miles in length and one in breadth, when the advanced corps of the American army was ſeen approaching, and ſoon afterwards deſcending into the plain from the ſame heights which the Britiſh army had juſt before quitted. About the ſame time intelligence was brought that large columns of the enemy were ſeen marching on both flanks. This intelligence confirmed the Britiſh general in his firſt opinion, that the deſign of the enemy was upon his baggage; and as that was now engaged in defiles which would continue for a conſiderable diſtance, no other mode of affording relief to general Knyphauſen's diviſion appeared to him ſo eligible as that of making a vigorous attack upon the corps which appeared in his rear, and, if ſucceſsful, of preſſing it ſo cloſely, that the detachments ſent forward on his flanks might be recalled to its aſſiſtance. A diſpoſition was accordingly made for commencing the attack in the plain; but before it could be carried into execution the provincials retired, and took poſt on the high ground from which they had before deſcended. This was a ſtrong poſition: But it was neceſſary to attempt ſomething deciſive for the relief of the baggage, and orders being given for the Britiſh troops to aſcend the heights, the attack was made with ſo much ſpirit, that the provincials were quickly obliged to give way. Their ſecond line, which was alſo ſtrongly poſted, now preſented itſelf to view. Here the reſiſtance was greater; but notwithſtanding the heat of the day, which was extreme, the Britiſh troops, fatigued as they were, advanced to the charge with ſo much order, firmneſs, and intrepidity, that their ſucceſs in this ſecond attack was not leſs complete than in the firſt. The

Battle of Freehold Court-houſe in the county of Monmouth.

CHAP. XXII. 1778. provincials now fled on all fides; when, in this critical moment, general Wafhington coming up with the main body of his army, took poffeffion of fome ftrong ground behind a defile, over which the Britifh troops muft neceffarily pafs in purfuit of the fugitives; and by his timely arrival, and the judicious pofition which he took, probably faved his advanced corps from total ruin. Already part of the fecond Britifh line had moved to the front, and occupied fome ground upon the left flank of the enemy, which was actually turned by the light-infantry and queen's rangers; but the Britifh general having reconnoitred their pofition, and feeing, in confequence of the difficulty of the defile, the impoffibility of attacking them in front with any profpect of fuccefs, and being alfo confident that the end was gained for which the attack had been made, recalled his victorious troops, ready to fink under the heat and fatigue of the day, and retiring to the advantageous pofition where the firft attack had been made, fuffered them to reft till ten in the evening; when he refumed his march to join general Knyphaufen's divifion with the baggage, carrying his wounded along with him, except fuch as could not with fafety be moved. Some attempts had been made upon the baggage by the enemy's light troops, which were quickly repelled through the able difpofition made by general Knyphaufen for its fecurity; and the two brigades of the enemy which had been fent forward on this fervice, one on each flank, were foon recalled, in confequence of the events which happened in the rear. In the different engagements of this day, the whole lofs of the Britifh army in killed, wounded, miffing, and thofe who died of fatigue, amounted to three hundred and fifty-eight men, including twenty officers. Amongft the flain the officer of greateft note was the honourable lieutenant-colonel Monckton, who fell at the head of the fecond battalion of grenadiers, greatly and defervedly lamented: And fuch was the extreme heat of the day, that three ferjeants, and fifty-fix men, dropped dead without a wound. Colonel Monckton had been felected for the hazardous duty to which he was this day appointed, on account of the cool intrepidity of his character. By his military qualities, and amiable virtues, he acquired the efteem and the affection of both the officers and the men. Thefe paid the moft marked tribute of refpect to his memory. During the confufion of a dangerous cannonade, the battalion in parties relieved each other, until, with their bayonets (being deftitute of more proper tools), they perfected a grave, where they laid the body of their beloved commanding officer, placing over it with their hands the earth they had moiftened with their tears.

The lofs of the Americans exceeded, by a little, that of the Britifh army; for, according to their own accounts, it amounted to three hundred and fixty-one men, including thirty-two officers.

The events of this day were celebrated by the provincials as a victory; but with what juftice the particulars which we have related will ferve to fhew. And, independently of thefe, it is apparent that general Wafhington had, in this day's engagement, received fuch a check as determined him to draw off his troops towards the North River, and moleft his retreating enemy no farther. Wafhington, in his public letter, fays that he lay clofe to the Britifh army after the action; but that it went off in fuch filence, as to give no alarm of its retreat to the Americans. This filence, however, it is well known, met with one interruption; for, juft as the Britifh were beginning to move, fome horfes or cattle were ftraggling through a wood, and a battalion of light-infantry, taking them for the enemy, began a fire upon them, which continued for five minutes. But general Wafhington dates his letter to Lee, on that fame night, from Englifh Town, three miles from the field of battle.

The

CHAP. XXII. 1778.

The conduct of general Lee on this day, which was so severely arraigned, and unjustly punished by the Americans, was worthy of applause and admiration. He had been betrayed across some narrow passes of a marsh by the persuasion that he had to deal with a rear-guard of only two or three battalions. When he suddenly perceived six thousand men, including the British light-infantry and grenadiers, forming to receive him, he retired with such quickness of decision, though not attacked, that he had repassed the marsh before our line was in readiness to move. Had he, in expectation of support, maintained his ground on the plain, until the British had attacked him, he must have been overpowered, and would not have had any retreat. On the other hand, the conduct of the commanders in chief of the contending armies, though each of them claimed a victory, was made the subject of animadversion. Why, it was asked, did general Clinton encumber himself with so enormous a train of baggage? Why, when a rapid retreat was his object, did he halt the army, without being fatigued by long marches, for two days at Freehold? It was undoubtedly his business to gain a communication with the fleet as quickly as possible; as it was of Washington again to cut it off. At no time on the march did general Clinton shew any other disposition than that of retreating to New York. General Washington's caution is therefore censurable. He ought to have attacked so encumbered an army with all his light troops, and, in spite of partial defeats, contended, in such favourable circumstances, for ultimate victory. The check that the advanced guard of the American army sustained did not, it was said, appear to be so great as to justify a declination of all farther attempts against the British army, even at that very time. Having come up with the main body of his army, fresh and untired troops, he should have endeavoured to turn one of general Clinton's flanks. Had he succeeded,

ſucceeded, that part of the Britiſh army muſt have been deſtroyed, as, immediately after quitting the plain, any regular mode of retreat would have been impracticable; for, on one ſide, the road was commanded by a pine barren precipice; while below, on the other, it was frightfully interſected and cut up by frequent gullies and ravines. Theſe, continued on both ſides for five or ſix miles, precluded the action of flanking parties, at the ſame time that the ſummit of the precipice, open to an aſſailing army, would have poured eaſy deſtruction on a retreating enemy. Succeſs in this quarter would have ſecured equal ſucceſs on the part of the army that was encumbered with baggage. And to all theſe circumſtances, ſo much in favour of the American general, was added the almoſt immediate appearance of a French fleet on the coaſt of America.

Yet, in ſuch a conjuncture of affairs, it was obſerved the Britiſh general riſked, and even courted an action, while the American ſuffered the important occaſion to paſs by, when he might have terminated the war by one great and deciſive effort.

The Britiſh army proceeded on its march, until, the baggage having reached Sandy Hook, there was no farther apprehenſion for its ſecurity. The fleet from the Delaware was there ready to receive it; and whilſt preparations were making, by a bridge of boats, for tranſporting the troops acroſs an inlet of the ſea which ſeparates Sandy Hook from the continent, ſir Henry Clinton, with the army, lay encamped at the diſtance of ſome miles in the country, eagerly expecting general Waſhington to come up, and fully determined to give him battle. But Waſhington was, by this time, on his march to the North River; and the Britiſh general having remained for two days in this ſituation, without ſeeing any thing of the provincials, proceeded from thence to Sandy Hook, where the army was embarked on the fifth of July, and the ſame day landed at New York.

It

CHAP. XXII.

1778.
The British army arrives at New York. July.

It may be mentioned as a fact in natural history, but not unconnected with this narrative, that the peninsula of Sandy Hook, by the storms of the preceding winter, had been converted into an island, which made it necessary to pass the troops across the channel by a floating bridge. The queen's rangers, who formed the rear guard when the bridge was broken up, embarked from the Jersey side in boats.

CHAP. XXIII.

The French Fleet sets sail from Toulon to North America—Thither also a British Fleet sets sail under Vice-Admiral Byron—The Count D'Estaing, missing the British Army in Philadelphia, comes to an Anchor off New York—The Harbour of this Place defended by a small Fleet, under Lord Howe—D'Estaing sets sail to the Southward—but changes his Course, and arrives at Rhode Island—American Preparations for an Attempt on Rhode Island—frustrated—Naval Operations—Lord Howe resigns the Command of the Fleet to Admiral Gambier.

CHAP. XXIII. 1778. A French fleet sails from Toulon to North America.

THE French, as soon as they had determined to take an open and active part in behalf of the revolted colonies, began immediately to arm by sea. At Toulon they equipped a fleet of twelve ships of the line and six frigates; which, with a considerable number of troops on board, sailed from thence on the thirteenth of April, under the command of the count D'Estaing; but from adverse winds, did not pass the straits of Gibraltar till the fifteenth of May.

Thither also a British fleet sets sail from Plymouth, under vice-admiral Byron.

The British ministry, who were not unapprized of this equipment, got ready a fleet of an equal number of ships, the command of which was given to vice-admiral Byron. With this fleet the admiral left Portsmouth on the twentieth of May, and proceeding to Plymouth, finally sailed from thence on the ninth of June, after such advices had been received as no longer left it doubtful that the

CHAP. XXIII. 1778.

Toulon ſquadron was bound to North America. Theſe advices were brought by captain Sutton of the Proſerpine, who, from the ſtraits of Gibraltar, had followed the French fleet for ninety leagues on its paſſage. The count D'Eſtaing, thus poſſeſſed of the advantage of being firſt at ſea, proceeded on his paſſage, and arrived on the coaſt of Virginia on the fifth of July, the ſame day on which the Britiſh army had embarked at Sandy Hook. He probably expected to have found that army in Philadelphia, and lord Howe's fleet in the Delaware: And had he found them in this ſituation, it is not eaſy to determine what might have been the conſequence of a joint operation between him and general Waſhington. Some have thought that the fate of both the Britiſh fleet and army would have been perilouſly critical; whilſt others, leſs prone to deſpondence, have maintained with much confidence, that nothing was to be apprehended by either, ſo long as their proviſions laſted; of which they had a ſufficient ſtock to enable them to hold out till the arrival of admiral Byron.

The count D'Eſtaing, miſſing the Britiſh army in Philadelphia, comes to an anchor off New York.

The count D'Eſtaing, diſappointed in his firſt object by the evacuation of Philadelphia, of which he received intelligence whilſt he lay off the mouth of the Cheſapeak, coaſted along the American ſhore to the northward, and on the eleventh of July in the evening came to an anchor off New York, with an apparent deſign of attempting to enter the harbour.

The harbour of this place defended by a ſmall fleet under lord Howe.

The naval force under lord Howe, although much inferior to the fleet under the count D'Eſtaing, was nevertheleſs reſpectable; the ſhips being well manned, and moſt ably officered. It conſiſted of ſix ſhips of the line, and four of fifty guns, with a number of frigates and ſmaller veſſels: And, intelligence of the count D'Eſtaing's approach having been received ſome days before he came in ſight, a maſterly diſpoſition of this force, for the defence of the harbour, had already been made under the immediate direction of the admiral, whoſe

whoſe exertions were moſt nobly ſeconded by the univerſal ardour which prevailed not only in the navy, army, and tranſport ſervice, but amongſt all ranks and claſſes of people at New York, who ran in crowds to offer their ſervice as volunteers. A Britiſh fleet blocked up in one of its own ports was ſuch a phænomenon as filled them with indignation.

For ſome time after the count D'Eſtaing came to an anchor the wind was unfavourable to the execution of his ſuppoſed intention; but on the twenty-ſecond of July it changed to the eaſtward, and the French fleet were ſeen getting under way. The long-meditated attack, it was now ſuppoſed, was inſtantly to be made; and ſo confident were all, that it would prove abortive in conſequence of the preparations made for defence, that the critical moment which was to decide, not only the fate of the Britiſh fleet, but of the army, was waited for with impatience. But the count D'Eſtaing, to their great diſappointment, as ſoon as his ſhips had weighed anchor, inſtead of attempting to enter the harbour, made ſail to the ſouthward, and was ſoon out of ſight. Whether he ever ſeriouſly intended to make an attempt upon the harbour of New York, but, after reconnoitring its ſituation, with the diſpoſitions made for defence, relinquiſhed the deſign as impracticable; or whether his appearing before that harbour was only a feint to draw the attention of the Britiſh commanders from the place where his attack was really intended; is uncertain: But after quitting New York, and ſtanding to the ſouthward, as far as the mouth of the Delaware, he changed his courſe, and ſteered directly for Rhode Iſland, before which he arrived on the twenty-ninth of July. Here at leaſt it was ſoon obvious that he meditated a real attack, in which general Sullivan, with a detachment from Waſhington's army, and a force collected from the neighbouring country of New England, was to co-operate.

The count D'Eſtaing ſets ſail to the ſouthward;

but changes his courſe, and arrives at Rhode Iſland. July 29th.

CHAP. XXIII.

1778.

American preparations for an attempt on Rhode Island,

The expulsion of the British troops from Rhode Island had been in the contemplation of the provincials for several months past. In the spring of this year general Sullivan was sent to take the command in its neighbourhood, and made preparations for invading it. To these preparations major-general sir Robert Pigott, who commanded at Rhode Island, was not inattentive; he readily perceived their object, and in order to retard them, projected about the end of May two different enterprises into Providence Plantation; one conducted by lieutenant-colonel Campbell of the twenty-second, and the other by major Eyre, of the fifty-fourth regiment, both of which were successfully executed. In the first, under lieutenant-colonel Campbell, several houses at Bristol and Warren, filled with military and naval stores, some gallies and armed sloops, and one hundred and twenty-five boats, many of them fifty feet long, which had been collected or built on the Hickamuct river, for the purpose of the invasion, were burnt and destroyed; and eighteen pieces of ordnance, most of them of heavy metal, were rendered unserviceable. And in the last expedition under major Eyre, a large quantity of boards, plank, and other materials for ship-building, were burnt.

frustrated.

Naval operations.

The losses sustained by the provincials in these expeditions retarded their preparations so much, that when the count D'Estaing arrived off Rhode Island they were not in readiness for co-operation; and for the present he contented himself with stationing two of his frigates in the Seaconnet Passage on the east, and two of his line-of-battle ships in the Narraganset Passage on the west side of the island, to interrupt the communications of the garrison, whilst, with the remainder of his fleet, he anchored off Brenton's Ledge, at the south-east end of the island, in a situation open to the sea. In this position he remained until the eighth of August, when, every thing being in

August.

CHAP. XXIII. 1778.

in readineſs on the part of the provincials, he entered the harbour with his fleet, receiving and returning the fire from ſeveral batteries as he paſſed them, and came to an anchor between Newport and Conanicut. Upon the firſt appearance of the French fleet at Rhode Iſland, a diſpatch-boat was ſent to New York with intelligence of this; and on the ſixth of Auguſt lord Howe, after being detained for four days by contrary winds, put to ſea with the Britiſh fleet, which was now increaſed to eight line-of-battle ſhips, five ſhips of fifty guns, two of forty-four guns, and four frigates, with three fire-ſhips, two bombs, and a number of ſmaller veſſels. With this force his lordſhip appeared in ſight of Rhode Iſland on the morning of the ninth of Auguſt, and after having communicated with the garriſon, and informed himſelf exactly of the ſituation of the French fleet, came to an anchor the ſame evening off Point Judith, which forms the entrance on the ſouth-weſt ſide into the great bay, or baſon of water which encompaſſes Rhode Iſland, and the other ſmaller iſlands adjacent. If any advantage could have been gained by finding the count D'Eſtaing in a confined ſituation, where his large ſhips could not act with freedom, and where they were alſo liable to be annoyed by the batteries from the ſhore, it was loſt by the Britiſh admiral's coming to an anchor ſo far to the ſouthward, and at ſuch a diſtance from the mouth of the harbour: For on the following morning, the wind having changed to the north-eaſt, the French admiral embraced this opportunity of ſailing out of the harbour, with all his ſhips, and forming them in order of battle as they came out, bore down upon the Britiſh fleet. The Britiſh admiral, for the preſent, thought it prudent to decline an engagement, and ranging his ſhips in order of battle, ſtood to the ſouthward, in the hope that a ſhift of wind might enable him to gain the weather-gage. Thus arranged, and thus relatively ſituated, the two fleets continued in ſight of each other for two days; when the Britiſh admiral,

CHAP. XXIII. 1778. admiral, despairing of a change of wind, and having failed in his endeavours to gain the weather-gage, now waited, to leeward, the approach of the enemy, with a determination to engage; but, about this time, the wind freshening into a tremendous storm, not only parted the two fleets from each other, but separated and dispersed the individual ships of each squadron. The British admiral, in the Apollo frigate, to which ship he had shifted his flag from the Eagle, that he might be the better enabled to direct the operations of his fleet when in prospect of an engagement, on the day on which the storm began, now, when the weather cleared up, found himself left with only six ships; and the Apollo having sustained so much damage in the storm as rendered it necessary to send her immediately into port, he again shifted his flag to one of the other ships, to endeavour to collect his scattered fleet: But having in vain looked out for them for several days, he at length directed his course for Sandy Hook, which he reached on the seventeenth, and there found the rest of his squadron already at anchor. In his passage thither, the British admiral narrowly escaped the French fleet, having come in sight of ten of their ships, some of them at anchor in the sea, about twenty-five leagues to the eastward of Cape May.

The separation and dispersion of the two fleets gave occasion to the accidental meeting of single ships, and produced engagements between them, which terminated so much to the honour of British valour and seamanship, as to excite deep regret, that, after the British admiral had at last determined to engage, the storm should have intervened to prevent the action. In the evening of the thirteenth captain Dawson, in the Renown, of fifty guns, fell in with the French admiral's ship, the Languedoc, of eighty-four guns, dismasted; and notwithstanding her great superiority of force, resolutely assailed her with apparent advantage, until darkness put an end to the

the engagement, which would have been renewed the following morning, had not the appearance of six other ships of the enemy's fleet obliged the brave captain Dawson to desist. The same evening, a similar engagement happened between the Preston of fifty guns, commanded by commodore Hotham, and the Tonant, a French ship of eighty guns, with her main-mast only standing, the rest being carried away in the storm. The event of this engagement was similar to that of the former: It was bravely begun and sustained by commodore Hotham, till darkness put an end to it in the evening, and it could not be renewed in the morning, because of the appearance of the rest of the French fleet. But the last of the engagements, produced by this untoward occurrence, of ships of disproportionate force, puts all naval calculation from weight of metal at utter defiance, and gives the palm to undaunted bravery and superior skill and seamanship. In the afternoon of the sixteenth of August the Isis, a ship also of fifty guns, commanded by captain Raynor, fell in with the Cæsar, a French ship of seventy-four guns, not dismasted nor injured by the storm, but capable of chasing, and bravely engaged her for an hour and a half with such advantage, that at the end of this period the French ship sheered off, and putting before the wind, left the Isis incapable of pursuing from the damage which she had sustained in her masts, sails, and rigging. In other respects her damage was inconsiderable, and only one man was killed and fifteen wounded: Whereas the French ship had been so roughly handled, and so much injured in her hull, that she was obliged to bear away for the harbour of Boston to refit; and her killed and wounded amounted to fifty, including in the latter her captain, the celebrated Bougainville, whose arm was shot away in the action. If we reason by analogy, these spirited actions, thus nobly sustained against ships of such superior force, can leave no room to doubt that, had the two fleets come to action on the day on which an engagement was

CHAP. XXIII. 1778.

was expected, the event would have proved highly honourable to the British flag. Of the two fleets, the French appears to have suffered the most by the storm, but both of them had sustained considerable damage. The British ships which were disabled went into the harbour of New York to refit; and the French admiral, after collecting his shattered squadron, bore away for the harbour of Boston, in his passage to which he again anchored off Rhode island, for the purpose of communicating with the provincials, who had effected a landing upon that island the day before he sailed out of the harbour. On this second visit to Rhode Island he remained only one day, when he shaped his course for Boston.

As soon as lord Howe's squadron, which was now further increased by the arrival of the Monmouth, one of admiral Byron's fleet, was sufficiently refitted, he put to sea with it again, hoping, from the intelligence which he had received of the motions of the French fleet, that he might be able to reach the bay of Boston before it; but in this hope he was disappointed. Upon his entering that bay, on the thirtieth of August, he found the French fleet already in the harbour, and so well secured by lying within certain points of land, on which batteries had been erected to cover and command the anchorage ground, that all attempts against them, in this situation, appeared impracticable. Having advanced to the mouth of the harbour, and reconnoitred their position, he determined to quit the bay of Boston, and proceed to the relief of Rhode Island; but that island being evacuated by the provincials before his arrival, and his assistance in that quarter no longer being necessary, he returned with

September.

the fleet to New York, towards the middle of September. During his absence six more ships of admiral Byron's squadron had arrived at that port; and as, in consequence of these arrivals, the British naval force in America was now unquestionably superior to the fleet under the count D'Estaing, and would be still farther increased by the arrival

rival of admiral Byron, in the Princeſs Royal, who was daily expected from Halifax, his lordſhip thought this a proper moment for availing himſelf of the leave which he had ſome time before obtained of retiring from the American ſtation, on account of his health; and, reſigning the command of the fleet to admiral Gambier, took his departure for England.

CHAP. XXIII. 1778.

Lord Howe reſigns the command of the fleet to admiral Gambier.

CHAP. XXIV.

A particular Account of the Progreſs and Iſſue of the American Attempt on Rhode Iſland, already generally mentioned.

CHAP. XXIV. 1778.

AS our attention hitherto has been occupied in detailing the more momentous operations of the two fleets, and the invaſion of Rhode Iſland by the provincials has only been incidentally mentioned, we ſhall now briefly relate the progreſs and iſſue of that invaſion, which would not have been undertaken but in the proſpect of a co-operation from the count D'Eſtaing, and which was abandoned as ſoon as that proſpect was withdrawn. Previouſly to the arrival of the French fleet, Rhode Iſland was ſufficiently protected againſt an invaſion from the provincials, by the garriſon which was placed in it, and by the frigates and other ſmaller veſſels of war which were ſtationed round it for its ſecurity: and ſoon after the arrival of the French fleet upon the American coaſt, the garriſon was reinforced with five battalions under general Preſcot; for it was foreſeen that, if the French fleet ſhould appear before it, the Britiſh naval force ſtationed there would be rendered ineffective, and the ſecurity of the place muſt, for a time at leaſt, depend chiefly upon the ſtrength of the garriſon. The event juſtified this precaution; for as ſoon as the count D'Eſtaing had detached two of his line-of-battle ſhips into the Narraganſet Paſſage, and as many frigates into the Seaconnet Paſſage, the retreat of ſuch of the Britiſh ſhips as were advanced beyond them was cut off: They could neither put to fea nor return to the harbour of Newport; and in order to prevent them from falling into the hands of the French, were difmantled and burnt *. Sir Robert Pigott, too, being threatened with a defcent in feveral quarters at the fame time, was obliged, notwithftanding his reinforcement, to withdraw his out-pofts, and concentrate his force in an intrenched camp in the neighbourhood of Newport. Thus all the north part of the ifland was neceffarily left unguarded; and there the provincials, under general Sullivan, fuppofed to amount to ten thoufand men, effected a landing on the ninth of Auguft, the day after the count D'Eftaing had entered the harbour of Newport. They did not, however, make their appearance before the Britifh lines till the fourteenth, when, taking poffeffion of Honeyman's Hill, they began to conftruct batteries, form lines of communication, and make regular approaches, which were continued without intermiffion until the morning of the twenty-fixth. But the re-appearance of the French fleet, in its fhattered and difabled condition after the ftorm, and its final departure for the harbour of Bofton to refit, threw a fatal damp upon the fpirits of the men who compofed general Sullivan's army. Great part of it confifted of volunteers: And thefe, difheartened by the departure of the French fleet, returned home in fuch numbers, three thoufand of them having gone off in the courfe of one day, that, according to the American accounts, the force which at laft remained did not greatly exceed that of the Britifh garrifon. General Sullivan's army being thus weakened by defertion, he faw the impoffibility of fuc-

* Britifh Ships deftroyed at Rhode Ifland, to prevent them from falling into the Hands of the French:.

Juno	32 guns,	burnt.	Cerberus	32 guns,	burnt.
Lark	ditto	ditto.	Falcon	18 guns,	funk.
Orpheus	ditto	ditto.	King's Fifher	16 guns,	burnt.
Flora	ditto	funk.			

ceeding,

CHAP. XXIV. 1778.

ceeding, and took meaſures for effecting a retreat. Orders were diſpatched to repair and ſtrengthen the works in his rear, upon the north part of the iſland, and alſo at Briſtol and Tiverton upon the continent: Such parts of his heavieſt baggage as could be ſpared were ſent off; and every previous preparation that was neceſſary being made, he began his retreat in the night of the twenty-eighth of Auguſt. By evacuating his works in the night, general Sullivan gained a march of ſeveral hours, unperceived by the Britiſh army, and by poſting his light troops on various eminences in his line of march, and leaving them behind him with orders to ſkirmiſh with the Britiſh troops as they advanced, and then retire, he was enabled to make good his retreat with the main body of his army, his artillery and baggage, to a commanding ſituation at the north end of the iſland; which, as we have ſeen, he had previouſly ſtrengthened with ſome additional works, for the purpoſe of covering his retreat. Day-light in the morning of the twenty-ninth diſcovered to ſir Robert Pigott the retreat of the enemy; and a purſuit being inſtantly ordered, the whole day was ſpent in ſkirmiſhes, in which the covering parties of the provincials were ſucceſſively driven from the different poſts occupied by them, until they fell back upon the main body of their army, by this time encamped on the advantageous ground already mentioned. Theſe ſkirmiſhes were terminated by a ſharp action in front of the American encampment, obſtinately maintained for half an hour, at the end of which the troops engaged on both ſides were withdrawn. The loſs of the provincials in killed, wounded, and miſſing, during the various engagements of this day, amounted to two hundred and eleven men, including officers; and ſo obſtinately did they diſpute the ground with their purſuers, that the loſs of the Britiſh troops was not much inferior. The latter were now, in their turn, become the aſſailants, and during the following day preparations were made for attacking the provincials in their encampment; but, in the evening of that day, general Sullivan, after having purpofely exhibited every appearance of an intention to maintain his ground, filently ftruck his tents as foon as it was dark, and withdrew his troops unperceived; which, with the help of the numerous boats that attended upon him, were, in a few hours, tranfported acrofs the channel to the continent. His artillery and baggage had been paffed over during the preceding day.

Fortunately for the provincials, fir Henry Clinton, who was haftening with four thoufand men to the relief of Rhode Ifland, was detained for fome days by contrary winds in his paffage through the Sound, otherwife the retreat of general Sullivan and his army would in all probability have been cut off. Even after all the delays which occurred, fir Henry Clinton arrived at Rhode Ifland the day after it was evacuated.

CHAP. XXV.

Discontents and Clamours in the American States—Riots between the American and French Seamen at Boston—and at Charlestown, South Carolina—Expedition to Buzzard's Bay—Expeditions against Little Egg Harbour, a noted Rendezvous for Privateers—The Weather this Summer uncommonly boisterous in the Atlantic Ocean—Dispersion and Fate of the Fleet under Admiral Byron—The Admiral struggles in vain against adverse Fortune—The Count D'Estaing sets sail to the West Indies.

CHAP. XXV. 1778.

Discontents and clamours in the American states.

THE total failure of the expedition againſt Rhode Iſland occaſioned great murmuring throughout the American continent, particularly amongſt the inhabitants of the northern ſtates, who were moſt intereſted, and had in a more eſpecial manner exerted themſelves to promote its ſucceſs. In theſe ſtates the clamours of the people were loud againſt the count D'Eſtaing, for deſerting them in the midſt of an expedition which he knew was undertaken only in conſequence of his promiſe of co-operation. Theſe murmurings the governing powers prudently endeavoured to ſuppreſs, that they might not give offence to their new allies; but they were nevertheleſs, in part, the cauſe of a dangerous riot that happened at Boſton, between the American and French ſeamen; in which ſeveral of the latter were ſeverely wounded. Nearly about the ſame time, too, a ſimilar riot happened at Charleſtown, in South Carolina, between the ſame claſſes of people, but more fatal in the effects, as ſome lives on both ſides

Riots between the American and French ſeamen at Boſton; and at Charleſtown, South Carolina.

ſides were loſt. Indeed, the manners of the people were yet ſo little aſſimilated, that a cordial agreement could ſcarcely be expected. At both thoſe places, however, means were fallen upon to appeaſe the tumults, and great pains were taken to give ſatisfaction to the French, whom, at this early ſtage of the connexion, it would have been highly imprudent to diſguſt.

Sir Henry Clinton, having been diſappointed in cutting off the retreat of the provincials from Rhode Iſland, returned with the fleet of tranſports towards New York, as far as New London; at which place he propoſed making a deſcent, for the purpoſe of deſtroying a number of privateers, which, rendezvouſing at this port, greatly infeſted that part of the trade to New York which paſſed through the Sound. But as he approached the mouth of the river which, paſſing by New London, empties itſelf into the Sound, the wind became unfavourable, and prevented the fleet from entering: And as the appearance of the weather indicated a continuance of the ſame unfavourable wind, the commander in chief here left the fleet, and continued his paſſage to New York, having firſt given orders to major-general, now ſir Charles Grey, upon whom the command of the troops on board the tranſports now devolved, to proceed to the eaſtward upon a ſimilar expedition in Buzzard's Bay.

Expedition under general Grey to Buzzard's Bay.

The object of this expedition was to deſtroy the privateers upon the Acuſhnet river in Plymouth county in New England, together with a number of prizes which they had lately taken; and never was a ſervice more effectually performed. The fleet of tranſports having proceeded to the eaſtward with a fair wind, landed the troops on the banks of the Acuſhnet river at ſix in the evening of the fifth of September. And ſuch was the rapidity of the execution, that by noon of the next day they were all re-embarked, having, in the mean time, burnt and deſtroyed all the ſhips in the whole extent of the river, amounting to more than ſeventy ſail. They alſo burnt at Bedford

CHAP. XXV. 1778.

and Fairhaven, the one of these towns situated on the west, and the other on the east side of the river, a number of storehouses filled with provisions, merchandise, naval and warlike stores, and the cargoes of the prize-ships, with several wharfs, and two large rope-walks. They also dismantled and burnt, on the east side of the river, an inclosed fort mounting eleven pieces of heavy cannon, with a magazine, and barracks for two hundred men *: This service being performed with the loss of only one man killed, four wounded, and sixteen missing, in exchange for whom sixteen persons were brought from Bedford. The troops being re-embarked, the fleet proceeded to the island called Martha's Vineyard, where they also took or burnt several vessels, destroyed a salt-work, and obliged the inhabitants to deliver up their arms, and furnish a contribution of ten thousand sheep, and three hundred oxen; and with this seasonable supply of provisions the fleet returned to New York †.

Another

* Vessels, Stores, &c. destroyed on Acushnet River, the 5th of September 1778, by the Troops under Major General Grey.

8 sail of large ships, from 200 to 300 tons burden, most of them prizes.

6 armed vessels, from 10 to 16 guns.

A number of sloops and schooners, amounting in all to 70, besides whale-boats and others.

26 store-houses at Bedford, and several at M'Pherson's Wharf, Cran's Mills, and Fairhaven, filled with rum, sugar, melasses, coffee, tobacco, cotton, tea, medicines, gunpowder, sail-cloth, cordage, &c.

Two large rope walks.

13 pieces of ordnance destroyed at the fort, the magazine blown up, and the platform and barracks for 200 men burnt.

† Vessels, Stores, &c. taken or destroyed by the Troops under Major General Grey, at Falmouth, in the Vineyard Sound, and at the Island of Martha's Vineyard.

At Falmouth, 2 sloops and a schooner taken, and one sloop burnt.

At Martha's Vineyard, one brig of 150 tons, and one schooner of 70 tons burden, burnt; and four other vessels with 23 whale-boats, taken or destroyed.

A salt-work destroyed; and a considerable quantity of salt taken.

388 stand

CHAP. XXV.

1778.

Expeditions againſt Little Egg Harbour, a noted rendezvous for privateers.

Another expedition was ſoon afterwards planned againſt Little Egg Harbour, on the eaſt coaſt of New Jerſey, which was alſo a noted rendezvous for privateers. The vicinity of this, otherwiſe inſignificant, little port, to that tract of the ſea through which veſſels uſually paſs either in entering or coming from the harbour of New York to the ſouthward, rendered it a moſt convenient ſituation for annoying the trade of that place; and on that account the expedition againſt it became an object of ſome conſideration. To favour the ſucceſs of this, as well as to procure forage, and open the country on both ſides of the North River, for the admiſſion of proviſions, the army was put in motion. The firſt diviſion, under lord Cornwallis, advancing on the weſt ſide of the North River into the country of New Jerſey, took a poſition between that river and New-Bridge, on the Hackinſack, the right of this diviſion extending to the North River, and the left to the Hackinſack; whilſt general Knyphauſen, with the other diviſion of the army, took a parallel poſition on the eaſt ſide of the North River, his left reaching to that river at Wepperham, and his right to the Brunx. From the relative ſituations of the two diviſions ſeparated from each other only by the North River, the whole, by means of the flat-bottomed boats, could have been aſſembled on either ſide of the river in leſs than twenty-four hours; whereas general Waſhington, from not having the command of that river, could not have aſſembled his troops in leſs than ten days. Senſible of theſe diſadvantages, and probably foreſeeing that this advanced poſition of the Britiſh army was only a temporary movement, he did not attempt to draw his

388 ſtand of arms taken, with bayonets, pouches, flints, ſome gunpowder, and a quantity of lead.

300 oxen, and 10,000 ſheep.

1000l. ſterling in paper, the amount of a tax collected in Martha's Vineyard by the authority of the congreſs, was received of the collector.

CHAP. XXV. 1778.

troops together, but ſent forward detachments to interrupt and confine as much as poſſible the operations of the Britiſh foragers. One of theſe detachments was in front of lord Cornwallis's diviſion, and occupied the villages of Old and New Taapan; a regiment of light-horſe, commanded by lieutenant-colonel Baylor, being quartered at the firſt of theſe places, and a body of militia at the other. Intelligence of their poſition having been received, a plan was laid by lord Cornwallis for cutting them off. Lieutenant-colonel Campbell, with the ſeventy-firſt regiment, and the queen's rangers from general Knyphauſen's diviſion, was to paſs the North River, and attack the provincials at New Taapan, whilſt another column from lord Cornwallis's diviſion, led by major-general Grey, ſhould advance on the left, and attack thoſe at Old Taapan. By ſome delay which occurred in tranſporting lieutenant-colonel Campbell's column acroſs the North River, the boats not having arrived in time, and by the intelligence carried to the enemy by ſome deſerters from this column, the provincials at New Taapan were alarmed in time to make their eſcape. But the village of Old Taapan was ſo completely ſurrounded in the night by the left column, under major-general Grey, whoſe prompt execution and unrivalled ſucceſs in enterpriſes of this nature had been the terror of the provincials ever ſince the ſurpriſe of general Wayne, that very few of the regiment which was quartered in it were able to make their eſcape. The greateſt part either fell victims to the carnage incident to the confuſion and uncertainty of a nightly attack; or were fortunate to be made priſoners; and amongſt the latter was their commander, dangerouſly wounded. The regiment was entirely ruined; and the ſuddenneſs and ſeverity of this nightly enterpriſe ſtruck ſuch terror into the provincials that the Britiſh foragers were not afterwards interrupted.

In the mean time, the ſquadron deſtined for Little Egg Harbour, ſailed from New York under the direction of captain Collins of the

4 Zebra.

Zebra. This little ſquadron conſiſted of the Zebra, Vigilant, Nautilus, ſome gallies, ſmall armed veſſels, and tranſports. On board the tranſports were embarked three hundred troops from the fifth regiment, and the New Jerſey volunteers, the whole under the command of captain Patrick Ferguſon, of the ſeventieth regiment, an active, zealous, and able officer, who, in this expedition, was entruſted with the conduct of the land ſervice. Although this ſquadron left New York on the thirtieth of September, it did not arrive off Little Egg Harbour till the fifth of October in the evening, on account of contrary winds; and in the mean time the country had been alarmed by receiving intelligence of the place of its deſtination; which gave an opportunity to four privateers to put to ſea and make their eſcape, whilſt the other veſſels were carried up the river, as far as their draught of water would permit. As the commanders of this expedition learnt on their arrival at Little Egg Harbour that the country had been already alarmed, they determined to loſe no farther time in carrying it into execution. On the morning of the ſixth, the wind ſtill preventing the tranſports from entering the harbour, the troops were embarked on board the ſmaller veſſels, which, with the row-gallies, proceeded about twenty miles up the river to a place called Cheſnut Neck, where were ſeveral veſſels, and a ſmall village with ſtore-houſes, for the reception of prize-goods. Here the provincials had erected two batteries; one level with the water, and the other upon a commanding eminence; but neither of them yet mounted with artillery. Behind theſe batteries, and a breaſt-work which they had alſo thrown up, they at firſt made a formidable ſhew of reſiſtance; but as ſoon as the troops were landed under cover of the row-gallies, fled. The batteries, with the houſes and ſtores, were immediately demoliſhed by the troops, whilſt the ſeamen ſet on fire and burnt ten large prize ſhips, which in conſequence of the previous alarm had been ſkuttled by the provincials, and

could

CHAP. XXV. 1778.

could not be brought off. It had been propofed to penetrate by the fame river as far as a place called the Forks, the grand depot for prize-goods, within thirty-five miles of Philadelphia; but information was now received that the militia in that part of the country were reinforced by a detachment of foot, a fmall train of artillery, and a corps of light-horfe; and as, from the fhallownefs of the navigation, the troops could not be farther accompanied by the row-gallies, it was determined to abandon this part of the enterprife as impracticable. The troops were accordingly re-embarked, and proceeded down the river. In their paffage they were twice landed, and deftroyed three falt-works, and fome houfes and ftores belonging to perfons either concerned in fitting out privateers, or whofe activity in the caufe of America, and unrelenting perfecution of the loyalifts, marked them out as proper objects of vengeance. After the gallies and fmaller veffels had joined the fquadron in the harbour, they were prevented from putting to fea for fome days by contrary winds; and during this interval an officer and fome privates, deferters from Pulafki's American legion, having come on board, gave fuch an account of the pofition of that corps, lying only at the diftance of twelve miles up the river, as fuggefted to the active and enterprifing mind of captain Fergufon the probability of furprifing it. Pulafki's corps, confifting of three companies of foot, three troops of horfe, and a detachment of artillery, with one brafs field-piece, was quartered about a mile beyond a bridge, which captain Fergufon propofed to feize, for the purpofe of fecuring his retreat: And two miles beyond Pulafki's corps, lay a provincial colonel with a detachment of artillery, fome field-pieces, and the militia of the country. Captain Fergufon having minutely informed himfelf of their fituation, communicated his ideas to captain Collins; and it was agreed that the attempt fhould be made. At eleven at night, two hundred and fifty troops were embarked in the boats, which, rowing ten miles

up

up the river, landed them at four in the morning. The bridge being immediately fecured, and left under the guard of fifty men, the reft of the detachment pufhed forward, and furrounding the quarters of Pulafki's infantry, cut them to pieces. Very few efcaped, and only five were made prifoners. The Americans themfelves numbered fifty that were flain, and amongft thefe three officers; one of whom was of rank; the baron de Bofe, a lieutenant-colonel. As this furprife was effected within two miles of a force fuperior in number to the affailants, not only celerity of execution, but an immediate retreat, became neceffary, which, in confequence of the bridge having been previoufly fecured, was made with eafe and fafety. The troops were re-embarked without any other lofs than two men miffing, and one officer and two privates wounded; and as foon as the wind proved favourable the fquadron returned to New York.

The furprife of Baylor's dragoons at Old Taapan, and that of Pulafki's legion near Little Egg Harbour, both of which happened nearly about the fame time, gave frefh occafion to the Americans to pour forth much virulent invective againft the cruelty of the Britifh troops. But whilft we admit the feverity of the execution on both thefe occafions, candour requires us to add, that as both thofe attacks were made by furprife, and both in the night, and as the fuccefs of a furprife depends in a great meafure upon celerity of execution, it is impoffible, under fuch circumftances, for a commander, however humane, to prevent carnage. In the laft of thefe enterprifes, it is alfo to be remarked, that captain Ferguson's foldiers were highly irritated by intelligence immediately before received from the deferters, that count Pulafki had given it out in public orders to his legion, no longer to grant quarter to the Britifh troops. This intelligence afterwards appeared to be falfe; but in the mean time captain Fergufon's foldiers acted under the impreffion that it was true; and to his honour it is to be related, that although he did not

fcreen,

CHAP. XXV. 1778.

screen the guilty, he was careful to spare the innocent. The dwelling of a persecuting committee-man he razed to the ground, but saved from the flames the house of a peaceable, inoffensive Quaker, although it contained part of the baggage and equipage of Pulaski's legion, which it was an object to destroy, and which he had not time to destroy in any other way than by setting fire to the house; but the house, belonging to a peaceable man, was saved, and with it the baggage.

Before the squadron from Little Egg Harbour returned to New York, the British army was withdrawn from its forward position; and in this quarter nothing material was undertaken or atchieved on either side during the remainder of the season.

The weather this summer uncommonly tempestuous in the Atlantic ocean.

The weather, throughout the whole of this summer, appears to have been uncommonly boisterous in the Atlantic ocean. From this cause admiral Byron's fleet, which sailed from England on the ninth of June, to counteract the designs of count D'Estaing on the American coast, was not only delayed in its passage, but was at length, on the third of July, dispersed and separated by a storm. Some of the ships arrived singly at New York, in the manner we have already seen; and six of them, under admiral Parker, having been fortunate enough to keep together, reached that port on the twenty-ninth of August. But admiral Byron himself, in the Princess Royal, which ship was at last left alone, after having made good his passage within thirty leagues of Sandy Hook, came in sight of twelve ships, on the eighteenth of August, about ten miles to leeward of him, which, from their signals, he at length discovered to be the French fleet; and as these ships from their situation equally obstructed his course to New York or to Rhode Island, he was obliged, by a necessity of refitting, to bear away for Halifax; where he arrived on the twenty-sixth of that month, and found the Culloden, another of his fleet, already in the harbour. Both these shhips being refitted with the utmost

Dispersion and fate of the fleet under admiral Byron.

utmoſt diſpatch, he ſailed again on the fourth of September, and arrived at New York about the middle of that month. The ſhips of his ſquadron which arrived there before him were ſo ſhattered and torn to pieces in the different ſtorms they had encountered, that with all the diſpatch that could be uſed they were not in readineſs to proceed to ſea till the eighteenth of October. On that day the admiral ſailed again in queſt of the count D'Eſtaing, but his ill fortune ſtill continued to perſecute him. Scarcely had he reached the bay of Boſton, when, on the firſt of November, another tremendous ſtorm aroſe, drove his ſhips out to ſea, and ſo diſabled them that he was obliged to return to Rhode Iſland to refit, and leave the bay of Boſton unguarded. The count D'Eſtaing, whoſe ſhips were by this time completely reſitted, embraced the favourable opportunity of putting to ſea, which the departure of the Britiſh fleet had given him; and leaving the harbour of Boſton on the third of November directed his courſe to the Weſt-Indies.

The admiral ſtruggles in vain againſt adverſe fortune.

The count D'Eſtaing ſets ſail to the Weſt Indies.

CHAP. XXVI.

Expedition to the West Indies under the Command of General Grant —The British Commissioners return to England—Review of their Proceedings—Expedition against Georgia—Reduction of Savannah.

CHAP. XXVI. 1778.

THE season for active operation between the two grand armies being now over, and no greater force being necessary to be kept at New York, during the winter, than would be sufficient for the defence of the different posts occupied by the British troops; as soon as admiral Byron had failed from thence for the bay of Boston, a detachment of five thousand troops was put under orders for embarkation, to proceed to the West Indies, under the command of general Grant. This force failed from Sandy Hook on the third of November. The transports were escorted by a squadron of six ships of war, under the command of commodore Hotham. Towards the end of the same month another embarkation took place, the object of which was the reduction of the province of Georgia. The troops sent on this service were commanded by lieutenant-colonel Campbell, of the seventy-first regiment, and the naval force by commodore Hyde Parker.

Expedition to the West Indies under the command of general Grant.

The British commissioners return to England.

About the time of the last of these embarkations the British commissioners took a final leave of America, and failed for England. We shall here, therefore, interrupt the thread of hostile detail, for the sake of giving a summary account of their proceedings subsequent to the answer of congress to their first application. In that answer, the congress, as a preliminary to all negotiation, had required either an explicit acknowledgment of the independence of America, or else that the British fleets and armies should be withdrawn: And even then they confined the extent of the negotiation to such an agreement as should not be inconsistent with treaties already subsisting between them and foreign powers. Although the British commissioners, after receiving this answer, must have been convinced that all farther attempts at negotiation with the congress must be fruitless, they nevertheless thought it necessary to reply, that it might clearly appear to the world not to be owing to any backwardness in them, if the negotiation should not succeed. In this reply, dated at New York the eleventh of July, they rejected the last of the two alternative preliminaries, which regarded the withdrawing of the British fleets and armies, as entirely inadmissible; not only for the sake of guarding against the designs of the natural enemy of Great Britain, but for the safety of those who, in America, had taken an active part in favour of the mother-country: And, with respect to the first of the alternatives, they declared, that if the congress, by the independence of America, meant no more than the entire privilege of the people of that continent to dispose of their own property and to govern themselves without any reference to Great Britain beyond what is necessary to preserve an union of force for the safety of the whole empire, such an independence had been already acknowledged in the first letter from the commissioners. They also reminded the congress that they had furnished that assembly with a copy of the powers under which they acted, and as a reciprocal mark of confidence they expected that the congress would make known to them the powers with which they were entrusted by their constituents to contract alliances with foreign powers; and, as these alliances were to have an influence on the negotiation, so they also expected copies of the treaties on which they were founded. But the congress took no further notice of this second letter of the commissioners, than

Review of their proceedings.

CHAP. XXVI. 1778.

barely to enter a refolution upon their journals, importing that no anfwer fhould be given to it; as neither of the preliminary conditions upon which alone a negotiation could commence, had been yet complied with.

General Burgoyne's army being ftill retained in captivity, in direct violation of the convention under which it had furrendered, a remonftrance on this fubject, bearing date the feventh of Auguft, was the next paper addreffed to the congrefs by the Britifh commiffioners. In this remonftrance they complained with fome feverity of the detention of thofe troops, demanded a free entrance for tranfports into the harbour of Bofton to tranfport them to Great Britain, according to the terms of the convention; and, to remove every poffible difficulty, offered to renew and ratify on the part of Great Britain every article of that convention, more efpecially the article by which the troops were bound not to ferve againft America during the war; and to this reprefentation they demanded a fpeedy, direct, and explicit anfwer. But the congrefs, inftead of returning a direct anfwer, tranfmitted to them a remonftrance on the conduct of governor Johnftone, one of the commiffioners, in which he was charged with attempting to bribe and corrupt fome of their members: And this remonftrance was accompanied with a declaration that it was incompatible with the honour of congrefs to hold any farther communication or intercourfe with governor Johnftone, more efpecially upon affairs in which the caufe of liberty and virtue was interefted.

This charge was founded on letters written by governor Johnftone to individual members of congrefs *, with fome of whom he was per-

* In confequence of an order of congrefs, that all letters received by members of that body, or their agents, from any fubject of the king of Great Britain, of a public nature, fhould be laid before them, the following letters were laid on the table from governor Johnftone:

To Francis Dana, *Efq. (Private.)*

" Dear Sir,

" It gives me great pleafure to find your name among the lift of congrefs, becaufe I am per-

perſonally acquainted, and for others had received letters of introduction from their friends in England. Governor Johnſtone had not only

perſuaded, from perſonal knowledge of me, and my family and connexions, you can entertain no jealouſy that I would engage in the execution of any commiſſion that was inamicable to the rights and privileges of America, or the general liberties of mankind; while, on the other hand, your character muſt be ſo well known, that no man will ſuſpect you will yield any point that is contrary to the real intereſt of your country; and therefore it will be preſumed we will loſe no opportunity, from falſe punctilio, of meeting to diſcuſs our differences fairly, and that, if we do agree, it will be on the moſt liberal, and therefore the moſt laſting terms of union. There are three facts I wiſh to aſſure you of. Firſt, That Dr. Franklin, on the 28th of March laſt, in diſcuſſing the ſeveral articles we wiſh to make the baſis of our treaty, was perfectly ſatisfied they were beneficial to North America, and ſuch as ſhe ſhould accept. Second, That this treaty with France was not the firſt treaty that France had *exacted*, and with which Mr. Simeon Deane had put to ſea, but granted and acceded to after the ſentiments of the people of Great Britain had fully changed, after the friends to America had gained their points for reconciliation, and ſolely with a view to diſappoint the good effects of our endeavours. You will be pleaſed to hear the pamphlet wrote by Mr. Pulteney was a great means of opening the minds of the people of England to the real ſtate of the queſtion between us, and that it has run through thirteen editions. The third fact is, That Spain, unaſked, had ſent a formal meſſage, diſapproving of the conduct of France. All theſe I will engage to prove to your ſatisfaction. I beg to recommend to your perſonal civilities, my friend, Dr. Ferguſon. He is a man of the greateſt genius and virtue, and has always been a ſteady friend to America. Private. . . . .

" If you follow the example of Britain in the hour of her privilege, inſolence, and madneſs, and refuſe to hear us, I ſtill expect, ſince I am here, to have the privilege of coming among you, and ſeeing the country, as there are many men, whoſe virtues I admire above Greek and Roman names, that I ſhould be glad to tell my children about.

" I am, with eſteem and affection, dear Sir,

" Your friend and ſervant,

Philadelphia, June 10, 1778. " GEO. JOHNSTONE."

To General JOSEPH REED.

" SIR,

" YOUR near and worthy relation, Mr. Dennis de Berdt, has made me happy by favouring me with a letter to you. I have been informed by general Robertſon of your great worth and conſequence in the unhappy diſputes that have ſubſiſted between Great Britain and her

CHAP. XXVI. 1778.

only been an uniform but a ſtrenuous advocate in the Britiſh parliament for the rights originally claimed by the Americans; and there-

her deſcendants. Your pen and your ſword have both been uſed with glory and advantage in vindicating the rights of mankind, and of that community of which you was a part. Such a conduct, as the firſt and ſuperior of all human duties, muſt ever command my warmeſt friendſhip and veneration.

" In the midſt of thoſe affecting ſcenes, my feeble voice has not been wanting to ſtop the evils in their progreſs, and to remove, on a large and liberal footing, the cauſe of all jealouſy;—that every ſubject of the empire might live equally free and ſecure in the enjoyment of the bleſſings of life;—not one part dependant on the will of another with oppoſite intereſts, but a general union on terms of perfect ſecurity and mutual advantage.

" During the conteſt, I am free to confeſs, my wiſhes have ever been, that America might ſo far prevail as to oblige this country to ſee their error, and to reflect and reaſon fairly in the caſe of others, heirs to the ſame privileges with themſelves. It has pleaſed God in his juſtice ſo to diſpoſe of events, that this kingdom is at length convinced of her folly and her faults. A commiſſion under parliamentary authority is now iſſued for ſettling in a manner conſiſtent with that union of force on which the ſafety of both parties depends, all the differences that have or can ſubſiſt between Great Britain and America, ſhort of a total ſeparation of intereſts. In this commiſſion I am an unworthy aſſociate. Though no man can feel the deſire of cementing in peace and friendſhip every member of what was called the Britiſh empire, ſtronger than myſelf; yet I am ſenſible that it might have fallen to the lot of many perſons better qualified to attain the end propoſed. All I can claim is ardent zeal and upright intentions; and when I reflect that this negotiation muſt depend much more upon perfect integrity than refinement of underſtanding, where a ſenſible, magnanimous people will ſee their own intereſt, and carefully guard their honour in every tranſaction, I am more inclined to hope, from the good-will I have always borne them, I am not altogether unqualified for the taſk.

" If it be (as I hope it is) the diſpoſition of good men in the provinces to prefer freedom, in conjunction with Great Britain, to an union with the ancient enemy of both; if it is their generous inclination to forget recent injuries, and recall to their remembrances former benefits, I am in hopes we may yet be great and happy. I am ſure the people in America will find in my brother-commiſſioners, and myſelf, a fair and cheerful concurrence in adjuſting every point to their utmoſt wiſh, not inconſiſtent, as I ſaid before, with a beneficial union of intereſts, which is the object of our commiſſion.

" Nothing could ſurpaſs the glory you have acquired in arms, except the generous magnanimity of meeting on the terms of juſtice and equality, after demonſtrating to the world that the fear of force could have no juſt influence in that deciſion.

" The

therefore, probably, thought himſelf entitled to take greater liberties with thoſe whoſe cauſe he had ſo powerfully ſupported, than the

" The man who can be inſtrumental in bringing us all to act once more in harmony, and unite together the various powers which this conteſt has drawn forth, will deſerve more from the king and people, from patriotiſm, humanity, friendſhip, and all the tender ties that are affected by the quarrel and reconciliation, than ever was yet beſtowed on human kind.

" This letter from Mr. de Berdt I ſhall conſider as an introduction to you, which line of communication I ſhall endeavour by every means to improve, by public demonſtrations of reſpect, or private friendſhip, as your anſwer may enable me.

" I am, with great reſpect, Sir,

" Your moſt obedient, and moſt humble ſervant,

London, April 11, 1778. " GEO. JOHNSTONE."

To Robert Morris, *Eſq. (Private.)*

" Dear Sir, *Philadelphia, June* 16, 1778.

" I came to this country in a ſincere belief that a reconciliation between Great Britain and America could be eſtabliſhed on terms honourable and beneficial to both. I am perſuaded, and can prove, that the laſt treaty with France ſhould be no bar, and the firſt treaty, if ever you ſaw it, ſhould be an inducement.

" Suppoſing every obſtacle to prevent us from treating removed, we are then to conſider whether the terms propoſed are advantageous. I incloſe you my ſentiments on the ſubject at large; if they concur with yours, we ſhall join in the work with all the prudence, and all the means poſſible and virtuous. I believe the men who have conducted the affairs of America incapable of being influenced by improper motives. But in all ſuch tranſactions there is riſk, and I think that whoever ventures ſhould be ſecured, at the ſame time that honour and emolument ſhould naturally follow the fortune of thoſe who have ſteered the veſſel in the ſtorm, and brought her ſafely to port. I think that Waſhington and the preſident have a right to every favour that grateful nations can beſtow, if they could once more unite our intereſts, and ſpare the miſeries and devaſtations of war. I wiſh above all things to ſee you, and hope you will ſo contrive it. Do not think Great Britain is ſo low; remember ſhe never can be lower than you were at Trenton. It is the ſame blunderers who produced the war who have conducted it. When the ſenſe of the nation is rouſed, believe me ſhe can make ſtruggles that few have conceived, but which I ſhould be ſorry to ſee exerted on ſuch an occaſion.

" Whatever may be our fate, I ſhall ever retain the ſtricteſt private friendſhip for you and yours; but let me entreat you to recall all thoſe endearing ties to your recollection.

" I am, with affection and eſteem, dear Sir,

" Your obedient ſervant,

" GEO. JOHNSTONE."

other

CHAP. XXVI. 1778. other commiſſioners; and being alſo fully of opinion that the privileges now offered to the colonies, which were abundantly ſufficient for ſecuring their liberty, peace, and permanent happineſs, and more extenſive than thoſe originally claimed by themſelves, ought to be thankfully accepted, perhaps he was, for that reaſon, leſs ſcrupulous about the means of inducing acceptance.

Although, in the extracts of the letters which were publiſhed on this occaſion by the congreſs, there was nothing which amounted to the direct offer of a bribe, yet it cannot be denied that general expectations were held out both of honours and rewards, as naturally appertaining to thoſe who ſhould be inſtrumental in cementing the disjointed parts of the empire, and putting an end to the horrors and devaſtations of war. If we ſuppoſe the members of congreſs, to whom theſe letters were addreſſed, to have been actuated by the pure principles of virtue, patriotiſm, and love of their country, ſuch letters, which held out ſelfiſh conſiderations as motives to influence their conduct in a public concern of ſuch magnitude, muſt neceſſarily have been offenſive; and it was probably owing to ſome offended feeling of this ſort that governor Johnſtone's private correſpondence was at firſt diſcloſed, and afterwards became the ſubject of public reprehenſion. Upon the receipt of this complaint and declaration, governor Johnſtone immediately withdrew from the commiſſion, and in the public act executed by him on this occaſion to teſtify his reſolution, which was tranſmitted to the congreſs and bore date the twenty-ſixth of Auguſt, he ſeverely recriminated on that aſſembly, and indirectly charged them with laying hold of this pretence to avoid returning an anſwer to the requiſition of the commiſſioners on the ſubject of general Burgoyne's army; in the ſame manner as on a former occaſion they had paſſed reſolutions about the cartouch-boxes of that army, to afford a ſeeming juſtification for breaking through the convention by which it had ſurrendered.

And

And as he had accepted the office of a commiſſioner only from the deſire of furthering the work of peace and reconciliation, ſo he ſignified to them his determination, that no act done by him ſhould furniſh a pretence for retarding ſo deſirable an end. He therefore declared, that he would take no farther part in any thing that ſhould be done under the commiſſion, reſerving to himſelf, however, the privilege of publiſhing, if he ſhould think fit, a refutation of the aſperſions which the congreſs had attempted to throw upon him. The other commiſſioners at the ſame time tranſmitted a declaration, ſpecifying, that they were utter ſtrangers to the letters, and to the ſeveral things mentioned in the remonſtrance of the congreſs reſpecting governor Johnſtone, until they had ſeen them publiſhed in the newſpapers: That they neither meant to admit the conſtruction put upon thoſe letters by the congreſs, nor to enter into an explanation of governor Johnſtone's conduct, whoſe abilities and integrity required no vindication from them; but that, in juſtice to him and to themſelves, and for the honour of the commiſſion, they thought it neceſſary to declare, that in all the converſations held with him on the ſubject of their miſſion, the principle of his reaſoning ſeemed to be, that the terms which they were empowered to offer to America were calculated to promote and eſtabliſh the liberties, peace, opulence, increaſe, ſecurity, and permanent happineſs of the inhabitants of that continent, and that no other connexion or form of government could be equally conducive to thoſe ends. As the commiſſioners ſeem to have been of opinion that the recent connexion with France was the principal obſtacle which they had to encounter, they embraced this opportunity of adducing in their letter to congreſs ſome new topics of reaſoning to enforce their former communications on that ſubject, and endeavoured to demonſtrate, that the interference of that power was rather from enmity to Great Britain than friendſhip to America, and merely intended

CHAP. XXVI. 1778.

to prolong the conteſt, and fruſtrate the effects of the liberal conceſſions made by the mother-country. They concluded by intimating that, in their opinion, the general congreſs, upon the ground of their connexion with France, even if they had been legally authoriſed to enter into it, were not entitled to aſſume ſo deciſive a part as they had taken, without firſt conſulting with their conſtituents, the provincial aſſemblies, and laying before them a ſtate of facts upon which a true judgment might be formed. The commiſſioners, along with this declaration, diſpatched again their former remonſtrance on the detention of the Saratoga troops, ſigned only by the earl of Carliſle, ſir Henry Clinton, and Mr. Eden: And theſe were the laſt of their papers particularly addreſſed to the congreſs.

The congreſs were probably diſconcerted by the readineſs with which governor Johnſtone withdrew from taking any further part in the execution of the commiſſion. It was obviouſly their wiſh to detain the Saratoga troops as priſoners until they ſhould be redeemed by exchange. It was alſo their intention not to enter upon any negotiation with the Britiſh commiſſioners compatible with their powers, leſt they ſhould give umbrage, or create jealouſy in their new allies: And, to effect both theſe ends, it is probable that they would have willingly laid hold of the pretence of governor Johnſtone's conduct to break off all communication or correſpondence with the Britiſh commiſſioners, more eſpecially as they knew there was ſtill a moderate party in all the colonies, which thought the terms offered by the commiſſioners ſufficiently liberal to be accepted, and viewed with extreme concern and apprehenſion the new connexion formed with France; a kingdom which they had been taught to conſider as proverbially faithleſs. The ſtumbling-block being removed which the congreſs had endeavoured to raiſe in the perſon of governor Johnſtone, they were under a neceſſity, for their

own

own credit, of paying ſome attention to the remonſtrance of the Britiſh commiſſioners on the detention of the convention army; but inſtead of repelling the charges which had been brought againſt them, of having violated the law of nations by infringing a military convention, they again laid hold of a miſerable ſubterfuge, and adhering to a literal interpretation of their former reſolution regarding general Burgoyne's army, they paſſed another, bearing date the fourth of September, as an implied anſwer to the remonſtrance of the commiſſioners, which imported that no ratification of the convention of Saratoga that might be tendered in conſequence of powers which may reach that caſe by conſtruction and implication, or which may ſubject whatever is tranſacted relative to it to the future approbation, or diſapprobation, of the parliament of Great Britain, could be accepted. That this reſolution was evaſive is apparent, when we reflect that it was paſſed without any previous inquiry into the powers under which the commiſſioners offered to renew the convention. For any thing that the congreſs knew, the commiſſioners might have had ſpecial authority delegated to them by the king, for this particular purpoſe, and independent of their general commiſſion. But, to drive that aſſembly from every ſubterfuge, and to remove every previous objection, ſir Henry Clinton, on the nineteenth of September, tranſmitted to them an extract from an inſtruction ſent to him by the ſecretary of ſtate, and received ſince the date of the remonſtrance made by the commiſſioners, by which he was authoriſed, not in implied, but expreſs terms, to demand a performance of the convention made with general Burgoyne, and, if required, to renew and ratify, in the king's name, all the conditions ſtipulated in it. The offer of a ratification now made ſeemed to be of that poſitive and preciſe nature which ſubſtantially removed every previous objection. But the congreſs were not to be ſatisfied; and to fill up the climax of that ſyſtem of evaſion which they had purſued

CHAP. XXVI. 1778.

in all their deliberations on this subject, they affected to consider sir Henry Clinton's letter as deficient in respect, from the casual use of an expression of disapprobation, which, in the warmth of his feelings as a soldier, when vindicating the rights of soldiers grossly violated, he had incautiously suffered to escape him; and instead of answering or complying with the requisition, directed their secretary to write to the British general, "that congress gave no answer to "insolent letters." Thus those brave troops who had surrendered at Saratoga, upon the faith of a convention, which stipulated for their return to Great Britain, were, by the gross violation of it, obstinately persisted in by the congress, still destined to bear all the ills incident to a state of captivity.

The British commissioners, finding all efforts to open a negotiation with the congress vain and fruitless, at last, on the third of October, published a manifesto and proclamation, addressed not only to the congress, but to all the provincial assemblies, and to all the inhabitants of the colonies of whatever denomination*, in which they [illegible] briefly [illegible]

* "MANIFESTO AND PROCLAMATION.

"To the Members of the Congress, the Members of the General Assemblies or Conventions of the several Colonies, Plantations, and Provinces of New Hampshire, Massachusett's Bay, Rhode Island, Connecticut, New York, New Jersey, Pensylvania, the three lower Counties on Delaware, Maryland, Virginia, North Carolina, South Carolina, and Georgia, and all others, Inhabitants of the said Colonies, of every Rank and Denomination.

"By the Earl of Carlisle, Sir Henry Clinton, and William Eden, Esq. Commissioners appointed by his Majesty, in pursuance of an Act of Parliament, made and passed in the 18th. Year of his Majesty's Reign, to enable his Majesty to appoint Commissioners to treat, consult, and agree upon the Means of quieting the Disorders now subsisting in certain of the Colonies, Plantations, and Provinces in North America.

"HAVING amply and repeatedly made known to the congress, and having also proclaimed to the inhabitants of North America in general, the benevolent overtures of Great Britain towards a re-union and coalition with her colonies, we do not think it consistent either with

briefly recapitulated the different steps taken by them to accomplish the object of the commission, and the refusal of the congress even to open a conference with them. They again set forth the extent and beneficial

with the duty we owe to our country, or with a just regard to the characters we bear, to persist in holding out offers, which, in our estimation, required only to be known to be most gratefully accepted; and we have accordingly, excepting only the commander in chief, who will be detained by military duties, resolved to return to England, a few weeks after the date of this manifesto and proclamation.

"Previous however to this decisive step, we are led by a just anxiety for the great objects of our mission, to enlarge on some points which may not have been sufficiently understood, to recapitulate to our fellow-subjects the blessings which we are empowered to confer, and to warn them of the continued train of evils to which they are at present blindly and obstinately exposing themselves.

"To the members of the congress then, we again declare, that we are ready to concur in all satisfactory and just arrangements for securing to them, and their respective constituents, the re-establishment of peace, with the exemption from any imposition of taxes by the parliament of Great Britain, and the irrevocable enjoyment of every privilege consistent with that union of interests and force on which our mutual prosperity and the safety of our common religion and liberty depend. We again assert, that the members of the congress were not authorised by their constitution, either to reject our offers without the previous consideration and consent of the several assemblies and conventions of their constituents, or to refer us to pretended foreign treaties, which they know were delusively framed in the first instance, and which have never yet been ratified by the people of this continent. And we once more remind the members of the congress, that they are responsible to their countrymen, to the world, and to God, for the continuance of this war, and for all the miseries with which it must be attended.

"To the general assemblies and conventions of the different colonies, plantations, and provinces, above mentioned, we now separately make the offers which we originally transmitted to the congress; and we hereby call upon and urge them to meet, expresly for the purpose of considering whether every motive, political as well as moral, should not decide their resolution to embrace the occasion of cementing a free and firm coalition with Great Britain. It has not been, nor is it, our wish, to seek the objects which we are commissioned to pursue, by fomenting popular divisions and partial cabals; we think such conduct would be ill suited to the generous offers made, and unbecoming the dignity of the king and the state which makes them. But it is both our wish and our duty to encourage and support any men, or bodies of men, in their return of loyalty to our sovereign, and of affection to our fellow-subjects.

"To all others, free inhabitants of this once happy empire, we also address ourselves. Such

beneficial tendency of the terms which they were empowered to offer. Notwithstanding the obstructions which they had met with, they still declared their readiness to proceed in the execution of the powers

of them as are actually in arms, of whatsoever rank or description, will do well to recollect, that the grievances, whether real or supposed, which led them into this rebellion, have been for ever removed, and that the just occasion is arrived for their returning to the class of peaceful citizens. But if the honours of a military life are become their object, let them seek those honours under the banners of their rightful sovereign, and in fighting the battles of the united British empire against our late mutual and natural enemy.

"To those whose profession it is to exercise the functions of religion on this continent, it cannot surely be unknown, that the foreign power with which the congress is endeavouring to connect them, has ever been averse to toleration, and inveterately opposed to the interests and freedom of the places of worship which they serve; and that Great Britain, from whom they are for the present separated, must, both from the principles of her constitution, and of protestantism, be at all times the best guardian of religious liberty, and most disposed to promote and extend it.

To all those who can estimate the blessings of peace, and its influence over agriculture, arts, and commerce, who can feel a due anxiety for the education and establishment of their children, or who can place a just value on domestic security, we think it sufficient to observe, that they are made, by their leaders, to continue involved in all the calamities of war, without having either a just object to pursue, or a subsisting grievance which may not instantly be redressed.

"But if there be any persons, who, divested of mistaken resentments, and uninfluenced by selfish interests, really think that it is for the benefit of the colonies to separate themselves from Great Britain, and that so separated they will find a constitution more mild, more free, and better calculated for their prosperity than that which they heretofore enjoyed, and which we are empowered and disposed to renew and improve; with such persons we will not dispute a position which seems to be sufficiently contradicted by the experience they have had. But we think it right to leave them fully aware of the charge which the maintaining such a position must make in the whole nature and future conduct of this war; more especially when to this position is added the pretended alliance with the court of France.

"The policy, as well as the benevolence of Great Britain, have thus far checked the extremes of war, when they tended to distress a people still considered as our fellow-subjects, and to desolate a country shortly to become again a source of mutual advantage: But when that country professes the unnatural design, not only of estranging herself from us, but of mortgaging herself and her resources to our enemies, the whole contest is changed; and the question is, how far Great Britain may, by every means in her power, destroy or render useless a connexion contrived for her ruin, and for the aggrandizement of France.

"Under.

powers contained in their commiſſion, and to treat not only with deputies from all the colonies conjunctly, but with any provincial aſſembly or convention individually, at any time within the ſpace of

" Under ſuch circumſtances, the laws of ſelf-preſervation muſt direct the conduct of Great Britain; and if the Britiſh colonies are to become an acceſſion to France, will direct her to render that acceſſion of as little avail as poſſible to her enemy.

" If, however, there are any who think that, notwithſtanding theſe reaſonings, the independence of the colonies will, in the reſult, be acknowledged by Great Britain, to them we anſwer, without reſerve, that we neither poſſeſs or expect powers for that purpoſe; and that if Great Britain could ever have ſunk ſo low as to adopt ſuch a meaſure, we ſhould not have thought ourſelves compellable to be the inſtruments in making a conceſſion which would, in our opinion, be calamitous to the colonies for whom it is made, and diſgraceful, as well as calamitous, to the country from which it is required. And we think proper to declare, that in this ſpirit and ſentiment we have regularly written from this continent to Great Britain.

" It will now become the colonies in general to call to mind their own ſolemn appeals to heaven in the beginning of this conteſt, that they took arms only for the redreſs of grievances; and that it would be their wiſh, as well as their intereſt, to remain for ever connected with Great Britain. We again aſk them, whether all their grievances, real or ſuppoſed, have not been amply and fully redreſſed; and we inſiſt that the offers we have made leave nothing to be wiſhed, in point of either immediate liberty or permanent ſecurity: If theſe offers are now rejected, we withdraw from the exerciſe of a commiſſion, with which we have in vain been honoured; the ſame liberality will no longer be due from Great Britain, nor can it either in juſtice or policy be expected from her.

" In fine, and for the fuller manifeſtation, as well of the diſpoſition we bear, as of the gracious and generous purpoſes of the commiſſion under which we act, we hereby declare, that whereas his majeſty, in purſuance of an act of parliament, made and paſſed in the eighteenth year of his majeſty's reign, entituled, ' An act to enable his majeſty to appoint commiſſioners, with ' ſufficient powers to treat, conſult, and agree, upon the means of quieting the diſorders now ' ſubſiſting in certain of the colonies, plantations, and provinces of North America,' having been pleaſed to authoriſe and empower us to grant a pardon or pardons to any number or deſcription of perſons within the colonies, plantations, and provinces of New Hampſhire, Maſſachuſett's Bay, Rhode Iſland, Connecticut, New York, New Jerſey, Penſylvania, the three lower Counties on Delaware, Maryland, Virginia, North Carolina, South Carolina, and Georgia; and whereas the good effects of the ſaid authorities and powers towards the people at large, would have long ſince taken place, if a due uſe had been made of our firſt communications and overtures, and have thus far been fruſtrated only by the precipitate reſolution of the members of the congreſs not to treat with us, and by their declining to conſult with their conſtituents; we now, in making our appeal to thoſe conſtituents, and to the free inhabitants of

CHAP. XXVI. 1778.

of forty days from the date of their manifesto; and then, addressing themselves to persons of every description, whether in civil, military, or ecclesiastical capacities, or in private stations, and suggesting

of this continent in general, have determined to give to them, what in our opinion should have been the first object of those who appeared to have taken the management of their interests; and adopt this mode of carrying the said authorities and powers into execution. *We accordingly hereby grant and proclaim a pardon or pardons of all, and all manner of, treasons or misprisions of treasons, by any person or persons, or by any number or description of persons, within the said colonies, plantations, or provinces, counselled, commanded, acted, or done, on or before the date of this manifesto and proclamation.*

"And we farther declare and proclaim, that if any person or persons, or any number or description of persons, within the said colonies, plantations, and provinces, now actually serving either in a civil or military capacity in this rebellion, shall, at any time, during the continuance of this manifesto and proclamation, withdraw himself or themselves from such civil or military service, and shall continue thenceforth peaceably as a good and faithful subject or subjects to his majesty, to demean himself, or themselves, such person or persons, or such number and description of persons, shall become and be fully entitled to, and hereby obtain all the benefits of the pardon or pardons hereby granted; excepting only from the said pardon or pardons every person, and every number or description of persons, who, after the date of this manifesto and proclamation, shall, under any pretext or authority, as judges, jurymen, ministers, or officers of civil justices, be instrumental in executing and putting to death any of his majesty's subjects within the said colonies, plantations, and provinces.

"And we think proper farther to declare, that nothing herein contained is meant, or shall be construed, to set at liberty any person or persons, now being a prisoner or prisoners, or who, during the continuance of this rebellion, shall become a prisoner or prisoners.

"And we offer to the colonies at large or separately, a general or separate peace, with the revival of their ancient governments secured against any future infringements, and protected for ever from taxation by Great Britain.

"And with respect to such further regulations, whether civil, military, or commercial, as they may wish to be framed and established, we promise all the concurrence and assistance that his majesty's commission authorises and enables us to give.

"And we declare, that this manifesto and proclamation shall continue and be in force forty days from the date thereof, that is to say, from the 3d day of October, to the 11th day of November, both inclusive.

"And in order that the whole contents of this manifesto and proclamation may be more fully known, we shall direct copies thereof, both in the English and German language, to be transmitted by flags of truce to the congress, the general assemblies or conventions of the colonies, plantations,

gesting severally to the consideration of each of these classes such motives as might be supposed to have the greatest influence, adjured them all not to let pass so favourable an opportunity of securing their liberties,

CHAP. XXVI. 1778.

plantations, and provinces; and to several persons both in civil and military capacities within the said colonies, plantations, and provinces; and for the further security in times to come of the several persons, or numbers or descriptions of persons, who are, or may be, the objects of this manifesto and proclamation, we have set our hands and seals to thirteen copies thereof, and have transmitted the same to the thirteen colonies, plantations, and provinces, above mentioned; and we are willing to hope that the whole of this manifesto and proclamation will be fairly and freely published and circulated, for the immediate, general, and most serious consideration and benefit of all his majesty's subjects on this continent. And we earnestly exhort all persons who by this instrument forthwith receive the benefit of the king's pardon, at the same time that they entertain a becoming sense of those lenient and affectionate measures whereby they are now free from grievous charges which might have risen in judgment, or have been brought in question, against them, to make a wise improvement of the situation in which this manifesto and proclamation places them, and not only to recollect that a perseverance in the present rebellion, or any adherence to the treasonable connexion attempted to be framed with a foreign power, will, after the present grace extended, be considered as crimes of the most aggravated kind; but to vie with each other in eager and cordial endeavours to secure their own peace, and promote and establish the prosperity of their countrymen, and the general weal of the empire.

"And pursuant to his majesty's commission, we hereby require all officers, civil and military, and all other his majesty's loving subjects whatsoever, to be aiding and assisting unto us in the execution of this our manifesto and proclamation, and of all the matters herein contained.

"Given at New York, this 3d day of October 1788.

"(L. S.) CARLISLE.
"(L. S.) HEN. CLINTON.
"(L. S.) WM. EDEN.

"By their Excellencies command,

"ADAM FERGUSON, Secretary."

On the thirtieth of October the following Manifesto was published by Congress:

"*By the Congress of the United States of America.*

"MANIFESTO.

"THESE United States having been driven to hostilities by the oppressive and tyrannous measures of Great Britain; having been compelled to commit the essential rights of man to the decision of arms; and having been at length forced to shake off a yoke which had grown too burdensome to bear, they declared themselves free and independent.

"Confiding

CHAP. XXVI. 1778.

liberties, and their future prosperity and happiness, upon a permanent foundation. They also proclaimed a general pardon for all treasons and rebellious practices committed at any time previous to the

" Confiding in the justice of their cause, confiding in Him who disposes of human events, although weak and unprovided, they set the power of their enemies at defiance.

" In this confidence they have continued, through the various fortune of three bloody campaigns, unawed by the powers, unsubdued by the barbarity, of their foes. Their virtuous citizens have borne, without repining, the loss of many things which made life desirable. Their brave troops have patiently endured the hardships and dangers of a situation, fruitful in both beyond example.

" The congress, considering themselves bound to love their enemies, as children of that Being who is equally the Father of all, and desirous, since they could not prevent, at least to alleviate, the calamities of war, have studied to spare those who were in arms against them, and to lighten the chains of captivity.

" The conduct of those serving under the king of Great Britain hath, with some few exceptions, been diametrically opposite. They have laid waste the open country, burned the defenceless villages, and butchered the citizens of America. Their prisons have been the slaughter-houses of her soldiers, their ships of her seamen, and the severest injuries have been aggravated by the grossest insults.

" Foiled in their vain attempt to subjugate the unconquerable spirit of freedom, they have meanly assailed the representatives of America with bribes, with deceit, and the servility of adulation. They have made a mock of humanity, by the wanton destruction of men; they have made a mock of religion, by impious appeals to God, whilst in the violation of his sacred commands; they have made a mock even of reason itself, by endeavouring to prove, that the liberty and happiness of America could safely be entrusted to those who have *sold their own*, unawed by the sense of virtue or of shame.

" Treated with the contempt which such conduct deserved, they have applied to individuals; they have solicited them to break the bonds of allegiance, and imbrue their souls with the blackest of crimes; but fearing that none could be found through these United States, equal to the wickedness of their purpose, to influence weak minds, they have threatened more wide devastation.

" While the shadow of hope remained, that our enemies could be taught by our example to respect those laws which are held sacred among civilized nations, and to comply with the dictates of a religion which they pretend in common with us to believe and revere, they have been left to the influence of that religion, and that example. But since their incorrigible dispositions cannot be touched by kindness and compassion, it becomes our duty by other means to vindicate the rights of humanity.

" We, therefore, the Congress of the United States of America, DO SOLEMNLY DECLARE AND

the date of their manifesto, to such as should, within the term of forty days, already limited, withdraw from their opposition to the British government, and conduct themselves in future as faithful and loyal subjects; denouncing at the same time the utmost vengeance of the British nation against such as, after these benevolent offers, should obstinately persist in withholding their allegiance from their lawful sovereign. And, that all persons residing within the revolted colonies might be acquainted with the benevolent offers now made, and be enabled to avail themselves of the pardon proclaimed by the manifesto, thirteen copies of it were immediately executed under the hands and seals of the commissioners, one of which was transmitted by a flag of truce to each of the colonies.

In the mean time, the congress, by a preposterous kind of resolution, recommended it to the executive power in the different states to seize and detain in prison all such persons as, under a pretence of a flag of truce, should be concerned in distributing or delivering the manifesto of the British commissioners, as violators of the law of nations, by circulating seditious writings; whilst at the same time they ordered those seditious writings to be published in the newspapers. And some time afterwards they passed another resolution, threatening to take exemplary vengeance if any one should attempt to put in execution the severities denounced in the manifesto of the commissioners. The commissioners remained at New York beyond the time limited by their manifesto, which expired on the eleventh of November; but

AND PROCLAIM, That if our enemies presume to execute their threats, or persist in their present career of barbarity, we will take such exemplary vengeance as shall deter others from a like conduct. We appeal to that God who searcheth the hearts of men, for the rectitude of our intentions. And in his holy presence we declare, That as we are not moved by any light and hasty suggestions of anger or revenge, so through every possible change of fortune we will adhere to this our determination.

"Done in congress, by unanimous consent, the thirtieth day of October, one thousand seven hundred and seventy-eight.

"CHARLES THOMSON, Secretary."

 as

CHAP. XXVI. 1778.

as they neither received any overtures in confequence of it, nor faw any profpect of being able to effect a reconciliation, they clofed their commiffion, and embarked for England, after having made fome regulations for the benefit of the trade of New York and Rhode Ifland; the only two places that remained to Great Britain in the whole extent of the revolted colonies.

It was now at laft feen, that all attempts to recover the revolted colonies by lenient means were ufelefs; and that force alone could again fubject them to the authority of the mother-country: And the rapid fuccefs of the expedition againft Georgia, which we are next to relate, gave a pleafing hope that the war, if transferred to the fouthward, might be more fuccefsful in future, than it had been in times paft. As the land-force fent on this expedition confifted only of the feventy-firft regiment of two battalions, two battalions of Heffians, four battalions of North and South Carolina provincials, and a detachment of royal artillery, amounting in the whole to three thoufand five hundred men, major-general Prevoft, who commanded in Eaft Florida, the colony next adjoining to Georgia on the fouth, had previoufly received orders to enter that province by land, with the force under him, and make a junction with lieutenant-colonel Campbell, and take the command of the whole. But fo ably did the laft of thefe officers form his plans of attack, and fo well was he fupported by the fpirit and bravery of the little army which he commanded, and the cordial and zealous co-operation of commodore Parker and the naval force, that the reduction of the province was completed before general Prevoft could form a junction.

The fquadron which accompanied the tranfports on this expedition, confifting of fome of the fmaller fhips of war, arrived off the ifland of Tybee, at the mouth of the Savannah river, on the twenty-third of December.

It feems evident that the people of South Carolina and Georgia, apprehending themfelves fecure againft an invafion ever fince the unfor-

unfortunate attempt upon Charleſtown, made by ſir Peter Parker and ſir Henry Clinton in the year 1776, were rather occupied in planning and making preparations for the conqueſt of Eaſt Florida, than in providing for their own defence. Between the inhabitants of Eaſt Florida and thoſe of Georgia, a kind of predatory war had been carried on from the time when the laſt of theſe provinces joined the general confederacy; the object of which ſeems to have been ſometimes plunder, and ſometimes revenge. But during the laſt ſummer two incurſions into Georgia were made from Eaſt Florida, which had a more ſerious aſpect. The troops engaged in theſe incurſions conſiſted chiefly of irregulars, moſt of whom had been obliged to fly from the Carolinas and Georgia, on account of their loyalty to their ſovereign, and harboured all the reſentment againſt their perſecutors which can be ſuppoſed to ariſe from the unworthy treatment they had received. One of theſe bodies of men proceeded by the inlets along the ſea-coaſt, whilſt the other marched through the interior parts of the country by the river Alatamaha. The firſt advanced as far as the town of Sunbury in Georgia, the fort of which they ſummoned to ſurrender. A colonel M'Intoſh commanded the garriſon, and was reſolved to hold out to the laſt extremity. To the ſummons of the beſiegers for the ſurrender of the fort, he returned a defiance in this laconic anſwer: "Come "and take it." The beſiegers being either unprovided with ſufficient artillery, or thinking their force inadequate to the reduction of the fort, abandoned the enterpriſe, and returned towards Eaſt Florida. The other corps of theſe irregulars penetrated through the interior country as far as the river Ogeeche, about thirty miles from Savannah. Here colonel Elben, who with two hundred continental troops had been ſent to oppoſe them, prepared to diſpute their paſſage: And about the ſame time they were informed of the retreat of their companions from Sunbury. Diſheartened with this intelli-

 gence,

CHAP. XXVI. 1778.

gence, and dreading the oppofition which they were to meet in the paffage of the river, they fuddenly decamped and began a retreat. Thefe incurfions into Georgia were followed by another into Eaft Florida, on the fide of the provincials. The troops employed in this incurfion confifted of feveral regiments of continentals, with fome militia from Georgia and South Carolina, the whole commanded by major-general Robert How. His object was the reduction of St. Auguftine, with the province of Eaft Florida: But this expedition proved not more fuccefsful than thofe which had been undertaken againft Georgia; and to the misfortune of the peaceable inhabitants on both fides, general How's retreat from Eaft Florida, like that of the Britifh irregulars from Georgia, was marked with rapine, plunder, and general devaftation. From this unfuccefsful expedition general How had juft returned, and lay with his army encamped in the neighbourhood of Savannah, at the time of the arrival of the Britifh fquadron from New York.

On the day after its arrival, part of the Britifh fleet got over the bar, and entered the river; but the reft, in confequence of foutherly currents and boifterous weather, were unable to follow until the twenty-feventh. In the mean time a company of light-infantry was landed on Wilmington Ifland, to bring off fome of the inhabitants, and was fortunate enough to fecure two of them; from whom information was received of the ftate of the province, and the pofition of the military force appointed for its defence. This was of fuch a nature as determined the commanders of this expedition, although no intelligence had yet been received of the approach of general Prevoft, to lofe no time in commencing their operations.

Savannah, the capital of Georgia, lies on the fouth fide of the river of that name, about fifteen miles from the fea. In the vicinity of this place, major-general Robert How, with a force confifting of fome regiments of American regular troops, and the militia of the province, in the whole about fifteen hundred men, was encamped for its protection, and daily expected to be joined by a considerable reinforcement. The country between Savannah and the sea being low and marshy, and intersected by creeks and cuts of water, the first practicable landing-place was at the plantation of one Gerridoe, about twelve miles up the river; and there a descent was proposed to be made without delay.

In pursuance of this determination, the fleet, on the twenty-eighth of December, in the morning, proceeded up the river, led by the Vigilant ship of war, the Comet galley, the Keppel armed brig, and the Greenwich armed sloop, with the design of landing the troops at Gerridoe's plantation that evening; but several of the transports having got aground from the difficulty of the navigation, the descent was necessarily postponed till the following morning. With the rising of the tide, the transports being floated off, moved up to their station, and at daybreak of the twenty-ninth the debarkation began. From the landing-place, a narrow causeway with a ditch on each side led through a rice swamp to the high plantation ground, at the distance of six hundred yards; and captain Cameron, of the seventy-first regiment, having first reached the shore with his company of light-infantry, immediately formed them, and advanced along the causeway, at the end of which, and upon the high ground, was posted a body of provincials. These, as captain Cameron approached, received him with a general discharge of musketry; by which this brave officer and two of his company were killed, and five wounded; but the impetuosity natural to the highlanders prevented the provincials from repeating it. Rushing on to revenge the death of their beloved commander, they struck terror into the provincials, who quitted their advantageous ground, and fled to the woods. Whilst the rest of the troops were landing, lieutenant-colonel Campbell reconnoitred the position of general How's army, and determined

to

CHAP. XXVI. 1778.

to attack him before the evening. The Britiſh troops were accordingly put in motion, even before the laſt diviſion of them was landed, and having advanced within half a mile of the enemy, were formed in order of battle. The provincial general had drawn up his forces acroſs the main road leading to Savannah, and about half a mile from it. His right was covered by a thick woody ſwamp, and the houſes of a plantation filled with rifle-men; his left reached to the rice ſwamps upon the river, and the town and fort of Savannah covered his rear. One piece of cannon was poſted upon the right, another on the left, and two upon the great road in the centre; in front of which, at the diſtance of one hundred yards, where the high ground was narrowed by the approach of two ſwamps, a trench was cut acroſs the main road reaching from one ſwamp to the other; and about one hundred yards ſtill further in front, was a marſhy rivulet running parallel to the whole extent of the provincial line. The bridge over this rivulet had been burnt down, in order to retard the progreſs of the Britiſh army. Here the provincial general waited the approach of the Britiſh troops: And, had the attack been made only in front, perhaps the ground might have been obſtinately diſputed. But the Britiſh commander having received information of a private path leading through the ſwamp which covered the enemy's right flank, detached the light-infantry, under ſir James Baird, ſupported by the New York volunteers, to proceed by that path and gain the enemy's rear: And as it appeared by ſome movements of the enemy that they wiſhed and expected an attack upon their left, lieutenant-colonel Campbell, in order to induce a belief that this was intended, ordered the light-infantry, and New York volunteers, to file off by their right, as if the deſign had been to extend the front of the Britiſh line that way, until they reached a fall of the ground, by retiring within which to the rear, their ſubſequent movements in their progreſs to the ſwamp

were

were effectually concealed from the view of the enemy. By this manœuvre the attention of the enemy was drawn from that quarter where danger was to be moſt apprehended; and ſir James Baird, under the guidance of a negro, having ſafely conducted his detachment by the private path to the rear of the enemy, ſuddenly iſſued from the ſwamp, and attacked a body of militia, which was poſted to ſecure the great road leading from Ogeeche. Hitherto the Britiſh troops in front had remained quiet upon their ground, without firing a gun in return for the provincial artillery; but as ſoon as it was perceptible that the light-infantry had turned the flank of the enemy, the whole Britiſh line received orders to advance and move on briſkly; and the artillery, which had been previouſly formed behind a ſwell in the ground, to conceal it from view, was inſtantly run forward to the eminence, and began to play upon the enemy. Thus aſſailed, the provincials quickly gave way, and running acroſs a plain in front of ſir James Baird's light-infantry, which had by this time diſperſed the militia and taken their cannon, were again attacked by them; who, with their uſual promptitude, daſhing upon the flanks of the fugitives, completed their rout, and added to the brilliant ſucceſs of the day. The provincials flying in confuſion through the town of Savannah, were cloſely purſued by the Britiſh troops; and before night thirty-eight commiſſioned officers, and four hundred and fifteen men of the enemy, the town and fort of Savannah, with the artillery, ammunition and ſtores, conſiſting of a large quantity of indigo, rice, ſugar, rum, &c. the ſhipping in the harbour, and a great quantity of proviſions, were in the poſſeſſion of the conquerors, whoſe loſs, during the whole of this day, amounted only to ſeven killed and nineteen wounded*.

So

* Artillery, Stores, Ammunition, Shipping, &c. taken at the Reduction of Savannah, in the Year 1778.

48 pieces of cannon.	1 ſtand of colours.
23 mortars,	817 ſmall arms.

94 barrels

CHAP. XXVI. 1778.

So decifive a victory, gained at fo inconfiderable an expence, rarely occurs, and muft be attributed partly to the inexperience of the American general, but principally to the fuperior military fkill and addrefs of the Britifh commander in improving to the utmoft every favourable circumftance which prefented itfelf for the final fuccefs of the day, added to the zeal, vigour, promptitude, and exactnefs with which his orders were obeyed by the brave little army which he commanded.

By the unremitting exertions of lieutenant-colonel Campbell, aided by the zeal and activity of all who bore a fhare in this expedition, the remains of the provincial army were driven acrofs the Savannah river into South Carolina, the different pofts upon that river were fecured for fifty miles up, and the lower parts of the province were entirely at peace in lefs than ten days after the defeat of the American army at Savannah. A great majority of the inhabitants came in, and having taken the oath of allegiance, fubmitted themfelves again to the authority of the mother-country. Rifle companies of dragoons were formed out of thofe who came in to renew their allegiance, whofe duty it was to patrol the country between the advanced pofts, and give information of the incurfions of the enemy; and various other wife and prudent regulations were adopted for the future peace and fecurity of the province.

94 barrels of gunpowder. 78 bag ditto.
1545 cannon fhot. 32 cartridges filled for 4 pounders.
104 cafe ditto. 200 fhells.
9 tons lead pigtail, and a confiderable quantity of flints, nails, fpikes, &c.
3 large fhips, 3 brigantines, 2 floops, and 2 fchooners, fome of them with cargoes on board, taken; and 2 floops burnt.

CHAP. XXVII.

War between the Americans and Indians—War between France and England—Channel Fleet commanded by Admiral Keppel—Engagement between the French and Engliſh Fleets—Irreconcileable Difference between the Admirals Keppel and Palliſer—Inflamed by the Zeal of their reſpective Partizans—War in the Eaſt Indies.

CHAP. XXVII. 1778. War between the Americans and Indians.

SUCH were the principal events on the ſea-coaſt of the revolted colonies during the campaign of the year 1778: On their weſtern frontiers a deſultory war was ſtill carried on between them and the Indians, in the mode originally peculiar to theſe ſavages, but now too generally practiſed by their better-informed neighbours the white inhabitants bordering on their ſettlements. Mutual incurſions were made, and ruin and devaſtation followed on the ſteps of the ruthleſs invaders. Whole families were butchered, their houſes burnt, the growing corn cut up, and entire plantations laid waſte. In this barbarous warfare the flouriſhing new ſettlement of Wyoming, on the banks of the Suſquehanna, fell a ſacrifice to an incurſion of the Indians: And the Indian ſettlements of Unadilla and Anaquago, upon the upper parts of the ſame river, which were alſo inhabited by white people attached to the royal cauſe, were in their turn ravaged and deſtroyed by the Americans.

But we muſt now for a time quit the continent of North America, to purſue the courſe of the war through the various quarters to which it was transferred by the hoſtile intervention of the French.

CHAP. XXVII. 1778. War between France and England.

After the refcript had been delivered which announced to the court of London the connexion and alliance formed betwen the king of France and the congrefs of the revolted colonies; and after the Britifh ambaffador at Paris, and the French ambaffador at London, had feverally quitted the places of their refidence, and returned to their refpective courts, without the formality of taking leave, which, according to an etiquette long eftablifhed, is univerfally confidered as a prelude to hoftilities; both nations began to make the moft affiduous preparations for open war. From Toulon, as we have already feen, a fleet of twelve fhips of the line was fent to fea under the command of the count d'Eftaing; but the principal naval arfenal of the French is at Breft, and there every hand was employed, and every finew ftretched, to get ready fuch a fleet as might enable them to meet their opponents with advantage upon their own element. That they might the more effectually diftract the attention of the Britifh miniftry, the ftale device of threatening an invafion was again reforted to; and large bodies of troops were marched from the interior parts of the kingdom to the fea-coaft bordering on the Britifh channel.

In Great Britain the people had been a good deal divided on the fubject of the American war, and from a knowledge of this circumftance the miniftry were probaby deterred from acting with that decifion which alone could have promifed fuccefs. Had no foreign power interfered, perhaps the war might have gradually languifhed until fuch terms had been offered as would have been accepted by the Americans, whofe refources, without foreign aid, muft foon have failed. But the intervention of the French, in a domeftic difpute between a fovereign and a part of his fubjects, after the affurances which had been given to the contrary, was confidered not only as an act of the bafeft treachery, but as a proof of enmity and hatred againft the Britifh nation inveterately malignant; and to punifh this

this perfidious interference every heart was united, and every hand uplifted. If any abatement is to be made from thefe unqualified affertions, it muft be in favour of fome of the leaders of the oppofition, or their immediate adherents, who were fo much wedded to the caufe of America, that they not only deprecated the idea of reducing the revolted colonies to obedience by force, but even rejoiced in their victories *. But certain it is, that after the alliance entered into by the people of the revolted colonies with the court of France, they loft the favour and good opinion of all thofe moderate men in the Britifh dominions who had formerly efpoufed their caufe, from principle, whilft they confidered them as injured and innocent. But after the Americans had made themfelves guilty, if they were not fo before, by leaguing with the enemies of their country, the people of Great Britain became more united in the profecution of the war: Their refentment was kindled; the national fpirit was roufed with the profpect of the impending difficulties; the miniftry recovered from their defpondence; and warlike preparations were made with a fpirit and efficacy which our enemies little expected. To guard againft the poffibility of an invafion, the militia were called forth and embodied; and although the French, by being the aggreffors, had it in their power to adapt their open interference to the ftate of their preparations, yet fuch was the vigour of our exertions, that a Britifh fleet of twenty fhips of the line was cruifing in the channel before the grand fleet of France was in readinefs to come out of the harbour of Breft.

The Britifh fleet in the channel, commanded by admiral Keppel.

Admiral Keppel had been fixed upon to command the channel fleet, as being a brave and experienced officer, who was highly popular, and much beloved in the navy; and as he was attached to the oppofition, it was hoped that his appointment, if it did not entirely reconcile the leaders of that party to the meafures which were in

* See Parliamentary Debates for a late altercation between Mr. Fox and Mr. Burke, refpecting the French revolution.

CHAP. XXVII. 1778.

agitation, would at leaſt ſilence much of their clamour. In the Victory, of a hundred guns, he ſailed from Portſmouth on the twelfth of June; and during his cruiſe hoſtilities were formally commenced between Great Britain and France.

Whilſt the fleet was at ſea, on the ſeventeenth, two ſtrange ſhips being ſeen reconnoitring, orders were given to chaſe, and conduct them under the ſtern of the admiral's ſhip. One of them, the Licorne, a French frigate, of thirty-two guns, and two hundred and thirty men, being overtaken towards the evening by ſeveral ſhips of the fleet, conſented to ſail with them during the night, but in the morning diſcovering an intention of going off, by attempting to get upon a different tack, a ſhot was fired acroſs her, when in an inſtant ſhe poured a whole broadſide of her great guns and muſketry into the America, a Britiſh line-of-battle ſhip which happened to be neareſt to her, and immediately ſtruck her colours. Strange as this proceeding was, it was rendered ſtill more extraordinary by the following circumſtance that attended it: For at the very inſtant when the French frigate fired her cannon and muſketry, lord Longford, the commander of the America, was ſtanding upon the gunwale of his own ſhip, in friendly converſation with the French commander. A broadſide from the America, which at ſo near a diſtance would have probably ſunk the French frigate to the bottom, would have been a juſt retribution for ſo uſeleſs and audacious a bravado; but the noble commander wiſely reſtrained his reſentment, and ſatisfied himſelf with ſending the Licorne under the ſtern of the Victory. The other ſhip, which proved to be the Belle Poule, a large French frigate, carrying heavy cannon, and commanded by the ſieur de la Clocheterie, was alſo overtaken in the evening, but at a conſiderable diſtance from the reſt of the fleet, by the Britiſh frigate the Arethuſa, of thirty-two guns, commanded by captain Marſhall, who communicated to the French commander the admiral's requeſt to ſpeak with him, and his orders for conducting him into the fleet. With theſe

5 orders

orders the French commander repeatedly and peremptorily refuſed to comply. A ſhot from the Arethuſa was then fired acroſs the French frigate, which was returned with a broadſide from the latter, when a furious and bloody engagement began, which was obſtinately and reſolutely maintained on both ſides for more than two hours. It was almoſt a calm, and as the two frigates were near to each other, the damage done to both was very conſiderable; but the Arethuſa had ſuffered ſo much in her maſts, ſails, and rigging, that at laſt, from the ſcantineſs of the wind, ſhe became quite unmanageable, and floated upon the water like a wreck. Whilſt the Britiſh frigate remained in this ungovernable ſtate, the French commander ſet his foreſail, and with the help of a light breeze which ſprung up, made for the French coaſt, and anchored in a bay amongſt the rocks; from which ſituation his ſhip was towed out of danger the following morning by boats from the ſhore. If the comparative damage in the maſts, ſails, and rigging, was greateſt on board the Arethuſa, it was overbalanced by the greater loſs of men on board the Belle Poule. According to the French accounts the number of killed on board the Belle Poule was eſtimated at forty-eight, and the wounded at fifty-ſeven; whereas the Arethuſa had only eight men killed and thirty-ſix wounded. On the following morning another French frigate, the Pallas, of thirty-two guns, and two hundred and twenty men, which was alſo diſcovered reconnoitring, was conducted into the fleet, and in conſequence of the hoſtile procedure of the commanders of the Belle Poule and the Licorne was with the laſt of theſe ſhips ſent into Plymouth.

The ſeizure and detention of theſe ſhips furniſhed the French with a pretence for charging the Britiſh nation with being the aggreſſors in the war: But when two nations are in ſuch a ſtate of enmity, that hoſtilities muſt neceſſarily enſue between them, it ſeems to be a matter of little conſequence by which of them the war is begun; and on

CHAP. XXVII. 1778.

on the present occasion the first deliberate act of hostility had been indisputably committed long ago by the court of France, in leaguing with the rebellious subjects of the crown of Great Britain, which would have justified instant vengeance on the part of the latter. But on this point the British ministry seem to have been peculiarly delicate; for although admiral Keppel seized and detained two of the French king's frigates, for improper conduct in one of their commanders, he suffered the peaceful merchantmen to pass through his fleet unmolested; nor were letters of reprisal issued in Great Britain until some time after they had been issued by the court of France.

By the seizure of these frigates, admiral Keppel obtained such information of the strength of the French fleet fitting out at Brest, as determined him to return into port and wait for a reinforcement. The fleet accordingly came to an anchor at St. Helen's on the twenty-seventh of June. Thither the first lord of the admiralty immediately repaired, to concert measures for reinforcing the fleet; and with such expedition were these measures executed, that the admiral was again at sea by the middle of July, with an addition to his fleet of ten ships of the line. It now consisted of thirty ships of the line, one of them of the first rate, six of them of ninety guns, and the remainder of the third rate, which were formed into three divisions, the centre commanded by the admiral himself, and the other two divisions by vice-admirals sir Robert Harland and sir Hugh Pallifer.

By this time the French fleet, under the command of the count d'Orvilliers, was also at sea, having left the harbour of Brest on the eighth of July; and no sooner had it sailed than general letters of reprisal against the king of Great Britain and his subjects, grounded on the capture of the Pallas and Licorne, were issued by the court of France. The two fleets being thus at sea, in the summer season, it could not be long before they met. On the twenty-third of July, in the afternoon, they came in sight of each other, when the British fleet

Engagement between the French and English fleets.

fleet happened to be much difperfed. A fignal for forming the line was immediately thrown out; but night came on by the time the fhips were able to get into their proper ftations; and before the morning the French fleet had obtained the weather-gage. For four days fucceffively did the Britifh admiral, by chafing to windward, endeavour to bring the French fleet to an engagement; but his leeward fituation rendered all his endeavours fruitlefs. Although the fleet of the count d'Orvilliers outnumbered that of admiral Keppel by two fhips of the line, and a much greater proportion of frigates, he neverthelefs carefully kept the advantage of the wind, and with equal caution avoided an engagement. But on the morning of the twenty-feventh, whilft the Britifh fleet ftill chafed to windward, endeavouring to profit by a flight variation in its favour, a fudden fquall came on, at the very inftant in which the French fleet was in the act of performing an evolution, and fo very thick, that during its continuance, the two fleets were concealed from the view of each other. When the weather cleared up at the end of half an hour, it was perceived that the French fleet during the fquall had fallen to leeward, and was now fo near the leading fhips in the van of the Britifh fleet, commanded by fir Robert Harland, as to begin to cannonade them. At this inftant the fignal for battle was thrown out by the Britifh admiral; and an engagement began between the two fleets as they paffed on contrary tacks, and in oppofite directions, which lafted about two hours. When the fleets had paffed each other, and the firing had ceafed, the Britifh admiral wore his fhip to return upon the enemy, and threw out a fignal for the reft of his fleet to follow his example, and form the line; but at this moment, obferving that fome of his fhips, difabled in the engagement, had fallen to leeward, and were in danger of being cut off by the enemy, he was in the firft place obliged to take meafures for their fafety. By the manœuvres neceffary for this purpofe, and by the length of time required.

CHAP. XXVII. 1778.

quired for repairing the damages ſuſtained by the ſhips of the rear diviſion, under ſir Hugh Palliſer, which had come laſt out of the engagement, before they could be again brought into their ſtations in the line, the day was ſo far ſpent, that the battle could not be renewed that evening. In the mean time, the count d'Orvilliers ranged his fleet in order of battle to leeward, and put on every appearance as if he meant to wait the attack of the Britiſh admiral in the morning; but in the night he quitted his ſtation, and ſteered for the coaſt of France, leaving three of his frigates to ſhew lights at proper intervals, correſponding to the leading ſhips of the three diviſions of his fleet, thereby to conceal his flight from the Britiſh admiral. In the morning the French fleet was at ſuch a diſtance as ſcarcely to be diſcernible. A ſignal was made for chaſing the frigates, but it was found impracticable to overtake them; and the fleet to which they belonged being ſtill at a greater diſtance, with the wind favourable for carrying it into port, a purſuit was deemed uſeleſs. The Britiſh admiral returned to Plymouth to repair the damage done to his fleet, and to land the wounded men; and the count d'Orvilliers, after the action, made the beſt of his way to the harbour of Breſt, for a ſimilar purpoſe. The loſs of men on board the Britiſh fleet in this day's engagement amounted to one hundred and thirty-three killed, and three hundred and ſeventy-three wounded: What the loſs on the ſide of the French was, does not appear ever to have been made public; but it is highly probable that it was much greater, not only as a French ſhip carries a greater number of men than a Britiſh ſhip of equal force, but as the Britiſh ſeamen point their guns at the hull, whilſt the French ſeamen principally aim at the ſails and rigging.

Irreconcileable difference between the admirals Keppel and Palliſer.

One very unfortunate conſequence which followed from this engagement, was, an irreconcileable difference which it occaſioned between the naval commander in chief and ſir Hugh Palliſer, one of his

his vice-admirals, who commanded the rear diviſion of the fleet on the day of the engagement: A difference which, inflamed by the indiſcreet zeal of the partiſans on both ſides, roſe to ſuch a height, as had nearly created a fatal diſſenſion in the naval ſervice. At laſt both the admirals were in their turn tried by a court-martial for their conduct in this day's engagement, and both were acquitted; the acquittal of the commander in chief being attended with circumſtances particularly honourable. He was not only fully and honourably acquitted, but the charges againſt him were by the ſentence of the court-martial pronounced to be malicious. When the news of his acquittal reached London, very general illuminations, inſtigated by his political partiſans, took place for two ſucceſſive nights; and the thanks of both houſes of parliament were voted to him for his conduct. One member only, Mr. Sturt, had the firmneſs (for many it was believed had the inclination), when the queſtion was put for thanks to admiral Keppel, to ſay, in a very audible and impreſſive tone of voice, No. But after all theſe teſtimonies, ſo honourable to the naval commander in chief, ſo violently had this diſpute been agitated in the daily publications, and ſo confidently did the partiſans on each ſide charge the other with criminal miſconduct or neglect, that an opinion ſeems to have become rooted, and ſtill in a great meaſure prevails, notwithſtanding the acquittal of both the admirals, that ſo much was not done on the twenty-ſeventh of July as might have been done.

One happy circumſtance attending admiral Keppel's engagement, was, that it took place at a critical time, when ſeveral Britiſh fleets of homeward-bound merchantmen were expected in the channel: And as, after the engagement, the count d'Orvilliers was obliged to return into Breſt to refit, it fortunately happened, that during this interval theſe fleets arrived in ſafety.

Both the French and Britiſh fleets put to ſea as ſoon as their damage was repaired; but they did not again meet during the preſent year.

CHAP. XXVII. 1778.

year. By their reciprocal operations the trade of both countries ſuffered a little; but the balance of captures at the end of the year was conſiderably in favour of Great Britain.

War in the Eaſt Indies,

Whilſt the French, with almoſt equal ſucceſs, thus diſputed the empire of the ſea in Europe, they had nearly loſt all their poſſeſſions in the Eaſt. When a rupture was ſeen to be inevitable, ſo expeditiouſly had the Engliſh Eaſt India company tranſmitted their orders, and with ſo much promptitude were theſe orders executed, that the war broke out in India almoſt as ſoon as in Europe. Chandernagore and all the factories belonging to the French in Bengal, at Yanaon, and Karical, with their ſettlement at Maſſulipatam, were wreſted from them during the ſummer; and, in the month of October, the town and fortreſs of Pondicherry, the capital of the French poſſeſſions, and the ſeat of their government in India, with an immenſe train of artillery, and a garriſon of three thouſand men, nine hundred of which were Europeans, after being inveſted for two months and ten days by an army under major-general Hector Munro by land, and by a ſquadron of ſhips of war under commodore ſir Edward Vernon by ſea, was ſurrendered by capitulation.* And thus in leſs than four months from the commencement of hoſtilities, the French power in Bengal, and on the coaſt of Coromandel, was entirely annihilated.

But in the weſtern hemiſphere, to which we muſt now again return, the ſucceſs of theſe two great contending powers, in their al-

* Artillery, Arms, Ammunition, and Stores, taken at Pondicherry, in the Eaſt Indies.

210	pieces of iron ordnance	60	wall pieces.
58	pieces of braſs ditto	45	carbines.
6	howitzers	556	piſtols
20	braſs mortars.	930	ſwords.
2	iron ditto	80	barrels gunpowder
6182	muſkets	21708	ſhot of different ſizes.
168	rifle-barrel pieces		

ternate

ternate endeavours to wreſt from each other their foreign poſſeſſions, was much more equally balanced.

1778. and in the Weſt.

The French having been permitted by the treaty of Paris, in 1763, to ſhare in the Newfoundland fiſhery, which is juſtly eſteemed a moſt beneficial ſource of commerce; and being, by the ſame treaty, allowed during the fiſhing ſeaſon the temporary uſe of the two ſmall iſlands of St. Pierre and Miquelon, for the purpoſe of curing their fiſh, and preparing them for market; it was therefore thought to be an object of ſome importance to deprive them of theſe advantages ſo ſoon as it was apparent that they no longer held themſelves bound by the treaty through which ſuch privileges had been ſecured to them. No ſooner, therefore, had vice-admiral Montague, who commanded on the Newfoundland ſtation, received advices of the hoſtile operations of the count d'Eſtaing on the coaſt of America, than he, in purſuance of orders previouſly tranſmitted to him from England, diſpatched commodore Evans in the Romney, with a ſquadron of ſhips of war, having on board a party of artillery and two hundred marines, under the command of major Wemys, with orders to diſpoſſeſs the French of theſe two iſlands, and deſtroy their temporary ſettlements. This ſervice was performed without any difficulty. The ſquadron appeared in the road of St. Pierre on the fourteenth of September; and the French governor, being totally unprovided with the means of defence againſt ſuch a force, ſurrendered upon the firſt ſummons. The arms of the inhabitants, their fiſhing veſſels, and furniture, with a conſiderable quantity of oil, fiſh, and ſalt, were delivered up to the captors*; and the inhabitants themſelves, amounting

* Arms, Ammunition, Veſſels, Fiſh, &c. taken at St. Pierre and Miquelon, in Newfoundland.

173	muſkets, with bayonets and cartouch-boxes	165	ſhallops without decks
83	ſwords	82	canoes
106	belts	16135	quintals of fiſh
10	ſhallops with ſhifting decks	201	hogſheads of oil
22	ditto with fixed ditto	244	ditto of ſalt.

CHAP. XXVII. 1778.

to something more than two thousand men, were shipped off for France. Every thing valuable, which could not be removed, was destroyed; and the French settlements on these islands were entirely laid waste.

In the same month, and almost with the same ease, the marquis de Bouillé, governor of Martinique, the principal of the French windward islands in the West Indies, made himself master of the British island of Dominica. The contiguous situation of these two islands, and the defenceless state of the latter, rendered this an enterprise of little difficulty. In the evening of the sixth of September, two thousand men were embarked on board transports at Martinique, and with these, escorted by four frigates and ten smaller armed vessels, the marquis de Bouillé, early in the morning of the seventh, appeared off the south end of Dominica. A detachment was immediately landed to attack fort Cachacrou, situated upon a point of land jutting out into the sea, round which the fleet must pass to reach Roseau, the capital of the island; and from the weakness of the garrison, of which the marquis de Bouillé had been previously apprized, this fort became an easy conquest. The garrison was soon overpowered; and the fleet passed round the point unmolested. A general debarkation now took place at Point Michel; and as soon as a landing was effected, the French troops marched on towards Roseau. The battery of Loubiere lay in their way, but it was evacuated as they approached, after the garrison had expended all their ammunition. The regular troops in the island consisted only of a party of the royal artillery, and a detachment from the forty-eighth regiment. These, with all the militia which could be got together, did not amount to five hundred men; and it was soon perceived that their resistance against a force so superior, could not long avail. Detachments of the French were already in possession of the heights behind Roseau; their main body approached the town from the place of their debarkation: The frigates were advancing to batter the

the forts; and preparations were making for an aſſault. In this critical juncture, a deputation from the council and principal inhabitants of the iſland requeſted the governor to call a council of war: Their requeſt being complied with, and the opinion of the council of war being in favour of a capitulation, an offer for that purpoſe was made by the governor, which was immediately accepted by the marquis de Bouillé; and ſuch liberal terms of capitulation were granted as ſecured the inhabitants in the enjoyment of their property, and of all the rights, privileges, and immunities which they held under the Britiſh government, with the further advantage of exporting their produce to whatever part of the world they thought fit, upon the payment of ſuch duties as the inhabitants of the French iſlands had been accuſtomed to pay in the iſlands or in Europe. The inhabitants were even allowed to retain their arms, upon condition of not ſerving againſt France during the war. The garriſon of regular troops, after marching out with all the honours of war, and depoſiting their arms, were to be tranſported to Great Britain under the condition of not ſerving againſt the king of France until they were exchanged. And as a particular mark of reſpect for governor Stuart, he was to be at liberty to go where he pleaſed, and to continue in the ſervice of his prince without reſtraint. So haſtily was this buſineſs ſettled, that the capitulation for the ſurrender of the whole iſland was ſigned, and the French put in poſſeſſion of Fort Young before night. The marquis de Bouillé having thus made himſelf maſter of Dominica, returned without delay to Martinique, leaving fifteen hundred of his troops to garriſon the iſland. His return was probably haſtened by the riſk which he incurred of being intercepted by admiral Barrington, who was then at Barbadoes, with a fleet of two ſhips of the line and ſeveral frigates; and the ſame cauſe may account for the facility with which he granted in the terms of capitulation almoſt every thing which was aſked.

This

CHAP. XXVII. 1778.

This ſudden and ſucceſsful attack created an univerſal alarm in all the Engliſh Weſt India iſlands. But the French force at Martinique was ſtill inſufficient for any diſtant operation; and fortunately before the arrival of the count d'Eſtaing in the Weſt India ſeas, the reinforcement of ſhips and troops which, we have ſeen, ſailed from New York on the third of November, had reached Barbadoes, and joined admiral Barrington, who had been waiting there for ſome time in expectation of that junction.

The troops under general Grant being deſigned for immediate offenſive operations, were not diſembarked: And on the twelfth of December, only two days after their arrival, admiral Barrington, with the whole fleet, left Barbadoes, and ſailed for the French iſland of St. Lucie, where he arrived the following day. The iſland of St. Lucie, on the weſt ſide, is indented by three great bays, ſeparated from each other by narrow ridges of high and ſtrong ground jutting out into the ocean. The moſt northerly of theſe is called the Bay of Du Choque; that in the middle, the Carenage Bay, at the head of which ſtands Morne Fortune, the capital town of the iſland, and the ſeat of the government; and the moſt ſoutherly of theſe bays is called the Grand Cul de Sac. It was this laſt bay which the Britiſh fleet entered on the thirteenth of December. Brigadier-general, now ſir William Meadows, with the fifth regiment, and the grenadiers and light-infantry of the army, which compoſed the reſerve, being forthwith landed, forced the heights on the north ſide of the bay, occupied by the chevalier de Mecond, the governor, with the regular force which he had under him, and the militia of the iſland, and took poſſeſſion of a battery of four guns which had annoyed the fleet as it entered the bay: And in the mean time brigadier-general Preſcot was landed with five regiments, to ſecure the other poſts round the bay, and to preſerve a communication with the reſerve. On the following morning, the whole of the troops

2 being

being difembarked, and brigadier-general fir Henry Calder, with four battalions, being left to guard the landing-place, to preferve a communication with the fleet, and to occupy the different paffes in the mountains on the fouth fide of the bay, the referve, under general Meadows, fupported by general Prefcot's brigade, advanced towards the head of the Carenage, and without meeting with any material obftruction, took poffeffion of the town of Morne Fortune, with the government houfe, hofpital, barracks, and all the ftores and magazines belonging to the ifland; the governor having been obliged to retire from poft to poft as the Britifh troops advanced. From Morne Fortune brigadier-general Meadows proceeded on to the important poft called the Virgie, which commands the north fide of the Carenage harbour, and before the evening was in poffeffion of all the different batteries and pofts upon the neck of land which feparates the bay of the Carenage from that of Du Choque. Scarcely had this been accomplifhed, when the count d'Eftaing's fleet appeared in full view. That commander, upon his arrival at Martinique, had been joined by a fleet of tranfports, with nine thoufand troops on board, and with thefe and his fuperior fleet he was elated with the hope of crufhing the fmall naval force under admiral Barrington, and reducing moft of the windward Britifh iflands before admiral Byron could come to their affiftance. With hopes thus fanguine, he failed from Martinique; Barbadoes, St. Vincent's, Grenada, Tobago, were all in their turn threatened with fubjection to his irrefiftible force. But the unexpected attack upon St. Lucie, information of which was conveyed to him by a veffel which efcaped from the ifland, and met him at fea, difarranged all his fchemes, and for the prefent obliged him to give up his vifionary plans of conqueft. The relief of that ifland was firft to be provided for; and with his fuperiority of force he did not doubt of being able to accomplifh it. Thither, therefore, he directed his courfe, and appeared in fight, as we have already mentioned, almoft

CHAP. XXVII. 1778.

almoſt immediately after the Britiſh troops had completed the circuit of the Carenage, and ſecured the high grounds which command it on the north ſide. He was yet unapprized of the extent of their progreſs; and on the following morning ſteered with his whole fleet for the bay of the Carenage, ſuppoſing it not to be poſſeſſed by the Britiſh troops; but a battery which opened upon his fleet as it entered the bay, and ſtruck his own ſhip the Languedoc, ſoon convinced him of his miſtake, and obliged him, after returning this ſalutation with a broadſide, to ſtand out to ſea.

The count d'Eſtaing, being thus diſappointed in his attempt upon the Carenage, after diſcovering by his movements ſome degree of embarraſſment and heſitation, directed his courſe towards the Grand Cul de Sac, where admiral Barrington, in expectation of an attack, had already made a diſpoſition for repelling it. Never, perhaps, was a greater ſtake committed to the defence of a force in appearance ſo inadequate. Admiral Barrington, with only three ſhips of the line, as many ſhips of fifty guns, and the remaining part of his force conſiſting of frigates, was not only to defend himſelf againſt twelve ſhips of the line, with a numerous train of frigates and American armed ſhips and privateers, but alſo to protect a large fleet of tranſports, having on board the proviſions, ammunition, ſtores, and baggage of the army, which there had not yet been time to land; and thus the fate of the army on ſhore became implicated in that of the fleet. Yet ſuch was the confidence of the officers of the fleet in each other, but above all, in the naval ability and experience of their firm and undaunted commander, that never was a defence undertaken with more alacrity, or greater hopes of ſucceſs; nor did the event diſappoint their moſt ſanguine expectations. During the night, and in the morning, the tranſports being warped into the bay, and the ſhips of war ſtationed without them, in a line acroſs the entrance, ſo juſt a diſpoſition of his very inferior force did the

Britiſh

British admiral make, that the count d'Eſtaing was repulſed with loſs in two different attacks which he made during the day; the firſt with ten of his largeſt ſhips, and the laſt with his whole force. The loſs ſuſtained by the Britiſh fleet in theſe attacks, conſiſted only of two men killed and eight wounded. One ſolitary trophy fell into the enemy's hands, a ſingle tranſport, loaded with the baggage of ſome officers of the army, which there had not been time to warp within the line of ſhips of war. The count d'Eſtaing being thus completely foiled in his naval operations, both at the Carenage and the Grand Cul de Sac, determined to diſembark his troops, and try the effect of an attack upon general Grant by land; and on the following morning, after being joined by a frigate, which was ſeen ſtanding into his fleet, with a number of ſignals flying, he plied to windward beyond the Carenage Bay, and came to an anchor off Groſs Iſlet. In the night, and during the following day, his troops were landed from the tranſports, which had anchored in the bay of Du Choque; and as the poſſeſſion of the poſt of the Vergie would have enabled his fleet to enter the Carenage with ſafety, an attack upon that poſt was the firſt military operation that he projected. Two days before, the ſafety of the Britiſh army depended upon the ſucceſsful reſiſtance of the fleet; and now the ſafety of the fleet was in its turn to depend upon the exertions of the army: For ſhould the count d'Eſtaing ſucceed againſt general Grant by land, admiral Barrington could not long withſtand a combined attack from his ſuperior fleet by ſea, and his batteries on ſhore. The high grounds of the Vergie were occupied by brigadier-general Meadows, with the reſerve of the army; and he prepared to defend them with a reſolution ſuitable to their importance, and the high expectations formed from his known gallantry, and the bravery of the ſelect corps which he commanded. Every thing being in readineſs for the aſſault, the French on the eighteenth of December advanced in three columns, led by the count d'Eſtaing, the marquis de Bouillé, and the count Lovendahl. Thrice did they ruſh on to the attack,

 and

CHAP. XXVII. 1778.

and as often were they repulfed. In the emphatic language of general Grant, "their two firft attacks were made with the impetuo-"fity of Frenchmen; and they were repulfed with the determined "bravery of Britons." In the third attack they were foon broke, and fled in confufion. General Meadows, although wounded early in the day, would not quit the field; but on horfeback vifited every quarter where his prefence was neceffary, and continued to give his orders, notwithftanding the anguifh of his wound, until the triumph of the day was completed, in the final rout and difcomfiture of the French. In the different actions of this day, the French artillery which had been taken upon the ifland was turned againft themfelves, and did fatal execution. Four hundred were left dead on the field; and, according to their own accounts, their wounded were nearly three times that number. The magnitude of their lofs, exceeding in number the whole of the Britifh troops which were engaged, evinces the defperation and perfeverance with which the French made and fupported their attacks, and places far beyond the reach of praife the mafterly difpofition formed by general Meadows for the defence of his poft, and the bravery and firmnefs of the troops to whom that defence was entrufted. The whole lofs of the Britifh troops amounted to one hundred and feventy-one: Of thefe thirteen only were killed, one hundred and fifty wounded, and eight miffing. After this fevere defeat, the count d'Eftaing remained inactive until the twenty-eighth of December, in the night of which he reimbarked his troops, and on the following morning failed with his whole fleet to Martinique. Whilft the French fleet was yet in fight, the chevalier de Micond offered to capitulate for the furrender of the ifland; and although he was now deftitute of all hope of relief, and entirely at the mercy of the Britifh commanders, who might have infifted on a furrender at difcretion, fuch liberal terms were granted as his deferted and defperate fituation gave him little reafon to expect. The governor and his garrifon were allowed to

 march

march out of their posts with the honours of war, and to retain their baggage; and having delivered up their arms, were to be transported to Martinique, as prisoners of war, not to serve in any military capacity until exchanged. The inhabitants, on delivering up their arms and taking the oath of allegiance to the king of Great Britain, were to be secured in the possession of their habitations and property, and in the exercise of their religion, to be governed according to the established laws of the colony, and to be entitled to the same protection as British subjects, and not to be obliged to bear arms against the troops of the king of France. These terms being granted, all stores of ammunition and provisions, and every thing in general belonging to the king of France, were to be faithfully accounted for, and delivered up to the British commissioners*. CHAP. XXVII. 1778.

On the sixth of January 1779, admiral Byron's fleet, which had been so long expected, arrived at St. Lucie, just eight days after the departure of the count d'Estaing; and had it not been detained in the harbour of Newport, at Rhode Island, by contrary winds and stormy weather for fourteen days after it was ready to sail, it is probable, either that the retreat of the count d'Estaing to Martinique would have been cut off, or that a general engagement must have been risked in order to effect it. But all the proceedings of admiral Byron had hitherto been marred by the opposition of the elements; and even in his present passage from Rhode Island, the Fame, one of his ships, was dismasted. 1779.

By his arrival the British naval force in the West Indies became equal, if not superior, to that under count d'Estaing, who was henceforward obliged to act upon the defensive, and shelter his fleet within

* Ordnance, Ammunition, Stores, &c. taken at St. Lucie in December 1778.

59	pieces of ordnance of different sizes	200	whole barrels corned powder
5766	round shot	333	muskets
407	langridge ditto	18,100	musket cartridges filled with ball
2899	cartridges for ordnance	2	cwt. 2 qrs. musket ball.

C H A P. XXVII. 1779.

within the bay of Fort Royal. So apprehenſive did he appear to be of the effects of a general engagement, that for ſix months together he only ventured twice to put to ſea; and both times haſtily returned as ſoon as the Britiſh fleet was ſeen ſtanding towards him. The iſlands of Martinique and St. Lucie are ſo near to each other, that the French fleet could ſcarcely come out of Fort Royal Bay without being ſeen from St. Lucie; and ſome ſmall faſt-ſailing veſſels were alſo appointed to watch its motions. Frequent ſquadrons were ſent to cruiſe off the mouth of Fort Royal harbour, and, if poſſible, provoke the count d'Eſtaing to come out and riſk an engagement; but no mortification of this ſort could induce him to deviate from his defenſive plan. Both fleets were reinforced during the winter; that of admiral Byron by a ſquadron of ſhips from England, under commodore Rowley, who had under his convoy a fleet of merchantmen for the Weſt India iſlands; and that of count d'Eſtaing by a ſquadron from France, under the command of the count de Graſſe: But notwithſtanding this reinforcement, the count d'Eſtaing ſtill remained in the harbour of Fort Royal.

When the ſeaſon arrived for the departure of the Weſt India fleet of merchant-ſhips for England, admiral Byron was obliged to quit his ſtation, and put to ſea, for the purpoſe of enabling the ſhips from the different iſlands to aſſemble with ſafety at St. Chriſtopher's, which was appointed to be the place of general rendezvous. Thither, therefore, he directed his courſe, having left St. Lucie on the ſixth of June. The departure of the Britiſh fleet for the protection of the homeward-bound trade, was the ſignal for the French to commence their operations. A force, conſiſting of four hundred and fifty men, under the command of the chevalier de Trolong du Romain, was embarked at Martinique, on board of four veſſels, and ſailed for the iſland of St. Vincent's, where they arrived on the twelfth of June. A landing was immediately effected, and a communication opened with the Caribs, the original inhabitants of the iſland,

iſland, who yet retained the poſſeſſion of ſome part of it. Between them and the Britiſh ſettlers a war had broke out ſome few years before, which, after much bloodſhed on both ſides, terminated in the ſubjugation of the former. But the Caribs, compelled to ſubmit, were not reconciled: They ſtill retained their ancient reſentment. They conſidered the Britiſh ſettlers as unjuſt intruders upon their poſſeſſions, and were ready to join the French as ſoon as they landed. The garriſon of the iſland conſiſted of ſeven companies of the ſixtieth regiment, amounting to four hundred and ſixty-four men, rank and file, beſides officers, under the command of lieutenant-colonel Etherington, as appears by a return of it made on the firſt day of April in the preſent year; but of theſe only three hundred and fifty-ſeven were actually effective, the reſt being confined with ſickneſs either in the barracks or hoſpital. The French, joined by the Caribs, advanced againſt Kingſton, the capital of the iſland, without meeting with any oppoſition. On the ſixteenth of June they took poſſeſſion of the heights behind the town; and on the ſame day, without a muſket having been fired, the whole iſland was ſurrendered by Valentine Morris, eſquire, the governor, with the conſent of the commander of the garriſon, on terms ſimilar to thoſe which had been granted by the marquis de Bouillé to the inhabitants and garriſon of Dominica. The eaſy conqueſt of St. Vincent's ſeems to have been the cauſe of much ſurpriſe to general Grant, who commanded at St. Lucie: But although no ſatisfactory reaſon has been yet given to the public, for this tame ſubmiſſion on the part of the civil governor, and the commander of the king's troops in St. Vincent's, unleſs the dread of the Caribs, whoſe ferocity during the former war was ſtill remembered, can be admitted to be ſuch; it is nevertheleſs preſumable, that ſuch reaſons did exiſt, becauſe it is ſcarcely credible, that a Britiſh officer, bred in the army from his infancy, who had arrived at the rank of lieutenant-colonel, would

would have consented to surrender his troops in this quiet and inoffensive manner, if there had been any reasonable hope of a successful resistance.

The island of St. Vincent having thus become an easy conquest, the count d'Estaing, whose fleet had by this time been increased by another reinforcement of ships under the command of monsieur de la Motte Piquet, sailed from Martinique towards the end of June, to make an attack upon Grenada, during the absence of admiral Byron. His fleet consisted of thirty-four ships of war, besides a number of transports carrying nine thousand land forces. Of the ships of war, twenty-six were of the line, and the rest large frigates. With this formidable force he arrived at Grenada on the second of July. The fleet came to an anchor in the bay of Moliniere; and the troops were immediately landed. Detachments from these, during the night, took possession of some heights in the vicinity of the town of St. George, the capital of the island, from which the count d'Estaing, on the following day, was enabled to reconnoitre the defences of the place. These consisted of a fort, and an intrenched hill, upon which the hospital stood. This hill, which nearly commanded the fort, constituted the principal defence of the place, being steep and of difficult ascent, and strengthened also with pallisadoes, and some lines of entrenchment. The whole regular force of the island did not exceed one hundred and fifty men, of whom twenty-four were artillery recruits, and the rest belonging to the forty-eighth regiment: To these were joined about four hundred militia, consisting chiefly of French inhabitants, who had become subjects after the peace of 1763, and of people of colour; but in the night after the landing of the French, so many of the militia deserted, that the whole effective force of the garrison was reduced under three hundred men. To a summons sent by the count d'Estaing, demanding a surrender of the island, lord Macartney, the gover-

governor, refolutely anfwered, that he was unacquainted with the force of the befiegers, but that he knew his own, and was determined to defend himfelf as long as he could. The count d'Eftaing had hoped that the difplay which he had made of the magnitude of his force, both by fea and land, would have induced the governor to capitulate, from a conviction that all oppofition would be fruitlefs; but the anfwer which he now received announced an obftinate refiftance, from which the fiege, if carried on by regular approaches, might be protracted until the arrival of admiral Byron with the Britifh fleet. He therefore determined, after viewing the works, to ftorm the lines upon the hofpital hill, whatever number of men it might coft him. A difpofition was accordingly made; and the following night the lines were affaulted in three different places, the column which made the principal attack being commanded by the count d'Eftaing in perfon. The French were at firft repulfed, and fuffered feverely, not only from the fire of the garrifon, but from the guns of a fhip of war in the harbour, which enfiladed one of their columns. In the next attack, however, they were fuccefsful, forced the lines, notwithftanding a brave refiftance made by the garrifon, and gained the fummit of the hill. The cannon found on the hofpital hill were on the following morning turned againft the fort; and the fort being commanded by the hill, Lord Macartney was reduced to the neceffity of fending a flag of truce with an offer of furrendering the ifland by capitulation. In anfwer to his flag, he was allowed only an hour and a half to propofe his terms; and although thefe were got ready, and prefented in due time, they were inftantly and wholly rejected by the count d'Eftaing, who, inftead of them, made propofals fo extraordinary and inadmiffible, that the governor, with the confent of the principal inhabitants, rather than accept of them, agreed to furrender at difcretion; and in this manner, on the fourth of July, the count d'Eftaing became poffeffed of the ifland of Grenada,

In

In the mean time, admiral Byron, who had failed with the homeward-bound fleet from St. Chriftopher's, on the fifteenth of June, after accompanying them a proper diftance, and appointing a convoy to efcort them during the remainder of their paffage, returned with the reft of his fleet to his former ftation at St. Lucie, where, however, he did not arrive until the firft of July, having been for fome time retarded by a ftrong eafterly wind and lee-current, in his endeavours to weather the ifland of Martinique. At St. Lucie he was informed of the capture of St. Vincent's: And an arrangement for its recovery being inftantly made between him and general Grant, fo expeditioufly were the troops embarked, which were deftined for this fervice, that the whole fleet failed on the third of July. In the paffage to St. Vincent's, information was received that the count d'Eftaing had left Martinique, and was gone to attack Grenada. This intelligence produced a change in the plan which had been pre-concerted between the admiral and the general; and a determination was now made to proceed with all expedition to the relief of Grenada. Soon afterwards two veffels which had made their efcape, after the arrival of count d'Eftaing, and before the furrender of the ifland, met the Britifh fleet; and from the intelligence brought by them, the admiral was led to believe that the naval force at Grenada, under the count d'Eftaing, was inferior to his own: From the fame fource of intelligence he alfo learned that lord Macartney expected to be able to hold out for a fortnight. Admiral Byron's fleet, exclufive of tranfports, confifted of twenty-one fhips of the line, and one frigate; the count d'Eftaing's force was reprefented to be between fourteen and nineteen fhips of the line; and under the influence of this intelligence, which afterwards appeared to be erroneous, the admiral made his fubfequent arrangements for the attack of the French fleet. On the evening of the fifth of July the Britifh fleet being fo near that it muft neceffarily be in fight of Grenada on the following morning, the fhips of war were drawn

from

from amongſt the tranſports, and theſe were left to windward under the care of rear-admiral Rowley, with three ſhips of the line, who had, nevertheleſs, orders to quit the tranſports and join the reſt of the fleet whenever on the following morning a ſignal for that purpoſe ſhould be made. The van diviſion of the Britiſh fleet was commanded by admiral Barrington, in the Prince of Wales; the centre diviſion by admiral Byron, in the Princeſs Royal; and the rear by admiral Hyde Parker, in the Conqueror. In this order they ſailed during the night; and at dawn of day the following morning were in ſight of Grenada and the French fleet. One of the count d'Eſtaing's frigates had brought him intelligence, during the night, of the approach of admiral Byron, and he, in conſequence of this intelligence, had given orders for his fleet to get under way by daylight in the morning; ſo that when the French fleet was firſt deſcried by admiral Byron, part of it was already under ſail, and the reſt in a cluſter getting under way as faſt as they could, a ſituation in which it was impoſſible to aſcertain their number. A ſignal was immediately thrown out for a general chaſe towards the quarter where the French fleet lay, another for rear-admiral Rowley to quit the tranſports and join, and ſoon afterwards a third for a cloſe engagement; the ſhips to fall in and form the line as they got up. As the Britiſh fleet bore down, that of the count d'Eſtaing ſtretched out from the land, and formed a line to leeward. Its great ſuperiority was now perceptible; but if in conſequence of this diſcovery any alteration had been neceſſary in the diſpoſition of the Britiſh fleet, it was now too late to make it, as ſeveral of the advanced ſhips were already engaged. Admiral Barrington in the Prince of Wales, captain Sawyer in the Boyne, and captain Gardner in the Sultan, preſſing forward with that ardour which has at all times diſtinguiſhed the Britiſh naval ſervice, had ſoon cloſed with the enemy's fleet, and brought it to action, bravely ſuſtaining their ſpirited attack until they were joined by their companions. To ſuccour theſe advanced

 ſhips,

CHAP. XXVII. 1779.

ſhips, and, if poſſible, to make the action deciſive, the ſame ſignals were ſtill continued. But it was not the count d'Eſtaing's intention, notwithſtanding the great ſuperiority of his force, to riſk the fate of Grenada upon the uncertain iſſue of a cloſe engagement with an enemy, which, though inferior in number, was formidable enough to create apprehenſion; he therefere kept his fleet at a cautious diſtance, whenever the action had the appearance of becoming general, and cloſed only when ſingle ſhips of the Britiſh fleet, in conſequence of their advanced ſituation, were expoſed to the fire of ſeveral of his own. His ſhips, too, being cleaner than thoſe of admiral Byron, he had it too much in his power to increaſe or diminiſh his diſtance as it ſuited his purpoſe; whence it happened that ſome of the Britiſh ſhips were much diſabled, whilſt others were little injured, and ſome few not at all engaged. The three ſhips already mentioned, which commenced the action, ſuſtained conſiderable damage, and loſt a number of men: The brave admiral Barrington was amongſt the wounded. The Grafton, captain Collingwood, the Cornwall, captain Edwards, and the Lion, captain Cornwallis, happening during ſome part of the action to be to leeward of the Britiſh line, ſuſtained the whole fire of the French fleet as it paſſed, and were greatly diſabled; as was the Monmouth, captain Fanſhawe, who gallantly bore down to ſtop the van of the enemy, and bring them to cloſe action. The Britiſh admiral ſeeing the diſabled condition of ſo many of his ſhips, hauled down the ſignal for chaſe, but continued that for cloſe action; keeping at the ſame time to windward, and forming his line as well as circumſtances would permit, to prevent the enemy from doubling upon him, and cutting him off from his tranſports, an intention which ſome of their movements plainly indicated. The deſign of the count d'Eſtaing againſt the tranſports being thus fruſtrated, he tacked to the ſouthward with his whole fleet about three in the afternoon. The Britiſh admiral inſtantly did the ſame, that he might be in readineſs to protect the Grafton,

Grafton, Cornwall, and Lion, three of his disabled ships, which were far astern, and the last of them greatly to leeward. The Lion had lost some of her masts, and her sails and rigging were so much cut to pieces that captain Cornwallis found it impossible to beat to windward: As soon, therefore, as the French fleet had tacked, and appeared to stand towards him, he bore away before the wind, and went with all the sail he could set to the westward. The other two ships stood for the British fleet, and from the extreme caution of the count d'Estaing, were fortunate enough to rejoin it: So studiously did he avoid every thing which could lead to a close engagement, that he made no effort to intercept them, although it was apparently much in his power. Night at last put an end to the action, the French fleet being then about three miles to leeward.

At the time when the British fleet in the morning was nearest to the town of St. George, the white flag was seen flying on the fort and the different batteries, an appearance which left no doubt in the mind of the British admiral that the French were already in possession of the island; and as in the present crippled state of his fleet nothing effectual could be done for recovering it, he sent orders in the evening to the transports to make the best of their way to St. Christopher's, whilst he with the ships of war should keep between them and the enemy. And the Monmouth, which had suffered so much as to stand in need of immediate repair, was ordered to the same place. As the French fleet was only three miles to leeward at the close of the engagement in the evening; and as the count d'Estaing during the action must have clearly perceived his great superiority over the British fleet in point of number; admiral Byron expected to have been attacked as soon as day-light appeared in the morning; but in the morning the French fleet was not to be seen. It had returned during the night to Grenada: And as nothing farther could at present be attempted for the recovery of the island, the British admiral fol-

CHAP. XXVII. 1779.

lowed the tranſports to St. Chriſtopher's, in order to refit his diſabled ſhips. The Lion, which we have mentioned to have ſtood to the weſtward at the time when the French fleet tacked on the day of the engagement, was ſo entirely diſabled, that captain Cornwallis was obliged to bear away for Jamaica to get her damage repaired. In maſts, ſails, and rigging, the damage done to the Britiſh fleet was great; but in men the loſs of the French was beyond all compariſon greater. Endeavours were uſed to conceal it; but the beſt accounts made it amount to one thouſand two hundred killed, including twenty-one officers, and nearly two thouſand wounded; whereas the loſs on board the Britiſh fleet amounted only to four officers and one hundred and ſeventy-nine men killed, and the ſame number of officers and three hundred and forty-two men wounded *.

* Return of killed and wounded on board Admiral Byron's Fleet, the 6th of July 1779, in the Action with the French Fleet off Grenada.

	Ships.	*Commanders.*	*Men.*	*Guns.*	*Killed.*	*Wounded.*
Van Diviſion.	1. Suffolk	Rear Admiral Rowley / Captain Chriſtian	617	74	7	25
	2. Boyne	Captain Sawyer	520	68	12	30
	3. Royal Oak	Captain Fitzherbert	600	74	4	12
	4. Prince of Wales	Vice Admiral Barrington / Captain Hill	617	74	26	46
	5. Magnificent	Captain Elphinſton	600	74	8	11
	6. Trident	Captain Molloy	500	64	3	6
	7. Medway	Captain Affleck	420	60	—	4
Centre.	8. Fame	Captain Butchart	600	74	4	9
	9. Nonſuch	Captain Griffith	500	64	—	—
	10. Sultan	Captain Gardner	600	74	16	39
	11. Princeſs Royal	Admiral Byron / Captain Blair	770	90	3	6
	12. Albion	Captain Bowyer	600	74	—	2
	13. Stirling Caſtle	Captain Carkett	500	64	2	6
	14. Eliſabeth	Captain Truſcott	600	74	1	2
Rear.	15. Yarmouth	Captain Bateman	500	64	—	—
	16. Lion	Captain Cornwallis	500	64	21	30
	17. Vigilant	Sir Digby Dent	500	64	—	—
	18. Conqueror	Rear Admiral Parker / Captain Harmood	617	74	—	—
	19. Cornwall	Captain Edwards	600	74	16	27
	20. Monmouth	Captain Fanſhawe	500	64	25	28
	21. Grafton	Captain Collingwood	600	74	35	63
					183	346

The

The iſland of Grenada having been ſurrendered at diſcretion, the governor, garriſon, and inhabitants, were ſubjected to the will of the conqueror, except ſo far as the law of nations, independent of all poſitive ſtipulation, impoſed limits to his authority. But even theſe, it is ſaid, were ſhamefully tranſgreſſed; and the inhabitants experienced all the rigorous oppreſſion and ſeverity which flow from uncontrolled power, when exerciſed by an unfeeling and unprincipled deſpot.

C H A P. XXVIII.

General Alarm throughout the Britiſh Weſt India Iſlands—Quieted by the Departure of Count d'Eſtaing to Hiſpaniola—Reduction of Sunbury in Georgia—Colonel Campbell's Expedition to Auguſta—Circuit for the Encouragement of the Loyaliſts performed by Colonel Hamilton—Colonel Hamilton quits Auguſta and returns to Savannah—Attempt of General Lincoln to ſtraiten the Britiſh Quarters—Fruſtrated by Colonel Prevoſt—Unſucceſsful Attempt of General Prevoſt on Charleſtown—General Prevoſt retires from Charleſtown, and takes Poſt at John's Iſland.

C H A P. XXVIII. 1779. General alarm throughout the Britiſh Weſt India iſlands,

THE balance of conqueſts in the Weſt Indies was now greatly in favour of the French; St. Lucie, the only Britiſh acquiſition, being but a poor recompence for the loſs of Dominica, St. Vincent's, and Grenada; and the great ſuperiority of the French fleet in that quarter threatened to make the balance ſtill greater, and filled the inhabitants of the remaining Britiſh Weſt India poſſeſſions with general alarm and apprehenſion. But the approach of the hurricane ſeaſon, added to the loſs of men in the laſt action, ſet bounds for the preſent to the ambitious projects of the count d'Eſtaing.

quieted by the departure of count d'Eſtaing to Hiſpaniola.

After remaining ſome time at Grenada, for the purpoſe of ſettling the government, he ſailed with his fleet for Cape François, in Hiſpaniola. And here we ſhall leave him, in order to reſume the relation of ſuch events as happened on the American continent ſince the commencement of the preſent year.

The

1779. Events on the North American continent.

The rigour of winter ſuſpended all military operations between the two great armies in the province of New York, until the return of ſpring; but in the more ſoutherly climate of Georgia, the winter is the properest ſeaſon for action, and in this laſt province it may be remembered that lieutenant-colonel Campbell began his victorious career as late as the end of December. We left him, after he had defeated the provincials, and driven them acroſs the Savannah into South Carolina, receiving the inhabitants of Georgia under the protection of Great Britain, forming them into military corps for their own defence, and framing other regulations for the future peace and ſecurity of the province. He had alſo projected, and was making preparations for proceeding on an expedition up the Savannah to Auguſta, the principal town in the interior part of the province, as ſoon as the arrival of general Prevoſt ſhould enable him to undertake it. That general had met with many difficulties and delays in his march towards Georgia, from the want of horſes and carriages to tranſport his artillery, ammunition, baggage, and proviſions. Theſe were carried in open boats, through the different inland water-courſes, with which the ſea-coaſt of Eaſt Florida, as well as Georgia and the Carolinas, every-where abounds; and the boats were frequently obliged to make large circuits, in order to avoid the enemy's gallies. During theſe circuits the troops, for want of other proviſions, were ſometimes obliged to ſubſiſt for ſeveral days together on oyſters, which the inlets from the ſea fortunately afforded. At laſt, however, they penetrated into Georgia, and reached Sunbury about the beginning of January, the fort of which they immediately inveſted, being the only place of ſtrength remaining in the poſſeſſion of the Americans in the lower parts of the province. Lieutenant-colonel Prevoſt, the brother of the general, by making a forced march with part of the troops, had previouſly ſurrounded it to prevent the garriſon from eſcaping, the commander of which at firſt ſeemed

CHAP. XXVIII. 1779. Reduction of Sunbury in Georgia.

ſeemed determined to make an obſtinate reſiſtance; but after trenches were opened, and ſome pieces of artillery had been brought up, he thought fit, on the ninth of January, to ſurrender the fort at diſcretion, with upwards of forty pieces of ordnance, and a conſiderable quantity of ammunition*; an acquiſition made with the loſs of only one man killed and three wounded. The loſs of the garriſon in killed and wounded was equally inconſiderable; but the ſurvivors, amounting to two hundred and twelve, were made priſoners of war. General Prevoſt, after the reduction of Sunbury, proceeded to Savannah, where he arrived about the middle of January; and as ſoon afterwards as the neceſſary arrangements were completed, lieutenant-colonel Campbell ſet out on his expedition to Auguſta.

In war much depends upon the promptitude with which a commander ſeizes and improves thoſe opportunities of action that are preſented by fortuitous circumſtances. This obſervation has been already exemplified in the conduct of lieutenant-colonel Campbell, on the day on which he defeated the American troops before Savannah, with ſo little loſs on his own ſide; and it is further verified by all the proceedings of this officer during his command. Had he not commenced his operations at the critical moment when he did commence them, without waiting for the junction of general Prevoſt, and had he not improved his firſt ſucceſs by rapidly purſuing the enemy after their defeat, until they were finally driven out of

* Artillery, Stores, &c. taken at Sunbury in Georgia, in January 1779, when the Fort was ſurrendered to General Prevoſt.

24 pieces of braſs ordnance	3002 muſket cartridges, 500 carbine ditto
1 braſs ſeven-inch mortar	150 muſket ball, 1,800 cwt. lead in pigs
20 pieces of iron ordnance	28 powder barrels
824 round ſhot of different ſizes	400 muſket flints
100 caſe and grape ſhot, 30 ſhells, 50 hand grenades	150 cartridge boxes, 72 pouches with powder horns
180 muſkets with bayonets, 12 rifles, 40 fuſees and carbines, and 4 wall pieces	30 claw handſpikes with ladles, wad-hooks, and ſpunges.

5 the

the province, it is probable that the conqueſt of even the lower parts of Georgia, inſtead of being effected in leſs than ten days, might have been a work not only of time, but of difficulty; as a large reinforcement was haſtening towards it, which reached the northern banks of the Savannah juſt in time to collect the ſcattered remains of the American general How's defeated army.

The delegates from South Carolina and Georgia, with a view to the conqueſt of Eaſt Florida, had ſolicited the congreſs to appoint general Lincoln to the command of the troops to the ſouthward. That officer was the ſecond in command in the army which captured general Burgoyne, a circumſtance which of itſelf was ſufficient to give him eclat. But his judicious, brave, and ſpirited conduct on the occaſion, gave him ſtill better pretenſions to fame, and entitled him, in the opinion of the Americans, to no ſmall ſhare in the glory of the atchievement. He was, in September of the laſt year, appointed by congreſs to the command of the ſouthern army, and arrived at Charleſtown in South Carolina about the beginning of December.

Long before Lincoln's arrival at Charleſtown, general Waſhington, through his ſpies at New York, had received intelligence of the intended expedition againſt Georgia; and as ſoon as this information was conveyed to the ſouthward, the provincial government of North Carolina, with a deciſion which did them credit, embodied two thouſand of their militia to ſerve for five months, and without delay ſent them on to Charleſtown, under the command of generals Aſhe and Rutherford, where they were to be provided with arms. Theſe troops arrived in time at Charleſtown to have reached general How at Savannah before he was attacked, had they been immediately furniſhed with arms. But the government of South Carolina refuſed to ſupply them, until it was finally aſcertained by the proceedings of the Britiſh, that Georgia, and not South Carolina,

CHAP. XXVIII. 1779.

was the object of their expedition. The reinforcement which we have already mentioned to have met general How, as ſoon as he had croſſed the Savannah, conſiſted of a detachment of theſe troops, with two regular regiments from Charleſtown, amounting in the whole to nine hundred and fifty men; and with theſe and the remains of the Georgia army, general Lincoln, on the third of January, eſtabliſhed his head-quarters at Puryſburg, on the north ſide of the river, about fifteen miles above the town of Savannah.

Colonel Campbell's expedition to Auguſta in Georgia.

The inhabitants of ſeveral of the interior counties of North Carolina were known to be well affected to the Britiſh government. The expedition up the Savannah, the courſe of which led towards theſe inhabitants, had, therefore, a double object, and was intended to open and eſtabliſh a communication with them, as well as to reduce the remaining part of Georgia. Auguſta, the ſecond town in Georgia, lies upon the ſouthern bank of the river Savannah, and is diſtant from the ſea-coaſt about one hundred and fifty miles. The previous arrangements neceſſary for marching through ſuch an extent of country, in many places thinly, and in ſome not at all inhabited, were ſo well adjuſted by lieutenant-colonel Campbell, that he met with few interruptions, except ſuch as aroſe from the water-courſes in his way, the bridges over which were in moſt places deſtroyed. Upon his approach to Auguſta, a body of provincials, under the command of brigadier-general Williamſon, quitted the town, and retreated acroſs the river. Here, as well as at Savannah, the inhabitants flocked in, took the oath of allegiance, and, for their own defence, were formed into companies, under officers of their own choice. From Auguſta lieutenant-colonel Hamilton of the North Carolina regiment was detached towards the frontiers of Georgia, with two hundred infantry, mounted on horſeback, to encourage ſuch of the inhabitants as were attached to the Britiſh government, and to diſarm the diſaffected. In his progreſs he ſoon diſcovered

Circuit for the encouragement of the loyaliſts, performed by colonel Hamilton.

that,

that, although many of the people came in to take the oath of allegiance, the professions of a considerable number were not to be depended upon; and that some came in only for the purpose of gaining information of his strength and future designs. In various quarters he met with opposition; and all their places of strength held out until they were reduced. The reduction of most of these was not, however, a work of great difficulty, as they consisted only of stockade forts, calculated for defence against the Indians. At last, having nearly completed his circuit, he was attacked by a colonel Pickens, with five hundred militia, who had marched against him from the district of Ninety-six, in the province of South Carolina; but the militia were soon repulsed and obliged to fly. The bodies of nine or ten who had been killed in the action were afterwards found in the woods covered with leaves; their wounded they carried off. During the progress of lieutenant-colonel Hamilton, a number of loyalists in the interior parts of North Carolina had embodied themselves under a colonel Boyd, and attempted to force their way into Georgia, and form a junction with the British troops. It was to oppose these, as well as to check colonel Hamilton's progress, that colonel Pickens had assembled his militia; and finding that he could make no impression upon the latter, he turned his arms against the loyalists, who had by this time forced a passage across the Savannah in the face of a detachment which he had left to oppose them. He came up with them at Kettle Creek, and an engagement ensued, in which the loyalists, after an obstinate resistance, were defeated with the loss of their commander, colonel Boyd, and a considerable number killed and wounded. About three hundred of them, by keeping together, afterwards found means to join the British army. The rest were dispersed, some flying back to North Carolina, and others into South Carolina, where they threw themselves upon the mercy of their countrymen. Of those who

 fled

CHAP. XXVIII. 1779.

fled into South Carolina, ſeventy were tried and convicted of treaſon againſt the new government, but five only were put to death.

February.

Lieutenant-colonel Campbell having received orders to retreat from Auguſta, recalled the detachment from the frontiers, and about the middle of February retired down the Savannah by eaſy marches until he reached Hudſon's Ferry, about twenty-four miles above Ebenezer, now the head-quarters of the army. At Hudſon's Ferry he left the advance of the army under the command of lieutenant-colonel Prevoſt, and returned to Savannah, to eſtabliſh ſome civil regulations in the province, previous to his departure for England, which took place ſoon afterwards.

Colonel Campbell quits Auguſta, and returns to Savannah.

The poſt at Auguſta was found too diſtant to be ſupported; for as the Britiſh troops extended themſelves along the ſouthern banks of the Savannah, the provincials did the ſame on the oppoſite ſide; and general Lincoln, whoſe force was every day increaſing, had not only eſtabliſhed ſeveral poſts in force on the north ſide of the river, but was alſo enabled to detach general Aſhe, with one thouſand five hundred militia, and ſome regular troops, to ſtrengthen the provincial poſt oppoſite to Auguſta, and to improve any opportunity which might offer for croſſing the river, in order to ſtraiten the Britiſh quarters. General Aſhe, upon his arrival at the poſt oppoſite to Auguſta, found that town already evacuated by the Britiſh troops, who had retired down the river: He therefore, in purſuance of his orders, croſſed the river, and followed them as far as Brier Creek, behind which he took poſt, about thirteen miles above Hudſon's Ferry.

Attempt of general Lincoln to ſtraiten the Britiſh quarters

General Lincoln was now forming a plan in concert with general Aſhe, for confining the Britiſh troops within ſtill narrower limits; but before he could carry it into execution, lieutenant-colonel Prevoſt, with a detachment conſiſting of three grenadier companies of the ſixtieth regiment, ſir James Baird's light-infantry, the ſecond battalion of the feventy-firft regiment, captain Tawes's provincial troop of light dragoons, and fome rangers and militia, amounting in the whole to nine hundred men, by making a circuit, and croffing Brier Creek fifteen miles above the place where general Afhe was encamped, found means to get into his rear unperceived; and whilft major Macpherfon, with the firft battalion of the feventy-firft regiment, and fome irregulars, with two field-pieces, appeared in front of the Americans, in order to draw their attention that way, they were on the third of March attacked in the oppofite quarter by lieutenant-colonel Prevoft, and totally routed and difperfed, with the lofs of feven pieces of cannon, feveral ftand of colours, almoft all their arms, and the whole of their ammunition and baggage. About one hundred and fifty of the enemy fell in the field of action and in the purfuit; twenty-feven officers, including brigadier-general Elbert, the fecond in command, with two hundred men, were made prifoners; and a much greater number perifhed in the river endeavouring to make their efcape. Of thofe who did efcape, many returned home: And of the whole detachment under general Afhe, which was fuppofed to exceed two thoufand men, only four hundred and fifty rejoined general Lincoln. The lofs of the Britifh troops amounted only to five private foldiers killed, and one officer and ten privates wounded. The plan of this furprife was well imagined, and the execution admirably conducted; and both ferve to exhibit in a very fuperior point of view the military talents of lieutenant-colonel Prevoft. In confequence of this fignal victory, the communication was again opened between the Britifh pofts and the frontier fettlements.

frustrated by colonel Prevoft.

In the mean time a new governor was elected for South Carolina, and to him and his council were delegated powers almoft dictatorial for the defence of the province. In confequence of the rigorous exercife of thofe powers, the army under general Lincoln was foon after-

CHAP. XXVIII. 1779.

afterwards reinforced with a body of one thousand militia; and this reinforcement enabled him to resume his former design of entering Georgia by the way of Augusta, in order to interrupt the communication which lieutenant-colonel Prevost's victory had opened: He had also another powerful motive for marching towards that place at present, which was to protect the provincial delegates for Georgia, who had agreed to meet and hold a convention at Augusta in the month of May. General Lincoln's force now amounted to five thousand men: Of these he left about one thousand to garrison Purysburg and Black Swamp, the former of these places under the command of colonel Macintosh, and the latter under general Moultrie; and with the rest, on the twenty-third of April, he began his march up the Savannah. Five days after his departure general Prevost, with a view of obliging him to return, passed over the greatest part of his army into South Carolina. The American posts at Purysburg and Black Swamp were immediately abandoned; and general Moultrie, unable to withstand the force to which he was opposed, retreated hastily towards Charlestown, destroying all the bridges in his rear as he passed them. Expresses were immediately dispatched after general Lincoln; but he concluded that the irruption of the British troops into South Carolina was only a feint to divert him from his principal object, and unmoved proceeded on his march, after detaching three hundred chosen troops to reinforce general Moultrie. The British general's original intention was no other than what Lincoln supposed; but meeting with scarcely any opposition or impediment in his progress, except what arose from the destruction of the bridges, and receiving at the same time information of the defenceless state of Charlestown on that side on which he would approach it, he began to cherish the hope of being able to reduce it before general Lincoln could come to its relief; and the farther he advanced, his expectations became the more sanguine,

guine, in conſequence of the general ſcope of the intelligence received from the inhabitants of the province, who joined him on his march.

At Charleſtown all was buſtle and confuſion; and the inhabitants were for ſome time in a ſtate of the moſt anxious ſuſpenſe, between the hope of being relieved by general Lincoln, to whom expreſſes were daily ſent, and the fear of being attacked before his return. Charleſtown ſtands upon a point of land between the rivers Aſhley and Cooper, which uniting juſt below it, and incloſing the town between them, form a bay, opening into the ſea, at the diſtance of ſome miles eaſtward. Towards the bay, and the rivers on each ſide, batteries had been erected, as in theſe quarters the town was expoſed to an attack from a naval force; but towards the land ſide ſcarcely any precautions had been taken for its defence, as on that ſide they had hitherto apprehended no danger. It was in this quarter, however, that at preſent all their danger lay; and the greateſt efforts were made to put it into ſome tolerable ſtate of defence. The ſlaves, with which South Carolina abounds, were now of the greateſt uſe. The houſes in the ſuburbs being burnt down, and an immenſe number of ſlaves being employed, lines and abbatis were in a few days carried acroſs from Aſhley to Cooper River, and cannon were mounted at proper intervals. Fort Johnſton, on the ſouth ſide of the bay, as being at preſent of no uſe, was diſmantled, and the garriſon withdrawn to Charleſtown. General Moultrie, with the remains of his retreating army, entered the town, governor Rutlege arrived with a body of militia from the interior country, and colonel Harris with the three hundred light troops detached by general Lincoln. Count Pulaſki too, with his legion, croſſed Cooper River to Charleſtown the ſame day on which it was inveſted by general Prevoſt. The arrival of theſe different reinforcements all nearly about the ſame time, infuſed ſome ſpirit into the inhabitants, and encouraged

CHAP. XXVIII. 1779.

raged them to ſtand upon their defence. If numbers could give them confidence, they had indeed every reaſon to expect ſucceſs; as, in conſequence of theſe reinforcements, the garriſon exceeded general Prevoſt's army in number by at leaſt one third.

May. Unſucceſsful attempt of general Prevoſt on Charleſtown.

On the tenth of May, in the evening, the Britiſh troops reached Aſhley Ferry, and, having paſſed the river, appeared before the lines at Charleſtown on the following day, the remainder of which was ſpent in ſkirmiſhes of little moment. On the twelfth the town was ſummoned to ſurrender; and favourable terms of capitulation were offered, which however were rejected. But as it was of conſequence to the garriſon and the people of the town to gain as much time as poſſible, things were ſo contrived that the whole day was ſpent in ſending and receiving meſſages; in the courſe of which a propoſal was made on their part for the neutrality of the province during the war, and that at the end of the war its fate ſhould be determined by the treaty of peace. But after various meſſages and explanations of this propoſal, it was utterly rejected by general Prevoſt; and the commiſſioners from the town were told, that as the garriſon was in arms, they muſt ſurrender as priſoners of war. This declaration put an end to the negotiation; and the inhabitants of the town now expected nothing elſe than an aſſault. But on the following morning they were agreeably ſurpriſed when they found that the Britiſh troops had been withdrawn during the night, and had re-croſſed Aſhley Ferry. After taking a view of the lines at Charleſtown, general Prevoſt was convinced, that, although unfiniſhed, they were not to be forced without ſuch a loſs of men as he could not ſpare. He alſo knew that the garriſon, reinforced as it had been, was now more numerous than the troops which he had to lead againſt it *; and that general Lincoln was by this time haſtening to its relief

* General Prevoſt's force was about 2400 men; the garriſon 3300, including militia.

from

from the back country, with a force ſtill greater. The Britiſh general was therefore, at laſt, prudent enough to retire, although with that loſs of credit which ariſes from making an abortive attempt, the original deſign of which appears to have been unwiſe, and the means uſed to accompliſh it incompetent and ineffectual. If general Prevoſt had not a ſufficient force to maintain the poſt at Auguſta, and preſerve the proper communications with it; that force was ſtill leſs adequate to garriſon Charleſtown, even if he had taken it, and at the ſame time preſerve a communication with Georgia, or indeed leave a ſufficient force for its defence. But if this conſideration had been out of the queſtion, he had not with him a train of artillery ſufficient to cover an aſſault.

The Britiſh troops having croſſed Aſhley River, after foraging for ſome days, retired towards the ſea-coaſt; which, being interſected by a chain of inland water-courſes, leading all the way to the Savannah River, afforded them, in conſequence of their ſhipping, not only the eaſieſt, but the ſafeſt means of effecting their retreat to Georgia, and tranſporting their baggage, unmoleſted. From the main land they paſſed to James Iſland, and from thence to John's Iſland, where they took poſt until the arrival of a ſupply of ammunition, which had for ſome time been expected from New York.

In the mean time general Lincoln had proceeded as far as Auguſta, notwithſtanding the intelligence he received of general Prevoſt's irruption into South Carolina. But whilſt he remained at this place, the daily expreſſes which arrived from Charleſtown, with information of the rapid progreſs of the Britiſh troops, ſoon convinced him that ſomething more was now intended by this irruption, than a mere feint: And after eſtabliſhing a poſt at Auguſta, and marching for three days down the ſouth ſide of the river Savannah, a route which was preferred, as the diſtance was nearly the ſame, for

CHAP. XXVIII. 1779.

the purpose of displaying his force, and reanimating the almost desponding hopes of such of the inhabitants of Georgia as were still attached to the American cause, he re-crossed the Savannah, and returned with hasty marches towards Charlestown, until he reached Dorchester, at the entrance of what is called Charlestown Neck; and here he established his head-quarters, until the British troops retired from Ashley Ferry towards the sea-coast.

CHAP. XXIX.

General Prevoſt departs from John's Iſland to Savannah—Succeeded in the Command at John's Iſland by Lieutenaut Colonel Maitland—Britiſh Troops under Colonel Maitland attacked by General Lincoln—The Americans repulſed—General Prevoſt having eſtabliſhed a Poſt in the Iſland of Port Royal, retires with the reſt of the Army to Georgia.

JOHN's Iſland, of which general Prevoſt had taken poſſeſſion, is ſeparated from the main land by an inlet to which has been given the name of Stono River; and the communication between the one and the other is preſerved by a ferry. Upon the main land, at this ferry, a poſt was eſtabliſhed, as well for the ſecurity of the iſland as for the protection of the Britiſh foraging parties; which was thought of ſo much conſequence, that for ſome time the garriſon conſiſted of fifteen hundred men under the command of lieutenant-colonel Prevoſt. For the defence of this poſt in front, three redoubts were thrown up, which were joined by lines of communication; and its rear was covered by Stono Inlet, acroſs which, to John's Iſland, a kind of bridge was formed by the numerous ſloops, ſchooners, and other ſmaller veſſels that attended the army.

Although it was neither the intereſt nor inclination of Lincoln to riſque a general engagement with the Britiſh troops, it was obviouſly his wiſh to attack their out-poſts, and cut them off in detail. With this view, on the fourth of June, he appeared with his army in front of the poſt at Stono Ferry; but, after viewing the lines,

CHAP. XXIX.

1779.

General Prevoſt departs from John's Iſland to Savannah: Is ſucceeded in the command at John's Iſland by lieutenant-colonel Maitland.

thought proper to retire. Not long afterwards, on the ſixteenth of June, lieutenant-colonel Prevoſt departed for Savannah, carrying with him the grenadiers of the ſixtieth regiment, and all the veſſels which had formed the bridge of communication except an armed flat, capable of containing twenty men. About this time it ſeems to have been determined to evacuate the poſt; and upon lieutenant-colonel Maitland, who at Prevoſt's departure was appointed to ſucceed him in the command, devolved the care of conducting that ſervice which the injudicious conduct of his predeceſſor, in carrying away the veſſels that preſerved the communication with John's Iſland, had rendered both difficult and dangerous. But every thing was done which could be expected from the zeal, ability, and experience of this diſtinguiſhed officer. The ſeventeenth, eighteenth, and nineteenth days of June were employed in tranſporting acroſs the inlet the ſick and wounded, the negroes and Indians, with the baggage and horſes belonging to the garriſon, and in deſtroying all unneceſſary huts and buildings, and putting the poſt in a proper ſtate of defence againſt a ſudden attack. Such precautionary meaſures had become the more neceſſary in conſequence of the preſent feeble ſtate of the garriſon, which conſiſted of the firſt battalion of the ſeventy-firſt regiment, much weakened and reduced in its numbers, part of a Heſſian regiment, part of the North and South Carolina regiments of provincials, and a detachment of artillery, the whole not much exceeding five hundred men, really effective, and fit for duty. The weak ſtate of the garriſon, which was not unknown to general Lincoln, tempted him to renew his deſign of cutting it off; and on the twentieth of June he advanced againſt it with a force conſiſting of two brigades of continental troops, a corps of light-infantry, ſeveral regiments of North and South Carolina militia, and a detachment of artillery with eight pieces of cannon, the whole eſtimated by general Prevoſt, in his official letter, at five thouſand men.

1779.

An attack made upon the Britiſh picquets advanced a conſiderable diſtance in front of the works, about ſeven in the morning, which was attended with a ſmart firing of muſketry, gave the firſt alarm to lieutenant-colonel Maitland. The garriſon was immediately ordered under arms, and two companies of the ſeventy-firſt regiment, under the command of captain Campbell, were ſent out on the right to feel the ſtrength of the enemy. The highlanders are not the beſt qualified for ſuch a ſervice: Their impetuoſity is apt to hurry them on too far, and their obſtinate bravery indiſpoſes them to retreat until it is often too late; and ſo it happened on the preſent occaſion. This detachment had proceeded only a little more than a quarter of a mile when it fell in with the left wing of the provincial army already formed: An engagement immediately commenced, which was ſo obſtinately maintained by the highlanders againſt ſo great a ſuperiority of force, that they did not retreat until all their officers were either killed or wounded; and of the two companies, only eleven men were able to make good their retreat. The whole provincial line now advanced within three hundred yards of the works, and a general engagement began with cannon and muſketry, which was ſupported by the provincials with more than uſual firmneſs. The fierce attack made by the highlanders upon their left, inſtead of intimidating, ſeemed to have animated them to copy their brave example. A regiment of Heſſians on the left of the Britiſh line unfortunately gave way, and the provincials preſſing forward, had already reached the abbatis of the works. At this critical juncture a judicious and rapid movement of part of the ſeventy-firſt regiment, which was ordered from the right to the left of the Britiſh line, ſtopped the progreſs of the Americans, and reſtored the fortune of the day. By the great exertions of lieutenant-colonel Maitland, and the officers in general, the Heſſians were rallied and again brought into action. The provincials were, in their turn, now obliged to retreat; but they retreated in good

Britiſh troops under colonel Maitland attacked by general Lincoln.

The Americans repulſed.

CHAP. XXIX. 1779.

good order, carrying with them ſome of their killed and all their wounded. The horſes belonging to the garriſon had, in the view of its evacuation, been tranſported to John's Iſland before the day of the attack, ſo that no purſuit could be made. The whole loſs of the Britiſh troops in this day's action amounted to one hundred and twenty-nine: Of theſe, three officers and twenty-three men were killed, and ten officers and ninety-three men wounded, one only being miſſing. The loſs of the provincials does not appear ever to have been publiſhed, and perhaps never was fully aſcertained. A liſt of their killed and wounded officers, however, has been publiſhed, amounting to twenty-ſix, juſt double the number of Britiſh officers who were killed or wounded: And if we ſuppoſe the loſs of men in proportion to officers, to have been nearly the ſame on both ſides, we ſhall have reaſon to conclude, that the whole loſs of the provincials in killed and wounded did not much fall ſhort of three hundred men. The greateſt praiſe was due to lieutenant-colonel Maitland for the ſucceſsful defence of his poſt, with a handful of men, againſt a force ſo ſuperior, in which he was bravely ſupported by all the officers of the garriſon. Lieutenant-colonel Hamilton of the North Carolina regiment, and majors M'Arthur, Fraſer, and Skelly, in a particular manner diſtinguiſhed themſelves. The artillery was moſt excellently ſerved, and did great execution under the direction of captain Fairlamb, and lieutenants Wilſon and Wallace, all of whom were wounded, and the latter ſo ſeverely, that he died a few days after. It would be endleſs to point out the merits of all who were entitled to praiſe; but the ſingular gallantry of an action performed by captain Moncrieff of the engineers in the ſight of both armies cannot be omitted. That officer was on John's Iſland with the troops under general Prevoſt at the commencement of the action; but as ſoon as the firing was heard, he rode in all haſte to Stono Ferry, and croſſing over, contributed by his diſtinguiſhed

guiſhed ſervices, during the remainder of the action, to the ſucceſs of the day. With twenty men only he ſallied out in the face of the whole provincial army, took an ammunition waggon, and brought it ſafe within the lines. This was a moſt ſeaſonable ſupply of what was greatly wanted; for ſuch was the ſcarcity of ammunition in the Britiſh garriſon, that the laſt charges were in the guns when the provincials gave way. The troops on John's Iſland were put in motion by general Prevoſt as ſoon as he received intelligence of the attack, but they did not arrive at Stono Ferry in time to take any part in the action. The appearance of a reinforcement coming to the aſſiſtance of the garriſon, might, nevertheleſs, have contributed to damp the ardour of the Americans and haſten their repulſe.

The militia under general Lincoln were diſheartened by this unſucceſsful attack; and the greateſt part of them ſoon afterwards quitted the army and returned home. The Britiſh troops were no farther moleſted: The poſt at Stono Ferry was evacuated; and the army retiring along the ſea-coaſt, paſſed from iſland to iſland until it reached Beaufort in the iſland of Port Royal. At Beaufort general Prevoſt eſtabliſhed a poſt, the garriſon of which he left under the command of lieutenant-colonel Maitland, and returned with the reſt of the army to Georgia; that the troops might reſt during the hot and ſickly ſeaſon, which in this ſouthern province prevents the operations of an army as effectually, as the rigour of winter does in a more northerly climate. For the ſame reaſon the American army retired to Sheldon; and nothing of any conſequence was attempted by either during the months of July and Auguſt.

General Prevoſt, having eſtabliſhed a poſt in the iſland of Port Royal, retires with the reſt of the army to Georgia.

The only real advantage gained by this irruption into South Carolina, was a ſupply of proviſions for the troops, the want of which had begun to be felt in Georgia, and the eſtabliſhing a poſt at Beaufort. But the American accounts have charged the army under general

CHAP. XXIX.

1779.

general Prevoſt with gaining other advantages not of ſo honourable a kind, and with ſuch an appearance of truth, that a regard to impartiality obliges us not to paſs them over unnoticed. By theſe accounts they have been charged with plundering the inhabitants indiſcriminately, and enriching themſelves at their expence; an imputation, if true, of a moſt diſgraceful nature and ruinous tendency, not only to the army, but to the intereſt of the Britiſh nation; as ſuch a rapacious conduct muſt have irritated the inhabitants in general againſt the Britiſh army, and alienated the attachment even of thoſe who were the beſt affected to government.

CHAP. XXX.

The Count d'Estaing sets sail for the American Continent—and arrives on the Coast of Georgia—Efforts Military and Naval for the Preservation of Savannah—Count d'Estaing summons Savannah to surrender to the Arms of his Most Christian Majesty—General Prevost succoured by Colonel Maitland—The combined Armies of France and America besiege Savannah—attack the British Lines—repulsed with considerable Loss—raise the Siege—The Campaign to the southward of North America concluded—Campaign in other Parts of the American Continent spent in desultory Operations—Naval Operations of Sir George Collier.

CHAP. XXX. 1779.

ALTHOUGH general Prevost had been obliged to retire from Charlestown without reducing it, and although all the upper country of Georgia was now in the possession of the Americans; yet so long as the British troops maintained a footing in the lower parts of that province, with a post at Beaufort, the inhabitants of South Carolina were exposed to incursions similar to that which we have already related, and could not be free from the most uneasy apprehensions. The post at Beaufort in the island of Port Royal was secure against an attack so long as the British maintained their superiority by sea; and so long as that post was maintained, general Lincoln could not even occupy his former quarters at Purysburg, without the danger of being inclosed between the British troops at Savannah and those at Beaufort. On the other hand, if the British

 lost

CHAP. XXX. 1779.

loſt their ſuperiority by ſea, the ſeparation of their force into two diviſions would render each of them an eaſier conqueſt. Moved by ſuch conſiderations, Rutledge, the governor of South Carolina, Lincoln, the commander of the ſouthern army, and monſieur Plombard, the French conſul at Charleſtown, ſeverally wrote letters to the count d'Eſtaing, who by this time had arrived at Cape François, after the conqueſt of Grenada. In theſe they repreſented to him the ſtate of affairs in the ſouthern provinces, and pointed out the advantages which might be expected, ſhould he, during the hurricane months in the Weſt Indies, viſit the American coaſt with his fleet, and co-operate with general Lincoln in the recovery of Georgia. The count d'Eſtaing, who had diſcretionary orders from his court for ſuch a co-operation, fluſhed with his ſucceſs at Grenada, indulged the ambitious but vain hope of being able, not only to ſweep the American coaſt with his ſuperior fleet, but by acting in conjunction with the provincials to reduce the different poſts occupied by the Britiſh troops within the limits of the revolted provinces, and thereby put an end to the war even during the preſent campaign. To a man who entertained ſuch viſionary projects, the applications from South Carolina, with their propoſals for co-operation, could not fail to be highly acceptable; and they met with his immediate concurrence. Georgia, it was ſuppoſed, would be an eaſy conqueſt, and was, therefore, the fitteſt for the commencement of his victorious career. In compliance with the requiſition which had been made to him, the count d'Eſtaing ſailed forthwith for the American continent, proceeding by the windward paſſage. Two ſhips of the line, with three frigates, were diſpatched as ſoon as he had got through the windward paſſage, to announce his approach to the inhabitants of Charleſtown; and with the reſt of his fleet, conſiſting of twenty ſhips of the line, two ſhips of fifty guns, and eleven frigates, having on board a conſiderable land force, he arrived on the coaſt of Georgia about

The count d'Eſtaing ſets ſail for the American continent,

and arrives on the coaſt of Georgia.

September.

about the beginning of September. So ſudden and unexpected was the count d'Eſtaing's appearance on this part of the American coaſt, that the Experiment of fifty guns, commanded by ſir James Wallace, and two ſtore-ſhips under his convoy, unapprehenſive of danger, had the misfortune to fall in with the French fleet off the bar of Savannah river, and were of courſe taken, but not till after a deſperate reſiſtance made by the Experiment, although ſhe had been previouſly diſmaſted in a ſtorm. The Ariel of twenty-four guns, which had been on a cruiſe off Charleſtown bar, ſhared the ſame fate.

As ſoon as intelligence of the arrival of count d'Eſtaing reached South Carolina, general Lincoln, with the force which he had then with him, inſtantly marched towards Georgia: Orders were alſo iſſued for aſſembling the militia, who were, with all expedition, to follow general Lincoln; and veſſels of a proper draught of water were diſpatched from Charleſtown to aſſiſt in landing the French troops.

It does not appear that the Britiſh commanders in Georgia were appriſed of the arrival of count d'Eſtaing until the fourth of September, when his whole force, conſiſting of forty-one ſail, was ſeen to the ſouthward of Tybee plying to windward. Information was immediately ſent to general Prevoſt; in conſequence of which, meaſures were taken for increaſing the fortifications at Savannah, and putting the town in a proper poſture of defence. The garriſon at Sunbury, under lieutenant-colonel Cruger, was withdrawn; and orders were diſpatched to Beaufort for lieutenant-colonel Maitland with the troops, and captain Chriſtian of the navy, with the ſhips and gallies under his command, to repair in all haſte to Savannah.

Efforts military and naval for the preſervation of Savannah.

In the mean time, captain Henry, who commanded the Britiſh naval force in the river Savannah, was taking precautions as well for its ſafety as for rendering it ſerviceable in the defence of the town.

 The

CHAP. XXX. 1779.

The leading marks upon the ſhore, which point out the channel to ſhips paſſing the bar, were cut down; and the ſquadron under captain Henry, which conſiſted only of the Fowey, Roſe, Keppel armed brig, and Germaine provincial armed ſhip, with ſome gallies, was ſo ſtationed that it might retire with ſafety towards the town of Savannah whenever future circumſtances ſhould render it expedient.

The retreat of this ſmall ſquadron ſoon became a meaſure of abſolute neceſſity. On the ninth of October the French fleet came to an anchor off the bar; and as the line-of-battle ſhips, from their great draught of water, could not paſs it, nor come near the ſhore, the ſmall coaſting veſſels ſent from Charleſtown were employed in receiving the troops from the French ſhips, and landing them at Beaulieu in Oſſabaw Sound, an inlet of the ſea ſome miles ſouth of the mouth of the river Savannah. On the following day four French frigates entered the anchorage ground at Tybee, and rendered it neceſſary for the Britiſh naval force to move up the river to Savannah. Upon its arrival the guns were landed from the ſhips, and mounted on the batteries. The marines were incorporated with the grenadiers of the ſixtieth regiment; and the ſeamen were put on ſhore to aſſiſt in working the artillery. The Roſe, and Savannah armed ſhip, with four tranſports, were ſunk acroſs the channel below the town, to prevent the French frigates from coming higher; and above it ſome ſmaller veſſels were ſunk, and a boom was laid acroſs to prevent fire-rafts from being ſent down. The Germaine armed brig alone retained her guns; and ſhe was ſtationed off *Yamiraw*, above the town, to flank the right of the Britiſh lines. Theſe diſpoſitions were made on the river, whilſt on ſhore the troops, aſſiſted by ſome hundreds of negroes, were employed in ſtrengthening the old, and erecting new works for the defence of the town.

As ſoon as the debarkation of the French troops was completed, the count d'Eſtaing marched againſt Savannah, and without waiting for

CHAP. XXX. 1779.

for a junction with the American army, which was every instant expected to come up, summoned general Prevost to surrender the town to the arms of his most christian majesty, displaying in his summons, in terms bordering on extravagance, the magnitude of his force, and the valour of his troops, who had so lately stormed the fortifications at Grenada, and in so short a time atchieved the conquest of that island, and threatening to make general Prevost answerable in his own person, should he, after this premonition, wilfully persist in making a fruitless defence. This hasty proceeding of the count d'Estaing, without waiting for general Lincoln, or joining the American states in the summons for a surrender, had nearly created a difference between him and his allies. By some it was thought to be a plain indication that the French meant to conquer for themselves; but upon a remonstrance being afterwards made by general Lincoln, the count d'Estaing gave such an explanation of his motives and intentions as was deemed satisfactory. General Prevost, to whom it was of the utmost importance to gain time, returned a civil message to the count d'Estaing, acknowledging the receipt of the summons, and desiring twenty-four hours to consider of an answer, and to prepare the terms on which a surrender might be made, should that be his ultimate determination. The request was granted without any difficulty; the count d'Estaing expecting nothing less than a surrender of the town at the expiration of the time fixed for an answer: But it was made with a very different view by general Prevost. He hoped that the troops under lieutenant-colonel Maitland might arrive during the interval; and in this hope he was not disappointed. That officer, after struggling with difficulties during some part of his route, which, to a mind less determined, would have appeared insurmountable, arrived at Savannah before the expiration of the truce, with the best part of his detachment, amounting to about eight hundred men. As the French were in possession

General Prevost succoured by colonel Maitland.

of

CHAP. XXX. 1779.

of all the lower part of the river, he had no other way left of effecting a junction with general Prevoſt but by tranſporting his troops in boats through the marſhes by an inland water-courſe called Wall's Cut, which for two miles was ſo ſhoal, that the men, wading up to their middle, were obliged to drag the boats by main force through the mud. The reſidue of the garriſon at Beaufort, which for want of a ſufficient number of boats could not be tranſported, remained with the ſhips and gallies under the command of captain Chriſtian; and their retreat being now cut off, they took a new poſition in Callibogie Sound, where, by erecting batteries on the ſhore, they made ſuch a ſtrong diſpoſition for defence, that neither the French nor Americans attempted to moleſt them during the ſubſequent ſiege of Savannah.

The ſafe arrival of ſo conſiderable a reinforcement, and that too of choſen troops, but above all, the preſence of the officer who commanded them, in whoſe zeal, ability, and military experience ſo much confidence was deſervedly placed by the army, inſpired the garriſon of Savannah with new animation: An anſwer was returned to the count d'Eſtaing, that the town would be defended to the laſt extremity: The zeal and ardour of both the officers and men were, if poſſible, increaſed; and new defences were daily conſtructed under the judicious eye and maſterly direction of that able engineer, captain Moncrieff.

After the arrival of general Lincoln with the American army, ſome time was required for landing and bringing up the heavy artillery from the ſhips, which, on account of their diſtance from the ſhore, and a ſcarcity of horſes and carriages, was a work of conſiderable labour and difficulty. Retarded by ſuch impediments, the combined armies of French and Americans did not begin to break ground for the purpoſe of carrying on their approaches until the twenty-third of September, nor were their batteries ready to open until the

fourth

CHAP. XXX.

1779. October.

The combined armies of France and America besiege Savannah.

fourth of the following month. During this interval, attempts were made to interrupt their operations by two different forties; the firſt of which, under major Graham of the ſixteenth regiment, reached the lines of the enemy, and threw them into confuſion; and when this detachment retired, it was incautiouſly purſued ſo cloſe to the Britiſh lines, that the confederates in their retreat loſt a great number of men, by a well-directed fire from the works. The other ſortie under major M'Arthur, was ſo artfully conducted, that it produced a firing between the French and American camps.

On the morning of the fourth of October the batteries of the beſiegers having opened with a diſcharge from fifty-three pieces of heavy cannon and fourteen mortars, a requeſt was made by general Prevoſt that the women and children might be permitted to leave the town and embark on board veſſels in the river, which ſhould be placed under the protection of the count d'Eſtaing, and wait the iſſue of the ſiege: But this propoſal, dictated by humanity, was rejected with inſult. Fortunately, however, for the inhabitants as well as the garriſon, although an inceſſant cannonade from ſo many pieces of artillery, was continued from the fourth to the ninth of October, leſs injury was done to the houſes in the town than might have been expected; few lives were loſt, and the defences were in no reſpect materially damaged.

The French troops landed from the ſhips amounted to about five thouſand men, and no doubt being entertained amongſt the Americans of the fall of Savannah, the militia poured in as to a certain triumph, and joined general Lincoln in ſuch numbers, that the combined armies, it is ſaid, amounted to more than ten thouſand men. The force in Savannah, under general Prevoſt, did not exceed two thouſand five hundred of all ſorts, regulars, provincial corps, ſeamen, militia, and volunteers. But the diſparity in numbers was in ſome degree compenſated by the extraordinary zeal and ardour which animated

CHAP. XXX. 1779.

animated the besieged, from the commander in chief down to the humble African, whose incessant and cheerful labours, in rearing those numerous defences which were completed with so much expedition as to astonish the besiegers, ought not to be forgotten in a history of this memorable siege. When the French were first landed, not more than ten or twelve pieces of artillery appeared upon the fortifications at Savannah: But so incessantly did the garrison labour in strengthening and enlarging the old works, and in erecting new redoubts and batteries, that before the conclusion of the siege near one hundred pieces of cannon were mounted.

The town of Savannah being situated upon the southern bank of the river of that name, had two of its sides secured by natural boundaries, one by the river behind it, and the other by a thick swamp and woody morass communicating with the river above the town. The other two sides were originally open towards the country, which in front of them for several miles was level and entirely cleared of wood: But they were by this time covered with artificial works, the right and left being defended by redoubts, and the centre by seamen's batteries in front, with impalements and traverses thrown up behind to protect the troops from the fire of the besiegers; and the whole extent of the works was surrounded with an abbatis. The redoubts on the right towards the swamp were three in number: That in the centre was garrisoned by two companies of militia, with the North Carolina regiment to support them, under the command of lieutenant-colonel Hamilton. Captains Roworth and Wylie, with the provincial corps of king's rangers, were posted in the redoubt on the right; and captain Tawse, with his corps of provincial dragoons dismounted, in that on the left, called the Springhill Redoubt, supported by the South Carolina regiment. To the right of the whole was a sailors battery of nine-pounders, covered by a company of the British legion, under the command of captain Stewart; and

2 between

between the centre and Springhill redoubt, was another of theſe batteries, under the direction of captain Manby, behind which were poſted the grenadiers of the ſixtieth regiment, under the command of lieutenant-colonel Glazier with the marines which had been landed from the ſhips of war. And the whole of this force on the right of the lines was under the command of lieutenant-colonel Maitland. On the left of the lines were two redoubts ſtrongly conſtructed with a maſſy frame-work of green ſpongy wood filled up with ſand and mounted with heavy cannon, one of them commanded by lieutenant-colonel Cruger, and the other by major Wright, having under him the Georgia loyaliſts. Behind the impalements and traverſes in the centre of the works were poſted the two battalions of the ſeventy-firſt regiment, two regiments of Heſſians, the New York volunteers, a battalion of Skinner's brigade, one of Delancey's, and the light-infantry of the army under the command of major Graham; all which corps were ready to act as circumſtances ſhould require, and to ſupport any part of the lines that might be attacked.

Such was the ſtate of the works at Savannah, and ſuch the poſition of the troops for its defence, at the time when the count d'Eſtaing, grown impatient under the unexpected reſiſtance which he had met with, reſolved to diſcontinue his regular approaches, and ſtorm the Britiſh entrenchments. He had already ſpent more time before Savannah, without having made any ſenſible impreſſion upon the garriſon, than he had aſſigned for the completion of the whole enterpriſe. His fleet, lying at anchor in the open ſea, was expoſed to the danger of being driven off the coaſt, at this late ſeaſon of the year, by tempeſtuous weather, and leaving him and his troops behind: But this danger was nothing, compared to what might have been apprehended had the Britiſh fleet followed him from the Weſt Indies, and made an attack upon his ſhips whilſt they were weakened by the number of men and guns that had been landed for carry-

CHAP. XXX. 1779.

ing on the ſiege of Savannah. Theſe conſiderations, the force of which was heightened by a joint repreſentation from his naval officers, added to the natural impatience of temper which characteriſed the count d'Eſtaing, determined him to riſque an aſſault under all its preſent diſadvantages, rather than waſte longer time in carrying on the ſiege by regular approaches. To facilitate the ſucceſs of the enterpriſe, an officer with five men, on the eighth of October, advanced under a heavy fire from the garriſon, and kindled the abbatis; but the dampneſs of the air, and the moiſture of the green wood of which the abbatis was compoſed, ſoon extinguiſhed the flames.

Attack the Britiſh lines.

The morning of the ninth of October was fixed upon for making the aſſault; and two feigned attacks by the militia were to draw the attention of the beſieged to their centre and left, whilſt a ſtrong body of choſen troops from the combined armies ſhould advance on the right of the Britiſh lines, and in two columns make the real attack. The principal of theſe columns was commanded by the count d'Eſtaing in perſon, aſſiſted by general Lincoln, and was deſtined to attack the Springhill redoubt in front, whilſt the other column, commanded by count Dillon, ſhould ſilently move along the edge of the ſwamp, paſs the redoubts and batteries, and get into the rear of the Britiſh lines. The troops which compoſed theſe two columns conſiſted of three thouſand five hundred French, ſix hundred provincial regulars, and three hundred and fifty of the Charleſtown militia, a number more than double that of the whole Britiſh garriſon, and were in motion long before daylight. Fortunately the column commanded by count Dillon miſtook its way, from the darkneſs of the morning, and was entangled in the ſwamp, from which it was unable to extricate itſelf until broad daylight appeared, and expoſed it to the view of the garriſon and the fire from the Britiſh batteries. This was ſo hot, and ſo well directed, that it was never

able

CHAP. XXX. 1779.

able even to form, and far leſs, by penetrating into the rear of the Britiſh lines, to accompliſh its original object. In the mean time the column led by the count d'Eſtaing advanced againſt the Springhill redoubt, juſt as daylight appeared: And ſuch was the darkneſs of the morning, that it had approached very near before it was diſcernible. But, as ſoon as it was diſcovered, it became expoſed to a continued blaze of muſquetry from the redoubt, and to a deſtructive croſs fire from the adjoining batteries, which mowed down whole ranks of the allies as they advanced. From the numbers which fell, the head of the column was ſeveral times thrown into confuſion; but their places being inſtantly ſupplied by others, it ſtill moved on until it reached the redoubt, where the conteſt became more fierce and deſperate. The brave captain Tawſe fell in defending the gate of his redoubt with his ſword plunged in the body of the third enemy he had ſlain with his own hand, and a French and American ſtandard were for an inſtant planted upon the parapet. The conflict for the poſſeſſion of the redoubt nevertheleſs continued to be obſtinately maintained on both ſides, and the event remained in ſuſpenſe; when lieutenant-colonel Maitland, ſeizing the critical moment, ordered the grenadiers of the ſixtieth regiment, with the marines, to move forward and charge the enemy's column, already ſtaggering under the obſtinate reſiſtance it had met with at the redoubt, the ſlaughter which had been made by the artillery from the different batteries, and now alſo from the Germaine armed brig. This well-timed movement decided the fate of the attack. The aſſailants were repulſed, driven out of the ditch of the redoubt, and routed with redoubled ſlaughter, leaving behind them, in killed and wounded, ſix hundred and thirty-ſeven of the French troops, and two hundred and ſixty-four of the Americans. No purſuit was ordered, becauſe the beſiegers, although they had ſuffered greatly in the aſſault, were ſtill three times more numerous than the garriſon; but in their

Repulſed with conſiderable loſs.

 flight,

CHAP. XXX. 1779.

flight, as in advancing, they were expoſed to a heavy fire from the Britiſh artillery, which was well ſerved under the direction of captain Charlton.

In this aſſault count Pulaſki, who commanded an American corps, received a mortal wound; and the count d'Eſtaing, who was ſeen by the garriſon to behave with great gallantry, was wounded in two places, but in neither of them dangerouſly.

No good agreement, it has been ſaid, ſubſiſted between the French and Americans from the commencement of the ſiege; and their mutual diſlike was now increaſed by their diſappointment. After the aſſault the French could no longer conceal their contempt for their new allies; they ſtyled them inſurgents, in common converſation, and even in written memorials. But the haughty demeanour of the count d'Eſtaing towards the garriſon ſeems to have been ſoftened by his misfortunes: An apology was made for refuſing leave to the women and children to retire to a place of ſafety, the blame of which was laid upon the Americans, and an offer was now made for their accommodation. This offer came too late to be accepted, eſpecially after a previous inſulting refuſal of what was now tendered; and it was with great propriety rejected by general Prevoſt.

Raiſe the ſiege.

The iſſue of the aſſault determined that of the ſiege. The French and Americans kept poſſeſſion of their lines only until the artillery and heavy baggage were withdrawn, and re-embarked on board the fleet. As ſoon as this was accompliſhed the ſiege was raiſed, and the allies ſeparated, the Americans retreating into South Carolina, and the French returning to their ſhips; on board which they had ſcarcely embarked when their fleet was diſperſed by a ſtorm. The count d'Eſtaing, with part of the ſhips, returned to France, and the reſt proceeded to the Weſt Indies.

Such was the termination of the ſiege of Savannah, during which it is ſaid that the allied armies loſt in killed, wounded, and by deſertion,

sertion, more than one thousand five hundred men; whereas the loss of the garrison in the whole did not exceed one hundred and twenty.

It is impossible to do particular justice to all who by their exertions contributed to the successful issue of the siege. The officers, naval and military, vied with each other who should render the most essential services to their king and country. The seamen and soldiers were animated with the same sentiment; and no small share of praise is due to the former for their brave assistance and peculiar adroitness in managing the artillery at the batteries. The cool, steady, prudent, and firm conduct of general Prevost, assisted by the able counsels and services of that distinguished officer lieutenant-colonel Maitland, the second in command, who in a peculiar degree enjoyed the love, esteem, and confidence of the garrison; the skilful designs, prompt execution, and indefatigable exertions of captain Moncrieff in his department, as commanding engineer; the active and able services of captain Charlton of the artillery; the wise precautions taken by captain Henry of the navy for the security of the river; the tried courage, manly firmness, and obstinate resistance of the provincial regiments and militia on the right of the lines, to whose lot it fell to bear, and nobly to withstand, the fury of the assault; and the bold, decisive, and irresistible charge made by lieutenant-colonel Glazier with the grenadiers and marines, which completed the overthrow of the enemy; are all deserving of the highest commendation, and rank the successful defence of Savannah amongst the most brilliant atchievements of the war.

One circumstance alone served to cloud the joy of the garrison on their recent success. This was the death of that highly-esteemed and much-beloved officer the honourable lieutenant-colonel Maitland, who fell a martyr to a bilious disorder contracted from the pestilential vapours which arise from the marshes during the hot and sultry season in that unwhole-

CHAP. XXX. 1779.

unwholefome climate. He was attacked by it before he left Beaufort. It gathered ftrength in his route through the marfhes to Savannah, and, preying upon him during the fiege, foon afterwards put a period to the exiftence of this gallant officer; whofe memory will be dear to Britons, fo long as manly fortitude, unftained honour, and highly-improved military talents, are held in eftimation.

The campaign to the fouthward of North America concluded.

With the raifing of the fiege of Savannah ended the campaign to the fouthward, which, although it clofed with an atchievement fo honourable to the Britifh arms, was neverthelefs unproductive of thofe advantages which had been expected at the commencement of it.

Campaign in the other parts of the North American continent fpent in defultory operations.

The campaign in the other parts of America was fpent in defultory operations and partial expeditions, the object of which feems to have been to diftract the attention of the Americans by their multiplicity, and to weaken them by cutting off their refources, and deftroying their magazines of naval and military ftores.

Naval operations of fir G. Collier.

Admiral Gambier, who fucceeded lord Howe in the command of the Britifh fleet on the American coaft, was recalled in the fpring of the prefent year, and in the month of April refigned the command to fir George Collier. This brave and zealous officer, who now fucceeded to the command of the Britifh navy in North America, had been employed on the Halifax ftation from the commencement of the war. In the Rainbow of forty-four guns he made one of a convoy which efcorted a fleet of tranfports with the firft divifion of the Heffian troops, and a detachment of the guards, to America, in the year 1776. This fleet arrived at Sandy Hook in Auguft of that year, a little before general Howe began his operations againft the provincials; and foon after their defeat on Long Ifland fir George Collier received orders to repair to Halifax and take the command of his majefty's fhips upon that important ftation, in the room of commodore Arbuthnot, who was recalled. On this ftation he con-

2 tinued

tinued until the ſpring of the preſent year, and during the whole time of his command diſtinguiſhed himſelf as a brave, zealous, active, enterpriſing, and vigilant officer. The timely relief of Fort Cumberland, at the head of the bay of Fundy, which was inveſted by the provincials from the eaſtern parts of Maſſachuſets Bay, ſoon after his arrival at Halifax: The capture of the Hancock of thirty-four guns and two hundred and ninety men, commanded by commodore Manley, the largeſt of a fleet of ſhips of war which were fitted out at Boſton to annoy the trade on the coaſt of Nova Scotia, and the Britiſh fiſhery on the Banks of Newfoundland: The driving off and diſperſing the provincials, who in ſmall veſſels had a ſecond time made a deſcent near St. John's River in Nova Scotia; and, at a ſubſequent period, the deſtruction of the proviſions, clothing, and military ſtores, which with great pains they had collected at Machias, in the eaſtern parts of Maſſachuſets Bay, for accompliſhing their favourite object, the invaſion of Nova Scotia; and in the deſtruction of theſe ſtores, the defeating the deſigns of the Americans againſt that province: The ſcouring of the eaſtern coaſts of New England with his cruiſers, keeping them in a conſtant ſtate of alarm, and taking their privateers, running up their rivers with his ſhips, appearing before their towns and ſhewing the practicability of a bombardment in caſe their hoſtile conduct ſhould demand ſuch a puniſhment, and thereby convincing them that it was their intereſt to be quiet, and not farther moleſt the peaceable inhabitants of Nova Scotia: The number of prizes carried into Halifax, and of Britiſh veſſels retaken from the enemy when they were upon the point of carrying them into their own ports: The trade of Nova Scotia protected, and the fiſhery in the gut of Canſo ſecured againſt moleſtation: Theſe are but a few of the many meritorious ſervices performed by this officer during his command at Halifax, for which, on more than one occaſion, he received the thanks of the

CHAP. XXX. 1779. the colony conveyed to him through the governor, council, and aſſembly.

From ſuch a line of uſeful and active ſervice ſir George was called to New York to take the command of the Britiſh fleet on the North American ſtation; and not long after his arrival an expedition to the Cheſapeak in Virginia, was concerted between him and ſir Henry Clinton, the commander in chief of the army. By the exports of tobacco from the Cheſapeak, the credit of congreſs with foreign nations was principally, if not wholly, ſupported; and by the inland navigation of that bay large quantities of ſalted proviſions, the produce both of Virginia and North Carolina, were conveyed to the middle colonies for the ſubſiſtence of the American army. The eſtabliſhment of a permanent poſt in Virginia, in ſuch a ſituation as to obſtruct the commerce of the Cheſapeak, both foreign and domeſtic, was an object of the utmoſt importance: But the feeble ſtate of the army would not admit of a ſufficient force to be detached for that purpoſe. A deſultory expedition to interrupt the commerce of the bay for a few weeks, and to deſtroy ſuch magazines, whether of proviſions, merchandiſe, or naval and military ſtores, as were acceſſible, was all the commander in chief, under the preſent ſituation of affairs, could conſent to. A detachment from the army, conſiſting of the grenadiers and light-infantry of the guards, the forty-ſecond regiment, a regiment of Heſſians, and the royal volunteers of Ireland, with a detachment of artillery, amounting in the whole to one thouſand eight hundred men, under the command of brigadier-general Matthew, was aſſigned for this purpoſe, and embarked on board tranſports. The commodore, in the Raiſonable of ſixty-four guns, attended by the Rainbow, Otter, Diligent, Haarlem ſloop, and Cornwallis galley, and ſome private veſſels of war, undertook to convoy them, and to conduct in perſon the naval part of the expedition. The troops being embarked, the fleet,

fleet, with a favourable wind, paſſed the bar at Sandy Hook on the fifth, and entered between the Capes of Virginia on the eighth of May. The Otter ſloop, with the privateers, was immediately ſent up the Cheſapeak, and the reſt of the fleet, with the tranſports, on the following morning proceeded to Hampton Road, a large baſon of water formed by the confluence of Elizabeth, Nanſemond, and James rivers. Some miles above its mouth Elizabeth River is ſeparated into two branches, one called the eaſtern, and the other the weſtern branch, and below the confluence of theſe branches, on the eaſtern ſide, once ſtood Norfolk, the principal commercial town in Virginia, and oppoſite to it, on the weſtern ſide, Portſmouth, a place of ſome trade, which, although not equal to Norfolk, was annually increaſing, and in time threatened to rival it. A little above theſe, upon a point of land intervening between two of the branches of the river, was Goſport, where the government of Virginia, ſince the commencement of the war, had eſtabliſhed a marine yard, and collected an immenſe quantity of timber for ſhip-building. As a defence for this yard and the adjoining docks, they had with great labour and expence conſtructed a fort upon the bank of the river, about half a mile below Portſmouth, which towards the water was already finiſhed and mounted with cannon; the walls of which conſiſted of an outward caſe of logs of timber ſtrongly dove-tailed together, with the intermediate ſpace filled up with hard-rammed earth, being fourteen feet in height, and fifteen feet thick.

Portſmouth was the place which the commanders on this expedition propoſed to occupy; and the reduction of the fort was of courſe the firſt thing to be attempted. As the Raiſonable, from her great draught of water, could proceed no higher than Hampton Road, the commodore ſhifted his broad pennant on board the Renown; and on the morning of the thirteenth of October the whole fleet, except the Raiſonable, got under way, and entered the mouth of Elizabeth

CHAP. XXX. 1779.

River. The ebbing of the tide ſoon obliged the ſhips to come to an anchor, but the troops being embarked on board the boats, proceeded, and effected a landing under cover of the Cornwallis galley, and ſome gun-boats, about three miles below the fort, at a place called the Glebe, the firſt diviſion at two in the afternoon and the ſecond before ſun-ſet. No oppoſition was made to their landing, except an ineffectual cannonade from the fort, which was too diſtant to do any miſchief. It was propoſed that the troops ſhould, on the following morning, ſtorm the fort on the land ſide, where the fortifications were yet unfiniſhed, whilſt the Rainbow ſhould move up and batter it from the water: But a forward movement of the troops having been made that ſame evening as ſoon as the ſecond diviſion had landed, the provincial garriſon, fearful of being ſurrounded, and having their retreat cut off, haſtily evacuated the fort, leaving behind all the artillery, ammunition, baggage, and ſtores. Such was their trepidation, that they did not even wait to ſtrike the American flag, but left it flying. General Matthew having thus eaſily poſſeſſed himſelf of the fort, took a ſtrong poſition with the army between Portſmouth and the country, the right wing reaching to the fort, the left to the ſouth branch of Elizabeth River, and the centre covered in front by an impenetrable ſwamp. Detachments were ſent to Norfolk and Goſport; and all the veſſels in Elizabeth River, except ſuch as were burnt by the provincials before their retreat, with an immenſe quantity of naval and military ſtores, merchandiſe, and proviſions, were either taken or deſtroyed by the Britiſh troops. Detachments were alſo ſent to Kemp's Landing, in Princeſs Ann county, and to the town of Suffolk in Nanſemond county, and at each of theſe places, particularly the latter, an immenſe quantity of proviſions and ſtores of all ſorts, with ſome veſſels richly laden, were either taken or deſtroyed.

The Otter ſloop, and the privateers which went up the Cheſapeak, were alſo ſucceſsful, and took a number of prizes. In the mean time the fort was demoliſhed, and the marine yard burnt, with all the timber it contained. Theſe ſervices being performed, the troops were re-embarked; and the whole fleet, with the prizes, having quitted Virginia, arrived at New York before the end of the month, having been abſent only twenty-four days. The damage done to the provincials was aſtoniſhingly great, and has been eſtimated at half a million ſterling. The Americans themſelves, before their flight from Portſmouth, ſet fire to a ſhip of war of twenty-eight guns belonging to congreſs, and ready for launching; and alſo to two French merchantmen in the river, one loaded with bale-goods, and the other with a thouſand hogſheads of tobacco. Beſides theſe, eight other ſhips of war, in different forwardneſs upon the ſtocks, and ſeveral merchantmen, were burnt by the Britiſh troops; and, excluſively of all other loſſes, the number of veſſels alone which were taken or deſtroyed, during this ſhort expedition, amounted to one hundred and thirty-ſeven.

CHAP. XXXI.

Reduction of two strong Posts on Hudson's River—Expedition against Connecticut—Ravages—Murmurs in Connecticut—Fort Stoney Point surprised by General Wayne—Stoney Point evacuated by the Americans—Again possessed by the British—British Settlement in Penobscot—Attacked in vain by the Americans—Reinforcement brought to the British Army by Admiral Arbuthnot, who succeeds Sir George Collier in the Command of the Navy—American Incursions into the Country of the Indians—Incursions of the Indians into the American Settlements.

CHAP. XXXI. 1779. May.

PREVIOUSLY to the arrival of the fleet from Virginia, sir Henry Clinton had made preparations for attacking two strong pcsts on Hudson's River, about sixty miles above New York, which the provincials were then fortifying. These were the important posts of Verplank's Neck and Stoney Point, on opposite sides of the river, commanding the passage at King's Ferry, which was the most direct and convenient course of communication between the northern and middle colonies. To gain these posts was an object of some consequence, as, by the loss of them, the provincials, in order to maintain an intercourse between the provinces on the east and west sides of Hudson's River, would be obliged to make a circuit of more than sixty miles through the mountains. A detachment from the army at New York was already embarked on board of transports, and these being joined by the transports with the troops from Virginia, the whole, on the thirtieth of May, proceeded up the North River, under

under the direction of ſir George Collier, who, as well as the commander in chief of the army, accompanied this expedition. The principal diviſion of the army, under major-general Vaughan, was landed on the eaſtern ſide of the river, about ſeven miles below Fort Fayette, on Verplank's Neck, and the commander in chief, with the other, proceeded onward within three miles of Stoney Point, where, on the weſtern ſide of the river, that diviſion was landed alſo. Stoney Point, by its high and commanding ſituation, is a place of great natural ſtrength; but, as the works were yet unfiniſhed, the provincials were afraid to riſque an aſſault, and quitted it as ſoon as the Britiſh fleet appeared in view, having firſt ſet fire to a block-houſe which they were conſtructing upon the ſummit of the eminence. It was taken poſſeſſion of towards the evening, and ſome heavy cannon and mortars were immediately landed from the fleet. Theſe were with much labour dragged up the hill during the night; and ſuch expedition was uſed under the direction of major-general Pattiſon, of the artillery, to whom this ſervice was committed, that, by five the next morning, a battery of cannon and mortars from the ſummit of Stoney Point opened upon Fort Fayette on the oppoſite ſide of the river. Fort Fayette was a ſmall but complete work, incloſed with palliſades, a double ditch, chevaux de frize, and abbatis, and had a block-houſe in the centre, which was bomb-proof; but as it was commanded by the ſuperior height of Stoney Point, the cannonade from the latter, as well as from the gallies and armed veſſels upon the river, ſoon made a ſenſible impreſſion. During the cannonade it was inveſted by general Vaughan on the ſide towards the country, and the gallies being ſo ſtationed as to prevent an eſcape by water, the garriſon, ſurrounded in every quarter, ſurrendered as priſoners of war, without ſtipulating for any other condition than a promiſe of good uſage. And thus theſe two important poſts were gained with the trifling loſs of only one man wounded. Orders were given for

com-

CHAP. XXXI. 1779.

completing the fortifications at Stoney Point; and garrifons having been appointed for both the forts, the fleet, with the reft of the troops, fell down the river, and returned to New York.

Expedition againft Connecticut.

Soon afterwards an expedition was planned againft the province of Connecticut, which, abounding with men as well as provifions, was a principal fupport to the American army. One purpofe of this expedition was to convince the people of Connecticut that their province was not inacceffible, and that it was owing only to the forbearance of the Britifh government, which rather wifhed to reclaim than to punifh, that their country had not yet experienced the calamities and devaftations of war; and another object was, to oblige general Wafhington to quit his ftrong fituation upon the North River, and defcend into the low country for the defence of the fea-coaft. On the fourth of July the tranfports, with the troops deftined for this expedition, which amounted to two thoufand fix hundred men, weighed anchor at the entrance into the found, and proceeded towards New Haven, the capital of Connecticut. The command of the land force was given to major-general Tryon; and the commodore, in the Camilla frigate, accompanied by the Scorpion floop, Halifax brig, and Huffar galley, efcorted the tranfports, and took upon himfelf their direction. At fome diftance below the town of New Haven, brigadier-general Garth, of the guards, difembarked with the firft divifion of troops, and notwithftanding a continued oppofition from the inhabitants during a march of feven miles, which he was obliged to make in order to pafs the head of a creek, he at laft forced his way and took poffeffion of the town. Major-general Tryon, with the fecond divifion of the troops, landed on the oppofite fide of the harbour, and took poffeffion of a fort upon the heights, by the guns of which the harbour was commanded. A communication was opened between the two divifions of the army; and brigadier-general Garth remained in poffeffion of of the town during the night. All the artillery, ammunition, and public ftores, and all the veffels in the harbour, were either taken or deftroyed; but the town itfelf was faved, and private houfes as much as poffible exempted from plunder. This was a degree of lenity which the conduct of the inhabitants fcarcely merited; for befides the oppofition made to the troops in their march to the town, they were annoyed from the windows, even after they had poffeffion of it; and feveral of the centinels placed at private houfes to prevent plunder were wounded upon their pofts. On the following day, after a proclamation calling upon the inhabitants to return to their allegiance, in which cafe they were promifed protection, fupport, and encouragement, and denouncing vengeance and punifhment if they fhould ftill perfift in a rebellious oppofition to the mother-country, had been diftributed, and after the fort was difmantled, the troops were re-embarked and left New Haven.

From New Haven the fleet proceeded to Fairfield, where the troops were again landed. Here a refiftance and oppofition were experienced more obftinate and inveterate than at New Haven: And as the lenity and forbearance fhewn at the laft of thefe places feemed to have produced no effect, the prefent was thought a fit moment to give an example of feverity. At Fairfield not only the public ftores of all forts, with the veffels in the harbour, were either taken or de-ftroyed, but the town itfelf was laid in afhes. As the fleet and troops proceeded in fulfilling the purpofes of the expedition, the op-pofition which they met with feemed to increafe with the extent of their progrefs: Norwalk, therefore, and Greenfield, at each of which places the troops were fucceffively landed, fhared the fame fate as the town of Fairfield. A defcent at New London, which was a rendezvous for privateers, was the ultimate object of the expedition; but as a greater oppofition was expected there than at either of the other places, it was thought neceffary to obtain a further fupply of ammu-

CHAP. XXXI. 1779.

ammunition and a reinforcement of troops before they made the attempt *. For this purpose the fleet returned to Huntington Bay in Long Island, and the commodore proceeded to Frog's Neck, to confer with the commander in chief of the army on the subject of their future operations.

During this short expedition, which had lasted only nine days, the injury sustained by the inhabitants of Connecticut in the loss of property both public and private, was very considerable: But notwithstanding the conflagration of so many towns on the sea-coast, general Washington could not be prevailed upon to abandon his strong situation in the neighbourhood of the North River. His apparent apathy, and that of the congress, with respect to Connecticut, produced murmurs amongst the inhabitants, which at length broke forth into open complaints. Some of the principal inhabitants, considering protection and allegiance to be reciprocal duties, began to think of withdrawing their subjection from a power which seemed to neglect them in their distress, and of making terms with the British commanders for themselves. Such certainly was the import of the intelligence from Connecticut communicated to sir Henry Clinton, about the present period; and the conference between him and the commodore at Frog's Neck, was on the subject of this intelligence, and with a view of arranging matters, so that the intended expedition against New London might serve to impress the inhabitants more strongly with those sentiments which they had already begun to entertain.

But, whilst the British commanders were thus devising measures for improving the disposition which had manifested itself in Connecticut, general Washington had already atchieved an enterprise which disconcerted all their present designs against that province, and

* The loss of the British troops in this expedition was 20 killed, 96 wounded, and 32 missing.

called

called their attention to a different quarter. This was the ſurpriſe of the fort at Stoney Point, which was taken by aſſault in the night of the fifteenth of July. As the Americans had been but lately diſpoſſeſſed of this poſt, it is preſumable that they were well acquainted with all the acceſſible approaches which led to it, as well as with thoſe parts of the works which were moſt aſſailable. But even with theſe advantages it was an enterpriſe of difficulty and danger; and the American general Wayne, who conducted it, deſerved great praiſe for his gallantry and good conduct, as did the troops which he commanded for their bravery. Theſe being divided into two columns, entered the works in oppoſite quarters, and met in the centre of them about one in the morning of the ſixteenth of July. The ſurpriſe was not ſo complete but that reſiſtance was made; and the loſs in killed and wounded was nearly equal on both ſides. Lieutenant-colonel Johnſon of the ſeventeenth regiment commanded the Britiſh garriſon, which conſiſted of the ſeventeenth regiment, the grenadier company of the ſeventy-firſt, a company of the regiment of loyal Americans, and a detachment of artillery, amounting in the whole to about ſix hundred men. Of theſe one hundred and fifty-two were either killed or wounded, and the reſt, with their commander, were made priſoners. The force under general Wayne has not been aſcertained; but, from the number of corps of which it conſiſted, it may be ſuppoſed to have amounted to fifteen hundred, all of them choſen men.

The conduct of the Americans upon this occaſion was highly meritorious; for they would have been fully juſtified in putting the garriſon to the ſword: Not one man of which was put to death but in fair combat. Colonel Johnſon's conduct was moſt deſervedly and juſtly cenſured.

The plan formed by general Waſhington for theſe operations on the North River comprehended Fort Fayette as well as Stoney Point.

 Both

CHAP. XXXI. 1779.

Both were to have been attacked the same night; but the detachment under the American general How, which was sent against Fort Fayette, did not arrive in time. Still, however, it was advancing; and, to favour the attack, general Wayne, as soon as he possessed himself of Stoney Point, turned the cannon of that garrison against Fort Fayette, where lieutenant-colonel Webster commanded, with a garrison consisting of the thirty-third regiment, part of the regiment of loyal Americans, a detachment from the seventy-first regiment, and another of royal artillery.

Intelligence of the capture of Stoney Point, and the danger of Fort Fayette on Verplank's Neck, having been brought to sir Henry Clinton just after his conference with sir George Collier, the expedition against New London was for the present laid aside, the transports and troops were recalled from the Sound, and the army made a forward movement to Dobb's Ferry, on the North River. Brigadier-general Stirling, with a detachment, was sent up the river in transports, to the assistance of lieutenant-colonel Webster; and the commander in chief, with a greater force, soon afterwards followed, from an expectation that general Washington might be tempted to quit his fastnesses, and risque an engagement for the possession of Stoney Point. But this was not general Washington's intention; and therefore, when intelligence was received of a British reinforcement advancing up the North River, orders were given for evacuating Stoney Point, which was done after as many of the works had been destroyed as the time would permit. In the mean time lieutenant-colonel Webster defended his post on Verplank's Neck with prudence and bravery. To the cannonade from Stoney Point he returned not a shot, as it would have been useless and ineffectual: But, against the provincials under general How, who were advancing to attack him on the other side, every effort was made that could prevent their success; and, before they were able to make any impression

Stoney Point evacuated by the Americans:

1779.

preſſion upon the fort, the arrival of brigadier-general Stirling with his detachment, put an end to their hopes, and obliged them to retreat. The poſt at Stoney Point was again taken poſſeſſion of; and upon the arrival of the commander in chief, orders were iſſued for repairing the works. A larger garriſon was aſſigned for its defence, and brigadier-general Stirling was appointed to command it. As it was now apparent that general Waſhington did not mean to quit his ſecure poſition in the high lands for the ſake of conteſting the poſſeſſion of Stoney Point, the tranſports were ordered to fall down the river, and the troops returned to their former quarters.

Again poſſeſſed by the Britiſh.

Scarcely had ſir George Collier reached New York, on his return from accompanying ſir Henry Clinton upon this expedition, when he received intelligence that a fleet of armed veſſels, with tranſports and troops, had ſailed from Boſton to attack a Britiſh poſt, which general Maclean was then endeavouring to eſtabliſh at Penobſcot, in the eaſtern part of the province of Maſſachuſet's Bay. Orders were immediately iſſued for getting in readineſs ſuch of his majeſty's ſhips as were then at New York; and on the third of Auguſt the commodore in the Raiſonable, accompanied by the Greyhound, Blonde, Virginia, Camilla, Galatea, and Otter ſloop, ſailed from thence for the relief of the garriſon at Penobſcot.

British ſettlement in Penobſcot,

In the month of June general Francis Maclean, who commanded the king's troops in Nova Scotia, with a detachment of ſix hundred and fifty men from the ſeventy-fourth and eighty-ſecond regiments, embarked in tranſports, and, eſcorted by three ſloops of war, arrived in the bay of Penobſcot, in order to form a ſettlement, and eſtabliſh a poſt which might not only ſerve to check the incurſions of the provincials into Nova Scotia, but be the means of obtaining a conſtant ſupply of ſhip timber, with which the neighbouring country abounded, for the uſe of the king's yards at Halifax and other places. The bay of Penobſcot is about ſeven leagues

 in

CHAP. XXXI. 1779.

in breadth at the mouth, and ſeventeen leagues in length, terminating where the river Penobſcot empties itſelf into the head of it; and the lands all round were then covered with wood, ſcarcely any ſettlements having been made upon them. About nine miles below the mouth of Penobſcot river, on the eaſtern ſide of the bay, is a ſmall but convenient harbour, which ſtill retains its ancient Indian name of Majabagaduce; and a peninſula, or point of land, forming one ſide of that harbour, was the ſpot fixed upon by general Maclean for erecting a fort to protect the ſettlement. The land was firſt to be cleared of the wood that grew upon it, which was a work of great labour and difficulty. This being done, the outlines of a fort were marked out, which was intended to be of a ſquare form with a baſtion at each angle, incloſing a ſpace of ground capacious enough to admit of a cavalier or block-houſe in the centre, with barracks for the men, and apartments for the officers; and every exertion was made to get this work in forwardneſs, which was to ſerve for their future defence.

In the mean time, intelligence of what was doing at Penobſcot having been carried to Boſton, the executive government of Maſſachuſet's Bay determined to ſit out an armament with the utmoſt diſpatch, in order to obſtruct or finally ruin the ſettlement. An embargo was immediately laid upon all the ſhipping in Boſton harbour, and bounties were offered to ſuch perſons as would engage in the Penobſcot expedition. By ſuch means a ſquadron was ſoon got in readineſs, which conſiſted of nineteen armed ſhips and brigantines, the largeſt carrying thirty-two, and the ſmalleſt ten guns. To theſe were added twenty-ſeven tranſports, having on board three thouſand troops; the fleet being under the direction of commodore Saltonſtall, and the troops under the command of general Lovel. Againſt ſo conſiderable a force it was thoug htthat general Maclean, with his handful of men, could not long defend himſelf: And upon the departure

parture of the fleet, his furrender, and the ruin of the fettlement, were confidered by the people of Maffachufet's Bay as events, of the completion of which no doubt could be reafonably entertained.

Intelligence of the failing of this armament was brought to general Maclean on the twenty-firft of July, only four days before its arrival at Penobfcot. All that time, two of the baftions of the intended fort were not begun, and the other two, with the curtains, were in no part above five feet in height, and twelve in thicknefs. The ditch in moft parts was not more than three feet deep; no platform was laid, nor any artillery mounted. But upon the arrival of this alarming intelligence, all prefent thoughts of finifhing the fort were laid afide, and the troops were employed day and night on fuch works as were immediately neceffary to fecure them againft an affault; a mode of attack which they had the greateft reafon to apprehend would be purfued by the enemy, in confequence of their very fuperior force.

Although the provincials arrived in the bay of Penobfcot on the twenty-fifth of July, they were unable to effect a landing until the twenty-eighth. The three floops of war, under the direction of captain Mowat, being fo ftationed as to command the mouth of the harbour, prevented the provincial fleet from entering and effecting a landing on that fide of the peninfula; and on the other fide the natural fteepnefs and ruggednefs of the fhore rendered it an enterprife of difficulty and danger. At length, however, they effected their purpofe before day in the morning of the twenty-eighth, at a place which had been thought inacceffible; and on the thirtieth opened a battery againft the works, at the diftance of feven hundred and fifty yards. From the inceffant labour of the garrifon, during the interval between the twenty-firft and thirtieth of July, the gorge of one of the unfinifhed baftions was filled up with logs of timber; and the

attacked in vain by the Americans.

CHAP. XXXI. 1779. the other, containing the well which supplied the garrison with water, was surrounded with a work of fascines and earth, ten feet thick; platforms were laid, and artillery mounted; a sort of chevaux de frize was carried round the fort; and the whole inclosed with an abbatis; so that by the time the enemy had opened their battery, general Maclean and his garrison thought themselves tolerably prepared to resist an assault. The enemy's fleet made frequent attempts to enter the harbour, but were constantly repulsed by the fire from the ships of war, and a battery erected to support them on shore. The provincial land force, nevertheless, continued to make approaches, and erect new batteries; and a brisk cannonade was kept up between them and the garrison for near a fortnight. Frequent skirmishes too happened without the fort, the garrison being under the necessity of preserving a communication with the shipping and the battery which covered it. August. On the twelfth of August intelligence was conveyed to general Maclean by a deserter, that on the following day an assault was to be made on the fort, and an attack upon the ships of war at the same time; and every necessary preparation was made by the general for repelling them. But the approach of the squadron under sir George Collier, as it afterwards appeared, prevented the provincials from executing their intention; and, on the morning of the fourteenth, the garrison, to their great surprise, discovered that the works had been evacuated during the preceding night, and that the provincial troops, with the greatest part of the cannon, were re-embarked on board the ships. The cause of this sudden retreat was then unknown to the garrison; but by ten in the forenoon the appearance of the British squadron standing up the bay quickly unveiled the mystery. The provincial fleet appeared to be in disorder; and for some time the commanders seemed undetermined what to do. At length an ignominious flight took place; every one endeavouring to provide for his own safety, and

and none daring to wait the ſhock of the Britiſh ſquadron. Two of the provincial armed ſhips endeavoured to get to ſea by paſſing round Long Iſland, which lies in the middle of the bay; but they were ſoon intercepted, the firſt being taken, and the other run a-ſhore and blown up by her crew. The reſt of their fleet, with the tranſports, fled in the utmoſt confuſion to the head of the bay, and entered the mouth of Penobſcot river. They were purſued by the Britiſh ſquadron. By this diſgraceful flight the provincials became expoſed to a danger almoſt as great as that which they had eſcaped. They were landed in a wild uncultivated country, without proviſions or any other neceſſaries, and had to explore their way for more than an hundred miles through this pathleſs deſert before they could reach a place from which ſupplies might be obtained. In this forlorn and deſtitute ſituation mutual reproaches paſſed between the ſeamen and landſmen; and each accuſed the other of being the cauſe of their preſent misfortunes. A battle enſued, in which fifty or ſixty were ſlain; and a much greater number, exhauſted with famine and fatigue, before they could reach the ſettled parts of the province, periſhed miſerably in the woods. Such was the iſſue of the provincial expedition againſt the Britiſh ſettlement at Penobſcot; for the ſucceſsful defence of which, under ſo many diſadvantages, general Maclean is entitled to the greateſt praiſe. And in the progreſs and iſſue of this expedition we ſee how much may be effected by a very inconſiderable force, when Britiſh officers act with zeal and unanimity in the ſervice of their king and country *.

The

* The loſs of the garriſon amounted to 70, killed, wounded, and miſſing. The loſs on board the fleet was 15 killed and wounded.

The American fleet taken or deſtroyed on this expedition was as follows:—

Warren of 32 guns, 18 and 12 pounders. Monmouth 24. Vengeance 24. Putnam 22. Sally 22, blown up. Hampden, 20 guns, taken. Hector 20, blown up. Hunter, 18, taken. Black Prince 18; and Sky Rocket 16; blown up.

Brigs

CHAP. XXXI.

1779.

Reinforcement brought to the British army by admiral Arbuthnot, who succeeds sir G. Collier in the command of the navy.

The relief of the garrison at Penobscot, with the total destruction of the naval armament that had been sent against it, was the last of those meritorious services performed by sir George Collier during the short but active period in which he had the command of the British fleet on the coast of North America. On his return to New York he found himself superseded by the arrival of admiral Arbuthnot from England with some ships of war and a fleet of transports, bringing a reinforcement of troops, and a supply of provisions and stores. To the admiral he resigned the command, and soon afterwards embarked for England.

The reinforcement brought by admiral Arbuthnot had been long and impatiently expected by sir Henry Clinton, who, from the feeble state of the army, was unable, until its arrival, to engage in any enterprise of importance. Although it was now late, the season for action was not yet entirely over; but the appearance of the count d'Estaing with his formidable fleet on the coast of Georgia, intelligence of which, as well as of his threatened attack against New York, was brought about this time, obliged the commander in chief to give up all thoughts of offensive operations during the remainder of the campaign, and to concentre his force, that he might be prepared to meet the shock which he was to expect from a combined attack of the French by sea and the Americans by land. In this view, Rhode Island was evacuated, and the garrison withdrawn to New York. And in this respect alone, by obliging sir Henry Clinton to change his system, and act upon the defensive during the remainder of the campaign, the expedition of the count d'Estaing to the coast of North America, otherwise unfortunate, may be said to have been serviceable to the American cause.

Brigs—Active 16 guns; Defence 16; Hazard 16; Diligence 14; Tyrannicide 14; Providence sloop 14; blown up. Spring Bird 12, burnt. Nancy 16, Rover 10, taken. Together with 24 sail of ships and vessels, as transports, all burnt.

Nothing

CHAP. XXXI.

1779.

Bold attack by the Americans on Paulus Hook.

Nothing elſe of moment happened upon the ſea-coaſt, except a bold and ſucceſsful attack made by the American major Lee upon the Britiſh poſt at Paulus Hook, on the Jerſey ſhore, oppoſite to New York, which, although it had no effect upon the general iſſue of the campaign, nevertheleſs merits notice, as it ſerves to ſhew how dangerous it is for the beſt-diſciplined troops to live in a ſtate of ſecurity, even when oppoſed to an enemy which they deſpiſe; and alſo as it affords one example out of many how well the provincials were furniſhed with intelligence of every thing that paſſed within the Britiſh lines. Major Sutherland, who had the command of the poſt at Paulus Hook, detached on the nineteenth of Auguſt a part of the garriſon to proceed on ſome particular ſervice, into the country; and intelligenee of this movement being immediately communicated to major Lee, who commanded ſome provincials in the neighbourhood, he reſolved to avail himſelf of the opportunity, which the abſence of a part of the garriſon afforded, to make an attempt upon the poſt. The deſign which he had formed was carried into execution the following night. Advancing, with three hundred men, to the gate of the works, he was miſtaken by the centinel for the officer who commanded the party that had marched into the country in the morning, and was ſuffered to paſs, together with his detachment; and in ſuch an unſoldierly ſtate of ſecurity did he find the garriſon, that he ſeized a block-houſe and two redoubts, before the alarm was given. Major Sutherland now threw himſelf into a redoubt, with ſixty Heſſians, and by keeping up an inceſſant fire upon the provincials, ſoon obliged them to quit the poſt, without their attempting to ſpike up the cannon, or doing any injury to the works; and ſo precipitately as to give occaſion to ſir Henry Clinton to remark, in his official diſpatches, that their retreat was as diſgraceful as their attack had been ſpirited and well-conducted. They nevertheleſs carried off with them about

 forty

CHAP. XXXI. 1779.

forty prifoners. It was not their intention to remain in poffeffion of the poft; the object of the attack being no other than to give fome eclat to the American arms, and to promote a fpirit of enterprife amongft the officers and foldiers.

In the interior country the war of devaftation was ftill carried on between the provincials and Indians. Againft the latter an expedition, of more than ordinary magnitude, was planned by the congrefs, to revenge the bloody incurfions of the preceding year. The command of it was given to major-general Sullivan; and the force employed amounted to five thoufand men. With this force, formed into two divifions, and accompanied by fome artillery and field-pieces, general Sullivan entered the Indian country. The Indians, feeing no profpect of being able to oppofe fuch a force, quitted their fettlements as he approached them, and fled into other parts. The war of devaftation now commenced; and the barbarous favage had the mortification to find that the civilized inhabitant of the fea-coaft could outdo him in deliberate acts of mifchief. Eighteen of their towns were laid in afhes, and more than one hundred and fifty thoufand bufhels of corn were deftroyed: Their gardens were laid wafte: Even their fruit-trees were cut down; and nothing was fuffered to remain that could be fuppofed to afford them any fuftenance. But whilft the provincials were thus laying wafte the Indian towns, the Indians on their part were making inroads into the provincial fettlements, and much mifchief was done on both fides. Revenge for an injury received is a point of honour which an Indian never gives up: A fevere retribution was therefore to be expected for the ravages committed by general Sullivan. The Indians were irritated but not fubdued, and had not deigned to fue for peace: Whence it may be doubted whether this expedition was of any real utility. But if any benefit was derived from it, it was not equal to the expence which it coft, or the expectations which had been formed

American incurfions into the country of the Indians.

Incurfions of the Indians into the provincial fettlements.

formed from it; and all who were concerned in planning it ſeem to have been diſappointed. The congreſs was diſſatisfied; General Waſhington did not approve of the conduct of the expedition; and general Sullivan, ſoon after his return from the Indian country, reſigned his employments in diſguſt, and retired from the public ſervice. CHAP. XXXI. 1779.

This expedition was undertaken againſt the northern Indians, which border on the provinces of Penſylvania and New York. Similar expeditions were alſo ſet on foot in the ſouthern colonies againſt the Indians on their frontiers, which, although not ſo expenſive as that of general Sullivan, were proportionably more efficacious: And, during this ſummer, both the northern and ſouthern Indians ſuffered a ſevere chaſtiſement.

CHAP. XXXII.

The Confederacy against Great Britain joined by Spain—French Attack on Jersey—Repelled—Naval Transactions—The combined Fleets of France and Spain threaten an Invasion of Great Britain—Engagement between Captain Paul Jones and the Convoy of a British Fleet from the Baltic—Blockade of Gibraltar—Incursion of the Americans into West Florida—West Florida reduced by the Spaniards—The Spaniards attack the British Logwood-cutters in Honduras—Reduction of the Spanish Fort Omoa, the Key of the Bay of Honduras—Protection afforded to the British Commerce—General Retrospect of British Affairs at the Conclusion of 1779.

CHAP. XXXII. 1779. The confederacy against Great Britain joined by Spain.

FROM America we must now pass to Europe, where, through the intrigues of the court of France, one power openly joined the confederacy against Great Britain, and another, her ancient and much-favoured ally, became so lukewarm in her attachment, that her friendship was no longer to be depended upon.

When France first determined to acknowledge the independence of the American colonies, and to enter into a treaty with them, Spain was solicited to join in it. But, however desirous this branch of the house of Bourbon, as well as the other, might be to reduce the power of Great Britain, the proposition was at that time rejected; very probably from an apprehension that Great Britain might be disposed to retaliate by stirring up a rebellion in the Spanish colonies. The court of France, nevertheless, unceasingly continued its

its ſolicitations, which, in the fall of the preceding year, appear to have become effectual. The king of Spain, in the month of September of that year, interpoſed ſo far as to offer to mediate between the belligerent powers.

However unſuitable, in point of impartiality, it might appear for one branch of the houſe of Bourbon to undertake to mediate between another branch of the ſame houſe and a third power, Great Britain nevertheleſs accepted the mediation of Spain; and the propoſals of the court of France, for putting an end to the differences which ſubſiſted between it and Great Britain, were preſented to the court of London by the Spaniſh ambaſſador. Theſe were found to be ſo totally inadmiſſible, as to create a ſuſpicion that the king of Spain had engaged in the mediation only for the purpoſe of furniſhing himſelf with a pretext to take a part in the war; and they were inſtantly rejected by the court of Great Britain. The king of Spain, in his character of mediator, now preſented other terms, as from himſelf, which he called ultimate propoſals: But theſe were ſo nearly the ſame in ſubſtance with thoſe offered by the court of France, that they were equally inadmiſſible. They were however rejected with much civility; and, in the anſwer delivered to the Spaniſh ambaſſador, a wiſh was expreſſed that nothing that had paſſed might interrupt the harmony ſubſiſting between Great Britain and Spain.

Although it was generally underſtood, long before the end of this negotiation, that, if it failed in effect, Spain was to become a party in the war; yet no declaration of that nature was made for a conſiderable time after the anſwer to his ultimate propoſitions had been received by the king of Spain. His preparations were not at that time in a ſufficient ſtate of forwardneſs: And the addreſs of his miniſters, in timing the proper moments of interpoſition, was as conſpicuous as their general policy in ſuffering him to be led into the

CHAP. XXXII. 1779.

the war was utterly reprehensible. In the preceding year, the offer of mediation was not made until after the return of the ships and troops that had been employed in America, during the late disputes between Spain and Portugal, and the arrival of the rich annual fleets, which bring home the treasures of Mexico and Peru. And, in the present year, the declaration which announced war was not delivered to the British ministry until it was morally certain, that the junction of the French and Spanish fleets, both of which were then at sea, could not be impeded. A momentary attention to dates will put this matter beyond a doubt. The French fleet sailed from Brest on the fourth of June, and steered for the coast of Spain; the British fleet being then, and for ten days afterwards, in harbour. On the sixteenth of June the hostile rescript was delivered to the British ministry, which announced the determination of the Spanish court to join with France in the war; and on the twenty-fourth of the same month a junction was made between the French and Spanish fleets. Thus it is apparent, that the Spanish ministry delayed coming to an open rupture, until, from the certainty of uniting their naval force with that of France, they had reason to expect, not only to be able to protect their own trade from molestation, but, by the magnitude of the combined fleets, to wrest the empire of the sea from the British nation.

To foreign powers the situation of Great Britain, at this critical moment, seemed beyond measure perilous. Thirteen of her colonies in open insurrection, and two powerful maritime states of Europe combined for her destruction, without a single ally disposed to stretch forth a helping arm, were, to them, certain indications of her approaching downfall; and they viewed the prospect with a malignant pleasure, or, at the least, with indifference. But it soon appeared that those who entertained such sentiments were not sufficiently acquainted with the extent of the national resources, or the firmness

of

of the Britiſh ſpirit, which diſdained tamely to yield to any hoſtile combination, however powerful. The union of Spain with France had for ſome time been foreſeen; and the moſt vigorous preparations were made to reſiſt the impending ſtorm. Gibraltar, where an attack was expected, was, in the ſpring of the year, reinforced with troops, and plentifully ſupplied with proviſions, ammunition, and ſtores. A fleet of tranſports, with a reinforcement of troops, and a large ſupply of proviſions and warlike ſtores, under the convoy of admiral Arbuthnot, with a ſquadron of ſhips of war, was ready to ſail for America by the beginning of May: And it was propoſed, with the channel fleet, to block up the harbour of Breſt, ſo as to prevent a junction between the French and Spaniſh fleets, a meaſure which it was ſuppoſed would be attempted, as ſoon as Spain ſhould throw off the maſk and declare for war. But unfortunate incidents frequently mar the beſt-concerted deſigns; and part of this arrangement was prevented from taking place, and another conſiderably impeded, by the conſequences of an unexpected attack made upon the iſland of Jerſey.

French attack on Jerſey,

Whilſt admiral Arbuthnot was proceeding down the channel with his convoy, on the ſecond of May, he received intelligence of this attack, and immediately ſailed, with part of the ſquadron, for the relief of the iſland; leaving the reſt, with the convoy, to proceed to Torbay, and wait his return. Upon his arrival off Guernſey he found that the French had been repulſed, and prevented from landing in Jerſey, and were returned to the coaſt of France. And as his aſſiſtance was no longer neceſſary, he altered his courſe, and ſailed for Torbay to rejoin the convoy.

repelled.

Although the French had been repulſed, the expedition againſt Jerſey was not abandoned. The ſmall ſquadron which accompanied it, conſiſting of three frigates, a cutter, and ſome ſmaller veſſels, ſtill

CHAP. XXXII. 1779.

ftill hovered on the coaft of France, waiting for an opportunity to renew the attack. But, during this interval, fir James Wallace in the Experiment, with the Pallas, Unicorn, Fortune, and Chabot brig, who had been fent in purfuit of it, got fight of the French fquadron, and drove it into Concalle Bay, where all the fhips were run a-fhore under cover of a battery. Sir James Wallace was neverthelefs determined either to take or deftroy them. The Experiment was already fo near as to be confiderably annoyed by the battery; and the pilots refufing to take charge of her any farther, her brave commander, with the characteriftic boldnefs of a Britifh feaman, took the charge upon himfelf, laid her a-breaft of the battery, and foon filenced it. The French fhips were now abandoned by their crews, and boarded by the boats from the Britifh fquadron. The French cutter was fcuttled as fhe lay on the fhore, two of the frigates were burnt, and the third, with the fmaller veffels, was towed off in triumph *. And by this gallant action the ifland of Jerfey was freed from all prefent apprehenfions of danger.

Naval tranfactions.

The neceffary deviation from his courfe made by admiral Arbuthnot for the relief of Jerfey, although as little time as poffible was loft by it, was neverthelefs unfortunately, and without any blame to be imputed to him, the caufe of much fubfequent delay. His fleet, which had anchored in Torbay, was prevented from failing for near a month by contrary winds: And, when it did fail, the paffage became fo tedious, in confequence of the wefterly winds that prevail in the Atlantic in the latter part of the fummer, that he did not arrive at New York, as we have already feen, until the campaign was

* Ships and Veffels taken and deftroyed at Concalle Bay.

La Danae, 34 guns, taken.	Le Reclufe, 24 guns, burnt.
La Valeur, 26 guns, burnt.	Le Dieppe, 16 guns, fcuttled.

A brig and two floops taken, and feveral fifhing-boats, and other fmall craft, deftroyed.

almoft

almoſt over. Another conſequence, that followed from this delay, was not leſs injurious. It was feared that, during the interval of detention, the French might have become acquainted with the force under admiral Arbuthnot, and the value of his convoy, which was immenſe, and thence been tempted to form ſome ſcheme for attacking him on his paſſage, and intercepting the convoy. To prevent the effect of ſuch a ſcheme, if it was formed, and for the greater ſecurity of the convoy, ten ſhips from the channel fleet were detached, under admiral Darby, to accompany Arbuthnot a certain diſtance on his paſſage: And the weakening of the channel fleet, by ſending away ſo conſiderable a detachment, was the cauſe of delaying the execution of the plan for blocking up the harbour of Breſt. The French did not fail to profit by the delay: So eager were they to ſend the Breſt fleet to ſea, that eight thouſand land-forces were embarked to ſupply the want of ſo many ſeamen; and with this kind of equipment it ſailed from Breſt on the fourth of June. Count d'Orvilliers, who commanded it, had two objects in view: One was, to intercept the ſquadron under admiral Darby in its return; and the other, to form a junction with the Spaniſh fleet. In the firſt he failed, admiral Darby having returned in ſafety to the channel; but in the ſecond he ſucceeded, and joined the fleet of Spain on the twenty-fourth of June. The two fleets, when united, amounted to more than ſixty ſail of the line, with nearly an equal number of frigates; and ſoon after the junction they ſteered for the Britiſh channel.

The Britiſh fleet, under ſir Charles Hardy, who was appointed to the command upon the reſignation of admiral Keppel, was by this time alſo at ſea. It conſiſted of thirty-eight ſhips of the line, with ſometing leſs than its due proportion of frigates, and cruiſed in that part of the ſea which, in nautical phraſeology, is called the chops, or mouth, of the channel. The great ſuperiority of the

 com-

CHAP. XXXII.

1779.

The combined fleets of France and Spain threaten an invasion of Great Britain.

combined fleet, in the number of ſhips, guns, and men, ſeemed to juſtify the forebodings of thoſe who prognoſticated the ruin of the Britiſh empire; and, to add to the dangers of the preſent moment, preparations were made on the French coaſt, and an invaſion of Great Britain was threatened under cover of the combined fleet. On the other hand, every precaution was taken by the Britiſh government, which prudence ſuggeſted, for defeating the expected attack. A proclamation was iſſued, ordering the cattle and draught-horſes to be driven from thoſe parts of the ſea-coaſt on which a landing ſhould be effected; the militia was embodied; and numerous cruiſers were ſtationed in the narrow ſeas, to watch the enemy's motions. And theſe efforts of the government were nobly ſeconded by thoſe of private individuals; for ſuch energy had the national ſpirit acquired under the proſpect of the difficulties that ſurrounded, and the dangers that threatened, that meetings were held in moſt of the principal towns, and voluntary contributions made to raiſe men for the defence of the nation.

About the middle of Auguſt, count d'Orvilliers, with the combined fleet, paſſed the Britiſh fleet under ſir Charles Hardy, in the mouth of the channel, without either fleet having diſcovered the other, and proceeded on as far as Plymouth; taking in the way the Ardent, a Britiſh ſhip of war, on her paſſage to join ſir Charles Hardy. The count d'Orvilliers made no attempt to land, but continued for ſeveral days parading with the combined fleet in ſight of Plymouth, until a ſtrong eaſterly wind ſet in, and compelled him to quit the channel. As ſoon as this abated, he returned to the coaſt of England, and cruiſed off the Land's End. The ſame eaſterly wind had alſo driven the Britiſh fleet to ſea; but, on the laſt day of Auguſt, ſir Charles Hardy regained his former ſtation, and entered the channel in full view of the enemy, who did not attempt to moleſt him. He now endeavoured to entice them into the narrower part of the channel,

channel, where their great ſuperiority in number would have leſs availed them; and they followed him as high as Plymouth, but choſe to proceed no farther. Their crews were ſaid to be ſickly; their ſhips to be in bad condition: And the ſeaſon for equinoctial gales was faſt approaching. They therefore ſoon afterwards quitted the Engliſh Channel, and entered the harbour of Breſt. Thus all the apprehenſions which had been raiſed were quickly diſſipated: And nothing was done anſwerable to the mighty expectations that had been formed from the union and co-operation of two ſuch powerful fleets. Even during their cruiſe, commodore Johnſtone, with a ſquadron of Britiſh ſhips, hovered on the coaſt of France and kept it in alarm. The trade of the enemy was every-where annoyed by the Britiſh cruiſers, and their merchant-ſhips taken, even at the entrance of their harbours. On the other hand, the Britiſh trade was leſs injured than in the preceding year: One of her homeward-bound fleets from the Weſt Indies, conſiſting of one hundred and twenty-five ſail, arrived in ſafety juſt before the combined fleets entered the channel; and ſcarcely had they left it, when another fleet from the Eaſt Indies was equally fortunate. Sir Charles Hardy continued to cruiſe with the channel fleet until it was late in the ſeaſon: And, notwithſtanding the apparent ſuperiority of the enemy, Great Britain, in effect, ſtill remained maſter of the ſea.

The only one of the homeward-bound Britiſh fleets that ſeemed to be in any danger, was that from the Baltic, under the convoy of the Serapis, captain Pierſon, and the Counteſs of Scarborough, captain Piercy, the firſt a ſhip of forty-four, and the other of twenty guns. This fleet was attacked near Scarborough, on the northern coaſt of England, by a ſquadron under the command of captain Paul Jones, in the ſervice of congreſs, a man of a ſavage and ferocious diſpoſition, hardened by his crimes, and rendered deſperate by the fear of puniſhment. Jones's ſquadron conſiſted of the Bon Homme

 Richard,

CHAP. XXXII.

1779.

Engagement between captain Paul Jones and the convoy of a Britifh fleet from the Baltic.

Richard, a fhip of forty guns; two frigates, one of thirty-fix, and the other of thirty-two guns; the Vengeance brig of twelve guns, and a cutter; and was fitted out from Port l'Orient in the end of July, for the purpofe of intercepting the Britifh fleet from the Baltic. But by the good conduct and perfevering bravery of captain Pierfon, the convoy was faved, although both the king's fhips were taken. As foon as the enemy was difcovered, a fignal was made for all the fhips of the convoy to run in fhore, and endeavour to make a harbour, whilft captain Pierfon fet all the fail he could to get between them and the enemy; and as foon as he came near enough to difcover the fuperior force which he had to contend with, another fignal was made for the Countefs of Scarborough to join him. Jones fhewed no backwardnefs to engage: He fteered directly for the Serapis, and brought-to within mufket-fhot of her larboard bow, about half after feven in the evening. An engagement immediately commenced, and not more than two or three broadfides were exchanged, when Jones attempted to board the Serapis; but he was foon repulfed, and obliged to fheer off. In a fecond attempt the two fhips became entangled, and dropped alongfide of each other fo clofe, that the muzzles of the guns touched the fides of the oppofite fhip. In this fituation the engagement was continued till half an hour after ten, during which the Serapis was frequently fet on fire by the combuftibles thrown into her from the Bon Homme Richard; and, in the confufion, a cartridge took fire, which, communicating to others, blew up all the officers and men ftationed abaft the main-maft, and rendered the guns in that quarter of the fhip totally unferviceable. Throughout the whole of the action, the Alliance, the largeft of Jones's frigates, failed round, and, as opportunities offered, poured her broadfides into the Serapis; and, towards the conclufion of the engagement, coming under her ftern, raked her fore-and-aft, and killed or wounded fo many of her

men,

men, that captain Pierſon, ſeeing no proſpect of being able to extricate the Serapis, thought it cruelty to his people longer to continue the action, and ſtruck his colours. The Counteſs of Scarborough, although ſo much inferior in force, had engaged the Pallas, a French frigate of thirty-two guns, for nearly two hours, but was at length obliged to ſtrike; her rigging being cut to pieces, ſeven of her guns diſmounted, four of her people killed, and twenty badly wounded: And, to cut off all hopes of ſucceſs from a further reſiſtance, juſt before ſhe ſtruck, the other frigate came up on her larboard quarter, and was ready to join in the action. The carnage on board the Serapis was great: It amounted, according to the beſt account that captain Pierſon was enabled to give, to forty-nine killed, and ſixty-eight wounded; but he had reaſon to believe, although this was all the loſs which he was able to aſcertain with preciſion, that in reality it was much greater. His ſhip too had ſuſtained very conſiderable damage; and the mainmaſt went by the board juſt as ſhe ſtruck. But the ſcene which preſented itſelf on board the Bon Homme Richard was horrible beyond deſcription. Her quarter and counter on the lower deck were entirely driven in, and the whole of her guns on that deck diſmounted. She was on fire in two different places; had ſeven feet of water in her hold; and her decks ſtreamed with the blood of the killed and wounded, which, according to captain Pierſon's account, amounted to three hundred and ſix, a number more than three-fourths of her crew. Under ſuch circumſtances of accumulated horror and diſtreſs, none but a deſperado would have continued the engagement; but their ruffian commander was ſeen ſeveral times during the action without his coat, and with his ſhirt-ſleeves tucked up beyond his elbows, running about the ſhip, and brandiſhing a naked cutlaſs to keep his men at their quarters. To him, who, it ſeems, was a native of Galloway in Scotland, and who, it is ſaid, had, by his crimes, forfeited his life

CHAP. XXXII. 1779.

to the laws of his country, before he entered into the ſervice of congreſs, it was eligible to fall in battle rather than by the hands of the executioner: But, to a commander of any humanity, the lives of the people entruſted to his care, are an object of the utmoſt attention; and, to ſuch a commander, reſiſtance appears unjuſtifiable, after it becomes hopeleſs. The iſſue of the engagement in favour of the Bon Homme Richard may therefore be aſcribed to the different circumſtances under which the two commanders acted, as much as to the diſparity of force. The damage done to the Bon Homme Richard was ſo great that it could not be repaired; the water gained upon her ſo faſt, that ſhe ſunk in leſs than two days afterwards, with ſome of her wounded men on board. By this engagement two of his majeſty's ſhips were loſt; but a valuable convoy were ſaved. The brave reſiſtance made by captain Pierſon gave the ſhips of the convoy time to eſcape; and enabled them to take ſhelter in the different harbours on the ſea-coaſt before they could be overtaken.

The declaration which announced hoſtilities on the part of the Spaniſh nation was not made until every thing had been previouſly prepared for acting with effect. The grand Spaniſh fleet had either failed, or was ready to ſail: Troops were in motion to occupy the works at St. Roque, and inveſt Gibraltar by land, whilſt a naval force was proceeding to block it up by ſea: And orders had been diſpatched to the governors of their foreign poſſeſſions to prepare them for the rupture. With the help of ſuch previous arrangements it was hoped, whilſt Great Britain was embarraſſed with the complicated operations of ſo extenſive a war, that Spain might with eaſe recover back ſome of the poſſeſſions that had been wreſted from her in leſs auſpicious times; and Gibraltar in Europe, and the province of Weſt Florida in North America, appear to have been marked out as the firſt objects of attack.

General

General Elliott, that brave and gallant veteran, commanded at Gibraltar; and the garrifon had been largely reinforced. With fuch advantages, added to the natural ftrength of the place, the reduction of it was thought impracticable, in any other way than by blockade: It was therefore invefted both by fea and land; and the blockade was formally notified to all the maritime powers in amity with Spain, that they might not attempt to furnifh it with fupplies. But in this refpect the Britifh miniftry had anticipated the views of Spain, and, under the apprehenfion of a rupture, had not only largely reinforced Gibraltar with troops, but plentifully fupplied it with provifions and ftores; fo that an attack upon a place of fuch ftrength, fo amply provided with every thing neceffary to hold out againft a fiege, in which the enemy might unprofitably wafte their blood and treafure, was rather to be wifhed than regretted.

Blockade of Gibraltar.

It was far otherwife with Weft Florida, a province of large extent, thinly fettled, and defended by an inconfiderable force. Its weftern extremity, at a great diftance from Penfacola, the feat of the government, bordered on the Spanifh province of Louifiana, from which it was feparated only by the river Miffiffippi. Weft Florida was therefore peculiarly expofed to an attack, not only from its weak ftate of defence, but from its contiguity to the Spanifh territories. And Don Bernardo de Galves, the governor of Louifiana, having been previoufly inftructed, had made all neceffary preparations, and was ready to pafs the boundary, as foon as he fhould receive information of the commencement of hoftilities, intelligence of which, it appears, was communicated to him early in Auguft, and long before it reached the governor of Weft Florida.

Incurfion of the Americans into Weft Florida.

In the preceding year a predatory incurfion had been made into this province by a captain Willing, an American partizan, who, from having been a fettler upon the Miffiffippi, previous to the war, was well acquainted with the countries bordering upon that river.

CHAP. XXXII. 1779.

river. He ſet out from Fort Pitt, and, deſcending by the courſes of the Ohio and Miſſiſſippi, arrived at a Britiſh ſettlement in Weſt Florida, called Manchac, at the confluence of the river Ibberville with the Miſſiſſippi; and ſuch was the weakneſs of this frontier ſettlement, that with twenty-five men only he entered it, took by ſurpriſe a Britiſh merchant-ſhip, mounting ſixteen guns, that lay there loading with tobacco and indigo, and made himſelf maſter not only of that ſettlement, but of ſome others that adjoined it upon the river Amit. Some of the principal inhabitants made their eſcape, and flying to Penſacola, applied to the governor for aſſiſtance. At that time there were not more than five hundred regular troops in the province, a number not more that ſufficient to garriſon Penſacola, and the fort at Mobille; from which ſervices none of them could be ſpared. But the ſuperintendant for Indian affairs, having conſented to permit a few of the hunters, who were attached to his department, to aſſiſt the inhabitants of Manchac in the recovery of their poſſeſſions; with this ſmall reinforcement they returned, drove out the Americans, and re-poſſeſſed themſelves of their former eſtates and habitations. This irruption of the Americans, together with the apprehenſion of the hoſtile intentions of Spain, was the cauſe of a reinforcement being ſent to Penſacola in the beginning of the preſent year. It conſiſted of a regiment of Germans, and the Maryland and Penſylvania regiments of provincials, under the command of brigadier-general John Campbell; and the whole regular force of the province, after the junction of this detachment, amounted to about one thouſand eight hundred men.

Weſt Florida reduced by the Spaniards.

Soon after the arrival of general Campbell, he detached lieutenant-colonel Dickſon, with five hundred men, to build a fort near the mouth of the Ibberville, for the defence of that part of the frontier. But, from various unexpected obſtructions that occurred, the fort

was

CHAP. XXXII. 1779. August.

was not nearly finiſhed when Don Bernardo de Galves, about the end of Auguſt, entered the province with two thouſand men, having firſt intercepted ſeveral veſſels with ſupplies for the fort, and taken every practicable precaution for preventing intelligence of his operations from being carried to general Campbell. On the twelfth of September he approached Baton Rouge, where lieutenant-colonel Dickſon had taken poſt with his detachment, and thrown up ſome works that were yet unfiniſhed. The place was immediately inveſted, and approaches were made and continued until the twenty-firſt of September, when a battery of heavy cannon was opened upon the works. Theſe, after an inceſſant cannonade for three hours, were found to be untenable: A flag of truce was ſent out with propoſals; and a capitulation was finally entered into for the ſurrender of the poſt. Honourable terms were obtained not only for the garriſon but the inhabitants of the neighbouring diſtricts; and in this manner the Britiſh ſettlements upon the Miſſiſſippi, from the Natches downward, were yielded to the crown of Spain. But this loſs was ſoon afterwards in part compenſated by an acquiſition made in a different quarter.

The Spaniards attack the Britiſh logwood-cutters in Honduras.

It ſeems evident that the ſame proviſionary orders for hoſtilities had been ſent to all the governors of the Spaniſh provinces that bordered on any Britiſh ſettlement; for nearly at the ſame time when Don Bernardo de Galves entered the province of Weſt Florida, the Spaniſh governor of Honduras made an unexpected attack upon the Britiſh logwood-cutters, took many of them priſoners, and expelled the reſt from their principal ſettlement at St. George's Key. General Dalling, governor of Jamaica, who, in conſequence of the rupture with Spain, was apprehenſive that ſuch an attack would be made, had already diſpatched captain Dalrymple, with a ſmall detachment of the Iriſh volunteers, to the Muſquito ſhore, to collect a force for the aſſiſtance of the logwood-cutters in the Bay of Hon-

 duras.

CHAP. XXXII. 1779.

duras. The tranſports which conveyed this detachment, carried alſo a ſupply of arms, ammunition, and ſtores, and arrived at Black River on the Muſquito ſhore on the twenty-ſeventh of September. The ſame day on which they arrived, intelligence was received of the attack made by the Spaniards on St. George's Key; and in conſequence of this intelligence the ſquadron again put to ſea, as ſoon as captain Dalrymple had enliſted ſome volunteers, and collected about ſixty Indians. In their paſſage to Honduras they fell in with a ſquadron of ſhips of war under the command of commodore Luttrell, conſiſting of the Charon, and the Loweſtoff and and Pomona frigates, that had been ſent by ſir Peter Parker, admiral on the Jamaica ſtation, to intercept ſome Spaniſh regiſter-ſhips, of which he had received intelligence.

From commodore Luttrell, information was received that the ſettlers at Honduras, with their ſlaves, had retired to Truxillo, and the iſland of Rattan, on the Muſquito ſhore; that the Spaniards had been already diſpoſſeſſed of St. George's Key, by his majeſty's armed ſchooner Racehorſe; and that the regiſter-ſhips, which were the object of commodore Luttrell's cruiſe, had taken ſhelter in the harbour of Omoa, and were too ſtrongly protected by the fortifications on ſhore to be attacked by ſea. Under ſuch circumſtances it was agreed between the commodore and captain Dalrymple to unite their force, proceed againſt Omoa, and attack it both by ſea and land. The united ſquadron accordingly ſailed firſt for Truxillo, where a number of bay-men and logwood-cutters were collected, armed and embodied; and from thence proceeded againſt Omoa.

Reduction of the Spaniſh fort Omoa, the key of the Bay of Honduras.

On the ſixteenth of October in the evening, the land-force, which, even with the marines and muſquetry-men of the ſhips, and the reinforcement from Truxillo, did not much exceed five hundred men, was diſembarked at Porto Cavallo, a harbour which was ſuppoſed to be not more than nine miles diſtant from Omoa. It had been in-

tended

tended to march forward in the night, ſurpriſe the fort, and take it by eſcalade, before the morning; but the country through which the march was to be performed was difficult, being in ſome parts interſected by lagoons and moraſſes, and in others by ſteep precipices, rendered almoſt impaſſable by the late rains; and through this difficult country only a narrow path led to the fort, which, in the darkneſs of the night, they were obliged to explore with lighted ſplinters of the cabbage-tree: The diſtance too was found to be greater than had been repreſented. By theſe obſtructions the march was ſo much retarded, that, when morning appeared, captain Dalrymple found himſelf ſtill ſix miles from the fort, and his men much fatigued. He ſuffered them to refreſh themſelves for two hours, and then continued his march, putting the Indians in front to ſcour the woods. A body of the enemy was diſcovered lying in ambuſh, about a mile from the fort, and quickly diſloged. The heights round the town, and the fort, with the roads leading to them, were ſecured: Poſts were eſtabliſhed; and ſome of theſe being galled by a ſcattering fire from the houſes in the town, captain Dalrymple found it neceſſary to burn it down. Whilſt the town was in flames, commodore Luttrell's ſquadron entered the bay; and the fort was now inveſted both by ſea and land. Some days were ſpent in landing cannon, and erecting batteries; but, after they were opened, it was quickly perceived, that, although they annoyed the garriſon exceedingly, they made no impreſſion upon the walls of the fort; and that, in this mode, the ſiege might be protracted to an indefinite length. It was therefore determined to cut the matter ſhort by attempting to take the fort by eſcalade, eſpecially as the ditch was obſerved to be dry. The attempt was to be made at four in the morning, by one hundred and fifty Europeans, conſiſting of ſeamen and marines, with a few of the loyal Iriſh, under cover of a cannonade from the ſhips in the bay, and the batteries on the heights. At

CHAP. XXXII. 1779.

three the detachment allotted for this ſervice moved down from the heights; and in the valley, being formed into four columns, waited with impatience for the ſignal of attack. A little after four the cannonade began, which ſo engaged the attention of the enemy, that the aſſailants, with their ſcaling-ladders, advanced, unperceived, cloſe to the ramparts. As they were ready to enter the ditch, they were diſcovered: The enemy's drums beat to arms, and the alarm was given. The aſſailants, for a moment, ſhrunk back, but, almoſt inſtantly recovering themſelves, ruſhed on into the ditch. The ſcaling-ladders were applied; and the ſeamen mounted the walls with alacrity. Two, who firſt reached the top of the ramparts, preſented their pieces at a body of the enemy aſſembled to oppoſe them, but, according to their orders, reſerved their fire until they were joined by more of their companions. Theſe followed ſo cloſely, that the Spaniards were ſtruck with conſternation, and ſeemed to loſe the power of reſiſtance, notwithſtanding the exertions of their officers to encourage them. About one hundred eſcaped over the walls on the oppoſite ſide of the fort; the reſt fled to the caſements; and the governor and principal officers, now ſeeing their ſituation deſperate, came and ſurrendered their ſwords, with the keys of the fort, to captain Dalrymple. Such was the humanity of the aſſailants, and ſuch the good order preſerved in the aſſault, that only two Spaniards were wounded with the bayonet, while in the act of reſiſtance, and not one was plundered. An inſtance of heroiſm in a ſeaman is mentioned, to which hiſtory affords nothing in its kind ſuperior. He had ſcrambled up the walls with a cutlaſs in each hand, and meeting with an unarmed Spaniſh officer, the generous tar diſdained to take advantage of his helpleſs ſituation; but, preſenting him with one of his cutlaſſes, added—"Now you will be on a footing with me." The Spaniſh gentleman was too much affected with the ſingular generoſity of the action to accept of the offer, and quietly ſurrendered. Unfortunately the name of this brave ſeaman has not been preſerved. The Spaniards, during the ſiege, loſt, in killed and wounded, about thirty men; and three hundred and ſixty-five, with a conſiderable number of officers, were made priſoners. The whole loſs of the beſiegers, in killed and wounded, did not exceed twenty.

Thus eaſily was acquired the important fortreſs of Omoa, the key of the Bay of Honduras, and, in time of war, the receptacle of the treaſure ſent from Guatimala. The fort was built of ſtone, raiſed out of the ſea, and brought from the diſtance of twenty leagues. Its walls were eighteen feet thick; and, although it had coſt the Spaniards twenty years labour, the out-works were not then finiſhed. But, to the captors, the moſt important part of the acquiſition was the two regiſter-ſhips, the value of which, with that of ſome other prizes of leſs note taken in the harbour, was eſtimated at three millions of dollars. A convention was made for an exchange of priſoners; and it was agreed, that thoſe who were taken in Fort Omoa ſhould be exchanged for an equal number of Britiſh ſubjects taken in the Bay of Honduras. The Spaniſh governor offered to ranſom the fort at the expence of three hundred thouſand dollars. But as Omoa was thought to be a poſt of great conſequence during a war with Spain, the offer, although an advantageous one to the captors, was immediately rejected; as was a ſimilar one for two hundred and fifty quintals of quickſilver, an article neceſſary for working the Spaniſh mines, and for which a ſum of money would have been given more than double its value.

When the Britiſh ſquadron quitted Omoa, a garriſon was aſſigned to it, ſuch as could be ſpared, and a ſloop of war left in the harbour for its further protection: But it did not long remain in the poſſeſſion of Great Britain. The weakneſs of the garriſon tempted the

CHAP. XXXII. 1779.

the Spaniards in the neighbourhood to collect a force and invest the fort. For a considerable time it was defended with great bravery: But, at last, both the officers and men, amongst whom an epidemical fever began to rage, and who, in the whole, amounted only to eighty-five, were so weakened and overcome with the fatigue of constant duty, one centinel being obliged, by shifting his place, to serve for five, that they saw it would be impossible to withstand an assault, which the enemy were preparing to make. They therefore determined to evacuate the fort; but to leave it as unserviceable as in their circumstances they could possibly make it. After the guns had been spiked, and the ammunition and military stores destroyed, the garrison, without losing a single man in the evacuation, embarked on board the vessels in the harbour, and took a final leave of Omoa.

Protection afforded to the British commerce.

It has already been observed, that had the British fleet under admiral Byron followed that of France under the count d'Estaing, when he made an unsuccessful attack upon Savannah, it is more than probable, that, to the disgrace of a repulse from that town, would have been added the loss of a great part of his fleet. But the British fleet, in the station on which it did remain, performed very eminent services to the state under the command of rear-admiral Hyde Parker, who succeeded admiral Byron in the fall of the present year. The British commerce in the West Indies was protected, whilst that of the enemy was almost ruined by the capture of their merchantmen. Great part of a convoy bound to Martinique was either taken or destroyed, in sight of the island, and of the French squadron at Fort Royal, under Monsieur de la Motte Piquet, who, in sailing out of the harbour to the relief of one of his frigates, was in imminent danger of having his retreat cut off by part of the British fleet, then cruising off the mouth of the bay.

bay. And to the captures of their merchantmen are to be added four of the count d'Eſtaing's frigates, on their return to the Weſt Indies from the coaſt of America *.

Thus Great Britain continued to make a noble ſtand againſt the machinations of her foes. And, although the year 1779 muſt be conſidered as unfortunate, in which ſhe loſt two valuable iſlands, without gaining from her enemies a territorial equivalent; it may, nevertheleſs, be doubted whether the loſs of theſe iſlands was not overbalanced by the damage done to the French and Spaniſh commerce, not only in Europe and the Weſt Indies, but in every quarter of the globe.

* The firſt of theſe frigates was taken on the 24th of October; and from her admiral Parker firſt learnt with certainty, that count d'Eſtaing had gone, with all his fleet, to North America.

CHAP. XXXIII.

Expedition under Sir Henry Clinton to South Carolina—Fortifications of Charlestown described—Garrison of Charlestown—Siege and Reduction of Charlestown—Incursion of the Spaniards into West Florida—Consequences of the Fall of Charlestown—Three new Expeditions set on foot by the British Commander—His Address to the Inhabitants of South Carolina—Its Effect—Defeat of the American Colonel Burford—Disposition of the British Troops in South Carolina—Administration of Earl Cornwallis there—Counter-revolution among those who had submitted to the Power of Britain on the Fall of Charlestown—Detachment from Washington's Army sent into North Carolina—Movements of the American Colonel Sumpter—His Attempt on the British Post on Rocky Point.

CHAP. XXXIII. 1780. Expedition under sir Henry Clinton to South Carolina.

SIR Henry Clinton having been cramped in his operations by the proceedings of the French fleet under the count d'Estaing, whose unsuccessful attack upon Savannah, together with his final departure from the American coast, has already been related; no sooner received certain information of the departure of d'Estaing than he set on foot an expedition, the object of which was the taking of Charlestown, and the reduction of the province of South Carolina. The troops designed for this expedition were immediately embarked on board the transports; and these, escorted by admiral Arbuthnot with an adequate naval force, sailed from Sandy Hook on the twenty-sixth of December 1779. Sir Henry Clinton accompanied the expedition, leaving the garrison at New

December.

New York under the command of lieutenant-general Knyphaufen. The paffage might have been expected to be performed in ten days; but fuch was the uncommon feverity of the feafon, that the fleet was very foon feparated, and driven out of its courfe by tempeftuous weather; and fcarcely any of the fhips arrived at Tybee, the appointed place of rendezvous, before the end of January. Some few ftraggling veffels were taken; fome others were loft; and all received more or lefs damage. Almoft all the horfes belonging to the artillery or cavalry perifhed during the paffage; and amongft the fhips that were loft was one which contained the heavy ordnance. Fortunately, however, the crews were all faved.

Thofe fhips being refitted that ftood in need of immediate repair, the fleet failed from Tybee to North Edifto Sound, in the province of South Carolina; and on the eleventh of February the troops were difembarked on John's Ifland, about thirty miles from Charleftown. Part of the fleet was immediately fent round to block up the harbour of Charleftown by fea; whilft the troops, flowly advancing through the country, paffed from John's to James Ifland; and from thence, over Wappoo Cut, to the main land, until they at length reached the banks of Afhley River, oppofite to Charleftown. So great were the impediments that they met with in their progrefs, or fuch the extreme caution of the commander in chief, in eftablifhing and fortifying pofts to preferve his communication with the fea, that it was not until the twenty-ninth of March that the advance of the army croffed Afhley River at the ferry, and landed on Charleftown Neck, fome miles above the town. The flat-bottomed boats had been brought from North Edifto Sound, through the inlets by which the coaft is interfected, until they entered Afhley River, by Wappoo Cut; and the paffing over of the troops was conducted with much addrefs by captain Elphinftone of

 the

CHAP. XXXIII. 1780.

the navy. On the following day the troops encamped in front of the American lines; and on the first of April began to break ground before Charlestown, at the distance of eight hundred yards from the provincial works.

Fortifications of Charlestown described.

The slow advance of the British army had given time to the provincials not only to strengthen, but greatly to enlarge, the defences of Charlestown. These now consisted of a chain of redoubts, lines and batteries, extending from Ashley to Cooper River, upon which were mounted upwards of eighty pieces of cannon and mortars. In front of the lines a canal had been dug, which was filled with water; and from the dam at either end a swamp oozed to each river, forming natural impediments where the artificial terminated. Behind these were two rows of abbatis, some other obstructions, and, immediately in front of the works, a double-picketted ditch. The works on the right and left were not only of great strength, but advanced so far beyond the range of the intermediate lines as to enfilade the canal almost from one end to the other: And in the centre was a horn-work of masonry, which, being closed during the siege, became a kind of citadel.

Such were the defences of Charlestown on the only side on which it could be approached by land; and, towards the water, numerous batteries covered with artillery forbad the approach of ships. But, besides the security which Charlestown derived from its numerous batteries, it was still more effectually protected by the bar, or sand-bank, at the mouth of the inlet that led from the sea. This bar was impassable by the larger ships of war, and rendered the entry of others difficult and dangerous; and, just within it, Five Fathom Hole, of a sufficient depth of water, furnished a convenient station for a squadron to command the bar, and render the passage of it still more difficult and dangerous. This station was occupied by the American

American commodore Whipple, with a ſquadron of nine ſail under his command, the largeſt carrying forty-four, and the ſmalleſt ſixteen, guns. After the perils and difficulties of the bar were ſurmounted, before a fleet could reach Charleſtown, Fort Moultrie, upon Sullivan's Iſland, was to be paſſed, the fire from which had, on a former occaſion, proved ſo deſtructive to a Britiſh ſquadron under ſir Peter Parker; and, ſince that period, the works on Sullivan's Iſland had been conſiderably ſtrengthened and enlarged. CHAP. XXXIII. 1780.

Garriſon of Charleſtown.

General Lincoln, truſting to thoſe defences, and at the ſame time expecting large reinforcements from the other colonies, inſtead of remaining with his army in the open country, ſhut himſelf up in Charleſtown, at the earneſt requeſt of the inhabitants, and with the force under his command, amounting to ſeven thouſand men of all denominations under arms, reſolved to defend it to the laſt extremity. Great expectations were, undoubtedly, at one time, entertained of the ſucceſsful defence of the bar, from the advantageous poſition of the American ſquadron; but it ſoon appeared that theſe were illuſory: For no ſooner did the Britiſh fleet, on the twentieth of March, approach the bar, with an intention to paſs it, than commodore Whipple quitted his ſtation and retired to Fort Moultrie, leaving admiral Arbuthnot to enter at his leiſure, and occupy the ſtation which the American ſquadron had juſt before quitted. Before the Renown, Roebuck, and Romulus could paſs the bar, it was neceſſary to lighten them, by taking out their guns, proviſion, and water; and in that deſtitute ſituation they lay for ſixteen days, before a favourable opportunity offered for making the attempt. But, when the attempt was made, they effected their paſſage without any oppoſition, except from ſome gallies left by commodore Whipple, which fired upon the boats of the fleet, and endeavoured to prevent them from ſounding the channel. Not long afterwards, commodore

CHAP. XXXIII. 1780.

Whipple retired to Charleſtown with his ſhips, part of which he ſtationed in Cooper River; and the reſt, with ſome other veſſels, were ſunk acroſs the mouth of it, to prevent the Britiſh fleet from entering. This was a moſt important precaution; for had the Britiſh fleet been permitted to gain the poſſeſſion of Cooper River, the larger ſhips might have been ſo ſtationed as to rake the American lines; the only communication that remained between the town and the country would have been interrupted; all hopes of obtaining ſupplies and reinforcements cut off, and the duration of the ſiege, in all probability, greatly ſhortened.

As ſoon as the Britiſh began to erect batteries againſt the town, admiral Arbuthnot embraced the firſt favourable opportunity that offered for paſſing Fort Moultrie; and, on the ninth of April, with a ſtrong ſoutherly wind and flowing tide, he weighed anchor, and effected his purpoſe with very little loſs. His ſquadron conſiſted of the Renown of fifty, the Romulus and Roebuck, each of forty-four guns; the Richmond, Blonde, Raleigh, and Virginia, frigates, and the Sandwich armed ſhip; and although, in paſſing, the ſhips were expoſed to a heavy cannonade from Fort Moultrie, their whole loſs of men, in killed and wounded, amounted only to twenty-ſeven; and the damage done to them in other reſpects was equally inconſiderable. As their entry into Cooper River was precluded, they anchored near Fort Johnſton, juſt without the range of ſhot from the batteries of the town.

The ſame day on which the fleet paſſed Fort Moultrie, the firſt parallel of the beſiegers was finiſhed; and the town being now almoſt completely inveſted, both by ſea and land, the Britiſh commanders ſummoned general Lincoln to ſurrender. His anſwer was ſhort, but firm, and conveyed an implied reflection againſt the Britiſh commanders for their ſuppoſed tardineſs in making their approaches:—" Sixty days," said he, " have passed since it has been " known that your intentions against this town were hostile, in which " time has been afforded to abandon it; but duty and inclination " point to the propriety of supporting it to the last extremity."

Siege of Charlestown.

The summons being ineffectual, the batteries of the first parallel were opened upon the town, and soon made a visible impression. But still the communication between the country and the garrison was kept open across Cooper River; and on the very day on which the summons was sent to general Lincoln, the American general Woodford passed Cooper River with seven hundred continental troops, and entered the town. To assist in preserving this communication, general Lincoln had left his cavalry without the lines, with orders to traverse and keep open the country to the eastward of Cooper River, as being that through which he expected to receive his reinforcements; and by the same route he hoped to be able to make good his retreat with the garrison, if at last he should find the town no longer tenable *.

To

* The underwritten Letter was intercepted and published by Sir Henry Clinton's orders during the siege of Charlestown.

South Carolina, May 11, 1780.

From B. Smith to Mrs. Benjamin Smith, dated Charlestown, April 30, 1780.

HAVING never had an opportunity of writing to her since the enemy began to act with vigour, and knowing that a thousand evil reports will prevail to increase her uneasiness—mine I have supported pretty well until last night, when I really almost sunk under the load:—Nothing remains around to comfort me but a probability of saving my life, - - - - - After going through many difficulties, our affairs are daily declining, and not a ray of hope remains to assure us of success. - - - - The enemy have turned the siege into a blockade, which, in a short time, must have the desired effect; and the most sanguine do not now entertain the smallest hope of the town being saved. The enemy have continued their approaches with vigour continually, since I wrote the inclosed, and are now completing batteries about two hundred yards distance from our lines; they fire but seldom from their cannon, but their popping off rifles and small-arms do frequent mischief, and every night throw out an amazing number of shells amongst our people at the lines, which, though not attended with the damage that might reasonably be expected, do some mischief. Our communication is entirely

CHAP. XXXIII. 1780.

To cut off the retreat of the garrison, and to prevent it from receiving reinforcements, were objects of such importance that they had not escaped the attention of the British general. But the maintaining his own communications with the sea had required all the troops he could spare from the immediate operations of the siege, until the British fleet passed Fort Moultrie, and gained the command of the water between it and Charlestown. From this time sir Henry Clinton felt no farther apprehension about his own com-

tirely cut off from the country (excepting by a small boat at great risque) by lord Cornwallis, who occupies every landing-place from Haddrill's Point, a considerable way up the river, with two thousand five hundred men. When I wrote last, it was the general opinion that we could evacuate the town at pleasure; but a considerable reinforcement having arrived to the enemy, has enabled them to strengthen their posts so effectually as to prevent that measure. The same cause prevents our receiving further supplies of provisions or reinforcements, and a short time will plant the British standard on our ramparts. You will see by the inclosed summons that the persons and properties of the inhabitants will be saved; and consequently I expect to have the liberty of soon returning to you; but the army must be made prisoners of war. This will give a rude shock to the independence of America; and a Lincolnade will become as common a term as Burgoynade: But I hope we shall in time recover this severe blow. However, before this happens, I hope I shall be permitted to return home, where I must stay, as my situation will not permit me to take any further an active part; and therefore my abandoning my property will subject me to many inconveniencies and losses, without being any way serviceable to the country. - - - This letter will run great risque, as it will be surrounded on all sides; but as I know the person to whose care it is committed, and feel for your uneasy situation, I could not but trust it. Assure yourself that I shall shortly see you, as nothing prevents Lincoln's surrender but a point of honour in holding out to the last extremity. This is nearly at hand, as our provisions will soon fail; and my plan is to walk off as soon as I can obtain permission. - - - - Should your father be at home, make him acquainted with the purport of this letter, and remember me to him; also to your mother, but do not let the intelligence go out of the house, - - - - but a mortifying scene must first be encountered: The thirteen stripes will be levelled in the dust, and I owe my life to the clemency of a conqueror.

Your ever affectionate husband,

(Signed) B. SMITH.

Note. Those parts filled up with *hyphens* contain expressions of tenderness to his wife, no way interesting to the public; for which reason we have omitted to publish them.

munications,

munications, and was enabled to detach lieutenant-colonel Webſter, with one thouſand four hundred men, to cut off thoſe of the enemy. By the advanced guard of this detachment, compoſed of Tarleton's legion and Ferguſon's corps, the American cavalry, with the militia attached to them, were ſurpriſed in the night of the fourteenth of April, at Biggin's Bridge, near Monk's Corner, thirty-two miles from Charleſtown, and completely routed and diſperſed, with the loſs of all his ſtores, camp equipage, and baggage *.

* Forty-two large waggons, one hundred and two waggon-horſes, eighty-two dragoon-horſes, and ſeveral officers horſes; a quantity of ammunition, flour, butter, clothing, camp and horſe equipage; harneſs for all the waggons; all the officers clothing and baggage; together with five puncheons of rum, ſix hogſheads of muſcovado ſugar, four barrels of indigo, a quantity of tea, coffee, ſpices, nails in caſks, ſome French cloth, three barrels of gunpowder, light-dragoon ſwords, &c. &c. found in a ſtore, which was ſet on fire, and blown up by the careleſſneſs of the centinel, who, in going to draw ſome rum, ſet it on fire, and in a ſhort time the ſtore was blown up. The loſs of the Americans, in men, was major Birnie of Pulaſki's legion of dragoons, three captains, one lieutenant, and ten privates, killed; fifteen privates, one captain, and two lieutenants, wounded; fifty-eight privates, two captains, and three lieutenants, taken priſoners, including the wounded. Major Birnie was mangled in the moſt ſhocking manner; he had ſeveral wounds, a ſevere one behind his ear. This unfortunate officer lived ſeveral hours, reprobating the Americans for their conduct on this occaſion, and even in his laſt moments curſing the Britiſh for their barbarity, in having refuſed quarter after he had ſurrendered. The writer of this, who was ordered on this expedition, afforded every aſſiſtance in his power; and had the major put upon a table, in a public-houſe in the village; and a blanket thrown over him. The major, in his laſt moments, was frequently inſulted by the privates of the legion: Some dragoons of the Britiſh legion attempted to raviſh ſeveral ladies at the houſe of ſir John Collington, in the neighbourhood of Monk's Corner. Mrs. ——— the wife of Doctor ——— of Charleſtown, was moſt barbarouſly treated; ſhe was a moſt delicate and beautiful woman. Lady ——— received one or two wounds with a ſword. Miſs ———, ſiſter to major ———, was alſo ill treated. The ladies made their eſcape, and came to Monk's Corner, where they were protected; a carriage being provided, they were eſcorted to the houſe of Mr. ———. The dragoons were apprehended and brought to Monk's Corner, where, by this time, colonel Webſter had arrived and taken the command. The late colonel Patrick Ferguſon (of whom we ſhall have occaſion to ſpeak hereafter) was for putting the dragoons to inſtant death. But colonel Webſter did not conceive that his powers extended to that of holding a general court-martial. The priſoners were however ſent to head-quarters, and, I believe, were afterwards tried and whipped.

By

CHAP. XXXIII. 1780.

By this defeat a paſſage was opened acroſs the head branches of Cooper River for the remainder of the detachment to move forward and occupy the country to the eaſtward of it. Some days afterwards, by the arrival of a reinforcement from New York, the commander in chief was enabled to ſend another detachment acroſs Cooper River; and the command of the whole was given to earl Cornwallis.

The force detached to the eaſtward of Cooper River was now ſo conſiderable as to cut off from the garriſon all reaſonable hopes of effecting a retreat. A council of war was called; and by their advice, an offer was made for ſurrendering the town on certain conditions: But the conditions propoſed were of ſuch a nature as could not be acceded to by the Britiſh commanders, and were of courſe inſtantly rejected. In the mean time the beſiegers were daily advancing their works: The ſecond parallel was completed on the twentieth of April, and the third on the ſixth of May. The laſt of theſe had been puſhed ſo near to the provincial works as to be cloſe to the canal; and the canal, for a conſiderable part of its extent, was quickly drained of its water by a ſap carried to the dam.

The misfortunes of the beſieged now crowded faſt upon them. On the ſame day on which the third parallel was completed, the garriſon of Fort Moultrie ſurrendered to captain Hudſon of the navy, who had been landed on Sullivan's Iſland, with two hundred ſeamen and marines, to attack the fort by land, whilſt the ſhips prepared to batter it from the water; and, on the ſame day alſo, the broken remains of the American cavalry, which had been collected with great care by a colonel White, were again defeated by colonel Tarleton on the banks of the Santee. Whilſt the Americans lay under the preſſure of theſe accumulated misfortunes, the Britiſh commanders, with a view of ſaving the effuſion of blood, thought proper once more to open a correſpondence with general Lincoln for the ſur-

ſurrender of the town: But the garriſon or the inhabitants were not yet ſufficiently humbled to accept of the terms that were offered; and hoſtilities were recommenced. The batteries of the third parallel opened upon the town, and did great execution; and at this ſhort diſtance the Heſſian yagers, poſted advantageouſly, fired their rifles with ſuch effect, that numbers of the beſieged were killed at their guns, and ſcarcely any eſcaped who ventured to ſhew themſelves over the lines. During this fire, which continued for two days without intermiſſion, the beſiegers gained the counterſcarp of the outwork that flanked the canal; the canal itſelf was paſſed; and the works were advanced almoſt to the verge of the ditch. The hopes of the inhabitants now forſook them: All the horrors of an aſſault preſented themſelves to their affrighted imaginations; and they joined in a petition to general Lincoln, praying him to accept the terms which had been offered. A flag of truce was accordingly ſent out with a propoſition to that effect. And, whatever ſevere juſtice might have dictated, the Britiſh commanders, unwilling to preſs to unconditional ſubmiſſion a reduced enemy, whom clemency might yet reconcile, accepted the propoſition, and agreed to grant the ſame terms which had been before rejected. The capitulation was ſigned on the twelfth of May; and on the ſame day the garriſon laid down their arms, and major-general Leſlie took poſſeſſion of the town.

Reduction of Charleſtown.

By the articles of capitulation the garriſon were allowed ſome of the honours of war: They were to march out and depoſit their arms between the canal and the works of the place; but the drums were not to beat a Britiſh march, nor the colours to be uncaſed: The continental troops and ſeamen, keeping their baggage, were to remain priſoners of war until exchanged: The militia were to be permitted to return to their reſpective homes as priſoners on parole;

 and,

CHAP. XXXIII. 1780.

and, while they kept their parole, were not to be molested in their property by the British troops: The citizens of all descriptions were to be considered as prisoners on parole, and to hold their property in the town on the same terms as the militia: The officers of the army and navy were to retain their servants, swords, pistols, and baggage, unsearched; they were permitted to sell their horses, but not to remove them out of the town: And a flag of truce was to be furnished to carry general Lincoln's dispatches to Philadelphia unopened.

The loss of the British troops, during the siege, amounted to seventy-six killed, and one hundred and eighty-nine wounded; that of the garrison was not, in the whole, quite so much: But in the number of the slain was greater. The prisoners taken in Charlestown, including the deputy governor, and the council of the province, seven general officers, a commodore, ten continental regiments, but much reduced; three battalions of artillery, with town and country militia, amounted to more than five thousand men; to whom must be added about one thousand American and French seamen, and near four hundred pieces of ordnance, with a considerable quantity of stores*.

A Return of the Ships and Vessels taken or destroyed at the Surrender of Charlestown.

The Bricole, pierced for 60, mounting 44 guns, twenty-four and eighteen pounders, sunk; her captain, officers, and company prisoners. The Truite, 26 twelve pounders, sunk; her captain, &c. prisoners. Queen of France, 28 nine pounders, sunk; her captain, &c. prisoners. General Moultrie, 20 six pounders, sunk; ditto. Notre Dame (brig), 16 ditto, sunk; ditto. Providence, 32 eighteen and twelve pounders, taken; captain and company prisoners. Boston, of the same force, taken; ditto. Ranger, 20 six pounders, taken; ditto.

French Ships. L'Avanture, 26 nine and six pounders, commanded by the Sieur de Brulot, Lieutenant de Vaisseaux, taken and company. Polacre, 16 six pounders, taken.

Some empty brigs, lying at the wharfs, with other small vessels, were also taken, and four armed galleys.

The

The commander in chief, in his public orders iſſued after the ſurrender of the town, and in his diſpatches to the ſecretary of ſtate, was laviſh in encomiums upon the officers who ſerved under him, and the troops he commanded. The aſſiſtance he received during the ſiege from his general officers, earl Cornwallis, major-generals Leſlie, Huyne, and Koſpotch, and brigadier-general Patterſon, is not only honourably remembered but thankfully acknowledged. The merits of captain Elphinſton of the navy, who conducted all the naval operations relating to the army in its progreſs from North Ediſto to Charleſtown, and in the paſſage of Aſhley River, and alſo of all the other officers and ſeamen ſerving on ſhore during the ſiege, are warmly recommended to the notice of the king, together with the ſervices of the officers and ſoldiers of the royal artillery, the corps of engineers, and in ſhort of every other corps, whether Britiſh or Heſſian, but more particularly of the yager detachment. The names of lieutenant-colonels Webſter and Tarleton, but above all of the chief engineer major Moncrieff, fill up the liſt of brave and meritorious officers that are particularly mentioned. The ſervices of the two firſt of theſe have been already noticed in the progreſs of the ſiege: By the bravery of the one, and the good conduct of the other, the country to the eaſtward of Cooper River was opened to the Britiſh troops, the American cavalry routed and diſperſed, and the communication between the town and the country cut off: And with reſpect to the laſt of theſe officers, no language can expreſs more forcibly than that of the commander in chief, the ſenſe which he entertained of his very extraordinary merit. Theſe are his words: "But to major Moncrieff, the commanding engi-
"neer, who planned, and, with the aſſiſtance of ſuch capable offi-
"cers under him, conducted the ſiege with ſo much judgment,
"intrepidity, and laborious attention, I wiſh to render a tribute of

CHAP. XXXIII. 1780.

"the very highest applause and most permanent gratitude; persuaded that far more flattering commendations than I can bestow "will not fail to crown such rare merit."

Of this officer it may be remarked, that he was not more happy in the possession of superior talents than fortunate in occasions to display them. The successive sieges of Savannah and Charlestown furnished him with opportunities of exemplifying his skill in the two principal branches of his profession, the art of defence, and that of attack: In both, his masterly designs were crowned with success; nor is it easy to determine in which of them his great attainments in his profession shone with brightest lustre.

Incursion of the Spaniards into West Florida.

Whilst the British arms were thus employed in South Carolina, the Spaniards made a fresh incursion into West Florida, and succeeded in reducing the town and fort of Mobille, with the adjoining country. In the month of January Don Bernardo de Galves sailed from New Orleans, with a fleet consisting of sixteen armed vessels, and a number of transports, having on board one thousand five hundred regular troops, and five hundred people of colour. On his passage he was overtaken by a storm, in which several of his vessels were lost, with a number of his troops, and great part of his provisions, artillery, and ammunition. With the rest he arrived off the entrance into Mobille Bay, and landed upon the point of land forming the eastern extremity of that inlet, where he remained until he obtained a reinforcement of men, and a fresh supply of provisions, artillery, and ammunition. When these arrived, Don Bernardo de Galves again embarked his troops, and, sailing up the Bay, landed at Dog River, about four miles from Mobille, on the twenty-fifth of February. From thence he advanced against the fort, and proceeded to make regular approaches, a waste of labour and time that seemed unnecessary against a place so totally unprovided for defence.

fence. The fort had been originally built only as a protection againſt the Indians; and, after it came into the poſſeſſion of Great Britain, had been ſuffered to go to decay, until the beginning of the preſent year, when captain Durnford, the chief engineer at Penſacola, was ſent to put it in a ſtate of defence. But this, it ſeems, was impoſſible, without an immenſe expence of money, and a greater length of time than intervened between his taking the command, and the arrival of the Spaniards. It was garriſoned by a company of the ſixtieth regiment, amounting to eighty-two men, including officers; and to theſe were added, upon the approach of the Spaniards, thirty-ſix ſailors, forty-five militia, and ſixty people of colour. On the fourteenth of March the Spaniards opened a battery upon the fort, of eleven pieces of heavy cannon, which, in twelve hours, damaged its defences ſo entirely, and rendered it ſo untenable, that the commanding officer thought fit to capitulate. Honourable terms were obtained; and, although it was ſcarcely poſſible for the garriſon to hold out longer, their ſurrender at this critical moment was, afterwards, a cauſe of regret, when they were informed that general Campbell, with ſeven hundred men, was then on his march from Penſacola to their relief, and at no great diſtance when the capitulation was ſigned.

Conſequences of the fall of Charleſtown.

By the fall of Charleſtown, the capture of the deputy governor, and the greateſt part of the council, and the defeat and diſperſion of the only regular force which general Lincoln had left without the lines, the war in South Carolina ſeemed entirely ſubdued: And three expeditions, ſet on foot by the commander in chief, immediately after theſe events, appeared well calculated to deepen the impreſſion that had been made, and to extinguiſh every idea of further reſiſtance amongſt the people of the interior country, if any ſuch idea could at that time be ſuppoſed to exiſt. The firſt of theſe ex-

Three new expeditions ſet on foot by the Britiſh commander.

peditions, under lord Cornwallis, was intended to overpower, or drive out of the province, a body of continental troops under a colonel Burford, who, arriving too late in the fiege to be able to throw fuccours into Charleftown, had taken poft on the northern banks of the Santee; and, being joined by thofe of the American cavalry who had furvived their laft defeat by Tarleton, made a fhew of oppofition to the Britifh intereft, and endeavoured to keep alive the expiring hopes of the Americans. The fecond of thefe expeditions was to proceed up the fouth-weft fide of the Santee to the diftrict of Ninety-fix, in order to confirm and encourage the loyal, and reduce the difaffected: And the third, with a fimilar intention, to move up the banks of Savannah to Augufta.

In the mean time the commander in chief, who had received information that a French armament, with tranfports and troops, might be expected on the coaft of America, to co-operate with general Wafhington, was bufily employed in preparing for his return to New York, and in eftablifhing fuch regulations for furthering and fecuring the Britifh intereft in South Carolina, as were neceffary, previous to his departure. A hand-bill was publifhed and circulated amongft the inhabitants, by which they were reminded, that as the commander in chief, upon his firft arrival in the province, had taken no ftep whatfoever to excite the loyal inhabitants to rife in favour of government, whilft the king's troops employed in the fiege of Charleftown might be unable to affift them in their efforts, nor wifhed to draw the king's friends into danger whilft any doubt could remain of their fuccefs; fo now, that fuccefs was certain, he trufted that one and all would heartily join, and by a general concurrence give effect to fuch neceffary meafures as might from time to time be pointed out. The helping hand of every man, it was faid, was wanted to re-eftablifh peace and good government. Thofe

His addrefs to the inhabitants of South Carolina.

who

who had families might form a militia to remain at home and preserve peace and good order in their own diſtricts; whilſt thoſe who were young, and had no families, it was expected would be ready to aſſiſt the king's troops in driving their oppreſſors, and all perſons whatſoever acting under the authority of congreſs, far from the province; and, for this purpoſe, that they ſhould prepare themſelves to ſerve with the king's troops for any ſix out of the next twelve months, under officers of their own choice, and with this expreſs ſtipulation, that they ſhould be allowed, when on ſervice, the ſame pay, ammunition, and proviſions, as the king's troops, and ſhould not be obliged to march beyond North Carolina on the one ſide, or Georgia on the other. Having ſerved for that period, it was ſaid, that they would have paid their debt to their country, would be freed from all further claim of military ſervice, except the uſual militia duty at home, and would be entitled to enjoy undiſturbed that peace, liberty, and ſecurity of property, which they had contributed to eſtabliſh. A proclamation was alſo iſſued by the commander in chief, on the twenty-ſecond of May, by which effectual countenanee, protection, and ſupport, were promiſed to the king's faithful and peaceable ſubjects, and the moſt exemplary ſeverity, with confiſcation of property, denounced againſt thoſe who ſhould hereafter appear in arms within the province againſt his majeſty's government, or who ſhould attempt to compel any others to do ſo, or who ſhould hinder or intimidate any of the king's faithful and loving ſubjects from joining his forces, or performing thoſe duties which their allegiance required. And on the firſt of June another proclamation was iſſued, in the name of ſir Henry Clinton and admiral Arbuthnot, as commiſſioners for reſtoring peace to the colonies, by which a full and free pardon was promiſed to all thoſe who, having been miſled from their duty, ſhould

May.

CHAP. XXXIII. 1780. ſhould immediately return to their allegiance, and a due obedience to the laws, excepting only ſuch as were polluted with the blood of their fellow-citizens, ſhed under the mock forms of juſtice for their loyalty to their ſovereign, and adherence to the Britiſh government: By the ſame proclamation, the promiſe of effectual countenance, protection, and ſupport, was renewed to the loyal and well-affected; and, as ſoon as the ſituation of the province would admit of it, a reinſtatement of the inhabitants in the poſſeſſion of all thoſe rights and immunities which they formerly enjoyed under the Britiſh government; and alſo an exemption from taxation, except by their own legiſlature. Its effect. Theſe meaſures ſeemed well calculated to encourage the loyal, and intimidate the diſaffected; and appear to have produced a conſiderable effect. Moſt of the people round Charleſtown came in, and offered to ſtand forth in defence of the Britiſh government; and not a few actually took up arms, and placed themſelves under the direction of major Ferguſon, who was appointed to command them. General Williamſon, and the militia of the diſtrict of Ninety-ſix, ſubmitted to the officer who commanded the expedition into that part of the country; and the inhabitants in the ſouthern parts of the province made the like ſubmiſſion to the Britiſh officer commanding at Beaufort. Nearly about the ſame time alſo, the commander in chief received the pleaſing intelligence that the continental troops and militia under colonel Burford had been completely routed and diſperſed by lieutenant-colonel Tarleton, who was ſent by lord Cornwallis in purſuit of them. Immediately after the ſurrender of Charleſtown, colonel Burford, whoſe force conſiſted of three hundred and eighty continental infantry, a detachment of Waſhington's cavalry, and two ſix pounders, quitted his poſt on the banks of the Santee, and began a retreat up the north-eaſt ſide of that river, with a view of retiring into the back country of North Carolina to join a reinforcement which he expected to meet him by that route. Earl Cornwallis did not begin his march in pursuit of him until the eighteenth of May, and then moved on towards Camden. After crossing the Santee, and marching some days on the road by which Burford had retreated, finding him too far advanced to be overtaken by the main body of his detachment, lord Cornwallis dispatched lieutenant-colonel Tarleton, with forty men of the seventeenth regiment of dragoons, one hundred and thirty of the cavalry of the legion, and one hundred mounted infantry of the same corps, to endeavour by forced marches to come up with him. By this officer, after a march of one hundred and five miles in fifty-four hours, Burford was overtaken at Waxhaws, on the borders of North Carolina, on the twenty-ninth of May, and defeated, with the loss of almost all his detachment, and the whole of his artillery, ammunition, and baggage. The execution done in this action was severe: One hundred and thirteen were killed on the spot, and two hundred and three made prisoners, of whom one hundred and fifty were badly wounded. Burford made his escape by a precipitate flight on horseback. The king's troops were entitled to great commendation for their activity and ardour on this occasion, but the virtue of humanity was totally forgot. The loss of the British troops was trifling; two officers and three privates being killed, and one officer and fourteen privates wounded *.

Defeat of the American colonel Burford.

The

* Upon the march to Camden the British troops were supported from the country through which they passed. A number of negroes, mounted on horses, were employed under proper conductors in driving in cattle for the support of the army, and, though they were in general very small, the army was plentifully supplied. The cattle were delivered alive to the regiments, who found their own butchers. On the 1st of June the royal army took possession of Camden, in a day or two after which colonel Tarleton joined the army at Camden, distant nearly one hundred miles from Charlestown. Upon the approach of the army to Camden the author, who had the honour of being commissary to the troops under lord Cornwallis, was by his lordship ordered to move on in front, to post centinels, and take charge of such stores as might be found in the town. In consequence of that order, a mill belonging to a colonel

 Kershaw

CHAP. XXXIII. 1780.

The last remains of the continental force in South Carolina being extirpated by the defeat of Burford at Waxhaws, and the inhabitants in most parts of the province having either submitted to the British government, or taken paroles from the officers commanding the detachments sent amongst them, the commander in chief, considering the province as completely reduced, thought fit, previous to his departure for New York, to alter the condition of those who had submitted upon parole; and, instead of considering them any longer as prisoners, to require of them the duties, and entitle them to the rights, of active citizens and loyal subjects. For this purpose a proclamation was issued, bearing date the third of June, declaring that all the inhabitants of the province who were prisoners on parole, except those who were in the military line, and those who were in Fort Moultrie, or in Charlestown, at the time of the surrender of those places, or who were then in actual confinement, should, from and after the twentieth of that month, be freed and exempted from all such paroles, and be restored to all the rights and duties of citizens and inhabitants: But, by the same proclamation, it was also declared that all persons under the above description, who should afterwards neglect

Kershaw was taken possession of; in it was found a quantity of wheat and flour. In a store belonging to Joseph and Eli Kerskaw was found a quantity of merchandize; 21 rice tierces, 3 hogsheads and a half of indigo, some tea, sugar, coffee, and linen, which were sent to the general hospital. A quantity of salt, 20 barrels of flour, 18 ditto Indian corn meal, one hogshead of rum, a quantity of bacon and hams, butter, brimstone, axes and wedges, sent to the engineer department. Rhubarb in root, damaged, sent to the general hospital. A number of hats, and some green cloth, distributed to the troops. In a barn near the river ninety hogsheads of tobacco, part of which was destroyed by the troops, the rest was ordered by lord Cornwallis to be sent to Charlestown. We shall have occasion hereafter to shew how the indigo and tobacco were disposed of. Near 100 head of cattle were found in and near the town, together with some sheep. Lord Cornwallis ordered the commissaries to give no receipt to colonel Kershaw for the property taken from him, as he was deemed a very violent man, and who was said to have persecuted the loyalists. We will hereafter assign our reasons for being so particular. A return was made every night to lord Cornwallis of all species of property taken in the course of the day, of its distribution, and of the amount in hand.

to

CHAP. XXXIII. 1780.

to return to their allegiance, and a due ſubmiſſion to his majeſty's government, ſhould be conſidered as enemies and rebels to the ſame, and be treated accordingly. Theſe general regulations having been eſtabliſhed, the commander in chief, on the fifth of June, embarked for New York, carrying with him all the troops that could be ſpared, leaving lieutenant-general earl Cornwallis in the command of thoſe that remained, with the charge of proſecuting the war in North Carolina as ſoon as the ſeaſon of the year, and other circumſtances, would permit.

June.

Diſpoſition of the troops in South Carolina.

The force left under lord Cornwallis amounted to about four thouſand men; and as the expedition into North Carolina was neceſſarily delayed, from the heat of the ſeaſon, the impoſſibility of ſubſiſting an army in that province until the harveſt was over, and the neceſſity of forming magazines, with a chain of communications properly ſecured before the expedition was begun, the troops were in the mean time ſo diſpoſed in cantonments as to cover the frontiers both of South Carolina and Georgia, and ſecure their internal quiet. The principal force upon the frontiers was at Camden, under the command of lord Rawdon: It conſiſted of the twenty-third and thirty-third regiments, the volunteers of Ireland, the legion cavalry, Brown's and Hamilton's corps of provincials, and a detachment of artillery. Major M'Arthur, with the two battalions of the ſeventy-firſt, was advanced to Cheraw Hill, upon the river Pedee, to cover the country between Camden and Georgetown, and to correſpond with the highland ſettlement on Croſs Creek, in North Carolina: And Georgetown was garriſoned by a detachment of provincials under captain Saunders of the queen's rangers. Camden was connected with the diſtrict of Ninety-ſix by a ſtrong poſt at Rocky Mount, upon the Wateree, garriſoned by the New York volunteers, and ſome militia, under lieutenant-colonel

CHAP. XXXIII. 1780.

Turnbull. At Ninety-ſix were ſtationed three battalions of provincials, and ſome companies of light-infantry; at firſt commanded by lieutenant-colonel Balfour, and afterwards by lieutenant-colonel Cruger. Major Ferguſon's corps of provincials, and a body of loyal militia, were not ſtationary, but traverſed the country between the Wateree and the Saluda, and ſometimes approached the confines of North Carolina. At Auguſta lieutenant-colonel Brown commanded with his own, and detachments from ſome other regiments. The reſt of the troops were ſtationed at Charleſtown, Beaufort, and Savannah: Brigadier-general Patterſon commanding at the firſt of theſe places, and lieutenant-colonel Alured Clarke at the laſt. And at Camden was to be formed the principal magazine for the intended expedition.

Adminiſtration of earl Cornwallis, commander in chief in South Carolina.

Upon earl Cornwallis, as commander in chief in South Carolina, devolved alſo the care of adjuſting the internal affairs, and eſtabliſhing ſuch regulations, whether civil or commercial, as might be neceſſary for its future proſperity; and, to enter upon this arduous taſk, he repaired to Charleſtown, as ſoon as he had fixed the poſts, and cantoned the troops in the manner already mentioned. A correſpondence had been kept up with the loyaliſts in North Carolina: And, as the expedition into that province was neceſſarily delayed, his lordſhip ſent emiſſaries amongſt them to requeſt the well-affected to attend to their harveſt, collect proviſions, and remain quiet till the king's troops were ready to enter the province, which would not be till the end of Auguſt, or beginning of September. But, unfortunately, this prudent and neceſſary admonition was not attended to. A number of loyaliſts in Tryon County having prematurely aſſembled in arms under a colonel More, towards the end of June, were quickly routed and diſperſed by a provincial force under general Rutherford. This unſucceſsful inſurrection furniſhed a pretence for perſe-

perſecuting the loyaliſts in other parts of the province; their gaols were filled with loyaliſts, and every day added a victim to their gibbets: Such were the ſufferings of the loyaliſts; and ſo haraſſed and oppreſſed were they, that about eight hundred of them, who had intended to wait the approach of the king's troops, at length loſt all patience, and, aſſembling under a colonel Bryan, quitted their habitations and marched towards South Carolina, where they were fortunate enough to arrive unmoleſted, and joined major M'Arthur's detachment at Cheraw Hill. Never was a finer body of men collected; ſtrong, healthy, and accuſtomed to the ſeverity of the climate; had they been properly diſciplined, they might have rendered the moſt important ſervices. Upon their marching into Camden they preſented to our view the horrors of a civil war. Many of them had not ſeen their families for months, having lived in the woods to avoid the perſecution of the Americans. Numbers of them were in rags, moſt of them men of property. There were men in Bryan's corps who poſſeſſed ſome hundred acres of land, farms highly cultivated, and well ſtocked: Theſe, with families and friends, they abandoned, to manifeſt their attachment to the Britiſh government.

In the mean time lord Cornwallis was buſily employed at Charleſtown in forming regulations for the internal government of South Carolina, and in forwarding to Camden the ſupplies wanted for the army upon the intended expedition. A board of police was eſtabliſhed for the adminiſtration of juſtice, until the ſituation of the province ſhould admit of the regular reſtoration of its former civil government. Commercial regulations were made for permitting to a certain extent the exportation of the produce of the country; and great pains were taken to inroll the militia, and prepare for aſſiſting in the defence of the province. In moſt caſes paroles were exchanged for protections, accompanied with a renewal of alle-

CHAP. XXXIII. 1780. Counter-revolution among those who had submitted to the power of Britain on the fall of Charlestown.

allegiance; and for ſome weeks an univerſal calm ſucceeded the agitations with which the province was lately diſtracted *.

But it was not long before the ſeeds of diſcontent appeared, which, when fully matured, produced a counter-revolution in the minds and inclinations of the people as complete and as univerſal as that which ſucceeded the fall of Charleſtown. Of thoſe originally attached to the American cauſe, who, ſince the capture of Charleſtown, had ſubmitted to the Britiſh government, either by taking the oath of allegiance, or obtaining a parole, ſome were influenced by the ruinous appearance of American affairs, the deſpair of ultimate ſucceſs, and a wiſh to ſave the remains of their property that had eſcaped the ravages and devaſtations of war; others were influenced by the fear of puniſhment, if they perſiſted longer in maintaining an oppoſition apparently fruitleſs; and not a few by the hope of being ſuffered to live quietly upon their eſtates, as priſoners upon parole, and enjoying a kind of neutrality during the remainder of the war. The determination of congreſs to ſend a part of general Waſhington's army to the aſſiſtance of their adherents in South Carolina, and the vigorous exertions of the colonies of Virginia and North Carolina to get a body of men in the field for the ſame purpoſe, quickly diſpelled the apprehenſions of the two firſt of theſe claſſes, and rouſed afreſh their hopes: And the laſt of theſe claſſes of men was very early diſguſted by the proclamation of ſir Henry Clinton, which, without their conſent, abrogated the paroles that

* From the time that the Britiſh army entered Camden, until this period, it was wholly ſupported by ſupplies from the neighbouring diſtricts. The militia were employed in collecting Indian corn to be ground into meal, which, iſſued when new, made a good ſubſtitute for wheat. They were alſo employed in collecting cattle and ſheep; they were allowed four ſhillings and eight-pence per head for cattle, and two ſhillings and eleven-pence ſterling per head for ſheep (for driving only). The owners had either a receipt, or a certificate, given them (unleſs avowedly hoſtile).

had

had been granted, and, in one inſtant, converted them either into loyal ſubjects or rebels. If it was proper policy at firſt to hold a middle courſe between theſe oppoſite extremes, the ſame policy required that it ſhould have been continued ſome time longer; and that the condition of the inhabitants ſhould have been altered, rather at their own application, either individually or collectively, than by the arbitrary fiat of the commander in chief. In this manner a proper diſcrimination might have been made between the inhabitants who were really loyal, and thoſe who were nominally ſo: But, by purſuing the oppoſite courſe, they were all blended indiſcriminately together. Even the violent revolutioniſt, unleſs he choſe to leave the country, was obliged to aſſume the appearance of loyalty: And thus the foundation of mutual jealouſy and diſtruſt was laid amongſt the inhabitants themſelves. The revolutioniſts complained that their condition was altered without their concurrence; and the loyaliſts murmured becauſe notorious rebels, by taking the oath of allegiance, and putting on a ſhew of attachment, became entitled to the ſame privileges with themſelves.

The detachment from general Waſhington's army ſent to North Carolina.

Whilſt theſe diſcontents began to prevail, intelligence arrived that major-general baron de Kalbe, with a detachment conſiſting of two thouſand men, from Waſhington's army, had advanced as far as Hillſborough, in North Carolina, and was preparing to move forward to Saliſbury, where colonel Porterfield, with three hundred Virginians, and Rutherford, with ſome North Carolina militia, had taken poſt: That Caſwell, with one thouſand five hundred militia of the ſame province, had marched from Croſs Creek to Deep River, in order to join the baron de Kalbe on the road to Saliſbury; that two thouſand five hundred Virginia militia were upon their march to the ſouthward; and that the aſſembly of Virginia had voted five thouſand men to be immediately draughted from the militia, who

were

CHAP. XXXIII. 1780.

were to ſerve as corps of obſervation. This intelligence increaſed the ill-humour of thoſe inhabitants of South Carolina who were diſaffected to the Britiſh government, and cheriſhed the ſpirit of revolt, which began to diſcover itſelf; when not long afterwards information was received that congreſs had determined to make a bold effort for the recovery of South Carolina and Georgia, and that major-general Gates, whoſe fame had been already eſtabliſhed at Saratoga, was appointed to the command of the ſouthern army. Beſides thoſe corps of the enemy already mentioned, a colonel Sumpter, who had fled out of the province after the conqueſt of Charleſtown, had influence enough to attach to himſelf a number of the people in that part of North Carolina where he had taken refuge, and with theſe, joined to ſome refugees from his own province, forming a kind of flying camp, he had advanced as far as the Catawba ſettlement. In conſequence of ſuch threatening movements on the part of the enemy, lord Rawdon found it neceſſary to make an alteration in the diſpoſition of his poſts, with a view of making them more compact; and major M'Arthur, whoſe poſt at Cheraw Hill was moſt expoſed, received orders to fall back.

Movements of the American colonel Sumpter.

About this time, that ſpirit of revolt, which had been hitherto reſtrained by the diſtance of the continental force now advancing to the ſouthward, burſt forth into action: And it made its appearance in two different quarters of the province nearly about the ſame inſtant of time. Ever ſince the fall of Charleſtown the command of the militia, in the diſtrict bordering on the rivers Tyger and Enoree, had been given to a colonel Floyd, their former commander, colonel Neale, a violent perſecutor of the loyaliſts, having fled out of the province. One Liſle, who had belonged to this corps whilſt it was under the command of Neale, and who had been baniſhed to the iſlands upon the ſea-coaſt as a priſoner upon parole, availing himſelf of the commander in chief's proclamation of the third of June, took the oath of allegiance, and exchanged his parole for a certificate of his being a good ſubject. Returning to his former abode, he obtained a command under colonel Floyd, and as ſoon as the battalion of militia was ſupplied with arms and ammunition, had the traiterous addreſs to carry it off to colonel Neale, his former commander, who had joined Sumpter in the Catawba ſettlement. This inſtance of treachery happened in the north-weſt quarter of the province; and nearly about the ſame time a ſimilar inſtance occurred in the north-eaſt part of it. When it became neceſſary for major M'Arthur to retire from Cheraw Hill, he embarked in boats the ſick of his detachment, amounting to near an hundred, and ordered them to fall down the Pedee, to the Britiſh poſt at Georgetown, under an eſcort of militia commanded by colonel Mills; but as ſoon as the boats had proceeded ſo far as to be out of the reach of aſſiſtance from major M'Arthur, the militia roſe upon their commanding officer, and carried the ſick into North Carolina as priſoners. Colonel Mills with ſome difficulty made his eſcape.

His attempt on the Britiſh poſt at Rocky Mount.

Sumpter being joined by the battalion of militia under Liſle, completely armed and furniſhed with ammunition, his active genius led him to undertake without delay ſome enterpriſe againſt the Britiſh out-poſts. Towards the end of July he marched from the Catawba ſettlement with nine hundred men; and on the thirtieth of that month made an attack on the Britiſh poſt at Rocky Mount, where lieutenant-colonel Turnbull commanded, with one hundred and fifty of the corps of New York volunteers, and ſome militia. Rocky Mount was ably defended by Turnbull, with his little garriſon; and Sumpter, after being repulſed in three different attacks, with a conſiderable loſs of men, was obliged to deſiſt. He re-

CHAP. XXXIII. 1780. treated again towards the Catawba ſettlement, without being diſcouraged by the want of ſucceſs; and, as ſoon as he had recruited a ſufficient number to make up for the loſs of men ſuſtained at Rocky Mount, he returned towards the Britiſh cantonments, and made an attack upon the poſt at Hanging Rock. This poſt was occupied by the infantry of the legion, part of Brown's corps of provincials, and colonel Bryan's North Carolina refugees; the whole being under the command of major Carden of the prince of Wales's American regiment. Sumpter directed his attack againſt that quarter of the poſt which was occupied by colonel Bryan and his refugees, and was fortunate enough to ſurpriſe them: This corps was but ill ſupplied with ammunition, and had no bayonets. It is difficult even for the beſt diſciplined men to withſtand the effects of a ſurpriſe; but, for undiſciplined men it is impoſſible. The refugees fled with the utmoſt precipitation, and ſpread confuſion through every quarter of the poſt. Sumpter, profiting by the confuſion, advanced with rapidity, and for a time ſeemed to carry every thing before him. At length the legion infantry, and the detachment from Brown's corps, by making three deſperate charges with the bayonet, checked his progreſs. Still, however, he perſevered, and the fate of the attack remained doubtful, when the appearance of a reinforcement changed entirely the fortune of the day. This reinforcement conſiſted only of forty mounted infantry of the legion who were returning from Rocky Mount: But the captains Stewart and Macdonald, who commanded it, by ordering the men to extend their files, gave it the appearance of a formidable detachment. The bugle horns were directed to ſound a charge: And the Americans, already kept at bay, were now fearful of being overpowered, and haſtily retreated, leaving behind them about one hundred of their killed and wounded.

CHAP. XXXIII. 1780.

The loſs of the Britiſh troops in repelling this attack, does not appear to have been exactly aſcertained, but it is admitted to have been conſiderable; and it fell principally upon the legion, and the detachment from Brown's regiment, the refugees having fled ſo early that few of them were either killed or wounded. Major Carden expoſed himſelf to cenſure and diſgrace, by reſigning the command to captain Rouſslet of the legion in the heat of action.

CHAP. XXXIV.

Earl Cornwallis ſets out from Charleſtown to Camden—Action between the Americans under General Gates, and the Britiſh under Earl Cornwallis, near Camden—The American Force under Colonel Sumpter ſurpriſed by Colonel Tarleton—Perfidy of the Americans—Reſtrained by Examples of Severity—Lord Cornwallis marches into North Carolina—Defeat and Fall of Major Ferguſon.

CHAP. XXXIV. 1780.

IN the mean time the different corps of continental troops and militia, commanded by the baron de Kalbe, Caſwell, Rutherford, and Porterfield, having formed a junction, entered the province of South Carolina. General Gates joined them on the twenty-ſeventh of July; and the whole, under his command, advanced by the main road towards Camden. In order to ſtop their progreſs, lord Rawdon moved forward, with the force under his command at Camden, and took a ſtrong poſition about fourteen miles in front of it, upon the weſt branch of Lynche's Creek. General Gates advanced on the oppoſite ſide; and the two armies continued for ſeveral days oppoſed to each other, with the creek only intervening between their advanced parties. Whilſt the oppoſite armies lay in this ſituation, orders were ſent to lieutenant-colonel Cruger to forward with all haſte to Camden the four companies of light-infantry ſtationed at Ninety-ſix; and intelligence being received of a movement made by the Americans towards their right, orders were ſent to the Britiſh officer commanding at Rugeley's Mills, to evacuate his

his poſt, which was expoſed on account of its advanced ſituation, and, after ſending part of his detachment to join the army, to retire with the reſt to Camden. By the evacuation of the poſt at Rugeley's Mills the road leading from Waxhaws to Camden was left unguarded; and lord Rawdon, fearing that general Gates might attempt to paſs him by this road, and get into his rear, found it neceſſary to fall back from Lynche's Creek, nearer to Camden, and took a new poſition at Logtown. By this time almoſt all the inhabitants between Black River and Pedee had openly revolted and joined the Americans; and, in other quarters, they ſeemed diſpoſed to follow the example, whenever it could be done with ſecurity. Sumpter, with his force increaſed by a detachment of continental ſoldiers, was ſent acroſs the Wateree to favour the revolt of the inhabitants on the ſouth-weſt ſide of that river, and to intercept the ſupplies and reinforcements on the road to Camden; and general Gates, in order to preſerve a communication with Sumpter, moved to his right up the north ſide of Lynche's Creek, and took poſt at Rugeley's Mills, intending to advance from thence, by the Waxhaw road, to Camden. Information of theſe movements on the part of the enemy being regularly tranſmitted by lord Rawdon to Charleſtown, earl Cornwallis thought it neceſſary to poſtpone the completion of the civil arrangements in which he had for ſome time paſt been engaged, and to proceed to Camden, where the threatening aſpect of affairs required all his immediate attention. He ſet out from Charleſtown in the evening of the tenth, and arrived at Camden in the evening of the thirteenth, of Auguſt. The following day he ſpent in examining the condition of his own force, and in obtaining information of that of the enemy: Nearly eight hundred Britiſh troops were ſick at Camden. The number of thoſe who were really effective, amounted to ſomething more than two thouſand, including officers, of whom about fifteen hundred were regu-

The earl Cornwallis ſets out from Charleſtown to Camden. Auguſt.

lars,

CHAP. XXXIV. 1780.

lars, or belonged to eftabliſhed provincial corps, and the reft, militia and refugees from North Carolina. The force under general Gates was reprefented to amount to fix thoufand men, exclufive of Sumpter's corps, which was eftimated at one thoufand: The American accounts, fince publiſhed, fay that general Gates's army, even including Sumpter's corps, did not much exceed five thoufand men; but we have ground for believing that general Gates's force was little lefs than fix thoufand ftrong. But almoft the whole country feemed upon the eve of a revolt *. The communication between Camden and Charleftown appeared in danger of being cut off by the enterprifing movements of Sumpter, whofe numbers were daily increafing by the junction of difaffected inhabitants. The fafety of the army depended upon preferving a communication with the fea-coaft; and fomething was neceffary to be done immediately for extricating it from its perilous fituation. At this juncture a retreat to Charleftown might have been effected without much difficulty; but the fick muft have been left behind, the magazines of ftores either

* The militia of South Carolina were in general faithlefs, and altogether diffatisfied in the Britiſh fervice. One great caufe of complaint with them was, that their horfes were frequently preffed for the cavalry and quarter-mafter-general's department; and that thofe who could obtain certificates for them at a fair price, were neverthelefs great lofers by difpofing of thofe certificates to men who purchafed them at an enormous difcount, a fpeculation which very much injured the public credit in that colony. It is to be obferved that a diftinction was made between a RECEIPT and a CERTIFICATE. Where the word Receipt was made ufe of, it was intended that the proprietor ſhould be paid upon his prefenting the receipt at Charleftown, and many of thofe receipts were afterwards actually paid by orders on the paymafter-general. Where the word Certificate was made ufe of, it was intended as an evidence in the hands of the holder, of fuch and fuch property being taken, its payment to depend on contingencies. This regulation governed the conduct of the commiffary until lord Cornwallis moved from Wynnefborough in January 1781; then, when receipts were given, they not only fpecified the property, but the value of that property, which gave them a negotiable authority. When certificates were given, the property was fpecified, but no value affixed. Its payment, as before, was to depend on the merit or demerit of the party at the end of the war. Receipts were frequently refufed; but certificates never, unlefs the perfon whofe property had been taken was known to be a decided enemy, and his character marked by acts of inhumanity towards the loyalifts.

aban-

abandoned or deſtroyed, and the loſs of the whole country would have neceſſarily followed, except indeed Charleſtown, in which there was already a ſufficient garriſon for its defence. A defeat could not be much more injurious in its conſequences than ſuch a retreat: And where the motives for action ſo ſtrongly preponderated, there was not much room for deliberation in the breaſt of an officer of ſo much enterpriſe as lord Cornwallis. Confiding in the valour and diſcipline of his troops, however inferior in number, he reſolved to move forward and attack the enemy, whoſe preſent ſituation at Rugeley's Mills inclined him to execute his intention without delay. Meaning to attack them early in the morning of the ſixteenth of Auguſt, and to point his attack principally againſt the continental regiments, whoſe poſition, from the information he had received, he knew to be a bad one, earl Cornwallis began his march towards Rugeley's Mills, at ten in the evening of the fifteenth of Auguſt, committing the defence of Camden to major M'Arthur, with ſome provincials, militia, convaleſcents of the army, and a detachment of the ſixty-third regiment, which was expected to arrive during the night. The army marched in the following order: The front diviſion, commanded by lieutenant-colonel Webſter, conſiſted of four companies of light-infantry, and the twenty-third and thirty-third regiments, preceded by twenty cavalry, and as many mounted infantry of the legion, as an advanced guard. The centre diviſion conſiſted of the volunteers of Ireland, the legion infantry, Hamilton's North Carolina regiment, and colonel Bryan's refugees, under the command of lord Rawdon. And the two battalions of the ſeventy-firſt regiment followed as a reſerve; the dragoons of the legion forming the rear-guard. It is not a little ſingular that the ſame night, nearly about the ſame time, and with a ſimilar intention, general Gates ſhould have left his encampment at Rugeley's Mills, and moved forward towards Camden. Both armies marching on the ſame

CHAP. XXXIV.

1780.

Action between the Americans, under general Gates, and the Britiſh, under the earl Cornwallis, near Camden.

ſame road, in oppoſite directions, their advanced guards met and fired upon each other about two in the morning. Some priſoners were made on both ſides; and from theſe the reſpective commanders became acquainted with the movements of the other: Both armies halted and were formed; and the firing ſoon afterwards ceaſed as if by mutual conſent. The ground on which the two armies had accidentally met was as favourable for lord Cornwallis as he could have wiſhed: A ſwamp on each ſide ſecured his flanks, and narrowed the ground in front, ſo as to render the ſuperiority of the enemy in numbers of leſs conſequence: He therefore waited with impatience for the approach of day; and as ſoon as it appeared made his laſt diſpoſition for the attack. The front line was made up of the two diviſions of the army already mentioned under lord Rawdon and lieutenant-colonel Webſter, Webſter's diviſion being to the right, and lord Rawdon's to the left. Theſe diviſions were diſpoſed in ſuch a manner, that the thirty-third regiment, on the left of Webſter's, communicating with the volunteers of Ireland, on the right of lord Rawdon's, formed the centre of the line; and to the front line were attached two ſix-pounders, and two three-pounders, under the direction of lieutenant Macleod of the royal artillery. The ſeventy-firſt regiment, with two ſix-pounders, formed a ſecond line, or reſerve, one battalion being poſted behind each wing; and in the rear of the whole, the cavalry were ready either to charge or purſue, as circumſtances might require.

The American army was alſo formed in two lines, general Giſt's brigade of continental troops being on the right, the North Carolina militia in the centre, and the Virginia militia, which had joined the army only the day before, with the light-infantry, and Porterfield's corps, being on the left. The firſt Maryland brigade formed a ſecond line or corps de reſerve: And the artillery was divided between the two brigades.

The

The oppofite armies being thus ranged in order of battle, and fome movement being obferved on the left of the provincial line, as if a change of difpofition had been intended, lord Cornwallis deemed this the critical moment for beginning the action, and gave orders to lieutenant-colonel Webfter to advance and charge the enemy. The order was immediately executed with fuch alacrity, and the charge made with fo much promptitude and fuccefs, that the Virginia militia, quickly giving way, threw down their arms and fled, and were foon afterwards followed by the greateft part of the militia of North Carolina. The American referve was now brought into action; and general Gates, in conjunction with general Cafwell, retiring with the militia, endeavoured to rally them at different advantageous paffes in the rear of the field of action, but in vain: They ran at firft like a torrent, and afterwards fpread through the woods in every direction. Lord Rawdon began the action on the left with no lefs vigour and fpirit than Webfter had done on the right; but here, and in the centre, againft part of Webfter's divifion, the conteft was more obftinately maintained by the Americans, whofe artillery did confiderable execution. Their left flank was, however, expofed by the flight of the militia; and the light-infantry and twenty-third regiment, who had been oppofed to the fugitives, inftead of purfuing them, wheeled to the left and came upon the flank of the continentals, who, after a brave refiftance for near three quarters of an hour, were thrown into total confufion, and forced to give way in all quarters. Their rout was completed by the cavalry, who continued the purfuit to Hanging Rock, twenty-two miles from the field of action. Between eight and nine hundred of the enemy were killed in the action, and in the purfuit, and about one thoufand made prifoners, many of whom were wounded. Of this number, were major-general baron de Kalbe, and brigadier-general Rutherford. The former of thefe officers, at the head

CHAP. XXXIV. 1780.

of a continental regiment of infantry, made a vigorous charge on the left wing of the British army, and when wounded and taken prisoner would scarcely believe that the provincial army had been defeated. He died of his wounds a few days after the action, much regretted by the Americans. One hundred and fifty waggons, a considerable quantity of military stores, and all the baggage and camp equipage of the provincial army, a number of colours, and seven pieces of cannon, were taken. General Gates, who retired with the militia to endeavour to rally them, finding all his efforts vain, gave up every thing as lost, and fled first to Charlotte, ninety miles from the place of action; and from thence to Hillsborough, in North Carolina, one hundred and eighty miles from Camden. General Gist alone, of all the American commanders, was able to keep together about one hundred men, who flying across a swamp on their right, through which they could not be pursued by the British dragoons, made good their retreat in a body. The loss of the British troops in this battle amounted to three hundred and twenty-five, of whom sixty-nine were killed, two hundred and forty-five wounded, and eleven missing. The weight of the action fell upon the thirty-third regiment in the left of Webster's division, and the volunteers of Ireland in the right of lord Rawdon's; and of course, by them the greatest loss was sustained, which amounted to two thirds of the whole. The road for some miles was strewed with the wounded and killed, who had been overtaken by the legion in their pursuit. The number of dead horses, broken waggons, and baggage, scattered on the road, formed a perfect scene of horror and confusion: Arms, knapsacks, and accoutrements found were innumerable; such was the terror and dismay of the Americans. The number of killed, wounded, and taken, exceeded the number of British regular troops in the action by at least three hundred. Lord Cornwallis's judgment in planning, his promptitude in executing, and his forti-

tude

tude and coolnefs during the time of action, juftly attracted univerfal applaufe and admiration. The lord Rawdon, who was only twenty-five years of age, bore a very confpicuous part in this day's action. Colonel Webfter's conduct was confiftent with his general character: Cool, determined, vigilant, and active in action, he added to a reputation eftablifhed by long fervice, the univerfal efteem and refpect of the whole army, as an officer of great experience and obfervation as well as bravery and rigid difcipline. In a word, every Britifh officer and foldier evinced in this day's action the moft perfect intrepidity and valour. The American wounded were treated with the utmoft humanity.

General Gates's conduct has been much cenfured. We are told no place was appointed for rendezvous in cafe of a defeat: His baggage fhould have been much farther in the rear: By delay Gates muft have added to his ftrength every hour, but he was confident of fuccefs.

General Gates's army being thus completely ruined and difperfed, the only provincial force in South Carolina which remained entire was that under Sumpter on the other fide of the Wateree. Had he been permitted to retire into North Carolina unmolefted, his force, fmall as it was, would have been fufficient to occupy a convenient ftation for collecting the fcattered remains of the American army: It was therefore of importance to ftrike at his corps, and endeavour to cut it off. An object of fo much confequence did not efcape the attention of the commander in chief; and in the evening of the day of the engagement orders were fent to lieutenant-colonel Turnbull, who, with the New York volunteers, upon evacuating the poft at Rocky Mount, had joined major Ferguson's corps on Little River, to endeavour to intercept Sumpter in his retreat. The light-infantry and the legion, who were deftined to proceed on the fame fervice, being exhaufted with the fatigues of the day, were fuffered to repofe themfelves during the night, but received orders to

CHAP. XXXIV. 1780.

The American force under colonel Sumpter surprised by colonel Tarleton.

be in readiness to march early the next morning, under the command of lieutenant-colonel Tarleton. On the following morning this active and enterprising officer, in pursuance of his orders, set out with his detachment, amounting to three hundred and fifty men, and receiving intelligence, during his march, of the retreat of Sumpter along the western banks of the Wateree, pursued so closely, that, after passing the river at Rocky Mount Ford, he overtook him at two in the afternoon of the eighteenth of August, near the Catawba Ford, when he was within a few hours march of reaching a friendly settlement. Sumpter, upon hearing of general Gates's defeat at Camden, immediately began his retreat, and moved with so much dispatch, that, thinking himself already out of all danger, he had encamped at this early hour to give his men some repose during the heat of the day. The surprise was so complete, that the British soldiers, both cavalry and infantry, entered the American camp, and cut off the provincials from their arms and artillery before they had time to assemble. Some opposition was however made from behind the waggons in front of the militia, but the universal consternation which prevailed rendered it ineffectual. One hundred and fifty of the provincials were either killed or wounded, and upwards of three hundred made prisoners. Sumpter's force consisted of one hundred continental soldiers, seven hundred militia, and two pieces of cannon: And he had in his train about two hundred and fifty prisoners, part of them British soldiers, and the rest loyal militia, and a number of waggons laden with rum and other stores for the British, which he had taken in the neighbourhood of Camden, on the opposite side of the river. The prisoners were all released, and the waggons retaken: And the whole of the provincial stores, ammunition, and baggage, with their artillery, and one thousand stand of arms, fell into the hands of the conquerors. Sumpter, by riding off without waiting to put on his coat, which he had laid aside on account of the

the heat of the weather, made his escape; but the rest of his detachment were all either killed, taken, or dispersed. The rapidity of Tarleton's march had been so great, that when he arrived at Fishing Creek, more than one half of his detachment, overpowered with fatigue, could proceed no farther. With only one hundred dragoons, and sixty of the light-infantry, he continued the pursuit; and with this small number the victory was atchieved. The loss of the British detachment was inconsiderable: It amounted to only nine killed, and six wounded; but unfortunately, amongst the former, was captain Charles Campbell, who commanded the light-infantry, a young officer of the most promising abilities, whose death was greatly lamented.

By the victory gained over general Gates at Camden, and the rout and total dispersion of his army, followed so soon after by the defeat and ruin of the corps under Sumpter, the provincial force to the southward seemed for a time entirely annihilated; and nothing prevented earl Cornwallis from proceeding immediately on his long-projected expedition into North Carolina, but the want of some supplies for the army, which were on their way from Charlestown. In the mean time emissaries were again sent into North Carolina, with instructions to the friends of government to take arms, and seize the most violent of their persecutors, with all the magazines and stores for the use of the American government, under an assurance that the British army would march without loss of time to their support.

The delay occasioned by waiting for the stores, gave time to the commander in chief again to employ his thoughts upon the internal affairs of the province, and to form some new regulations which recent events and circumstances had rendered more immediately necessary. It was now apparent, by the revolts that had taken place upon the approach of general Gates, and by the number of militia

Perfidy of the Americans

CHAP. XXXIV. 1780.

militia who had joined him after exchanging their paroles for protections, and ſwearing allegiance to the Britiſh government, that thoſe perſons were not to be depended upon, that the lenity which had been ſhewn to them had been abuſed, and that it was become neceſſary to reſtrain their perfidy by examples of ſeverity, and the terrors of puniſhment. With this view, the eſtates of all thoſe who had left the province to join the enemies of Great Britain, or who were employed in the ſervice, or held commiſſions under the authority of congreſs, and alſo of all thoſe who continued to oppoſe the re-eſtabliſhment of his majeſty's government within the province, were ordered to be ſequeſtered: A commiſſioner was appointed to ſeize upon them; and after a ſufficient allowance was made for the ſupport of the wives and families of ſuch delinquents, the reſidue of the annual produce of their eſtates was to be accounted for to the paymaſter-general of the forces, and to be applied to the public ſervice. Inſtant death was again denounced againſt thoſe who, having taken protections from the Britiſh government, ſhould afterwards join the enemy; and, to impreſs them with an idea that this puniſhment would be hereafter rigorouſly inflicted, ſome few of the moſt hardened of the militia, who had been taken in general Gates's army with arms in their hands, and protections in their pockets, were actually executed. But perfidy, it ſeems, was not confined to the lower ranks of men: By letters found upon ſome of the officers of general Gates's army, it was diſcovered that even perſons of ſuperior rank, priſoners upon parole in Charleſtown, had held an improper correſpondence with their friends in the country. In conſequence of this diſcovery, thoſe perſons, and ſome others, againſt whom there were ſtrong circumſtances of ſuſpicion, were at firſt put on board the priſon-ſhips, and afterwards ſent to St. Auguſtine, in Eaſt Florida, where paroles were again allowed to them, but under ſuch reſtrictions as their recent conduct rendered neceſſary.

Reſtrained by examples of ſeverity.

CHAP. XXXIV. 1780. Lord Cornwallis marches into North Carolina.

As ſoon as the neceſſary ſupplies arrived, lord Cornwallis on the eighth of September began his march from Camden, proceeding through the hoſtile ſettlement of Waxhaws to Charlotte-town, in the back parts of North Carolina. This march was no doubt projected with a view of bearing down all oppoſition: His lordſhip was to paſs through the moſt hoſtile parts of either province with the main army, whilſt major Ferguſon, with his corps of loyal militia, was to advance ſtill nearer to the frontiers; and lieutenant-colonel Tarleton, with the cavalry, and the light and legion infantry, to purſue an intermediate courſe, and move up the weſtern banks of the Wateree. On the right of his lordſhip's march, but at a conſiderable diſtance, was the friendly ſettlement of highlanders, at Croſs Creek, and on his left another friendly ſettlement in Tryon County. If he was able to reduce to obedience the inveterate inhabitants of the tract of country through which the main army marched, a communication might be opened between the friendly ſettlements on the right and left, a powerful aſſiſtance derived from their co-operation, and the ſpeedy reduction of the whole province reaſonably expected. The previous meaſures appeared well adapted to the end: And the reduction of the province of North Carolina was undoubtedly at this time confidently looked for. But to confound human wiſdom, and ſet at nought the arrogance and preſumption of man, unexpected incidents daily ariſe in the affairs of human life, which, conducted by an inviſible hand, derange the beſt-concerted ſchemes, as will be exemplified in the event of the preſent expedition.

The march of the main army was performed without any material occurrence, except that a number of the convaleſcents relapſed into their former ſtate of illneſs, and were left behind at Blair's Mills, under the care of major M'Arthur, who remained there, with the ſeventy-firſt regiment, for their protection, for the ſecurity of the mills, and for preſerving the communication with Camden.

Tarleton,

CHAP. XXXIV. 1780.

Tarleton, with the cavalry and light-infantry, received orders to paſs the Catawba at Blair's Ford: And Charlotte was taken poſſeſſion of after a ſlight reſiſtance from the militia towards the end of September. At this period, major Hanger commanded the legion, colonel Tarleton being ill. In the centre of Charlotte, interſecting the two principal ſtreets, ſtood a large brick building, the upper part being the court-houſe, and the under part the market-houſe. Behind the ſhambles a few Americans on horſeback had placed themſelves. The legion was ordered to drive them off; but, upon receiving a fire from behind the ſtalls, this corps fell back. Lord Cornwallis rode up in perſon, and made uſe of theſe words:—"Legion, remember you have every thing to loſe, but nothing to "gain;" alluding, as was ſuppoſed, to the former reputation of this corps. Webſter's brigade moved on and drove the Americans from behind the court-houſe; the legion then purſued them; but the whole of the Britiſh army was actually kept at bay, for ſome minutes, by a few mounted Americans, not exceeding twenty in number.

The vicinity of Charlotte abounded with mills*; and the army, during its ſtay, was ſufficiently ſupplied with proviſions, notwithſtanding the hoſtile diſpoſition of the inhabitants. So inveterate was their rancour, that the meſſengers, with expreſſes for the commander in chief, were frequently murdered; and the inhabitants, inſtead of remaining quietly at home to receive payment for the produce of their plantations, made it a practice to way-lay the Britiſh foraging parties, fire their rifles from concealed places, and then fly into the woods †. Nevertheleſs Charlotte, from its inter-

* In colonel Polk's mill was found twenty-eight thouſand weight of flour, and a quantity of wheat.

† There were ſeveral large, well-cultivated farms in the neighbourhood of Charlotte: An abundance of cattle; few ſheep; the cattle being moſtly milch-cows, or cows with

4

intermediate position between Camden and Salisbury, was a convenient situation to be occupied whenever the army should advance farther into North Carolina; and here, accordingly, lord Cornwallis intended to establish a post. But whilst he was taking measures for this purpose, the unwelcome news arrived of the defeat of major Ferguson; the fall of that officer, and the destruction, captivity, or dispersion of his whole corps. The total loss of so consider-

CHAP. XXXIV. 1780. Defeat and fall of major Ferguson.

with calf, which at that season of the year was the best beef; for the cattle in North and South Carolina run wild in the woods, and at this season are in general very poor. As an instance, when the army was at Charlotte, we killed upon an average 100 head per day. The amount of rations issued, including the army departments, militia, negroes, &c. was 4100 per day. The leanness of the cattle will account for the number killed each day. This was not confined to Charlotte, for they were poor at this season throughout the Carolinas; very few of the oxen were fit to kill. In one day no less than 37 cows in calf were slaughtered! Necessity only justified this measure. At this period the royal army was supported by lord Rawdon's moving with one half of the army one day, and colonel Webster, with the other half, the next day, as a covering party, to protect the foraging parties and cattle-drivers. This measure was rendered necessary from the hostile disposition of the inhabitants. Wheat and rye were collected in the straw, Indian corn in the husk, and brought in waggons to Charlotte, where (in the court-house) it was threshed out by the militia and negroes, and then sent to the mill. This was attended with much trouble and fatigue to the army; nevertheless meal was not wanting; cattle there were in abundance. When a cow calves in the Carolinas, the owner marks the calf, and turns it into the woods, where it remains for three or four, and even seven, years, without ever being brought out. Individual farmers have marked from twelve to fifteen hundred calves in one year. It would never answer to fodder such a number of cattle. The climate being very much to the southward, admits of their running in the woods all the winter, where a species of coarse wild grass grows most luxuriantly all the year. Pensylvania and Maryland do not raise black cattle sufficient for their own consumption. The drovers from Pensylvania go to the Carolinas, purchase these lean cattle at a very low price, and bring them to Pensylvania, where they are fatted in the rich meadows on the banks of the Schuylkill and Delaware rivers for market. This will explain, in some degree, why the Carolinas suffered so much during the war; for the planters property consisted chiefly in cattle and negroes, there not being white inhabitants sufficient to cultivate the land; the planters asserting, that, without negroes, indigo and rice could not be cultivated, the whites not being able to bear the heat of the climate. The negroes in general followed the British army.

 able

CHAP. XXXIV. 1780.

able a detachment, from the operations of which ſo much was expected, put a ſtop, for the preſent, to the farther progreſs of the commander in chief, and obliged him to fall back into South Carolina, for the protection of its weſtern borders againſt the incurſions of a horde of mountaineers, whoſe appearance was as unexpected as their ſucceſs was fatal to the proſecution of the intended expedition.

CHAP. XXXV.

The Americans under Colonel Clarke make an Attack on Augusta—Retreat of Clarke—The Detachment under Major Ferguson attacked and overpowered by American Mountaineers—Lord Cornwallis falls back to South Carolina—Colonel Tarleton checks the Inroads of the American Partizan Marion—Junction of the American Forces under Sumpter, Clarke, and Brannen—Action at Blackstock's Hill between Sumpter and Tarleton.

CHAP. XXXV. 1780.

IN order to trace the causes of an event so important in its consequences as the defeat of major Ferguson, it will be necessary to go a little farther back. A colonel Clarke, an inhabitant of Georgia, who had fled from that province after its reduction by colonel Campbell in 1779, having attached to himself some followers on the frontiers of North and South Carolina, made his way through these provinces, his numbers increasing as he advanced, until he reached the province of Georgia, where, during the march of lord Cornwallis from Camden to Charlotte, he made an attack upon the British post at Augusta. Here lieutenant-colonel Brown commanded, with a garrison of one hundred and fifty provincials; and as the town did not afford an eligible position for defence, he marched from thence with his garrison, and some friendly Indians whom he had called to his assistance, towards Garden Hill, an eminence on the banks of the Savannah. This hill he found was already occupied by the enemy; but, bringing his cannon to bear upon them, and at the

The Americans under colonel Clarke make an attack on Augusta.

same

CHAP. XXXV. 1780.

ſame time making a charge with his whole force, the enemy were diſlodged, after a deſperate conflict of twenty minutes, at the end of which, lieutenant-colonel Brown gained poſſeſſion of the hill, although with the loſs of his cannon, the troops which he had under him not being ſufficient in number to force the one and ſecure the other. This poſt, ſo gallantly won, he bravely maintained, under many diſadvantages, until lieutenant-colonel Cruger, who had intelligence of Clarke's motions, arrived from Ninety-ſix, and brought a detachment to his aſſiſtance. Clarke, receiving information of Cruger's march, endeavoured by menaces of cruelty to intimidate Brown into a ſurrender of the poſt; but finding his menaces ineffectual, he haſtily decamped, upon the nearer approach of the reinforcement, and retreated with his followers. Theſe had originally amounted to about ſeven hundred men; but in the different conflicts with the garriſon, and in the blockade of Garden Hill, Clarke had loſt about one ſixth part of his number. On the part of the Britiſh troops, captain Johnſon was killed, and lieutenant-colonel Brown wounded: The loſs in other reſpects was inconſiderale, and fell principally upon the Indians. The retreat of Clarke and his followers was ſo precipitate, that, although a purſuit was ordered, very few priſoners were made, but the Britiſh cannon were retaken. Still, however, it was hoped that Clarke's retreat might be cut off, as major Ferguſon, with his corps, traverſed the country between him and North Carolina; and intelligence was accordingly ſent to that officer, acquainting him with the route which he had taken. Major Ferguſon, whoſe zeal in the ſervice of his king and country was equal to his other great qualities as an officer, did not fail to take immediate meaſures for accompliſhing an object ſo deſirable, and advanced nearer to the mountains than the other purpoſes of his expedition probably required: But, unfortunately for his ſucceſs, another enemy appeared at this juncture, whoſe ſuperiority in numbers

Retreat of Clarke.

numbers it was hazardous to encounter, and whofe rapidity of movement rendered a retreat difficult in his prefent advanced fituation. This enemy was compofed of men who had affembled from different views and with different objects, and the union of their force againft Fergufon was in a great meafure accidental. The firft divifion of thefe men confifted of the wild and fierce inhabitants of Kentucky, and other fettlements weftward of the Alleganey Mountains, who, affembiing under the colonels Campbell and Boone, paffed the mountains, with an intention of feizing upon a quantity of prefents which they underftood were but flightly guarded at Augufta, and which were about that time to have been diftributed amongft the Creek and Cherokee Indians. After paffing the mountains they heard of Clarke's repulfe at Augufta, and from his failure conceiving their own force to be infufficient for attempting the poft, they turned their thoughts towards Fergufon, whofe movements on the frontiers, indicating an approach to their country, gave them confiderable alarm. In this new defign they were joined by a colonel Williams, an American partizan of the diftrict of Ninety-fix, with a confiderable number of followers. The other divifion of thefe men, confifting of the inhabitants about Holfton River, Powel's Valley, Berkeley, Botetourt, and Fincaftle, on the frontiers of Virginia, had affembled under the colonels Cleveland, Shelby, Sevier, Brandon, and Lacy, with a view of oppofing the advance of the Britifh army towards their fettlements: But after they had proceeded fome diftance on their march, thinking themfelves unable to attempt any direct oppofition to the army under lord Cornwallis, they too bent their force againft the devoted Fergufon, who they underftood had taken poft with his corps at Gilbert-town, in the vicinity of the mountains: Thither, therefore, they directed their march. Thefe men were all well mounted on horfeback and armed with rifles: Each carried his own provifions in a wallet, fo that

that no incumbrance of waggons, nor delays of public departments, impeded their movements. Ferguſon's vigilance nevertheleſs prevented a ſurpriſe: Whilſt they were yet at ſome diſtance he received intelligence of their approach, by means of his emiſſaries, and immediately began a retreat towards the Britiſh army, ſending forward meſſengers to acquaint lord Cornwallis with his danger; but theſe unfortunately were intercepted. When the different diviſions of mountaineers reached Gilbert-town, which was nearly about the ſame time, they amounted to upwards of three thouſand men. From theſe, fifteen hundred of the beſt were ſelected, who, mounted on fleet horſes, were ſent in purſuit of Ferguſon, and overtook him at King's Mountain on the ninth of October. At this place he had halted, upon the near approach of the enemy, and, after occupying the beſt poſition he could find, determined to wait the attack. King's Mountain, from its height, was undoubtedly an eligible ſituation for receiving an attack; but in another reſpect it was advantageous to the aſſailants: Being covered with wood, it afforded them an opportunity of fighting in their own way, by placing themſelves behind trees. When they approached the mountain they divided into different bodies, and under their reſpective leaders made the attack from different quarters. Colonel Cleveland's detachment firſt engaged, but was quickly obliged to retire from the approaching bayonet. Scarcely had this detachment given way, when another under colonel Shelby, from an unexpected quarter, poured in a well-directed fire; the bayonet, however, was again ſucceſsful, and obliged this detachment alſo to fall back. By this time the party under colonel Campbell had aſcended the mountain, and renewed the attack from a different quarter. Major Ferguſon, whoſe conduct was equal to his courage, quickly preſented a new front, and was again ſucceſsful. But as often as one of the American parties was driven back, another returned to its former ſtation, and, ſheltered behind the

The detachment under major Ferguſon attacked and overpowered by American mountaineers.

the trees, poured in an irregular but destructive fire. In this manner the engagement was maintained for near an hour, the mountaineers flying whenever they were in danger of being charged with the bayonet, and returning as soon as the British detachment had faced about to repel another of their parties. Already an hundred and fifty of major Ferguson's corps were slain, and a greater number wounded: Still, however, the unconquerable spirit of that gallant officer refused to surrender: He persevered, and repulsed a succession of attacks from every quarter, until he received a mortal wound. By the fall of major Ferguson his men were undoubtedly disheartened: Animated by his brave example, they had hitherto persevered under all their disadvantages: In the resources of his fruitful genius they deservedly placed the utmost confidence; and with him perished all their hopes of success. Under such circumstances, the second in command, judging all farther resistance to be vain, offered to surrender, and sued for quarter. The prisoners, including the wounded, amounted to eight hundred and ten: Of these, about one hundre[illegible]y were British regulars. The loss of the Americans, in the number of killed, was trifling, but they had a considerable number wounded: And brilliant as their success was, they shamefully stained the laurels they had won by cruelties exercised upon the prisoners, ten of whom were hanged immediately after the action.

CHAP. XXXV. 1780.

Much had been expected from the exertions of major Ferguson in collecting a force upon the frontiers: And by his unfortunate fall, and the slaughter, captivity, or dispersion of his whole corps, the plan of the expedition into North Carolina was entirely deranged. At Polk's Mill, near Charlotte, a small detachment of the twenty-third regiment was posted, commanded by lieutenant Guyon, a very young man. The Americans made an attack upon the mill, with a very superior force, but were repulsed. Lieutenant Guyon's

CHAP. XXXV. 1780.

conduct was highly applauded. The weſtern frontiers of South Carolina were now expoſed to the incurſions of the mountaineers; and it became neceſſary for lord Cornwallis to fall back for their protection, and to wait for a reinforcement before he could proceed farther upon his expedition. Fortunately the friends of government in North Carolina, rendered cautious by their misfortunes in former inſurrections, had not been ſo ready to take arms as was expected: No general riſing had taken place; ſo that the retreat of the Britiſh army did not much increaſe, although it prolonged their ſufferings.

Lord Cornwallis falls back to South Carolina.

On the fourteenth of October, which was as ſoon after lord Cornwallis received certain intelligence of the loſs of Ferguſon's detachment as the army could be put in motion, he began his march back to South Carolina. Nearly about this time lord Cornwallis fell ſick, and continued ill for ſome time; the command devolved on lord Rawdon. In this retreat the king's troops ſuffered much, encountering the greateſt difficulties; the ſoldiers had no tents; it rained for ſeveral days without intermiſſion; the roads were over their ſhoes in water and mud. At night, when the army took up its ground, it encamped in the woods, in a moſt unhealthy climate; for many days without rum. Sometimes the army had beef, and no bread; at other times bread and no beef. For five days it was ſupported upon Indian corn, which was collected as it ſtood in the field, five ears of which were the allowance for two ſoldiers for twenty-four hours. They were to cook it as they could, which was generally done by parching it before the fire. In riding through the encampment of the militia, the Author diſcovered them grating their corn, which was done by two men of a meſs breaking up their tin canteens, and with a bayonet punching holes through the tin; this made a kind of raſp, on which they grated their corn: The idea was communicated to the adjutant-general, and it was afterwards

2 adopted

adopted throughout the army. The water that the army drank was frequently as thick as puddle. Few armies ever encountered greater difficulties and hardſhips; the ſoldiers bore them with great patience, and without a murmur: Their attachment to their commander ſupported them in the day of adverſity; knowing, as they did, that their officers', and even lords Cornwallis and Rawdon's fare was not better than their own. Yet, with all their reſolution and patience, they could not have proceeded but for the perſonal exertions of the militia, who, with a zeal that did them infinite honour, rendered the moſt important ſervices. The continual rains had ſwelled the rivers and creeks prodigiouſly, and rendered the roads almoſt impaſſable. The waggon and artillery horſes were quite exhauſted with fatigue by the time the army had reached Sugar Creek. This creek was very rapid, it banks nearly perpendicular, and the ſoil, being clay, as ſlippery as ice. The horſes were taken out of ſome of the waggons, and the militia, harneſſed in their ſtead, drew the waggons through the creek. We are ſorry to ſay, that, in return for theſe exertions, the militia were maltreated, by abuſive language, and even beaten by ſome officers in the quarter-maſter-general's department: In conſequence of this ill uſage, ſeveral of them left the army next morning, for ever, chuſing to run the riſque of meeting the reſentment of their enemies rather than ſubmit to the deriſion and abuſe of thoſe to whom they looked up as friends *.

At

* The militia, moſt of them being mounted on horſeback, were not in ſo weak a ſtate as the regulars; but they were not without their ſhare of toil and trouble, added to their exertions already mentioned: For as ſoon as the army had taken up its ground for the night, to endeavour to procure a limited and ſcanty reſt, the duty of the militia began. They were aſſembled by the author, who always attended them in perſon, and went in queſt of proviſions, which were collected daily from the country through which the army marched: Nor were their difficulties on this ſervice trifling; they were obliged to ride through rivers, creeks, woods, and ſwamps, to hunt out the cattle. This ſervice was their conſtant and daily duty; they were frequently oppoſed; ſometimes worſted, and with no inconſiderable loſs. In ſhort, ſo eſſentially

CHAP. XXXV. 1780.

At length the army reached the Catawba, which was forded by the troops. This river is six hundred yards wide, and three and a half feet deep. Two hundred rifle-men placed on the opposite bank must have destroyed many of our men before we could have gained the shore. On the twenty-ninth of October the army arrived at Wynnesborough, an intermediate station between Camden and Ninety-six: The army, thus encamped, was at hand either to succour Camden or Ninety-six; and covered from the enemy's incursions all the country behind to the sea-coast. Lord Cornwallis, however, did not expect to remain long without such a reinforcement as would enable him to prosecute his further designs; as he had under his orders a detachment commanded by general Leslie, which had been sent to Virginia by sir Henry Clinton, as soon as he received information of the defeat of Gates at Camden. This detachment was sent to Virginia with a view of co-operating with lord Cornwallis, upon a supposition that he would proceed upon his expedition into North Carolina immediately after the battle of Camden; and the detachment was of course put under his lordship's orders. But as that expedition was necessarily postponed, earl Cornwallis sent orders to general Leslie to bring his detachment by water round to Charlestown, and join him at Wynnesborough.

In the mean time the mountaineers, contented with their success against Ferguson, had gone home and dispersed: But the north-east parts of the province were infested by the depredations of an enterprising partizan of the name of Marion. This man, previous to the defeat of general Gates, had been active in stirring up the inhabitants upon Black River to revolt; but after that event had

tially necessary was this unfortunate description of people, that it was impossible to have supported his majesty's army in the field without them. Cattle-driving was of itself a perfect business; it required great art and experience to get the cattle out of the woods. The commissary was under the greatest obligations to those people, without whose assistance he could not possibly have found provisions for the army.

thought it prudent for ſome time to retire out of the province. He had now again returned, and, traverſing the country between the rivers Pedee and Santee, without oppoſition, was ſo ſucceſsful in ſtirring up rebellion, that the whole of that diſtrict was upon the eve of a revolt. The number of his followers too had ſo increaſed that he was enabled to ſend parties acroſs the Santee, and threatened to interrupt the communication between Camden and Charleſtown. To repreſs his incurſions, lieutenant-colonel Tarleton was ſent againſt him with the light-infantry and legion. That officer, after obtaining information of Marion's ſtrength, which he found to be not ſo great as it had been repreſented, endeavoured, by concealing his own, to invite an attack, and had nearly ſucceeded. Marion advanced within two miles of the Britiſh encampment; but being then informed of his danger, immediately retreated amongſt the ſwamps and marſhes, through which it was impoſſible to follow him. This expedition was however ſerviceable in another reſpect, by convincing the inhabitants, that if they ſwerved from their allegiance, there was ſtill a power in the province capable of puniſhing them.

Colonel Tarleton checks the inroads of the American partizan Marion.

November.

Nearly about the ſame time, and whilſt the light-infantry and cavalry were abſent upon this expedition, Sumpter again made his appearance in the north-weſt part of the province. After his defeat on the eighteenth of Auguſt he had retired into a remote part of the province called the New Acquiſition, the inhabitants of which had not yet ſubmitted to the Britiſh arms. Here he was indefatigable in ſtirring them up to take arms; and the reputation he had already acquired, with his peculiar talent for enterpriſe, in a ſhort time procured him a number of followers. With theſe he now advanced towards the Britiſh quarters, intending to form a junction with colonels Clarke and Brannen, and with their united force to attack the Britiſh poſt at Ninety-ſix. Earl Cornwallis re-

CHAP. XXXV.

1780.

ceiving intelligence of his approach, laid a plan for ſurpriſing him in his camp at Fiſh Dam, upon Broad River, the execution of which was committed to major Wemyſs, of the ſixty-third regiment. That officer accordingly marched from Wynneſborough in the evening, with the ſixty-third regiment mounted, and about forty of the legion cavalry that had been left behind when Tarleton marched into the eaſtern parts of the province, intending to make his attack at day-break in the morning; but reaching the place of his deſtination ſooner than he expected, and fearful leſt the enemy ſhould diſcover him before it was light, and have time to eſcape, he ventured to make his attack in the night. At the head of his detachment he charged the enemy's piquet; but, unfortunately, from five ſhot only, that were fired before the piquet retired, he received two dangerous wounds; and to this accident Sumpter probably owed his ſafety. The command now devolved upon a young lieutenant, unacquainted with the plan, the ground, or the ſtrength of the enemy, and all was confuſion. Sumpter had time to draw out his troops; and the Britiſh detachment was repulſed, and obliged to retire, leaving behind their commander, and about twenty of their number killed or wounded. Sumpter now croſſed the Broad River, and formed the intended junction with Clarke and Brannen; and lord Cornwallis, alarmed for the ſafety of Ninety-ſix, ſent an expreſs to recall Tarleton with the light troops from the eaſtern parts of the province. He had orders to proceed by the neareſt route againſt Sumpter: The ſixty-third regiment was ſent forward to join him upon his march; and the ſeventy-firſt advanced to take poſt at Brierley's Ferry for ſupporting him. Sumpter moved forward with great confidence, becauſe he knew of the abſence of the Britiſh light troops in the eaſtern parts of the province; and Tarleton, after receiving lord Cornwallis's expreſs, came back with ſo much expedition, that he had nearly got behind Sumpter's corps before

Junction of the American forces under Sumpter, Clarke, and Brannen.

before the latter was aware of his return. In the night preceding the day on which Tarleton expected to effect his purpose, by marching up the banks of the Enoree, Sumpter was apprised of his danger by a deserter from the sixty-third regiment, and immediately began his retreat. Tarleton, while on his march the next morning, received information that Sumpter was retreating, and commenced a pursuit with his usual celerity. At a ford upon the Enoree, he came up with, and cut to pieces part of the rear-guard of Sumpter's detachment, which was waiting for the return of a patrole; the main body having passed the river some hours before. The rapid river Tyger crossed the line of march which Sumpter was pursuing at some distance in his front, and if he was suffered to pass it unmolested, it was feared that all farther pursuit would be fruitless. Tarleton, impressed with this idea, moved on with as much expedition as he could, consistently with another object, which a knowledge of Sumpter's force rendered it necessary for him to have steadily in view. This was to keep his detachment compact, that the infantry and cavalry might be at hand to support each other. But, at the hour of four in the afternoon of the twentieth of November, finding that, unless he altered his disposition, Sumpter would have time to pass the Tyger before he could come up with him, he took the resolution of pressing forward with the cavalry, and eighty mounted men of the sixty-third regiment, making in the whole, two hundred and fifty men, and left the infantry, who were much fatigued with their previous exertions, to come on at their own pace. After an hour's march, he overtook Sumpter, advantageously posted on an eminence called Blackstock's Hill, near the banks of the Tyger, and without waiting to be joined by the light-infantry, made a precipitate attack with the force which he had then with him. Sumpter's numbers, which were more than double the British

Action at Blackstock's Hill between Sumpter and Tarleton.

CHAP. XXXV. 1780.

Britiſh force at this moment oppoſed to him, perhaps would not have availed on equal ground; but the advantages of a ſtrong ſituation gave him a moſt decided ſuperiority, eſpecially over cavalry. "That part of the hill to which the attack was directed was "nearly perpendicular, with a ſmall rivulet, bruſhwood, and a railed "fence in front. The rear of the Americans, and part of their "right flank, were ſecured by the river Tyger, and their left was "covered by a large log barn, into which a conſiderable diviſion of "their force had been thrown, and from which, as the apertures "between the logs ſerved them for loop-holes, they fired with ſe"curity. Britiſh valour was conſpicuous in this action; but no "valour could ſurmount the obſtacles and diſadvantages that here "ſtood in its way. The ſixty-third regiment was roughly handled: "The commanding officer †, two others ‡, with one third of their "privates, fell. Lieutenant-colonel Tarleton, obſerving their ſitua"tion, charged with his cavalry; but unable to diſlodge the enemy, "either from the log barn on his right, or the height on his left, "he was obliged to fall back. Lieutenant Skinner, attached to the "cavalry, with a preſence of mind ever uſeful in ſuch emergencies, "covered the retreat of the ſixty-third; and in this manner did the "whole party continue to retire, till they formed a junction with "their infantry, who were advancing to ſupport them, leaving "Sumpter in quiet poſſeſſion of the field. This officer occupied the "hill for ſeveral hours, but having received a bad wound, and "knowing that the Britiſh would be reinforced before next morn"ing, he thought it hazardous to wait. He accordingly retired, "and taking his wounded men with him, croſſed the rapid river "Tyger. The wounded of the Britiſh detachment were left to the "mercy of the enemy; and it is but doing bare juſtice to ge-

† Major Money.

‡ Lieutenants Gibſon and Cope.

" neral

" neral Sumpter to declare that the ſtricteſt humanity took place " upon the preſent occaſion; they were ſupplied with every comfort " in his power *."

Although Tarleton was repulſed at Blackſtock's Hill, the immediate effects of the action were nearly the ſame as thoſe of a victory. Sumpter being diſabled by his wound from keeping the field, his followers diſperſed, after conveying him to a place of ſafety.

* The whole of this account of the action at Blackſtock's is taken from Mackenzie's Strictures on Tarleton's Campaigns. The account is there ſaid to have been compiled from the concurrent teſtimony of ſeveral officers preſent in the action; and it has been preferred to Tarleton's own account, becauſe his claim of victory is evidently inconſiſtent with ſome other circumſtances which he admits, particularly this, that he did not gain poſſeſſion of the field of action until the next morning, after it had been quitted by the Americans in the night.

CHAP. XXXVI.

Effects of the Defeat and Fall of Major Fergufon—General Gates refigns the Command of the Southern American Army to General Green—Danger arifing to the Britifh Garrifon in New York from the extreme Rigour of the Winter—Meafures taken for the Defence of New York—Unfuccefsful Attempt to eftablifh the royal Standard in the Jerfeys.

CHAP. XXXVI.

1780.
Effects of the defeat and fall of major Fergufon.

THE poftponing the expedition into North Carolina was not the only injurious confequence that followed from the defeat and fall of major Fergufon. By that unfortunate event the loyal inhabitants in both the Carolinas were difcouraged from joining the king's ftandard; and the expiring embers of the war were lighted up afrefh. The difafter which had befallen that brave officer was quickly circulated from one end of the continent to the other; and the friends of independence, cheered by the intelligence, recovered from that ftate of defpondence which followed the fucceffive defeats of Gates at Camben, and Sumpter near the ford of Catawba. The governments of Virginia and North Carolina continued to raife men and make draughts from their militia: And the officers who efcaped from Camden were indefatigably active in collecting the difperfed remains of their broken army. By thofe means fomething like a force was after a time affembled at Hillfborough, where general Gates eftablifhed his head-quarters. As this force increafed, head-quarters were advanced, firft to Salifbury, and afterwards

to

to Charlotte; and ftill more to encourage the reviving fpirits of the fouthern troops, general Green, who was fuppofed to enjoy the efteem and confidence of Wafhington more than any other officer of the army, was fent to command them. He arrived at Charlotte on the fecond of December, and on the following day general Gates refigned the command of the army. With thefe tranfactions clofed the campaign of the year 1780 in the fouthern colonies, the events of which, for the fake of perfpicuity, have been given in a connected feries.

General Gates refigns the command of the fouthern American army to general Green.

We muft now take a review of the military operations between the two grand armies in the vicinity of New York, and of the other principal events that occurred upon the continent of America from the beginning of the prefent year, and from thence pafs to thofe that occurred in other quarters of the world, to which the war in its progrefs extended itfelf.

Dangers arifing to the Britifh garrifon in New York, from the extreme rigour of the winter.

The winter that preceded this campaign was the fevereft ever remembered in North America. The rivers from Virginia northwards were frozen up for the greateft part of three months: And even the arms of the fea were in many parts paffable upon the ice. When fir Henry Clinton departed upon his expedition againft Charleftown, he left a garrifon fully adequate to the fecurity of New York in ordinary feafons: But by the unexpected rigour of the winter it was deprived of thofe defenfive advantages which its infular fituation at other times afforded, and became expofed to an attack from general Wafhington. By the middle of January the North River, which conftituted its greateft natural defence, was fo completely covered with thick ice, that the largeft army, with the heavieft artillery and baggage, might have paffed it on the ice with eafe. In other quarters, towards the country, New York was not lefs acceffible; whilft its communication with the fea was entirely cut off, the

 fhips

CHAP. XXXVI. 1780.

ſhips of war that remained for its defence, and all the other veſſels in the harbour, being frozen up in the ice.

Meaſures taken for the defence of New York.

In this perilous ſituation, the veteran lieutenant-general Knyphauſen, who commanded, took ſuch precautionary meaſures as prudence dictated. The ſeamen were landed from the ſhips and tranſports, and formed into companies: The inhabitants were embodied and officered, and took their routine of duty with the regular garriſon. In the mean time the danger to be apprehended from an attack was not the only evil to which the garriſon and inhabitants were ſubjected: They were deprived of thoſe ſupplies which a communication by water would have afforded, and in particular ſuffered ſeverely for want of fuel. Such was their diſtreſs for want of this article, that it became neceſſary to break up ſome old tranſports, and to pull down ſome uninhabited wooden houſes, to ſupply their moſt preſſing neceſſities. But the ſame zeal animated them, and the ſame ardour ran through the whole ſervice, as when, in a former year, the count d'Eſtaing anchored off Sandy Hook, and threatened to enter the harbour.

Had general Waſhington been in ſufficient force to have hazarded an attack, it is difficult to ſay what might ultimately have been the conſequence: It was however ſufficiently apparent, that he would have met with the moſt determined reſiſtance. But general Waſhington was in no condition to make the attempt: His army had been weakened by the large detachments drawn from it for the relief of Charleſtown; and amongſt the troops that remained with him a mutinous ſpirit began to appear, in conſequence of their ſufferings from the ſcarcity of proviſions and the want of all other neceſſaries. The deſtruction of the continental magazines by the deſultory expeditions of the preceding year, againſt different parts of the ſea-coaſt, probably laid the foundation of this ſcarcity: And the evil was increaſed by the rapid depreciation of the paper money iſſued by congreſs, which rendered it difficult for their contractors to procure ſupplies. Thus, in conſequence of the reciprocal weakneſs of the two armies, the winter paſſed without any thing material happening between them, except an ineffectual attempt made by the American general lord Stirling, about the middle of January, to take Staten Iſland. He marched over the ice from the Jerſey ſhore in the night, ſurpriſed a ſmall poſt, and made a few priſoners; but was ſoon obliged to retreat, and in his retreat loſt ſome of his own men, who ſerved to exchange for the priſoners that he had taken.

The enemy having eſtabliſhed a poſt at Young's Houſe, in the neighbourhood of the White Plains, which greatly annoyed the provincial loyaliſts, as well as the Britiſh army, by the interception of cattle and proviſions intended to be brought to New York, it became an object of importance with the governor and commander of his majeſty's troops, if poſſible, to diſlodge that party, conſiſting of about three hundred men. Much as it had been the wiſh of both to drive the enemy from this poſt, no means had been uſed for that end, on account of their diſtance, twenty miles from the out-poſts of our army, till the month of February 1780, when, after a great fall of ſnow, it was ſuggeſted that a detachment of ſoldiers might be conveyed in ſleighs in one night, and ſurpriſe the enemy by break of day. Major-general Mathew, who commanded at King's Bridge, on the ſecond of February communicated to lieutenant-colonel Norton of the guards the intention of general Tryon and lieutenant-general Knyphauſen, to ſend a detachment of troops to Young's Houſe in ſleighs, which would be ready at King's Bridge in the evening, and that lieutenant-colonel Norton was to command the party. The colonel, though highly gratified by this command, and unwilling to ſay any thing that might ſeem to retard the ſervice, or throw difficulties in the way of the intended expedition,

 yet

CHAP. XXXVI. 1780.

yet thought it his duty to point out the improbability of the ſleighs anſwering the purpoſe: And ſo convinced was general Mathew, from the reaſons which lieutenant-colonel Norton adduced, of the very little chance of ſucceeding by means of the ſleighs, that general Mathew, in the handſomeſt manner, in the event of the ſleighs upon trial not being found to anſwer, left lieutenant-colonel Norton at liberty to act with the detachment as he pleaſed; either to convert it to a foraging party, to proceed, or to return, as he ſhould think moſt adviſable. Under theſe circumſtances, lieutenant-colonel Norton, on the evening of the ſecond of February 1780, ſet out with the four flank companies of the guards, two companies of Heſſians, and a party of yagers, in the ſleighs; two three-pounders, a detachment of yager cavalry, and the mounted Weſt Cheſter refugees. The ſleighs, being ſoon found, inſtead of accelerating, to retard the progreſs of the troops, were ordered back, and the detachment moved on. Not long after the men had quitted the ſleighs, and were marching forward, word was brought to lieutenant-colonel Norton, that the horſes were not able to draw the guns through the ſnow; he was therefore obliged to leave the guns, and with them a guard ſufficient to enſure their return. The detachment continued its march through bye-ways, and acroſs the country, in order to avoid falling in with the enemy's patroles, ſtill in hopes, by perſeverance and exertion, to reach Young's Houſe by break of day. At ſun-riſe, they learned from the guides that they were yet ſeven miles ſhort of the enemy's poſt: A long way for men wearied with marching all night in bad roads, and with the ſnow in many places above two feet deep. Their ſituation was, now, not a little embarraſſing. As the guns, intended to open the doors of the ſtone houſe, were left behind, to ſurpriſe the enemy was impoſſible. To proceed, and not to carry the point, would be to expoſe the detachment, in their return, already fatigued with a long and toilſome march, to be haraſſed for the ſpace of twenty miles, by an enemy in force, freſh, and with a perfect knowledge of the country. In theſe circumſtances, the colonel, unwilling to return without accompliſhing ſome object that might anſwer the expectation of thoſe who had placed their confidence in him, determined, at all events, to march to the enemy's poſt, and then act according to circumſtances; availing himſelf of ſome axes he had found by the way, and an iron crow, the better to enable the grenadiers to force the doors and windows of the houſe. When the detachment arrived within two miles of the enemy, the cavalry were ordered to advance, and inveſt the houſe in ſuch a manner as to prevent either a retreat or reinforcement. This order, from the depth of the ſnow, could not be carried into execution, and the cavalry drew up on an eminence at ſome little diſtance from the houſe. As the flank companies of the firſt battalion of guards approached, parties of the enemy were obſerved marching very deliberately to reinforce lieutenant-colonel Thomſon, in Young's Houſe. The diſpoſition for attack was then ſoon made, by deſiring lieutenant-colonel Hall, with his company of light-infantry of the guards, to aſcend the hill on his right, below which ſtood the houſe, whilſt the firſt company of grenadiers inclined a little to the left, to cut off the retreat of a party that had advanced from Hammond's, a houſe at a ſmall diſtance from Young's. Very ſhortly after the ſeparation of the two leading companies, the fireing began between the party in the houſe and lieutenant-colonel Hall's men: Nor was it long before the grenadiers came up with the party of the enemy juſt mentioned, who were in readineſs waiting for them in the orchard adjoining to Hammond's houſe, and received them with a degree of coolneſs and courage that did the Americans honour. To ſuperior force they were obliged to give way; and by the timely arrival of lieutenant-colonel Pennington, with a part of the ſecond company of grenadier guards, who had advanced in a ſtraight line, the

CHAP. XXXVI. 1780.

the houfe was carried, and the enemy defeated. So fharp was the conflict, and fo fpeedily terminated, that the whole of lieutenant-colonel Pennington's company had not time to come up, which made it impoffible for the fecond company of light-infantry, commanded by lieutenant-colonel Guydickens, or the other troops, which were in the rear of the line of march, to fhare in the action *.

The prifoners, being put under a proper efcort, and the troops formed again in line of march, the detachment took the direct road to King's Bridge, which they reached by nine on the fame evening †.

For

* No accurate account was taken of the killed of the enemy, but from the numbers that lay dead around the houfe, there was reafon to believe not lefs than forty. Ninety were made prifoners, among which were the lieutenant-colonel commandant of the diftrict, 1 captain, 1 captain-lieutenant, 2 lieutenants, and 2 enfigns.

† Twelve of the prifoners were fo feverely wounded, that they were obliged to be left at different houfes on the road. Eighty-feven were conducted to New York.

The lofs fuftained by the detachment under colonel Norton:—Yagers, 3 men wounded. Refugees, 1 captain wounded. Firft light-infantry company of the guards, 1 rank and file wounded. Firft grenadier company ditto, 2 rank and file killed. Wounded, 1 lieutenant, 1 ferjeant, 12 rank and file. Second grenadier company of the guards, 1 ferjeant, 3 rank and file wounded. Total; killed, 2, wounded, 23.

Lieutenant-colonel Norton made his report on the 4th of February to major-general Mathew of the killed and wounded of the detachment, together with the number of prifoners taken. In the afternoon of the 4th, the major of the brigade, in a polite letter to lieutenant-colonel Norton, inclofed him a copy of the after-orders of the 4th inftant, viz.

Public Orders, King's Bridge, 4th of February 1780.

" Major-general Mathew returns his thanks to lieutenant-colonel Norton, and the officers and privates of the detachment under his command, for their conduct and fpirited behaviour on the morning of the 3d inftant, and for their intrepidity and perfeverance in that duty: The fuccefs of which claims the general's higheft approbation."

On the 5th of February 1780, the following Order was given out from Head Quarters at New York.

" His excellency lieutenant-general Knyphaufen defires his thanks may be given in public orders to lieutenant-colonel Norton of the guards, for his good conduct and gallant behaviour

in

For some days in the winter, general Washington's army was entirely without bread. Occasional supplies were afterwards received,

in attacking and forcing a considerable body of the rebels, advantageously posted at Young's House, in the neighbourhood of White Plains, on the morning of the 3d instant. His excellency returns his thanks to the officers and private soldiers of the different detachments employed on this service; and the general is particularly obliged to the officers and men of the West Chester refugees for their very determined behaviour upon this as well as former occasions."

Subsequent to the order of thanks, highly flattering to colonel Norton and the party, the generals having learnt more particularly the difficulties the detachment had encountered, and thinking that the extraordinary exertions of the troops merited yet further attention at their hands, lieutenant-colonel Norton was desired to make major-general Mathew a formal report of the excursion to Young's House, and to mention as many circumstances as he should deem worthy of notice, giving him to understand the report would be transmitted to England. Lieutenant-colonel Norton accordingly made his report to major-general Mathew, which was sent to sir Henry Clinton, the commander in chief, then at Charlestown; and from sir Henry forwarded to England by the earl of Lincoln, aid-du-camp to the commander in chief, by whom it was delivered in to the secretary of state's office. The only account given to the public of this expedition in the Gazette, was on the 26th of April 1780, in the extract of a letter from lieutenant-general Knyphausen to lord George Germaine, as follows:—

"General Mathew sent a detachment of guards, and provincial horse, under the command of lieutenant-colonel Norton, to attack a post at John's House, upon the White Plains. This did not succeed entirely to his wishes; but the rebels, who were posted in a house, were however attacked and dislodged; with the loss of 40 men killed and 97 made prisoners."

An act of generosity was upon this occasion displayed, which ought not to be passed over in silence: The wounded Americans were placed in houses, and a sum of money given by the British officers to the occupiers or inhabitants of those houses, as an encouragement or reward for the trouble they might be at in attending on the wounded Americans.

When the Gazette, giving an account of this expedition, arrived at New York, general Mathew immediately took it to general Knyphausen, and shewed it him. General Knyphausen exclaimed, "This is not my account! for my account of this expedition was perfectly agreeable to the order of thanks I gave, and my letter to the minister spoke in the handsomest manner of colonel Norton's conduct, and the officers and men under his command." But this mutilated, most untrue, and unjust account, was not without its object, it being intended to wound the feelings of the father through the son, the father, then sir Fletcher Norton, afterwards lord Grantley, having dared to hint that a frugal expenditure of the public money was expected by the commons. When, as speaker of the house of commons, he addressed his majesty upon presenting a bill, granting supplies to his majesty, on the 7th of May,

CHAP. XXXVI. 1780.

ceived, but fo fcanty, that the fufferings of the troops neceffarily produced difcontent; and towards the end of May two regiments actually mutinied. Means however were found to pacify them; and after fome time they returned to their duty.

By the thawing of the ice upon the approach of fpring, New York was reftored to its infular fituation; and all further apprehenfions for its fafety being at an end, the Britifh commanders there were at liberty to employ their force offenfively againft the enemy, and to take advantage of any favourable circumftances that might occur for annoying them. Intelligence of the mutinous difpofition of the American army being carried to New York, and information being alfo received that the inhabitants of the Jerfeys were difcontented with the new ftate of things, and wifhed to re-eftablifh their old form of government, general Knyphaufen was induced to detach a confiderable force under brigadiers-general Mathew and Sterling, which landed at Elizabeth-town, in the Jerfeys, on the feventh of June. If the inhabitants were difpofed to throw off the yoke of congrefs, the force fent to their affiftance would enable them to do it:

May 1777 (vide vol. i. page 273—275), fir Fletcher Norton's fpeech gave great offence to the minifters; and although generals Knyphaufen's and Mathew's moft favourable account of the expedition to Young's Houfe, together with the very handfome and well-deferved order of thanks to colonel, now the honourable major-general, Norton of the guards, and the detachment under his command, were delivered (by the earl of Lincoln, then aid-du-camp to fir Henry Clinton) to lord George Germaine in perfon, as the minifter for American affairs; yet we fee, from the Gazette account, how falfe a relation was given to the public.

There is a certain degree of fair fame, and honourable ambition, to which every good man looks up: But were that fame to be blafted for either private or party purpofes, all emulation, the great incentive to glorious actions, would be fuppreffed and deftroyed.

It is well obferved by the great Roman hiftorian TACITUS (of whofe admirable writings Mr. Murphy has, at a very feafonable time, prefented to the Englifh reader an excellent tranflation), "That it is incumbent on the writer of hiftory to rejudge the actions of men, to the end, that the good and worthy may meet with the reward due to eminent virtue; and that pernicious citizens may be deterred by the condemnation that waits on evil deeds at the tribunal of pofterity. In this confifts the chief part of the hiftorian's duty."

it: And if a mutinous difpofition ftill prevailed amongft the foldiers of the American army, fome advantage might probably be gained over general Wafhington. It foon however appeared that part of this intelligence was falfe, and the reft greatly magnified. Although the inhabitants of the Jerfeys had murmured in confequence of the depredations committed upon them by the American foldiers in the time of their diftrefs for want of provifions, they had never thought of deferting the American caufe: On the contrary, they made the greateft exertions to relieve the neceffities of thofe very men to whofe depredations they were expofed; and it was principally owing to thefe exertions that the American army had not been actually difbanded. A mutinous difpofition had alfo certainly difcovered itfelf amongft the foldiers of the American army: But it arofe from diftrefs, and not difaffection; and the two regiments which had already mutinied, were foon pacified. Under fuch circumftances the Britifh commanders experienced a grievous difappointment: Inftead of being received in the Jerfeys as friends, the militia very generally turned out to oppofe them. During their march from Elizabeth-town to Connecticut Farms, a diftance of only feven miles, they were annoyed by parties of militia the whole way; who, if they were unable to make any impreffion, or do any confiderable injury, fhewed at leaft that it was not from want of inclination: And when the Britifh troops approached Springfield, a detachment from that army, which was reprefented to be mutinous, was feen drawn up in force on the other fide of the river ready to difpute their paffage. It being now apparent that the information, upon which this expedition had been undertaken, was not to be depended upon, the Britifh troops in the evening returned to Elizabeth-town, and would have croffed the fame night to Staten Ifland, had not the ebbing of the tide, which on that fhore leaves a large fpace covered with deep mud between the high land and the water, rendered it

Unfuccefsful attempt to eftablifh the royal ftandard in the Jerfeys.

CHAP. XXXVI. 1780.

impoſſibe to embark the cavalry till the next morning; and to cover their embarkation it was neceſſary that the infantry ſhould remain with them. In the mean time, the Britiſh commanders had leiſure to reflect upon their diſappointment, and the conſequences of their fruitleſs expedition; and it was determined, for the credit of the Britiſh arms, to remain ſome days longer in New Jerſey, leſt their precipitate retreat ſhould be repreſented as a flight.

CHAP. XXXVII.

The Americans dislodged from Springfield, and that Town destroyed—A French Armament arrives at Rhode Island—A Scheme formed by one of General Washington's Officers, Arnold, for delivering an important Post into the Hands of the British Army—Adventure and Fate of the British Adjutant-General Major André—A general Exchange of Prisoners—The Troops on both Sides retire into Winter Quarters.

CHAP. XXXVII. 1780.

WHILST, in consequence of this determination, the British army lay at Elizabeth-town, sir Henry Clinton arrived from South Carolina; and the post at Springfield having been reinforced and put under the command of general Green, a resolution was taken to attack and dislodge him before the army returned to New York. In pursuance of this resolution the army marched at break of day in the morning of the twenty-third of June, and arrived at Springfield with very little interruption. The enemy appeared determined to dispute the further progress of the British troops at two different passes upon the river, but were dislodged from both after a considerable resistance, nearly about the same time, and forced to flee to the heights in their rear, where they again took post. The town of Springfield was burnt: And the British army, having rested a few hours after the action, returned the same day to Elizabeth-town, and in the evening, under cover of a redoubt that had been thrown up by the Americans, but now occupied by the British, passed over to Staten Island without molestation, by means of a bridge of boats.

The Americans dislodged from Springfield, and that town destroyed.

 Before

CHAP. XXXVII. 1780.

Before the Britiſh troops marched out from Elizabeth-town, ſome pains had been taken to miſlead general Waſhington, as to the real deſign of the Britiſh commander. The tranſports were aſſembled, and troops embarked, as if an expedition had been intended up the North River againſt Weſt Point; and by ſuch indications general Waſhington was ſo far alarmed, that he actually marched from his camp in the Jerſeys towards the North River. But he marched with great deliberation, cautiouſly intending not to remove too far from Morris-town, until the future movements of ſir Henry Clinton ſhould enable him to diſcover his real intention; and he had proceeded only fifteen miles, when information was brought to him, that the Britiſh troops, inſtead of going up the North River, were marching out in force towards Springfield. General Waſhington immediately halted, and ſent back a detachment to reinforce general Green; but before it arrived the action at Springfield was over, and the Britiſh troops had retreated to Elizabeth-town. The real object of the expedition was probably againſt the American magazines at Morris-town: But the oppoſition made at Springfield was an indication to the commander in chief, that every mile of his future march through a country naturally difficult, and abounding with ſtrong paſſes, would be not leſs obſtinately diſputed, and determined him to abandon an enterpriſe, which, even if it ſhould be ſucceſsful, might coſt him too much; more eſpecially as the expected arrival of a powerful French armament on the coaſt of America, obliged him not to engage in any expedition that would either require much time, or carry him a conſiderable diſtance from New York.

The Britiſh army having quitted New Jerſey, general Waſhington on his part planned an enterpriſe againſt a Britiſh poſt at Bergen Point, on the North River, oppoſite to New York, which was garriſoned by ſeventy loyaliſts. This enterpriſe had for its object not only the reduction of that poſt, but the carrying away of the cattle

upon

upon Bergen Neck, from which the garrifon of New York was occafionally fupplied with frefh provifions, through the poft occupied by the loyalifts: And the force appointed for carrying it into execution, amounted to about two thoufand men, under the command of general Wayne, who had rendered himfelf famous by the furprife of Stoney Point. At Bergen Point, the defences of which confifted of a block-houfe furrounded by an abbatis, this brave little band of loyal refugees defended themfelves againft a cannonade of three hours, and repulfed an attempt to take the place by affault: In the affault the Americans loft a number equal to the whole amount of the garrifon, and in their retreat fome ftragglers were made prifoners, and part of the cattle retaken, which they were attempting to carry off.

A French armament arrives at Rhode Ifland

In the mean time, on the tenth of July, the expected armament from France arrived at Rhode Ifland. It confifted of feven fhips of the line, fome frigates, and a number of tranfports, having on board fix thoufand troops; the fleet being commanded by the chevalier de Ternay, and the troops by the count de Rochambeau: And in order to prevent difcuffion, and obviate every difficulty that might arife upon the junction of the French troops with the American army, a commiffion was fent to general Wafhington, appointing him a lieutenant-general of France, which of courfe put the count de Rochambeau under his orders.

The arrival of fo confiderable a reinforcement diffufed a general joy amongft the adherents of congrefs throughout the American ftates, and excited them to frefh exertions. Thofe ftates, which had lately turned a deaf ear to the applications not only of general Wafhington, but of congrefs, were now eager to raife and fend forward their quotas of men: And the American army, which, from the various caufes already mentioned, had been reduced to a ftate of imbecility, began again to make a refpectable appearance. When the French arrived at Rhode Ifland, the Britifh fleet under admiral Arbuthnot was inferior to that of the chevalier de Ternay; and a

plan

CHAP. XXXVII. 1780.

plan was laid for attacking New York: But the arrival of ſix ſhips of the line from England, which followed cloſe on the track of the chevalier de Ternay, ſoon gave admiral Arbuthnot the ſuperiority; and the Britiſh commanders, inſtead of waiting to be attacked, made preparations in their turn for acting offenſively againſt the French at Rhode Iſland. Sir Henry Clinton, with the tranſports and troops deſtined for this expedition, proceeded to Huntington Bay, in the Sound, whilſt admiral Arbuthnot, with the ſhips of war, ſailed round Long Iſland, in order to co-operate by ſea. But in the mean time general Waſhington, whoſe army had been increaſed by the arrival of conſiderable reinforcements, ſuddenly paſſed the North River, and approached King's Bridge. So unexpected a movement obliged ſir Henry Clinton to abandon the expedition againſt Rhode Iſland, and return with the troops for the protection of New York, leaving admiral Arbuthnot to block up the French fleet by ſea. The object of this expedition was loſt, from a circumſtance but too frequent in the hiſtory of this country, a diſagreement between the commanders in chief of the land and naval ſervice. Upon the return of the Britiſh commander, general Waſhington drew off his forces to a greater diſtance, cautiouſly avoiding ſuch a poſition as might be the means of bringing on a general engagement.

About this time the count de Guichen was expected from the Weſt Indies, with a land force, and twenty ſhips of the line. In view of this aſſiſtance the New England militia had aſſembled very readily, and marched to Rhode Iſland, when their allies the French were threatened with an attack from ſir Henry Clinton: General Waſhington's army too, as has been already mentioned, had been greatly increaſed by the arrival of freſh reinforcements. And with theſe different bodies of men, when united, it was intended to attack New York by land, whilſt the count de Guichen, joined by the ſquadron under the chevalier de Ternay, ſhould block it up by ſea. But the count de Guichen, as we ſhall ſee hereafter, when we come

come to the tranſactions in the Weſt Indies, had been ſo roughly handled in his different engagements with admiral Rodney, and his ſhips were in ſo ſhattered a condition, that inſtead of proceeding to America, according to the original deſign, he returned with his fleet to France, taking under his convoy the trade from the French iſlands. The failure in ſo conſiderable a part rendered impracticable the further proſecution of the ſcheme againſt New York; and as ſoon as general Waſhington was made acquainted with the departure of the count de Guichen, it became neceſſary for him to concert new meaſures with the French commanders at Rhode Iſland, for their future operations. For this purpoſe an interview took place between them at Hartford in Connecticut, about half way between the French and American camps.

A ſcheme formed by one of general Waſhington's officers, Arnold, for delivering an important poſt into the hands of the Britiſh army.

Whilſt general Waſhington was abſent from his army upon this ſervice, a deep-laid ſcheme was formed by one of his own officers, for delivering up to ſir Henry Clinton the ſtrong poſt of Weſt Point, in the high lands upon the North River, the poſſeſſion of which would have nearly cut off all communication between the northern and middle colonies. The officer engaged in this deſign was the famous general Arnold, whoſe ſervices in the cauſe of America had been of the moſt meritorious kind, and whoſe brilliant actions in the field juſtly raiſed him to ſuperior notice and regard. After the evacuation of Philadelphia by the Britiſh troops in the year 1778, he was appointed to command the American garriſon that took poſſeſſion of it; and while he acted in that capacity had the misfortune to diſguſt many of the inhabitants, and even to fall under the diſpleaſure of congreſs. He lived expenſively, and, as was ſuppoſed, conſiderably beyond his ſtated income; but he was at the ſame time concerned in trading ſpeculations, and had ſhares in ſeveral privateers; and upon the profits expected from thoſe adventures, he probably relied, as means of enabling him to keep up the ſtate and ſtyle

CHAP. XXXVII. 1780.

of life he had assumed: He had also claims against the public to a considerable amount; and upon the payment of them he depended as a fund to satisfy the immediate demands of his creditors, who were beginning to become importunate. But the trading speculations in which he had engaged proved unproductive; his privateers were unsuccessful; and a considerable portion of his demand against the public was cut off, by the commissioners appointed to examine his accounts. From the decision of the commissioners, general Arnold appealed to the congress, who appointed a committee of their own members to revise the sentence: But the committee of congress were even less favourable to his views than the commissioners, from whose decision he had appealed. They reported that the balance already allowed by the commissioners was more than general Arnold was entitled to receive.

So many disappointments could not fail to ruffle a temper less irritable than general Arnold's: Recollecting his former services, he gave full scope to his resentment, and complained of ill-usage and ingratitude in terms better calculated to provoke than to mollify, and such as were peculiarly offensive to congress. His enemies availed themselves of his indiscretion to swell the tide of popular clamour which already ran strongly against him. A court-martial was appointed to examine into his conduct during his command in Philadelphia, and by the sentence of that board it was in general terms reprehended, and himself subjected to the mortification of receiving a reprimand from general Washington.

From this moment it is supposed that Arnold formed the design of quitting the American service and joining the British; and only delayed the execution of his purpose until an opportunity should offer of performing some essential service to the power which he was about to join, that might render his accession of more importance. A correspondence was opened with sir Henry Clinton: The delivering up the poſt at Weſt Point, where Arnold now commanded, was the ſervice he propoſed to perform; and the interval of general Waſhington's abſence, when he went to confer with the French commanders, was the time appointed for finiſhing the negotiation. To facilitate the means of carrying on the previous correſpondence, the Vulture ſloop of war was ſtationed in the North River, at ſuch a diſtance from Weſt Point as to excite no ſuſpicion, but near enough to ſerve for the intended communication; and as general Arnold required a confidential perſon to treat with, major André, aid-du-camp to ſir Henry Clinton, and adjutant-general of the Britiſh army, undertook to confer with him, and bring the negotiation to a concluſion. For this purpoſe he repaired on board the Vulture ſloop. At night, in purſuance of a previous arrangement, a boat from the ſhore carried him to the beach, where he met general Arnold; and day-light approaching before the buſineſs on which they had met was finally adjuſted, major André was told that he muſt be conducted to a place of ſafety, and lie concealed until the following night, when he might return on board the Vulture without the danger of being diſcovered. The beach where the firſt conference was held was without, but the place of ſafety to which major André was conducted to lie concealed during the day, was within the American out-poſts, againſt his intention, and without his knowledge. Here, however, he remained with general Arnold during the day; and at night, the boatmen refuſing to carry him on board the Vulture, becauſe ſhe had ſhifted her poſition during the day, in conſequence of a gun being brought to bear upon her from the ſhore, he was reduced to the neceſſity of endeavouring to make his way to New York by land. Laying aſide his regimentals, which he had hitherto worn, he put on a plain ſuit of clothes, and receiving a paſs from general Arnold, under the aſſumed name of John Anderſon, as if he had been ſent down the country on

Adventure and fate of the Britiſh adjutant-general major André.

CHAP. XXXVII. 1780.

public bufinefs, he fet out on his return to New York. His paffport fecured him from interruption at the American out-pofts; and he had already paffed them all, and thought himfelf out of danger, when three American militia-men, who had been fent out to patrol near the road along which he travelled, fuddenly fpringing from the woods, feized the bridle of his horfe and ftopped him. The fuddennefs of the furprife feems to have deprived major André of his wonted prefence of mind; and, although a man of the greateft addrefs, he was entrapped by the rude fimplicity of clowns. Having inquired from whence they were, and being anfwered, "From below;" "And fo," faid he, "am I." It was not long before he difcovered his miftake; but too late, it would appear, to remove the impreffion which his firft anfwer had made. The men who had made him prifoners fearched him for papers, and having taken from his boot a packet, in the hand-writing of general Arnold, determined to carry him without delay to their commanding officer. It was in vain that he offered them a purfe of gold and his watch, to fuffer him to pafs: His promifes of an ample provifion, and getting them promotion, if they would accompany him to New York, were equally unavailing. The unfortunate André, after thefe efforts to regain his liberty, feems to have been regardlefs of what might be his own fate, and was only anxious to fave general Arnold. Before the commanding officer of the militia he continued to perfonate the fuppofed John Anderfon, and requefted that a meffenger might be fent to general Arnold to acquaint him with his detention. A meffenger being accordingly difpatched, and fufficient time having elapfed for general Arnold to make his efcape, he no longer difguifed his real name, and avowed himfelf to be major André, adjutant-general of the Britifh army: He alfo wrote a letter to general Wafhington, in his real name, acquainting him that he was his prifoner, and accounting for the difguife which neceffity had obliged him

him to aſſume. The meſſage ſent to general Arnold, announcing the detention of John Anderſon, was ſufficient notice to him to provide for his own ſafety: He quitted Weſt Point without delay, got on board the Vulture ſloop, and in her proceeded to New York.

In the mean time general Waſhington returned from his interview with the French commanders, and being informed of what had paſſed during his abſence, together with Arnold's eſcape, he reinforced the garriſon of Weſt Point with a ſtrong detachment from his army, and appointed a board of general officers, to inquire into and report upon the caſe of major André. The candid, open, manly, and ingenuous explanation of his conduct, given by major André, before the board of officers, impreſſed with admiration and eſteem even his enemies who were about to ſhed his blood. Diſmiſſing from his thoughts all perſonal conſiderations of danger, he was only anxious that the tranſaction in which he had been engaged, ſhaded as it was by the intervention of unfortunate circumſtances, might be cleared from obſcurity, and appear in its genuine colours, at leaſt with reſpect to his intention, which was incapable of ſwerving from the paths of honour. But the board of officers fixing their attention upon the naked fact of his being in diſguiſe within their lines, without perhaps duly conſidering the unfortunate train of incidents which unexpectedly, and almoſt unavoidably, led him into that ſituation, were of opinion that he came under the deſcription, and ought to ſuffer the puniſhment, of a ſpy.

The concern felt at New York, in conſequence of the capture of major André, was in the mean time inconceivably great: His gallantry as an officer, and amiable demeanour as a man, had gained him not only the admiration, but the affection, of the whole army; and the uncertainty of his fate filled them with the deepeſt anxiety. Sir Henry Clinton, whoſe eſteem and regard he enjoyed in an eminent degree, immediately opened a correſpondence with general

CHAP. XXXVII. 1780.

Washington, by means of a flag of truce, and urged every motive which justice, policy, or humanity, could suggest, to induce a remission of the sentence. Finding his letters ineffectual, he sent out general Robertson, with a flag, to confer upon the subject with any officer that should be appointed by general Washington. An interview took place between general Robertson and general Green, who had been president of the court-martial. But all efforts to save the unfortunate André were unavailing: His doom was irrevocably fixed. The greatness of the danger which the American army had escaped by the discovery of Arnold's plot before it was ripe for execution, seems to have extinguished in the breast of the inexorable Washington, every spark of humanity that remained. Although entreated by a most pathetic letter from major André, written on the day previous to his execution, to change the mode of his death from that of a common malefactor to one more correspondent to the feelings of a soldier, he would not condescend to grant even this inconsiderable boon to the supplication of his unfortunate prisoner: And on the second day of October this accomplished young officer met his fate, in the manner prescribed by his sentence, with a composure, serenity, and fortitude, which astonished the beholders, and excited those emotions of sympathy that would have been more honourably and humanely exercised in averting than lamenting his fate.

Thus fell the unfortunate André. If intention is necessary to constitute guilt; and if guilt alone merits punishment, some doubt may be entertained with respect to the sentence of the board of officers. Major André did not, at first, knowingly enter within the American lines: He was then also in his regimentals: And when he actually found himself within those lines, contrarily to his intention, whatever he afterwards did, in order to extricate himself, by assuming a disguise, and using a feigned passport, ought rather to be ascribed to the imposed necessity of his situation than to choice.

But,

But, even if the ſentence pronounced againſt him ſhould be found agreeable to the letter of the law of nations, ſo unſuitable is the exerciſe of extreme juſtice to our imperfect ſtate, that we turn with diſguſt from thoſe tranſactions, in which the finer feelings of humanity have been ſacrificed to its rigour. Bright as the fame of Waſhington ſhall ſhine in the annals of America, as one of the moſt illuſtrious ſupporters of her independence, the ſons of freedom will lament the cold inſenſibility, that did not ſuffer him to interpoſe, in order to reſcue from his fate ſo gallant an officer, and even could withhold from him the poor conſolation of meeting death like a ſoldier; whilſt a glance of indignation ſhall dart from the eyes of her fair and compaſſionate daughters, ſoftened only by the tear of pity for the fate of the accompliſhed André.

From ſo tragic an event, tending by its ſeverity to increaſe, we paſs with pleaſure to an arrangement calculated to leſſen, the calamities of war. This was an agreement for a general exchange of priſoners, finally ſettled and adjuſted towards the cloſe of the preſent year, between major-general Philips, on the part of the Britiſh army, and major-general Lincoln, on the part of the Americans, the former having been an American priſoner ever ſince the convention of Saratoga, and the latter a Britiſh priſoner ſince the fall of Charleſtown.

The congreſs had, from policy, hitherto reſiſted all propoſals for a general exchange upon equitable terms. They knew the expence that attended recruiting the Britiſh army from Europe: They knew alſo that their own army would receive no great increaſe of ſtrength by a releaſe of the Americans detained as priſoners, becauſe the ſhort periods for which the American ſoldiers enliſted, during the firſt years of the war, would have generally expired before an exchange could have been effected. But the clamours of their people, ſo long detained in captivity, and for whoſe releaſe they had ſhewn ſo much indifference, had now become ſo loud; ſo many of their

CHAP. XXXVII. 1780.

regular ſoldiers had been made priſoners by the capture of Charleſtown, and the defeat of general Gates at Camden; and in conſequence of theſe diſaſters ſo much difficulty had been experienced in recruiting their army during the preſent year; that neceſſity, rather than choice, obliged them at laſt to yield to an equitable arrangement. An ineffectual attempt was made for the releaſe of the privates of general Burgoyne's army, who had been priſoners ſince the convention of Saratoga: But nothing could prevail upon the congreſs to depart from their former reſolutions; and the convention troops were deſtined to captivity during the remainder of the war.

The cold weather beginning to ſet in, put an end to all further active operations in the field. The Britiſh troops went into winter quarters in New York and its dependencies: The French troops remained at Rhode Iſland: And general Waſhington continued to occupy the high grounds bordering on the North River, from whence in a ſhort time he was obliged to diſcharge a conſiderable part of the new levies, in conſequence of a want of bread for their ſubſiſtence.

CHAP. XXXVIII.

Tranſactions in Europe and the Weſt Indies—Succeſſes of the Britiſh Fleet under Admiral Rodney—Relief of Gibraltar—Growing Differences between Great Britain and Holland—Armed Neutrality, or Aſſociation among Neutral Maritime Powers, for the Purpoſe of eſtabliſhing the Doctrine that Free Ships make Free Goods—Suſpenſion of the Treaties between Great Britain and Holland—Naval Tranſactions—Commercial Treaty between America and Holland—War on the Part of Great Britain againſt the Dutch.

CHAP. XXXVIII. 1780.

BUT the tranſactions in Europe and the Weſt Indies now demand our attention. Admiral Rodney, whom his ſervices in the preceding war had recommended to the notice of the miniſtry, being appointed to command the Britiſh fleet in the Weſt Indies, failed for that ſtation, with a reinforcement of ſhips, about the beginning of the preſent year; and advantage was taken of his convoy to ſend a freſh ſupply of proviſions and ſtores for the relief of the garriſon at Gibraltar, which had been blockaded by the Spaniards from the commencement of the war with that nation. That this ſervice might be performed without any danger of miſcarriage, a part of the channel fleet was put under admiral Rodney's command, which was to accompany him as far as Gibraltar.

It ſeems to have been reſerved for this commander to revive, by his ſucceſſes, the memory of our glorious atchievements in former wars.

CHAP. XXXVIII. 1780.

wars. He had been but a few days at ſea, when he fell in with and took a fleet of twenty-three ſail of Spaniſh ſhips bound from St. Sebaſtian to Cadiz, ſixteen of them laden with proviſions, naval ſtores, and bale goods, and the reſt ſhips of war belonging to the royal company of Caraccas that had been aſſigned to the others as a convoy. The ſame good fortune, about a week afterwards, brought him in ſight of a Spaniſh fleet of eleven ſhips of the line and two frigates, that were cruiſing off Cape St. Vincent, under the command of Don Juan Langara. A lee-ſhore at no great diſtance favoured the eſcape of the enemy, and rendered a purſuit from the Britiſh fleet hazardous; and the ſhortneſs of a winter's day, already far advanced, with tempeſtuous weather, increaſed the danger. But the gallant Rodney, like the intrepid Hawke, choſe to riſque ſomething, where the performance of a great national ſervice was the expected conſequence; and threw out the ſignal for a general chaſe, taking the lee-gage to cut off the enemy from the ſhore. Night came on; but the purſuit was ſtill continued. The ſhips of the Britiſh fleet cloſed with thoſe of the enemy as faſt as they could get up; and the action was not ended till two in the morning, when the Monarca, the headmoſt of the enemy's fleet, ſtruck to the Sandwich, admiral Rodney's ſhip. The San Domingo, one of the enemy's ſhips, blew up early in the engagement; and every ſoul on board periſhed. Four of their fleet, including the Phœnix of eighty guns, Don Juan Langara's ſhip, were taken and carried into Gibraltar. Two others had ſtruck; but after the officers had been ſhifted, were driven on ſhore by the tempeſtuous weather, and one of them was entirely loſt. The two frigates, and four ſhips of the line, alone eſcaped, two of the latter much damaged in the action. The enemy, although inferior in number, maintained a running fight with great bravery; and the victory was not obtained but at the expence of thirty-two killed, and one hundred and two wounded,

on

on board the Britiſh fleet. The weather continued ſo tempeſtuous, that it was with difficulty ſome of the Britiſh ſhips, on the day after the action, were able to extricate themſelves from the dangerous ſhoals of St. Lucar.

CHAP. XXXVIII. 1780.

Relief of Gibraltar.

The convoy being conducted ſafely to Gibraltar, and the proviſions and ſtores having been landed, admiral Digby, taking under his charge the Spaniſh prizes and homeward-bound tranſports, ſailed for England on the fifteenth of February, with the greateſt part of the fleet; and admiral Rodney, with the reſt, proceeded to his ſtation in the Weſt Indies. The homeward-bound fleet under admiral Digby got ſight of a French convoy, eſcorted by ſeveral ſhips of war, but at ſuch a diſtance that the greateſt part of it eſcaped by an early flight. The Prothée, a French ſhip of ſixty-four guns, one of the eſcort, was however taken, and ſome few of the merchant-ſhips.

Growing differences between Great Britain and Holland.

In the mean time the differences ſubſiſting between Great Britain and Holland were every day increaſing, and verging faſt towards a ſtate of hoſtility. The Dutch merchants, particularly thoſe of Amſterdam, had, from the beginning of the diſturbances in America, maintained a correſpondence with the people of that country, and in the progreſs of the war ſupplied them, not only with merchandiſe, but with warlike ſtores, without which the very unequal conteſt could not have been ſo long ſupported by the Americans. The carrying on a clandeſtine intercourſe of ſuch a nature, with thoſe whom Great Britain claimed as her ſubjects, was not to be endured, even in a nation ſtrictly neutral, and far leſs in one bound to her by the moſt ſolemn engagements of ancient friendſhip and alliance. Various remonſtrances on this ſubject were accordingly preſented by the Britiſh ambaſſador at the Hague, but no ſatisfaction was obtained. After the interference of France in the war, the unfriendly proceedings of the Dutch became ſtill more notorious: As they had

CHAP. XXXVIII. 1780.

heretofore supplied the Americans with whatever they wanted, and indeed still continued to do the same, so now they became the carriers of naval stores for the French. The remonstrances presented on this occasion having been found ineffectual, the commander of the British navy received orders to prevent a trade which the Dutch, from good faith, ought to have prohibited. In pursuance of these orders, such of the Dutch merchant-ships as were found laden with naval stores for the use of the French, were brought into British ports, from whence they were suffered to depart as soon as the prohibited articles had been landed; and in the mean time full satisfaction was made to the ship-owners for their freight. This proceeding, however equitable, produced much discontent among the Dutch merchants: They complained that by the seizure and detention of their vessels, the express letter of the treaties subsisting between Great Britain and the republic of the States General was grossly violated; whilst the real fact was, that they themselves, by furnishing the enemies of Great Britain with things necessary for carrying on the war, which this proceeding was calculated to prevent, were acting directly contrary to the spirit of all those treaties.

By the vigilance of the British cruisers this trade was in some degree checked; and the supplies, thus obtained by the French, became not a little precarious. But towards the beginning of the present year, a number of Dutch ships, laden with naval stores, being ready to sail for the ports of France, the owners availed themselves of the opportunity of the departure of a Dutch squadron that was proceeding to the Mediterranean, under the command of count Byland, to put their ships under his protection in their passage through the channel. Timely information of their design being conveyed to the British court, commodore Fielding was dispatched, with a sufficient force, to cruise in the channel, examine the Dutch convoy, and seize such of the ships as were found carrying on the trade

which

which Great Britain was determined to prohibit. The two fleets met in the channel on the third of January. Permiſſion to examine the convoy being refuſed, and the boats of the Britiſh fleet ſent for that purpoſe being fired upon, commodore Fielding fired a ſhot acroſs the way of the Dutch admiral, which was anſwered with a broadſide from the latter. The Britiſh commodore did not fail to return the ſalute, when the Dutch admiral ſtruck his colours. In the mean time the greateſt part of the convoy had borne away for the coaſt of France, and eſcaped: Thoſe that remained were ſafely conducted to Spithead, whither count Byland choſe to accompany them, to wait for orders from the States General, although he was told by commodore Fielding, that he was at liberty to proceed upon his voyage. This proceeding, bordering upon hoſtility, increaſed the clamours of the diſcontented in Holland, and added ſtrength to the party attached to France, which was already too powerful.

Armed neutrality, or aſſociation among neutral maritime powers, for the purpoſe of eſtabliſhing the doctrine, that free ſhips make free goods.

Whilſt Great Britain was thus availing herſelf of her maritime power to prevent the Dutch from ſupplying her enemies with the means of carrying on the war, another of her allies, upon whom ſhe had alſo ſtrong claims of friendſhip, was actively engaged in promoting a ſcheme for altering the received law of nations, and rendering ſuch a trade legitimate as the Dutch had been attempting to carry on with France. It was obviouſly the intent of the greater maritime powers, when engaged in war, that the ſhips of neutral nations ſhould be liable to a ſearch, and ſhould not protect enemy's property; and ſuch was hitherto held to be the law of nations, except in thoſe inſtances where it had been altered by treaties and conventions between particular powers: It was not leſs evidently the intereſt of the weaker commercial powers, when engaged in war, that the ſhips of neutral nations ſhould paſs free and unmoleſted; becauſe, whenever the ſtate of the war rendered them unable to carry on trade in their own ſhips, they might employ thoſe of neutral powers. The alteration propoſed

 by

by this scheme was, that a free ship should make free goods, or, in other words, that a neutral ship, although loaded with a cargo belonging to one of the powers at war, should pass as free and unmolested as in time of peace: A scheme evidently intended to wound Great Britain in her most essential interest; and, to her surprise, Russia was the power that brought it forward. In the war of the latter with the Turks some few years before, the conduct of Great Britain had been such as to entitle her to expect from Russia, support and assistance under her present embarrassments, rather than a regulation calculated to increase them. But with nations, if not with individuals, views of interest are the grand motives to action; and their policy consists in improving those opportunities that occur for promoting it: Friendship, gratitude, and the other virtuous affections that adorn private life, seem to have little influence upon their conduct. In a war between Great Britain and the kingdoms of France and Spain, the local situation of the former enables her in a great measure to cut off those supplies of naval stores which the north of Europe alone can furnish. Hence, in time of war between those powers, this kind of trade experiences considerable interruptions: Russia, Sweden, and Denmark, all partook of the loss arising from such interruptions: And the present embarrassed state of Great Britain was laid hold of as a fit opportunity for compelling her to submit to such a regulation as might remove the incovenience complained of by these northern powers. This scheme is said to have originated with the king of Sweden; but it was first promulgated by a declaration of the empress of Russia addressed to the belligerent powers, which was followed by declarations of the like import from the courts of Sweden and Denmark: The basis of the whole being, that neutral powers unconcerned in the war should be permitted to carry on their commerce in the same unlimited manner as in time of peace, those articles called contraband alone excepted. The other

neutral

neutral powers in Europe were invited to accede to the principles contained in thefe declarations; and as it was propofed to compel the practical execution of them by a maritime force, to be equipped by each of the contracting parties, hence the confederation gained the name of the armed neutrality.

The declaration of the emprefs of Ruffia being conformable to the prefent intereft of the courts of France and Spain, was received by them with the utmoft fatisfaction; and fuitable anfwers were returned. Great Britain alone was to fuftain an injury from it, and at another time, and under different circumftances, perhaps it might have been refented as an infult. But at prefent it was thought fit to return an anfwer which might neither give offence, nor derogate from the dignity of the Britifh nation by a tame fubmiffion to the claims of the northern powers. The anfwer was decent and refpectful: But, far from admitting the principles laid down by the emprefs of Ruffia, the general law of nations, as it had been hitherto underftood, was held out as the only rule of decifion in maritime cafes, except fo far as it had been altered by treaties between particular powers; and that between thofe powers the treaties of courfe furnifhed the rule. The emprefs was affured, that from the commencement of the war the ftricteft orders had been iffued to the Britifh naval commanders for refpecting her flag, and obferving all the ftipulations contained in the commercial treaty fubfifting between the two nations; and that the fame orders would be continued, and ftrictly executed. But fhould any infringement happen, the courts of admiralty, to whom the decifion in fuch cafes belonged, would afford redrefs in fo equitable a manner as fhould be perfectly fatisfactory to her imperial majefty.

By thefe proceedings of the northern powers it became fufficiently apparent that from them Great Britain was neither to expect affiftance nor fupport: And about this time it feems to have been determined

CHAP. XXXVIII. 1780.

mined in the Britiſh cabinet to put to the teſt the ſincerity of the Dutch, and try how far they were to be relied on for the performance of thoſe engagements to which they were bound by treaty. The ground of the alliance between Great Britain and Holland was mutual ſafety and protection; and in caſe either nation was attacked, the other was to furniſh certain ſuccours. Theſe had been already formally demanded, on the part of Great Britain, after Spain took a part in the war: But the States General had hitherto neglected either to furniſh the ſuccours, or give a ſatisfactory anſwer to the demand. The Britiſh ambaſſador at the Hague was now inſtructed to preſent a remonſtrance on the ſubject, to claim the ſuccours ſtipulated by treaty, and to declare, that, if a ſatisfactory anſwer was not given to this requiſition, within three weeks after the delivery of the remonſtrance, ſuch a neglect on the part of the States General would be conſidered as a declaration that they withdrew from the alliance between the two nations. The remonſtrance was accordingly preſented on the twenty-firſt of March, and no ſatisfactory anſwer being given within the time limited, the threat held out was put in execution. By an order of the king in council, bearing date the ſeventeenth of April, all the treaties ſubſiſting between the two nations were to be ſuſpended, and the ſubjects of the States General were in future to be entitled to no other privileges than thoſe enjoyed by neutral nations, unconnected with Great Britain by treaty.

Suſpenſion of the treaties between Great Britain and Holland. April.

By this deciſive meaſure the unfriendly diſpoſition of the Dutch towards the Britiſh nation was laid open, or, at leaſt, their total indifference about its fate: And it ſeems to have been wiſe policy in the Britiſh miniſtry to put that diſpoſition to the teſt; ſince it is ſafer to have an open enemy than an inſidious friend. Theſe ſeveral tranſactions, which happened ſoon after the beginning of the preſent year, diſcloſed the temper of moſt of the powers of Europe, upon whom Great Britain had any claim for aſſiſtance; and from them it became manifeſt, that ſhe muſt henceforward ſupport the conteſt againſt the united power of the houſe of Bourbon, not only without the aid of a ſingle ally, but under the conviction that the other nations of Europe viewed her danger with unconcern, and rather rejoiced in the proſpect of her ruin, than wiſhed to prevent it: A conviction mortifying no doubt in the extreme, but at the ſame time not entirely without its uſe, as it had a tendency to ſtimulate to the braveſt exertions thoſe who felt the genuine flame of patriotiſm, and whoſe love for their country was ſuperior to all the conſiderations of party.

May. Naval tranſactions.

Upon the death of ſir Charles Hardy, in the month of May, the command of the channel fleet was given to admiral Geary, who failed in queſt of the enemy, about the uſual time, with thirty ſhips of the line. During his cruiſe, in the beginning of July, he came in ſight of a fleet of about thirty ſail, which he afterwards found to be a convoy of French merchantmen from Port au Prince, in the Weſt Indies, bound to France. A general chaſe was immediately ordered; but it was evening before the headmoſt of the Britiſh fleet reached the enemy, and a fog ſoon afterwards coming on, twelve only of the merchantmen were taken. The reſt, with the two armed ſhips that accompanied them as a convoy, eſcaped in the fog.

The French and Spaniſh fleets again formed a junction this year, as they had done in the preceding one. They did not however attempt to enter the channel, but cruiſed in that tract through which the outward-bound trade from Great Britain to the Eaſt and Weſt Indies uſually paſſes, and from their number ſpread over an immenſe extent of ſea. A fleet for the Eaſt Indies, and another for the Weſt Indies, ſailed together from Portſmouth towards the end of July, under the convoy of captain Moutray of the Ramillies, attended by two frigates, and unfortunately, in the night of the eighth of Auguſt,

CHAP. XXXVIII. 1780.

August, fell in with that division of the combined fleet which was commanded by Don Lewis de Cordova. The Ramillies, with the two frigates, and a few merchantmen, escaped: All the rest, amounting to more than forty sail, were taken and carried into Cadiz. This misfortune was the more severely felt, as a number of the ships were loaded with naval and military stores for the use of the settlements in those parts of the world to which they were bound. Not long afterwads admiral Geary resigned his command, and was succeeded by admiral Darby.

The opposite grand fleets did not this year come in sight of each other: Of course nothing decisive was done by sea. But several hard-fought actions took place between single ships, in which British valour maintained its wonted superiority. In these actions the Belle Poule of thirty-two guns became a prize to the Nonsuch, commanded by sir James Wallace: The Artois and Pearl, two French frigates, were taken by commodore Johnstone, in the Romney; the Nymphe, by captain Peere Williams in the Flora; and the Count d'Artois, a private ship of war, mounting sixty-four guns, by captain Macbride in the Bienfaisant. Nor must we omit a gallant action performed by captain Moor, of the Fame, private ship of war belonging to Dublin, who alone attacked five French privateers, drawn up to receive him off Cape de Gat, and captured four of them.

The siege and blockade of Gibraltar was still continued by the Spaniards; but with no greater prospect of success than when it commenced. The danger of a famine, arising from the long continuance of the blockade, was averted by the supplies which admiral Rodney conveyed in the beginning of the year: And all the other efforts of the Spaniards to reduce it, were either prevented from taking effect by the vigilance of general Elliott, or successfully resisted by the determined spirit and persevering bravery of the garrison.

After

After relieving Gibraltar, in the manner already related, admiral Rodney proceeded to his ſtation in the Weſt Indies, and arrived at St. Lucie on the twenty-ſeventh of March. The reinforcement of ſhips, which he carried out, brought the contending fleets nearer to an equality; the ſuperiority in numbers ſtill, however, remaining with the French. But although, before the arrival of admiral Rodney, the French fleet was ſo much ſuperior to that of Great Britain in the Weſt India ſeas, no advantage was obtained proportioned to that ſuperiority: On the contrary, the trade of the enemy had been greatly annoyed, their force leſſened by the capture of ſeveral of their frigates, and the empire of the ſea diſputed with an undaunted firmneſs which no ſuperiority in number could diſmay. Only two days before the arrival of admiral Rodney, monſieur de la Motte Piquet, who was cruiſing with four ſhips of ſeventy-four guns, and two frigates, for the protection of the French trade, fell in with and attacked three Britiſh ſhips of war, one of them mounting ſixty-four, another fifty, and the third only forty-four guns, the largeſt commanded by the honourable captain Cornwallis. Notwithſtanding the great diſparity both in number and force, the Britiſh commander gallantly prepared to receive the enemy's attack, and to give a new diſplay of Britiſh valour on that element on which it ſeems peculiarly deſtined to ſhine. The engagement began about five in the afternoon, and was continued during the whole night, and part of the following day, when the combatants ſeparated, as if by mutual conſent, to repair their reſpective damages. On the third day in the morning, a Britiſh ſhip of ſixty-four guns, and two frigates, having appeared in ſight, captain Cornwallis reſolutely bore down upon the enemy to bring them again to action: But the French ſquadron had ſuffered ſo much in the firſt engagement, that monſieur de la Motte Piquet declined to renew it, notwithſtanding the ſuperiority of force he ſtill poſſeſſed. Alſo, previous to the arrival of admiral

CHAP. XXXVIII. 1780.

admiral Rodney, the count de Guichen, with twenty-five ſhips of the line, eight frigates, and a number of tranſports with troops, had appeared before St. Lucie, and diſcovered an apparent deſign of attacking it; but after viewing the diſpoſitions made on ſhore, by general Vaughan, and the judicious arrangement of the ſquadron under admiral Hyde Parker, for repelling the attack, he thought proper to return to Martinique, without making the attempt. This viſit was returned by ſir George Rodney ſoon after his arrival. On the ſecond of April he ſailed for Fort Royal Bay, in Martinique, to offer battle to the enemy, and approached near enough to exchange ſome ſhot with their batteries on ſhore. The count de Guichen however did not think fit to come out: And admiral Rodney, after remaining two days before Fort Royal, and endeavouring in vain to provoke the enemy to an engagement, returned to St. Lucie, leaving ſome faſt-ſailing veſſels to bring the earlieſt intelligence of any movement that ſhould be made by them.

Nothing happened till the fifteenth of April, when, in the middle of the night, the count de Guichen came out of Fort Royal harbour, and ſailed with twenty-three ſhips of the line, and a number of frigates. Immediate intelligence being conveyed to ſir George Rodney, he inſtantly put to ſea, with twenty ſhips of the line. On the ſixteenth, he got ſight of the enemy, and on the ſeventeenth, after various manœuvres practiſed on both ſides, by the one to elude, and by the other to force an engagement, the French fleet was brought to action. The firing began about one, and did not ceaſe till four in the afternoon. The Sandwich, ſir George Rodney's ſhip, after beating three of the enemy's fleet in ſucceſſion, out of the line, engaged with the Couronne, the count de Guichen's ſhip, ſupported by two others, the Triumphant and Fendant, and, although alone, maintained this unequal combat for an hour and a half, at the end of which the French admiral bore away. At this time the enemy might

might be ſaid to be completely beaten; but ſuch was the diſtance of the van and the rear from the centre of the Britiſh fleet, and ſuch the crippled ſtate of ſeveral of the ſhips, particularly the Sandwich, which for twenty-four hours was with difficulty kept above water, that an immediate purſuit could not be ordered with any proſpect of advantage. In the mean time every endeavour was uſed to refit the diſabled ſhips; and on the twentieth, the Britiſh commander again deſcried the enemy. He purſued them, for three days ſucceſſively, but without effect. They ſtudiouſly avoided an engagement, and endeavoured to puſh for Fort Royal in Martinique. From this retreat they were however cut off by ſir George Rodney, who had penetrated their intention in time to counteract it; and they were at laſt obliged to take ſhelter under Guadaloupe. In the action the loſs of men on board the Britiſh fleet amounted to one hundred and twenty killed, and three hundred and fifty-three wounded: That of the French in killed and wounded was ſaid to be near one thouſand. Although a victory was undoubtedly obtained, it is plain, from the Britiſh commander's diſpatches, that it was not ſo complete as he wiſhed, and had reaſon to expect at the beginning of the action: And although blame is not directly imputed to any of the officers under him, it is apparent that he thought himſelf not well ſupported by ſome of them. Sir George Rodney, finding, from an ineffectual purſuit of three days, that it was in vain to follow the enemy any farther, judged it beſt, as the next poſſible chance of bringing them again to action, to be off Fort Royal in Martinique before them, the only harbour in the Weſt Indies where they could repair their damages. To Fort Royal he accordingly directed his courſe, and continued to cruiſe off Martinique, until the condition of ſome of his own ſhips obliged him to return to Gros Iſlet Bay in St. Lucie to refit.

CHAP. XXXVIII. 1780.

The ſick and wounded having been landed, and the fleet watered and refitted, the Britiſh commander receiving information by his cruiſers, on the ſixth of May, that the French fleet was approaching to windward of Martinique, immediately ſailed in queſt of it with nineteen ſhips of the line, two ſhips of fifty guns, and ſome frigates. After beating to windward for ſeveral days, he at laſt got ſight of the object of his wiſhes: But it was not the intention of the count de Guichen to riſque an engagement, and being to windward, he had it much in his power to avoid it; yet not ſo effectually, but that the rear of his fleet was brought to action by the van of ſir George Rodney's on the fifteenth and nineteenth of May, and on both days the advantage was manifeſtly on the ſide of the latter. After the laſt of theſe actions the French fleet ſtood to the northward with ſuch a preſs of ſail, that in three days their whole fleet was out of ſight. Their ſuperiority in ſailing was ſuch, that all further purſuit ſeemed in vain; and ſir George Rodney, having been led in chaſe of them already forty leagues to windward of Martinique, proceeded to Barbadoes to refit ſuch of his ſhips as had been diſabled in the late engagements. The abſence of the Britiſh fleet afforded an opportunity to the count de Guichen, which he did not fail to embrace, of returning with his ſhattered ſquadron to the harbour of Fort Royal.

That ſir George Rodney ſhould put his fleet in the beſt poſſible ſtate, and that he ſhould occupy a windward ſtation, became the more neceſſary, in conſequence of information, received by him about this time, of the approach of a fleet from Spain, which if ſuffered unmoleſted to join that of France, would give to the latter a dangerous ſuperiority. The Spaniſh fleet, of which he received information, had ſailed from Cadiz on the twenty-eighth of April, under the command of Don Joſeph Solano, and conſiſted of twelve ſhips

ſhips of the line, a proportionable number of frigates, and eighty-three transſports, having on board near twelve thouſand troops, and a conſiderable train of artillery. That the Britiſh admiral might not loſe the opportunity of intercepting this armament, he uſed the greateſt diſpatch in refitting his fleet at Barbadoes; and having put to ſea as ſoon as it was in readineſs, cruiſed in that latitude, in which, according to the information conveyed to him, there was the greateſt chance of meeting with Don Solano. But the extreme caution of the latter proved the means of his ſafety, and defeated all the attempts of the Britiſh admiral to intercept him. Inſtead of ſailing directly to Fort Royal Bay in Martinique, the appointed place of rendezvous, he kept more to the northward, and ſtopped ſhort at Guadaloupe, diſpatching a frigate to acquaint count de Guichen of his arrival, and requeſting a junction where he then was. The count de Guichen, upon receiving this intelligence, immediately ſailed, with eighteen ſhips of the line, and keeping to leeward of the iſlands, joined the Spaniſh ſquadron under Dominique.

The combined fleet now poſſeſſed ſo great a ſuperiority, that it had nothing to fear from ſir George Rodney; and the land force, that accompanied it, was ſo conſiderable as to portend ruin to the Britiſh intereſt in the Weſt Indies by the ſucceſſive reduction of all the iſlands. It was generally ſuppoſed that the conqueſt of Jamaica was the principal object of the Spaniſh armament, in effecting which the French fleet, without doubt, was to co-operate. But the Spaniſh troops had been ſo crowded on board the tranſports, that a peſtilential diſtemper broke out amongſt them: And it raged with ſuch violence about the time of their arrival in the Weſt Indies, that it became neceſſary to land the men in order to check its progreſs. For this purpoſe the combined fleet proceeded to Fort Royal Bay in Martinique: And the allies were for a time obliged to ſuſpend their operations.

CHAP. XXXVIII. 1780.

Sir George Rodney having been disappointed in his design of intercepting the Spanish squadron, returned to Gros Islet Bay in St. Lucie, as the most convenient station for obtaining early intelligence of any movement made by the enemy. Although their numbers had been lessened by the contagious distemper, they were still in sufficient force to have attempted the conquest of Jamaica with every prospect of success: But a difference of opinion between the two commanders proved fatal to the expedition. After remaining inactive for several weeks in the bay of Fort Royal, the combined fleets put to sea in the night of the fifth of July, without making signals or shewing lights, and directed their course to Saint Domingo. Here they separated, the count de Guichen with the French fleet putting in to Cape François, whilst Don Solano with the Spanish fleet proceeded to the Havannah. The count de Guichen remained at Cape François only until the homeward-bound trade from the French islands had assembled, when, taking it under his protection, he sailed directly for Europe.

July.

Sir George Rodney probably concluded that the count de Guichen only meant to convoy the trade to a certain latitude, and then proceed to the continent of America to execute the plan concerted with general Washington; and that he might be in readiness to thwart the count's operations there, as he had already done in the West Indies, he sailed for New York with eleven ships of the line and four frigates, where he arrived in September, as has been already related. But the truth was, that the count de Guichen's fleet was not in a condition to execute his part of the plan: His ships had been so shattered in his different engagements with sir George Rodney, that he found it necessary to return as speedily as possible to Europe, to give them a thorough repair.

In the mean time an incident occurred, which opened more fully to the view of the British cabinet, the hostile designs of the Dutch.

So

So long ago as the month of September in the year 1778, a private interview had taken place at Aix la Chapelle, between William Lee, formerly an alderman of London, and then an agent for the American congreſs, and John de Neufville, a merchant of Amſterdam, acting under powers delegated to him by Van Berkel, grand penſionary of that city. The object of their interview was to plan the outlines of a commercial treaty, which might be proper to be entered into between the revolted colonies in America and the Seven United Provinces: And at the concluſion of their conferences, certain proviſionary articles were agreed upon, and ſigned by the reſpective agents, as thoſe upon the baſis of which a treaty might be hereafter formed. Duplicates of the articles were tranſmitted both to Holland and America; and great ſecrecy obſerved to prevent the tranſaction from coming to the knowledge of the Britiſh court. All this was done, whilſt the Dutch were pretending to act the part of good and faithful allies to the king of Great Britain, and at his requiſition formally prohibiting, in appearance, an intercourſe between their ſubjects and the revolted colonies: And perhaps it was not their original intention to carry the matter farther, but to ſuffer the clandeſtine commerce between the Dutch dominions and America, to be conducted agreeably to the proviſions of this unfiniſhed arrangement, during the continuance of the war, at the end of which the proceedings of John de Neufville might be either confirmed or diſavowed, as ſuited their intereſt; and accordingly nothing farther was done towards completing the treaty for near two years. But the finances of the congreſs had become deranged, and their paper money had been depreciated to ſuch an extent, that they ſaw it would be impoſſible to maintain the conteſt much longer without the aid of a foreign loan, which they found from experience could only be negotiated in Holland: And even there the monied men were averſe to truſting their property upon ſuch ſecurity as a people could

CHAP. XXXVIII. 1780.

could offer, whose sovereignty and independence were yet unacknowledged by the States General. Besides the general interest, therefore, which the congress had in getting the independence of the American states acknowledged by as many of the European powers as possible, they had a peculiar interest in procuring that acknowledgment from the States General, in order to facilitate the negotiation of the proposed loan; and they were encouraged to hope for success in their solicitations to that end, partly from the favourable disposition of the inhabitants of Amsterdam towards their cause, who had already tasted the sweets of the American commerce, and partly from the prevalence of a party which the intrigues of the court of France had raised in Holland in opposition to the Stadtholder and the British interest.

Commercial treaty between America and Holland.

Moved by such considerations, the congress in the present year appointed their late president, Henry Laurens, to proceed to Holland as their ambassador, with full powers to bring the commercial treaty to a conclusion. Mr. Laurens accordingly embarked at Philadelphia in a vessel bound to Holland, carrying with him all the papers that in any manner related to the object of his mission, and particularly the provisional commercial articles settled between William Lee and John de Neufville. But the vessel was taken on her passage to Europe, and with her Mr. Laurens and his papers; the box containing them, which had been thrown overboard, having been prevented from sinking by the alertness of a British seaman.

Mr. Laurens's papers having furnished the British ministry with full evidence of what they had long before suspected, the unfriendly disposition of the Dutch, their connexion with the revolted colonies, and the underhand practices of the pensionary Van Berkel to make that connexion still closer; they determined to demand instant satisfaction for the injury. For that purpose the papers, which afforded the evidence, were transmitted to the British ambassador at

the

the Hague, who was inſtructed to preſent a memorial to the States General, requiring them to diſavow the proceedings of the penſionary Van Berkel and his accomplices, and to inflict upon them a puniſhment ſuitable to the magnitude of their offence: He was further enjoined to declare, that, if ſatisfaction in theſe reſpects ſhould be either refuſed or delayed, the States General would be conſidered as making themſelves parties to the injury, and ſuch meaſures be purſued as the law of nations authoriſed for compelling a reparation of the wrong. The memorial was accordingly preſented; and no ſatisfactory anſwer being returned by the States General within the time expected, the Britiſh ambaſſador was recalled from the Hague, and on the twentieth of December, letters of repriſal were ordered to be iſſued againſt the Dutch. In the mean time Mr. Laurens, after an examination before the ſecretaries of ſtate, was committed on a charge of high treaſon a cloſe priſoner to the Tower of London.

War on the part of Great Britain againſt the Dutch.

CHAP. XXXIX.

French Attempt on the Iſland of Jerſey—Defeated—Naval Exertions of both France and Britain—Relief of Gibraltar—Capture of the Dutch Iſland St. Euſtatius—And of Demarary and Iſſequibo, Dutch Settlements on the Spaniſh Main—Fruitleſs Attempt of the French on St. Lucie—The Iſland of Tobago ſurrendered to the French.

CHAP. XXXIX. 1781.

HOSTILITIES againſt the Dutch began on the part of Great Britain by the detention of ſuch of their veſſels as were in Britiſh harbours, until it ſhould be known in what manner Britiſh veſſels were treated in their ports. The rich harveſt expected from the capture of the Dutch merchantmen excited a freſh ſpirit of enterpriſe amongſt the Britiſh ſhip-owners: Numerous privateers were fitted out; and in a ſhort time their trade was greatly annoyed. Meaſures were alſo taken, and orders ſent to the Britiſh commanders abroad, for ſeizing their foreign poſſeſſions: And ſo valuable did the Dutch commerce appear in every quarter, that the policy of the Britiſh miniſtry, in peremptorily requiring them to fulfil their engagements, and ſhew themſelves either ſincere and uſeful allies, or open and avowed enemies, ſeemed fully juſtified.

French attempt on the iſland of Jerſey,

The French began the year 1781, with renewing their attempt upon the iſland of Jerſey, in which they had failed two years before. The command of the expedition was given to the baron de Rullicourt, an officer of courage; but of a temper hot, intractable, violent, and ferocious. About two thouſand men were aſſigned for the ſervice: And with theſe embarked in tranſports he ſailed from the coaſt of France, in dark and ſtormy weather, hoping thereby more completely to ſurpriſe the iſland. Nearly one half of the tranſports were obliged to put back in diſtreſs to the coaſt of France; but with the reſt the baron perſiſted in his deſign, and having paſſed the dangerous ſhoals of La Roque Platte, where ſeveral of his veſſels were wrecked, and a number of his troops loſt, he landed unperceived in the night of the ſixth of January, with eight hundred men, at a place called the Baue de Violet. From thence he marched during the night to St. Helier's, the capital of the iſland, and early in the morning ſeizing the avenues, was in poſſeſſion of the town before the inhabitants were aware of his landing. Not long after the French reached St. Helier's, major Corbet, the lieutenant-governor, was made a priſoner; but not, it ſeems, till he had an opportunity of diſpatching meſſengers to give the alarm at the other ſtations occupied by the troops aſſigned for the defence of the iſland. The lieutenant-governor being a priſoner, the baron de Rullicourt required him to ſign a capitulation for the ſurrender of the iſland, threatening, if he refuſed, to reduce the town of St. Helier's to aſhes, and put the inhabitants to the ſword. To avoid ſuch dreadful conſequences, major Corbet too eaſily thought fit to comply, after having in vain repreſented, that no act done by him whilſt a priſoner could be binding, either upon the troops or inhabitants. Elizabeth Caſtle was then ſummoned to ſurrender under the terms of the capitulation; but captain Aylward, who commanded, aſſiſted by captain Mulcaſter, of the engineers, peremptorily refuſed: And the French, who had advanced to the gate, placing the lieutenant-governor in their front, were fired upon and compelled to retire.

In the mean time major Pierſon, upon whom the command of the troops devolved, after the lieutenant-governor became a priſoner, having collected them from their different ſtations, and aſſembled as many of the militia as could be got together, advanced againſt the

 town,

CHAP. XXXIX. 1781.

town, and ſeized the heights adjoining to it. Whilſt he lay in this ſituation he received a ſummons to ſurrender, agreeably to the capitulation; to which he gallantly anſwered, that unleſs the French themſelves laid down their arms, and ſurrendered within twenty minutes, they might expect to be attacked. An able diſpoſition of his troops was accordingly made; and at the end of that time, the town being aſſaulted on all ſides, the French were ſo fiercely charged, that they retreated from every quarter to the market-place. Here, their force being concentered, the action was renewed with freſh vigour under the eye of their general, who, diveſting himſelf of the magnanimity attached to the character of an officer, and even of the feelings belonging to a man, kept by his ſide the lieutenant-governor during the heat of the battle, expoſing him, although a priſoner, to the fire of the Britiſh troops. But at length, the baron de Rullicourt received a mortal wound: When the ſecond in command, ſeeing his troops unable any longer to withſtand the impetuoſity of the aſſailants, and his own ſituation hopeleſs, requeſted the lieutenant-governor to reſume his authority, and accept the ſubmiſſion of him and his troops as priſoners of war. In the attack of St. Helier's, the loſs of the aſſailants was not ſo great as might have been expected: Of the Britiſh regulars twelve only were killed, and thirty-ſix wounded; and of the militia four were killed, and twenty-nine wounded. But the death of the brave major Pierſon, who fell at the end of the action and in the moment of complete victory, filled every one with regret. To his gallantry and good conduct, and to the brave exertions of the officers and troops under him, his country was indebted on the preſent occaſion for the ſafety of Jerſey. Although moſt of the troops were new levies, they fought with the firmneſs of veterans: And the loſs ſuſtained by the militia ſhews that they were entitled to a full ſhare of merit for the ſucceſs of the day. Of the enemy not one eſcaped, all who ſurvived the action being made pri-

defeated.

ſoners of war. In this manner ended the ſecond expedition undertaken by the French againſt the iſland of Jerſey, under all its circumſtances more diſaſtrous to them than the firſt.

Naval exertions of both France and Britain.

In the mean time they were ſtraining every nerve to place their marine upon a more reſpectable footing, and to fit out ſuch a fleet as might give them a decided ſuperiority in the Weſt Indies during the following ſummer: Whilſt the Britiſh miniſtry on the other hand exerted themſelves not leſs ſtrenuouſly, to equip ſuch a force as might be adequate to the various ſervices which the war in its extenſion required them to provide for. That which was the moſt preſſing, and demanded their immediate attention, was the relief of the garriſon of Gibraltar, more endangered by the want of ſupplies, in conſequence of the blockade, than by the tremendous fire from the enemy's batteries. Gibraltar having received no ſupplies ſince thoſe conveyed by ſir George Rodney in the beginning of the preceding year, both the garriſon and inhabitants were at this time in the utmoſt diſtreſs for want of proviſions. The allowance to the garriſon had been reduced to a pound and a half in the week of ſalted meat for each man, which at length became ſo bad as to be ſcarcely eatable. Freſh proviſions, when they could be procured, ſold at the moſt enormous prices: Pigs at two guineas, turkies at three, geeſe at thirty ſhillings, fowls and ducks at ten ſhillings, damaged biſcuit at a ſhilling the pound, peaſe at eighteen-pence; and all other neceſſaries in proportion. Fuel was ſo ſcarce, that it was with difficulty enough was found for dreſſing their victuals. Theſe diſtreſſes were known in England: The neceſſity of attempting to relieve the garriſon was of courſe urgent; but the difficulty of accompliſhing it was great. The Spaniſh fleet, under Don Louis de Cordova, had orders to cruiſe upon the coaſt of Portugal, and was repreſented to conſiſt of thirty ſhips of the line: A French fleet, not much inferior, was almoſt in readineſs to put to ſea from Breſt; and all the force, which

which the Britiſh miniſtry could ſpare from other ſervices for the relief of Gibraltar, conſiſted only of twenty-eight ſhips of the line. Theſe, however, were commanded by the admirals Darby, Digby, and Roſs, all of them officers of great profeſſional reputation. With this fleet admiral Darby ſailed from Portſmouth on the thirteenth of March, taking under his convoy the trade bound to the Eaſt and Weſt Indies; and having touched at Cork to receive the tranſports with proviſions, and afterwards conducted the outward-bound trade as far as was thought neceſſary, he left them to purſue their voyage, and ſteered directly for the bay of Cadiz; into the harbour of which Don Louis de Cordova, upon receiving intelligence of admiral Darby's approach, had thought fit to retire with the Spaniſh fleet, without daring to riſque an engagement. Whilſt admiral Darby cruiſed off Cadiz and the mouth of the Straits, keeping the Spaniſh fleet in port, the tranſports with the proviſions and ſtores proceeded to the place of their deſtination, under the convoy of the diviſion of the Britiſh fleet commanded by admiral ſir John Lockhart Roſs: And thus, to the utter mortification of Spain, Gibraltar was a ſecond time relieved, and ſupplied with every thing neceſſary for ſuſtaining the ſiege.

Relief of Gibraltar.

Whilſt the Britiſh fleet was abſent on this ſervice, that of France deſtined for the Weſt India ſtation, and conſiſting of twenty-one ſhips of the line, ſailed from Breſt under the command of the count de Graſſe. The French poſſeſſions in that quarter, from the inferiority of the ſquadron left for their protection by the count de Guichen when he returned to France at the end of the preceding ſummer, had been expoſed to the attempts of the Britiſh commanders during the winter, and probably ſome of them owed their ſafety to the war with Holland. Sir George Rodney, after remaining at New York until the hurricane ſeaſon was over, returned to the Weſt Indies towards the cloſe of the former year, and in conjunction with general

general Vaughan was meditating a defcent upon fome of the French iflands, when he received information of the rupture with the Dutch, and inftructions to commence hoftilities againft their Weft India poffeffions. Of thefe the little ifland of St. Euftatius claimed the firft attention, not from its intrinfic value, but as being a general depot of merchandife, from whence not only the American colonies, but the French iflands alfo, derived confiderable fupplies: And it was the more obnoxious to Britifh vengeance, that the commerce between it and the American colonies, connived at by the States General, was the original caufe of difference between the two nations, which at laft produced an open rupture. Of fmall extent, of barren foil, and without any native productions of value, the ifland of St. Euftatius was of no importance, except from its commerce. Being a free port, it was inhabited by people of all nations, who reforted thither for the fake of carrying on commerce with their refpective countries; and during the prefent war, from the great demands for merchandife of all kinds in America, the trade of the ifland had increafed to an amazing extent. So confiderable was the importation of merchandife into St. Euftatius, that the bulkier articles, for want of room in the warehoufes, lay in the ftreets. The whole ifland was a kind of natural fortification, with only one convenient landing-place; but nothing had been done towards improving thofe defenfive advantages, nor was it even provided with any thing like a fufficient garrifon. Such was the fituation of St. Euftatius, when fir George Rodney and general Vaughan, on the third of February, appeared before it with a force of fhips and troops more proportioned to the importance than to the difficulty of the acquifition. A fummons was immediately fent to the governor, requiring him to furrender the ifland; with which, knowing its defencelefs ftate, and his utter inability to make any effectual refiftance, he thought it prudent without delay to comply: And thus the ifland of St. Euftatius, with all

February.

its

CHAP. XXXIX. 1781. Capture of the Dutch ifland St. Euftatius;

its ftores of merchandife, was furrendered at difcretion to the Britifh navy and army. The value of the merchandife thus furrendered was fuppofed to amount to four millions; and whatever parts of it belonged to the Dutch, the French, or the Americans, unqueftionably became lawful prize to the captors. But feveral Britifh agents having fettled there for the purpofe, as they pretended, of purchafing American produce under the implied fanction of an act of parliament, it became a queftion, whether the property of fuch perfons, confidered as inhabitants of St. Euftatius, was or was not fubject to confifcation. Perhaps fome diftinction ought to have been made between thofe Britifh agents, who had *bona fide* fettled in St. Euftatius for the purpofe aforefaid, and thofe who were alfo concerned in carrying on an illegal intercourfe, either with the revolted fubjects of Great Britain, or her open and avowed enemies; and poffibly it was not an eafy matter to make the proper difcrimination. However this might be, the proceedings of the Britifh commanders with refpect to the property of fuch perfons, became afterwards the fubject of much controverfy in the courts of law, and of great vexation to the captors themfelves, in confequence of the oppofite decifions given by fome of the tribunals before whom the St. Euftatius prize caufes were fucceffively carried.

A Dutch frigate of thirty-fix guns, five fhips of war of inferior force, and more than one hundred and fifty fail of merchantmen, were taken in the bay; and a fleet of thirty fhips richly laden, which had failed from St. Euftatius for Holland two days before its capture, were purfued, overtaken, and brought back, together with their convoy, a fhip of fixty guns, commanded by an admiral. The furrender of St. Euftatius was followed by that of the iflands of St. Martin and Saba in its vicinity; and the Dutch colours having been kept flying upon the forts of the captured iflands for fome time after the furrender, a number of French, American, and Dutch veffels veſſels were decoyed by the ſnare, and became an eaſy prey to the new poſſeſſors.

After the capture of St. Euſtatius, general Cunningham, governor of Barbadoes, ſent a ſummons, by captain Pender, of his majeſty's ſloop Barbuda, to the inhabitants of the Dutch ſettlements upon the Spaniſh main bordering on the river Demarary and Iſſequibo, informing them of that event, and requiring them to ſurrender to his majeſty's arms. Theſe were new ſettlements, but from the richneſs of their ſoil of great future expectation. Being totally unprovided for defence, the inhabitants, in anſwer to the ſummons, ſent a deputation to governor Cunningham, with an offer to ſurrender upon the ſuppoſed terms granted to St. Euſtatius. In the mean time a ſquadron of Britiſh privateers, chiefly belonging to the port of Briſtol, upon hearing of the Dutch war, united their force, and boldly entering the rivers Demarary and Iſſequibo, cut out even from under the Dutch forts and batteries, and brought off, almoſt all the Dutch ſhips of value in either river. The deputies ſent from theſe ſettlements to governor Cunningham, of Barbadoes, were by him referred to ſir George Rodney and general Vaughan at St. Euſtatius, who diſdaining to take any advantage of the improvident offer of the inhabitants to ſhare the ſame fate as the people of St. Euſtatius, and thinking that a line of diſtinction ought to be drawn between the inhabitants of thoſe Dutch colonies, who, previouſly to the commencement of hoſtilities againſt Holland, had openly aſſiſted the enemies of Great Britain, in violation of the treaties ſubſiſting between the two nations, and ſuch as, occupied in their own domeſtic affairs, had given no ſuch provocation, granted to the deputies, terms of capitulation ſufficiently liberal, by which the inhabitants of thoſe ſettlements were ſecured in the full poſſeſſion of their civil government and private property.

and of Demarary and Iſſequibo, Dutch ſettlements on the Spaniſh main.

CHAP. XXXIX. 1781. Whilſt ſir George Rodney remained at St. Euſtatius, and before he had finiſhed the variety of buſineſs in which he was involved, by the capture of that iſland, the diſpoſal of the merchandiſe found in it, and the claims of the Britiſh merchants, advice was brought to him of the ſailing of count de Graſſe from Breſt, with the French fleet deſtined for the Weſt Indies. Upon receiving this intelligence, ſir Samuel Hood and rear-admiral Drake were immediately diſpatched to windward with eighteen ſhips of the line, to endeavour to intercept and bring the count de Graſſe to action, before his force was increaſed by the junction of the French ſquadron already at Martinique. April. Theſe admirals accordingly proceeded to Fort Royal Bay, off which they cruized until the twenty-eighth of April, when the advanced ſhips announced by ſignal the approach of the French fleet. A general chaſe to windward was immediately ordered, and the line of battle a-head formed, which was continued during the whole night, in order more effectually to cut off the French fleet from the harbour of Fort Royal. In the morning the French fleet was ſtill to windward, and the convoy cloſe in with the land: It was of courſe in the power of the count de Graſſe, by bearing down, to engage when he pleaſed; but he kept at a diſtance, and avoided an engagement. Every exertion was made by the Britiſh commanders to bring him to action, and in the courſe of the various evolutions practiſed by them with this intention, the French ſquadron in Fort Royal Bay unfortunately found an opportunity of coming out and joining their admiral. By the junction, he acquired a ſuperiority of force over the Britiſh fleet, in the proportion of twenty-four to eighteen, but ſtill avoided a cloſe engagement. The endeavours of the Britiſh commanders to come up with him were nevertheleſs unremittingly continued; and they ſo far ſucceeded, as to bring on a partial action. Only the van and ſome ſhips of the centre of the Britiſh fleet could

could get near enough to engage; and in their ftruggles to clofe with the enemy, they were for a confiderable time expofed to a great fuperiority of fire, and fuftained much damage. The lofs of men was not great; but at the end of the engagement, which lafted about three hours, the Ruffel was found to have received fo many fhots between wind and water, that fhe was obliged to bear away for the ifland of St. Euftatius to refit: Four other fhips were alfo much difabled. The enemy did not efcape without damage; but their fuperiority of force ftill remained. The next morning fir Samuel Hood endeavoured to gain the wind of the enemy, that he might engage with lefs difadvantage; but it was to no purpofe. At laft, finding all his efforts ineffectual, and feveral of his fhips fo crippled as to be unfit for immediate action, he bore away for Antigua to get them refitted, and was followed by the count de Graffe, with the whole French fleet. The next day fome fhips in the rear of the Britifh fleet being in danger of being cut off, fir Samuel Hood bore down with the van and centre for their protection, and made fo refolute a ftand, that the count de Graffe, notwithftanding his great fuperiority, did not dare to perfift in the attempt; but foon afterwards gave over the purfuit, and returned to Martinique.

Whilft the Britifh fleet proceeded to Antigua to refit, an attempt was made by the French to regain poffeffion of the ifland of St. Lucie. In the night between the tenth and eleventh of May, a force from Martinique, commanded by the vifcount Damas, acting under the orders of the marquis de Bouillé, who accompanied him, landed upon the ifland in three different places, and early the next morning furprifed the town of Gros Iflet, and made prifoners fome fick of the forty-fixth regiment that were in the hofpital. Pigeon Ifland, which commanded the anchorage-ground in Gros Iflet Bay, and was garrifoned by a company of the eighty-feventh regiment, under the command of captain Campbell, and fome feamen under the direction of

May.

CHAP. XXXIX. 1781.

lieutenant Miller, of the navy, was immediately ſummoned to ſurrender, with a threat, that the garriſon, in caſe of refuſal, might expect to ſuffer all the ſeverities authoriſed by the laws of war: But captain Campbell, the commanding officer, bravely bid defiance to the enemy, and reſolved to defend his poſt to the laſt extremity. On the day after the landing of the troops, the count de Graſſe appeared with twenty-five ſhips of the line, and ſtood in for Gros Iſlet Bay, as if with intention to anchor; but was ſoon obliged to alter his deſign, and fall to leeward, in conſequence of a well-directed fire from the batteries on Pigeon Iſland. In the mean time general St. Leger, who commanded at St. Lucie, had made a moſt judicious diſpoſition of his little force for the defence of the iſland: And the fortunate arrival of a frigate and two ſloops of war, ſupplied him with a reinforcement of ſeamen to aſſiſt in manning the batteries. So determined an appearance of reſiſtance entirely diſconcerted the views of the French commanders, who had expected an eaſy conqueſt. The enterpriſe was in conſequence abandoned: Their troops were re-embarked in the night: And the next morning their whole fleet returned to Martinique.

Fruitleſs attempt of the French on St. Lucie.

This fruitleſs attempt upon St. Lucie was followed by another againſt the iſland of Tobago, which proved more ſucceſsful. A ſmall ſquadron of ſhips from Martinique appeared before it on the twenty-third of May, having on board twelve hundred troops, under the command of the ſieur Blanchelande, governor of St. Vincent's, who effected a landing the next day. The whole force that could be collected for the defence of the iſland, did not exceed five hundred men of all denominations, including regulars, militia, and ſome armed negroes. With theſe governor Ferguſon took a ſtrong poſition on Mount Concordia, having firſt diſpatched an advice-boat to Barbadoes, with intelligence of the attack. Mount Concordia was an eligible ſituation, becauſe from thence both ſides of the iſland might

might be diſtinctly ſeen; and in this poſition the governor, and major Stanhope, who commanded the regular troops, defended themſelves until the firſt of June. Immediately after the landing of the French troops, a ſummons was ſent to the governor to ſurrender the iſland, and an offer was made to grant the moſt favourable terms; but both were inſtantly rejected. Threats were then made, that unleſs the militia returned to their homes, their plantations would be burnt: But theſe alſo were diſregarded. The ſieur Blanchelande, ſeeing ſuch a ſhew of reſiſtance, diſpatched a veſſel to Martinique, requeſting a reinforcement. His requeſt was inſtantly complied with: And a powerful reinforcement, commanded by the marquis de Bouillé in perſon, and accompanied by the count de Graſſe, with the whole French fleet of twenty-five ſhips of the line, arrived at Tobago on the thirty-firſt of May. Upon the arrival of the French fleet with this reinforcement, a council of war was held between the governor and his garriſon: And the engineers being of opinion that Mount Concordia was no longer tenable againſt ſo ſuperior force, a reſolution was unanimouſly taken to retreat to a ſtill ſtronger poſition upon the main ridge, the approach to which was by a road of ſome miles in length, ſo narrow that two men could not walk abreaſt, and inacceſſible on each ſide by impenetrable foreſts. In purſuance of this reſolution the garriſon left Mount Concordia at one in the morning of the firſt of June, unperceived by the enemy, and without moleſtation reached the defile leading to the main ridge before eight.

No movement perhaps was ever more critically executed, preparations having been made by the enemy for ſtorming the Britiſh lines at Mount Concordia on the ſame morning on which the garriſon had evacuated them. And as the marquis de Bouillé, in conſequence of the great ſuperiority of his force, entertained no doubt of the ſucceſs of the attack; ſo his diſappointment was extreme, upon finding that

CHAP. XXXIX. 1781.

that the garrifon had efcaped to an inacceffible part of the ifland, where his own numbers could not avail, and where they might defend themfelves with eafe againft any force, fo long as their provifions lafted. His chagrin on this occafion feems to have betrayed him into unufual acts of feverity, inconfiftent with his former character for lenity and moderation. Fearful left the garrifon fhould hold out until the arrival of the Britifh fleet, which might fruftrate the whole expedition, he began to execute the threats made by the fieur Blanchelande. Two of the neareft plantations were immediately fet on fire: An order was iffued to burn four more within the fpace of four hours; and a flag of truce was fent to acquaint the governor and inhabitants, that the like execution would be repeated every four hours, until the ifland fhould be furrendered.

Thefe ruinous devaftations overcame the firmnefs of the militia. To fave their property, they determined to capitulate; and in this determination they were joined by the commanding officer of the troops. It was in vain that the governor reprefented the natural ftrength of the poft which they now occupied, and urged them to perfift in the defence of the ifland until the Britifh fleet fhould come to their relief. They had already held out for more than a week againft a very fuperior force, in daily expectation of relief: They had alfo by this time received information that a reinforcement coming to their affiftance had been obliged to put back on account of the arrival of the French fleet. They defpaired of further relief; and they faw their habitations in flames. Under fuch circumftances no remonftrances of the governor could prevail; and in order to obtain better terms for the inhabitants, he was at laft obliged to yield, and join in a meafure which he could no longer prevent. A treaty for a capitulation was entered upon, and terms were obtained for the inhabitants, not lefs beneficial than thofe granted to the inhabitants of Dominica. The difference of opinion, that had taken place between

1781.

The iſland of Tobago ſurrendered to the French.

the governor and the commanding officer of the troops, was the cauſe of their acting ſeparately in the treaty opened with the marquis de Bouillé; the terms which reſpected the inhabitants being ſettled by the governor with their concurrence, and thoſe regarding the regular troops by major Stanhope, without the participation of the governor.

In the mean time the ſhips of the Britiſh fleet, that had been diſabled in the late actions between vice-admiral ſir Samuel Hood and the count de Graſſe, having been repaired, and ſir George Rodney having as expeditiouſly as poſſible joined the vice-admiral with ſuch ſhips as had remained with him at St. Euſtatius, the whole fleet, then amounting to twenty ſhips of the line, proceeded under his command to Barbadoes, where it arrived on the twenty-third of May, the ſame day on which the French armament had firſt appeared off Tobago. Governor Ferguſon's diſpatch-boat with advice of that armament, and the attack on Tobago, reached Barbadoes early in the morning of the twenty-ſeventh; and on the following day, admiral Drake was diſpatched to its relief, with ſix ſhips of the line, three frigates, and ſome tranſports, having on board the ſixty-ninth regiment, and two companies of other regiments, under the command of brigadier-general Skeene. This was the reinforcement of which the governor and inhabitants of Tobago had received intelligence: But the previous arrival of the whole French fleet prevented it from landing. As ſoon as admiral Drake diſcovered the enemy's fleet lying between him and the iſland, he returned to Barbadoes, in purſuance of his orders, not to riſque his ſquadron againſt a ſuperior force. Sir George Rodney now put to ſea with the whole fleet; but before he reached Tobago, the iſland had ſurrendered.

A train of unfortunate circumſtances ſeems to have led to this event. The iſland might probably have been ſaved, had ſir George Rodney ſailed with his whole fleet to its relief as ſoon as he was apprized of its danger, inftead of fending only a fquadron of fhips with a reinforcement. The previous intelligence conveyed to the inhabitants, that admiral Drake was on his paffage with this reinforcement, rendered the difappointment greater, when they found that he was obliged to put back, and, added to the burning of their plantations, threw them into a ftate of defpair. But even after all thofe unlucky circumftances, had there been a more cordial co-operation between the governor and the commander of the troops, it is poffible that the militia, after the exertions already made by them, might have been prevailed upon to hold out longer: Or even if the militia were determined in all events to furrender, fuch was the nature of the defile, according to governor Fergufon's defcription, that the regulars themfelves might have defended it againft any force, until the arrival of fir George Rodney. On the fecond of June, the capitulation for Tobago was figned; and on the fourth fir George Rodney with the Britifh fleet appeared in fight of it.

The Britifh admiral, after receiving intelligence of the furrender, ftood to the northward, and on the fifth of June came in fight of the French fleet lying to leeward between him and the Grenadilles. Towards the evening the two fleets, fteering both the fame courfe, approached each other. Sir George Rodney, however, although to windward, did not think fit to bear down upon the enemy, left he fhould have got entangled amongft the iflands of the Grenadilles, and by the currents been driven to leeward into the channel between Grenada and the Spanifh main; whilft the French fleet could fhelter itfelf in the harbours and under the batteries of that ifland, and thus gaining a windward fituation, endanger the fafety of Barbadoes before the Britifh fleet could beat up to its affiftance. But, as he trufted that the French, from their fuperiority, might be induced to follow him, and thus be led into a track where there would be more fea-room and lefs danger of being driven to leeward, he kept on his courſe to windward of St. Vincent's, and gave orders for all the lights of his fleet to be made as conſpicuous as poſſible during the night, that the enemy, if they were diſpoſed to engage, might know that their wiſhes in the morning would not be diſappointed: In the morning, however, the enemy's fleet was not to be ſeen. In the night it had tacked and ſteered for Courland Bay, in Tobago; and during the remainder of the ſummer, the count de Graſſe, notwithſtanding his ſuperiority of five ſhips of the line, cautiouſly avoided to riſque a general engagement.

CHAP. XL.

Reduction of Penſacola by the Spaniards—The combined Fleets of France and Spain, to the Amount of ſeventy Sail, threaten Deſtruction to the marine Force of England—The Britiſh Admiral, with twenty-one Ships of the Line, prudently retires into Torbay—where the Enemy do not think it adviſable to attack him—Cauſes why the Combined Fleets enjoyed a temporary Superiority over that of Great Britain—Action between a Britiſh and a Dutch Fleet, near the Dogger Bank—Britiſh Armament ſent againſt the Dutch Settlement at the Cape of Good Hope—attacked by the French Admiral Suffrein—The Dutch Garriſon at the Cape reinforced by the French—Commodore Johnſtone makes Prizes of four Dutch Eaſt Indiamen—The Britiſh Armament under General Meadows ſails for the Eaſt Indies—Invaſion of the Carnatic by Hyder Ally—Defeat and Diſaſter of a Britiſh Detachment under Colonel Baillie—Ravages committed in the Carnatic by Hyder Ally—The Command of the Britiſh Army in the Preſidency of Madras committed to Sir Eyre Coote—Operations of the Britiſh Fleet in India.

CHAP. XL. 1781.

WHILST the French were thus availing themſelves of the embarraſſed ſtate of Great Britain, to wreſt from her her Weſt-India iſlands, the Spaniards were employed upon the continent of America, in recovering the poſſeſſions which had been taken from them in the former war. In each of the two preceding years, as we have already ſeen, they had conquered a part of Weſt Florida; and in the preſent year the conqueſt of the whole province was atchieved

CHAP. XL.

1781.

Reduction of Penfacola by the Spaniards.

chieved by the reduction of Penfacola. Don Bernardo de Galvez, intent on making this conqueft, went from New Orleans to the Havannah, in the fall of the preceding year, to folicit a force that might be adequate to the purpofe. In confequence of his reprefentations the expedition was undertaken, but the firft fleet that failed was difperfed by a ftorm, fome of the fhips loft, and the reft obliged to return in diftrefs. The perfeverance of Don Bernardo de Galvez was however not to be conquered. Another armament was got ready with all expedition. A land-force, amounting to five or fix thoufand men, with a large train of artillery, was embarked on board tranfports; and the whole, under the convoy of fome fhips of war, having failed from the Havannah in the month of February, arrived in fafety off the bar of Penfacola on the ninth of March.

General Campbell ftill commanded the Britifh troops in Weft Florida: But, reduced as they had been by the capture of lieutenant-colonel Dickfon's detachment on the Miffiffippi, and the garrifon under captain Durnford at Mobille, they did not at this time exceed nine hundred and fifty men, confifting of Britifh regulars, German auxiliaries, part of two provincial regiments, and fome militia.

Notwithftanding the great difparity of force between the befiegers and the garrifon, the Spanifh general thought fit to fend for a reinforcement. In the mean time the troops that he had with him were landed, and the Britifh works at Penfacola regularly invefted. After fome time the expected fuccours arrived, part of the Spanifh garrifon of Mobille having marched acrofs the country to join in the fiege, and a fleet of fifteen fhips of the line, under the command of Don Solano, having arrived from the Havannah, with an additional land force of three thoufand men. Although the defence made by the garrifon was brave and fpirited, and the progrefs of the befiegers hitherto proportionably flow; it was apparent, from the force with which it was invefted, that the place muft ultimately fall:

CHAP. XL. 1781.

But its fate was unexpectedly precipitated by the baseness and perfidy of a traitor. A man of the name of Cannon, formerly an officer in one of the provincial regiments in garrison at Pensacola, had been broke the year before by a court-martial for ungentlemanlike behaviour, and retired to the Creek country among the Indians, whence he returned as soon as he heard of the landing of the Spaniards, and joined them on the fifth of April. By him they were made minutely acquainted with the state and situation of all the British works, and were thus enabled to direct their fire towards those quarters where it was likely to produce the greatest effect. Indefatigable in his traiterous purpose, he used to climb to the top of a tall pine-tree, commanding a view of the British works, from whence he was enabled to inform the Spanish bombardiers where the shells discharged from their mortars took effect, and whether near or at a distance from the British magazines. Thus instructed, and improved by repeated trials, they acquired such a knowledge as at length enabled them to do fatal execution. On the morning of the eighth of May, a shell bursting at the door of a magazine in one of the advanced works, set fire to the powder within, which in an instant reduced the whole redoubt to a heap of rubbish. By the explosion seventy-six of the garrison lost their lives, and twenty-four were badly wounded. The enemy immediately advanced to take advantage of the confusion; but were repulsed in their first attempt by the fire from two flank works, which had been added to the redoubt after the commencement of the siege, and which fortunately were not injured by the blowing-up of the magazine. This repulse procured a short respite to the garrison, during which those who had been wounded by the explosion were carried off, some of the cannon removed from the flank works, which it was now judged necessary to evacuate, and the rest spiked up. The enemy, however, again advanced in greater force, and under cover of the flank works, which had been abandoned, kept up ſo hot a fire of muſquetry upon another redoubt, that the men could no longer ſtand to their guns. There was alſo, it ſeems, a ſcarcity of ordnance ſhot in the garriſon, from the great number that had been already expended. Under theſe circumſtances general Campbell thought fit to capitulate; and thus the province of Weſt Florida was once more re-annexed to the Spaniſh dominions.

In theſe military operations abroad the French and Spaniards acted ſeparately, but in Europe they undertook a joint expedition againſt the iſland of Minorca. The plan of the expedition had been laid in the beginning of the year; but the neceſſary preparations delayed the execution of it until the middle of ſummer. After the return of the Britiſh fleet from conveying ſupplies to Gibraltar, and whilſt it cruized near our own coaſts, for the protection of the homeward-bound trade, a French fleet of eighteen ſhips of the line ſailed from Breſt towards the end of June, and in the following month joined the Spaniſh fleet at Cadiz. At Cadiz was prepared the principal armament deſtined againſt Minorca: It conſiſted of ten thouſand men, with a ſuitable train of artillery, and was commanded by the duke de Crillon, a French general of great reputation. When every thing was in readineſs, the armament ſailed about the end of July, under the convoy of the combined fleets, and being accompanied by them as far as any danger was to be apprehended, arrived in ſafety at Minorca. On the twentieth of Auguſt the Spaniſh troops were landed, and being ſoon afterwards joined by ſix thouſand French from Toulon, St. Philip's Caſtle, the principal fortreſs of the iſland, was regularly inveſted: But, as the duration of the ſiege was protracted, in conſequence of the brave defence made by the garriſon, until the month of February 1782, the account of its progreſs and termination will more properly belong to the tranſactions of that year.

The

CHAP. XL.

1781.

The combined fleets of France and Spain, to the amount of seventy sail, threaten destruction to the marine force of England.

The combined fleets having convoyed the armament against Minorca as far as the straits of Gibraltar, and seen it safely into the Mediterranean, altered their course, and sailed for the coast of England, with orders to fight the British fleet. Arriving off the mouth of the channel, they extended themselves in a line across it from the islands of Scilly to Ushant, amounting in all to seventy sail, fifty of them being of the line, and some of these of the largest rate. The attention of all Europe was again directed to the operations of so powerful a fleet, and the destruction of the marine force of England was confidently expected: But the race is not always to the swift, nor the battle to the strong. Admiral Darby, who was then cruizing in the channel, with only twenty-one ships of the line, having fortunately met with a neutral vessel that had passed through the combined fleets a few days before, received from her information of their approach, as well as of their great strength, and prudently withdrew into Torbay, to wait for a reinforcement. In this situation the enemy, vast as their superiority was, and although their orders were to fight, did not dare to attack him. The count de Guichen, who commanded the French fleet, and Don Vincent de Dos, the second in command of the Spanish fleet, were eager to make the attempt, but in a council of war, held for deliberating on the subject, their opinions were over-ruled by a great majority. The design of attacking admiral Darby in Torbay being given up, the commanders of the combined fleets next turned their whole attention to intercepting the homeward-bound British trade, but met with no success. The crews of their ships being sickly, and their ships themselves in bad condition, the stormy month of September quickly obliged them to put an end to their cruize. Early in that month they separated, the fleet of France steering for Brest, and that of Spain for Cadiz, where they severally arrived much shattered and disabled. In the mean time great apprehensions were entertained in England for the safety

The British admiral, with twenty-one ships of the line, prudently retires into Torbay,

where the enemy do not think is advisable to attack him.

CHAP. XL. 1781.

ſafety of the homeward-bound convoys, more eſpecially as admiral Darby was prevented from ſailing by contrary winds, for ſome time after he received his reinforcements: But fortunately none of the merchant fleets that were expected, arrived upon the coaſt until after the combined fleets had ſeparated and returned to port; and by the time of their arrival, admiral Darby, with thirty ſhips of the line, was at ſea for their protection.

Cauſes why the combined fleets enjoyed a temporary ſuperiority over that of Great Britain.

By the various ſervices, upon which, in conſequence of the extenſion of the war, it became neceſſary to employ ſeparate ſquadrons, the grand channel fleet was unavoidably weakened; and the combined fleets thereby obtained a more conſiderable temporary ſuperiority. The war with Holland required that a ſquadron ſhould be ſent into the north ſea, as well for the ſafety of the Britiſh trade to the Baltic, as for the obſtruction of that of the Dutch. This ſquadron conſiſted of an old eighty-gun ſhip, that carried no heavier metal than a fifty, an old ſixty-gun ſhip that had been diſcharged, but was lately refitted for ſervice, two ſeventy-fours, a ſixty-four, a fifty, a forty-four, and four frigates; and the command of it was given to admiral Hyde Parker, a veteran officer of diſtinguiſhed bravery. Their Baltic trade being of the utmoſt importance to the Dutch, they ſtrained every nerve to fit out a ſtrong ſquadron for its protection, which, when it went to ſea, conſiſted of eight ſhips of the line, and ten large frigates, under the command of admiral Zouttman. It ſo happened, that whilſt admiral Parker was on his return to England, with a large fleet under his convoy, admiral Zouttman ſailed from Holland, having under his convoy a Dutch fleet bound to the Baltic. The two ſquadrons ſailing nearly in the ſame track, and in oppoſite directions, met upon the Dogger Bank on the fifth of Auguſt; and both without delay prepared for action, after taking ſuch previous meaſures as were neceſſary for the ſafety of their reſpective convoys. One of the Dutch line-of-battle ſhips

 had,

CHAP. XL. 1781.

had, from some cause or other, returned into port, but a forty-four gun ship, carrying heavy metal, being substituted in her room, admiral Zouttman's line still consisted of eight ships of two decks: That of admiral Parker consisted only of seven, and of these one mounted only fifty, and another forty-four, guns. His two smallest frigates were sent off with the convoy, and the two largest stationed so as to be in readiness to tow off any of the ships of the line that might be disabled in the action. The British fleet being to windward, of course bore down upon that of admiral Zouttman, who, unlike some modern naval commanders, practised no manœuvres to avoid a decisive engagement; but rather seemed to court it, and prepared to dispute the day with his opponent by dint of hard fighting. No gun was fired on either side, until the two squadrons came so near as to be within half musquet-shot, when admiral Parker, ranging alongside the Dutch admiral, and the other ships of his squadron bearing down in like manner upon those of the enemy that were opposed to them, the action began and continued with unremitting fury for three hours and a half; at the end of which both fleets were so disabled, that neither of them could form the line and renew the action. They lay-to for some time, at a small distance from each other, repairing their damages, when the Dutch admiral, with his convoy, bore away for the Texel; and the British fleet was so disabled as not to be in a condition to pursue. Although no ship was taken on either side, this was by far the hardest-fought battle of any that had yet happened by sea during the war. The obstinate resistance made by the Dutch incontestably proved that however much their navy, in a long course of peace, had been suffered to decline, their officers and seamen possessed the same intrepidity and desperate valour as in the days of Van Tromp and De Ruyter: And although admiral Parker obtained no trophy of victory, the gaining an advantage, with an inferior force, over such an enemy, was

Action between a British and Dutch fleet near the Dogger Bank.

CHAP. XL. 1781.

was a ſufficient proof that Britiſh ſailors, when boldly led to action, without waſting their time in nautical manœuvres, ſtill ſupported their claim to that pre-eminence by ſea, which has been ſo long the pride and boaſt of the nation. That an advantage was gained by admiral Parker was very apparent, from the Dutch admiral being the firſt that bore away: The object of his ſailing was alſo completely defeated, as the convoy which he had under his charge, was obliged to put back, and could not, after the action, proceed with ſafety on their voyage. The Britiſh fleet alſo ſuffered much; and the loſs of men was great. It amounted to one hundred and four killed, and three hundred and thirty-nine wounded, amongſt whom were a number of valuable officers. But the Dutch ſhips were ſo miſerably torn and ſhattered, that it was with difficulty moſt of them were kept above water until they reached a port; and the Hollandia, one of them, actually ſunk the night after the engagement, with all her wounded people on board. The loſs of men ſuſtained by the Dutch has never been publiſhed by authority: It was, however, known to be great, and, according to private accounts from Holland, amounted to near twelve hundred men.

Beſides the loſs of one of their capital ſhips, and the unſerviceable condition of ſome of the reſt, in conſequence of the damage ſuſtained in the action, it was a grievous mortificatton to the Dutch to ſee their Baltic convoy obliged to return, and one of the moſt beneficial branches of their commerce, for this year at leaſt, entirely interrupted. But this was not the only remaining mortification which the fortune of war in this eventful year ſubjected them to bear. For not long after the action with admiral Parker, intelligence arrived in Europe of the capture of five of their Eaſt India ſhips in Saldanha Bay, on the coaſt of Africa, by a Britiſh ſquadron under the command of commodore Johnſtone.

CHAP. XL. 1781.

Previous to the commencement of the Dutch war, this squadron was in some state of preparation, and is said to have been designed to favour an insurrection in the Spanish colonies of South America. And as in another part of this work the interference of foreign powers in disputes between a sovereign and his subjects has been generally condemned, and pronounced to be illegal and unwarrantable, it will be proper in this place to observe, that however true such an assertion, generally taken, must be admitted to be, yet the conduct of the British ministry, had they executed the design here ascribed to them, would have been fairly justifiable upon the ground of retaliation, after the Spaniards had taken a part in the war between Great Britain and her colonies, and actually assisted the latter in their opposition. But this plan, which appears to have been well laid, was never carried into execution *: The rupture with Holland appears to have produced a change of the plan; and the armament was now primarily destined to act against the Dutch possessions at the Cape of Good Hope. The squadron consisted of one ship of seventy-four guns, another of sixty-four, three fifty-gun ships, three frigates of thirty-two guns, two sloops of war, two cutters, a bomb-ketch and fire-ship, two ordnance store-ships, eleven transports, five victuallers, and thirteen Indiamen. On board the transports and Indiamen was distributed a land force consisting of the second battalion of the forty-second regiment, with Fullarton's and Humberstone's regiments, of one thousand men each, but all newly raised, four companies from other regiments, and a detachment of the royal artillery. The land force was commanded by general Meadows, who

British armament sent against the Dutch settlement at the Cape of Good Hope.

* Two new regiments, of one thousand men each, viz. the 98th and the 100th, were completed in January 1781, by William Fullarton, Esq. the author of the plan, the representative of an ancient family of that name in Airshire; and Mr. Makenzie Humberstone, a young gentleman of great hopes, of the family of Seaforth.

had

had gallantly diſtinguiſhed himſelf, as may be ſeen in a former part of this work, in the ſucceſsful defence of the poſt of the Virgie againſt the furious attack of the count d'Eſtaing in the year 1778.

With this ſquadron, commodore Johnſtone ſailed from St. Helen's on the thirteenth of March, in company with the grand fleet under admiral Darby, when it went to the relief of Gibraltar, and proceeding on his deſtination, without any material occurrence, until he arrived at St. Jago, one of the Cape de Verd Iſlands, there, on the tenth of April, anchored his ſquadron in Port Praya Bay, for the purpoſe of procuring ſupplies of freſh water and proviſions. As the iſland of St. Jago belonged to the Portugueſe, a neutral nation, Praya Bay was of courſe a neutral port: And by the law of nations the ſhips and veſſels of either of the powers at war, when lying in a neutral port, are exempted from inſult or moleſtation by the others. In ſuch a ſituation no danger was apprehended, more eſpecially as an enemy's ſquadron was neither known nor ſuſpected to be in thoſe ſeas; from whence it happened that commodore Johnſtone's ſhips were ſuffered to ſpread themſelves about in the bay, without much order, and rather with a view to their own convenience in readily ſupplying their wants, whereby much time would be ſaved, than for the purpoſe of defence. In this ſtate of ſecurity they were ſuddenly attacked on the ſixteenth of April, by a ſuperior French ſquadron under monſieur de Suffrein. Although commodore Johnſtone's expedition was to be a ſecret one, it ſufficiently appears from what happened, that both the Dutch and the French had either by their ſagacity penetrated into the intention of the Britiſh miniſtry, or by their emiſſaries and ſpies diſcovered the real object of the expedition. The former, conſcious as they were of the weakneſs of the garriſon at the Cape, and ſeeing in all their extent the ruinous conſequences that would follow its capture, were nevertheleſs unable to equip a fleet in time for its protection, and in their diſtreſs applied to the

CHAP. XL. 1781.

French for affiftance: And the latter, in order to give an earneft of good faith to their new affociates in the war, readily complied with the requifition. A fquadron, fuperior in force to commodore Johnftone's, was with all difpatch fitted out at Breft, and failed from thence only nine days after the commodore left St. Helen's. The fquadron confifted of five fhips of the line, and feveral frigates, with a number of Eaft India fhips and tranfports, having on board a confiderable land force, and a train of artillery. Monfieur de Suffrein, who commanded it, received orders to counteract the operations of commodore Johnftone wherever he might happen to meet with him, but in an efpecial manner to provide for the fecurity of the Cape of Good Hope. With fuch orders he proceeded on his expedition, and having difcovered the Britifh fquadron at anchor in Port Praya Bay, took the fudden refolution of attacking it, although in a neutral port, expecting probably, in that fituation, to find it unprepared for action, and to obtain an eafy conqueft. In the former of thefe expectations he appears not to have been miftaken, but in the latter was grievoufly difappointed. When the alarm was firft given, at leaft fifteen hundred perfons are faid to have been abfent from the fhips of the Britifh fquadron, employed in the neceffary fervices of watering, fifhing, and embarking live-ftock, and other frefh provifions. The commodore's firft fignal was for all perfons to return from the fhore, which he enforced by the firing of a gun; another was foon afterwards made to unmoor, and a third to prepare for action. But the French commodore gave them little time for preparation. The appearance of his fquadron was firft communicated by fignal from the Ifis, lying near the mouth of the bay, between nine and ten in the morning; and before eleven monfieur de Suffrein, having feparated from his convoy, entered the bay with five fhips of the line. In the Heros, of feventy-four guns, he led the way, and, firing at the Ifis as he paffed, kept on his courfe until he was within a cable's length

attacked by the French admiral Suffrein.

length of the Monmouth and Hero, two of the largeſt ſhips of the Britiſh ſquadron, and there dropped his anchor; the next French ſhip that followed was the Annibal, which ſhot a-head of monſieur de Suffrein, and there dropped anchor; the third, the Arteſien, anchored about the ſame diſtance aſtern: And in this ſituation they began a heavy cannonade, ſprings having been paſſed on their cables before they entered the bay. The other two French ſhips, the Sphynx and the Vengeur, did not anchor, but ranged about the bay, firing at every ſhip as they paſſed, and endeavouring to board the merchantmen; but in this they had little ſucceſs. Notwithſtanding the ſuddenneſs of the attack, the fire of the French ſquadron was returned with vigour and effect by ſuch of the Britiſh ſhips as could bring their guns to bear. Captain Alms, in the Monmouth, kept up a well-directed fire; and from the Hero, captain Hawler iſſued a conſtant, awful, heavy diſcharge of artillery. On board the laſt of theſe ſhips commodore Johnſtone removed, ſoon after the beginning of the action, finding that the Romney, from her particular ſituation, was likely to have no great ſhare in it: He was accompanied by general Meadows, and captain Saltern. Captain Paiſley, in the Jupiter, by working hard from the beginning of the buſineſs, had got a ſpring upon his cable, by which means every ſhot from his ſhip took effect. Even the Eaſt India ſhips, recovering after a time from their ſurpriſe, materially aſſiſted in the action. It was not long before the Arteſien, that had anchored aſtern of monſieur de Suffrein, quitted her ſtation, and went out to ſea, carrying with her the Hinchinbroke Eaſt Indiaman. She had alſo boarded the Fortitude; but her decks were quickly cleared of Frenchmen by the gallantry of captain Jenkinſon, of the ninety-eighth regiment, who, with his company, poured in upon them a conſtant and well-directed fire of muſquetry. They had afterwards the ſatisfaction of taking out of the water, and ſaving two of the enemy, who in the conflict had been

CHAP. XL. 1781.

been forced overboard, and could not regain their own ſhip by ſwimming. About three quarters of an hour after the commencement of the action, the French commodore, finding his ſituation too hot to be longer endured, cut his cable and followed the Arteſien. The Annibal, the only remaining French ſhip, was now left as a mark to be fired at by every Britiſh ſhip that could bring her guns to bear upon her, and in a ſhort time was reduced to an apparent wreck. Such a picture of diſtreſs, it is ſaid, was ſcarcely ever ſeen. Having remained in this ſituation for near a quarter of an hour, her cable was either cut or ſhot away, when the ſhip turning round on her heel, drifted out to ſea before the wind, her maſts tottering, her yards hanging different ways, and her ſails in rags. As ſhe paſſed along, her mizen-maſt firſt, and afterwards her main-maſt, fore-maſt, and part of her bowſprit, in ſucceſſion fell into the ſea. After ſhe got clear of the Britiſh ſhips, ſome of her companions took her in tow, and, to the ſurpriſe of every one, the Annibal, notwithſtanding her diſabled ſituation, had the good fortune to eſcape. The commodore, after ſummoning by ſignals all his captains, and receiving from them a report of the ſtate of their ſhips, ordered a purſuit; and, in the Romney, was the firſt that got out of the bay. He was followed in ſucceſſion by the reſt of his ſquadron, except the Iſis, captain Sutton, who being employed in repairing his damages, did not obey his ſignal for near three hours, although it was enforced by the repeated firing of guns. It is to be remarked, that although the Iſis, lying near the mouth of the bay, had very little ſhare in the action, ſhe had ſuſtained ſome damage from the fire of the French ſhips as they paſſed and repaſſed her. The Iſis having at laſt come out, the purſuit was continued; but ſo much time had been already waſted in waiting for her, that before the commodore could come near the French ſquadron the ſun had ſet, and the wind become boiſterous. If he diſcontinued the purſuit, fuit, the probability was, that monfieur de Suffrein would reach the Cape before him: If he continued it, and engaged as foon as he came up, an action in the night was liable to fo much uncertainty as fcarcely to be reconcilable with the main object of the expedition: On the other hand, if he purfued, but deferred the engagement until the morning, he would in the mean time be led fo far to leeward after the French fhips, which were running before the wind with all their fails fet, that it would be impoffible for him afterwards to beat to windward and rejoin his convoy, whereby the expedition would be at once fruftrated, and a valuable convoy left unprotected. A fituation prefenting fo many difficulties muft have been a trying one to any commander, but efpecially to one of the commodore's impatience and irafcibility. However, after confidering the matter in every point of view, he determined to follow that courfe which feemed moft confiftent with the nature of his inftructions. This was, to rejoin his convoy without delay; which he effected with fome difficulty, after plying to windward for feveral days. The Hinchinbroke Eaft Indiaman was retaken the day after the engagement, with twenty-five Frenchmen on board; and the Infernal fire-fhip, which had been alfo carried off by the enemy, was abandoned by them in the night, and, after fome days, reached Port Praya Bay in fafety: So that monfieur de Suffrein retained no trophy to confole him for his repulfe. The lofs of men in this engagement was not fo great as might have been expected, confidering the clofenefs of the action, the fmoothnefs of the water, and the crowded fituation of the fhips. It amounted to forty-three killed, and one hundred and thirty-four wounded, including officers, and was fo equally divided, that almoft every fhip in the fquadron and convoy bore a part. Some of the fhips having been difabled, particularly the Hinchinbroke Eaft Indiaman, they were refitted

CHAP. XL. 1781.

with all possible dispatch; and on the second of May the whole squadron sailed from Port Praya Bay.

As it was much to be feared that monsieur de Suffrein would reach the Cape before the British squadron, which might render an attempt upon it not only extremely hazardous, but perhaps altogether impracticable, the commodore, on the twelfth of June, dispatched four of his smaller fast-sailing vessels to proceed a-head of the rest of the squadron, for the purpose of gaining intelligence, with orders to rejoin him in a certain latitude. The detached squadron, having proceeded to the southward of the Cape, fortunately, on the first of July, fell in with and took a Dutch ship bound for Ceylon, laden with stores and provisions, and forty thousand pounds in bullion, which had left Saldahna Bay only a few days before. From her they learnt that monsieur de Suffrein, with his squadron, and part of his convoy, had arrived at the Cape on the twenty-first of June, where he had landed five hundred men to reinforce the garrison, amongst whom were eighty or ninety artillery men. They also received information that five Dutch East India ships, homeward-bound, and richly laden, were lying in Saldahna bay, about forty miles north from the Cape. With this intelligence, and their prize, the detached squadron returned, and on the ninth of July joined the commodore at the appointed place of rendezvous. A consultation was now held between the commodore and general Meadows, on the subject of the intelligence received by the Dutch prize; and the attempt upon the Cape was given over as impracticable. At this consultation colonel Fullarton was present, and urged the most forcible reasons for resuming (now that the design against the Cape had miscarried) the original project of an attack on the Spanish settlements in South America; from whence they might afterwards proceed to the East Indies, through the Pacific Ocean.

The Dutch garrison at the Cape reinforced by the French.

CHAP. XI. 1781.

Ocean: But the commodore determined either to take or destroy the ships that lay in Saldahna Bay. In prosecution of this design he steered for the land, and, as he approached the shore, took the pilotage upon himself, judging his distance from it by the depth of water. So ably was this enterprise conducted, that the British squadron, arriving off the mouth of the bay in the night, entered it with so much rapidity, the commodore in the Romney leading the way, that although the Dutch ships were run a-shore, and set on fire by their crews, as soon as they discovered an enemy's squadron, the boats of the British fleet nevertheless arrived in time to extinguish the flames in all of them, except the Middleburgh, on board of which the fire raged so violently that it was impossible to save her. It was now necessary to tow the burning ship to a distance from the rest; a work which was undertaken with alacrity, and performed with success, although with imminent danger, as she blew up with a violent explosion in ten minutes after the boats quitted her. The other prizes were got afloat the same evening. Both the French and British commanders had secondary objects to which their instructions extended, besides what related to the Cape of Good Hope. Monsieur de Suffrein, after providing for the security of the Cape, was to proceed with his squadron to the East Indies: And the instructions to the British commanders imported, that after either the success or failure of the expedition against the Cape, a certain number of the ships should be sent to the East Indies, to reinforce sir Edward Hughes; and in case of failure, part of the troops was also to be sent, and the remainder to proceed to the leeward islands in the West Indies. But the intelligence received by the Dutch prize of the invasion of the Carnatic by Hyder Ally, and of the cutting off of a strong detachment of British troops under colonel Baillie, determined the British commanders to deviate from their instructions, and instead of dividing the land force, to send the whole to the

Commodore Johnstone makes prizes of four Dutch East India-men.

CHAP. XL. 1781. The British armament under general Meadows sails for the East Indies.

East Indies, to replace the loss of colonel Baillie's detachment. Accordingly, the Dutch prizes, after being fitted for sea, were dispatched without a convoy to St. Helena; and the commodore having accompanied the detachment of ships bound to India with his whole force to the fourth degree of longitude beyond the Cape, there separated from it, and, with the Romney and frigates, returned to St. Helena to join his prizes, and conduct them to England. In their way thither they were separated by a storm; and two of the prizes were unfortunately lost.

In a former part of this work we have already seen that in the first year of the war with the French, the power of that nation in India was almost annihilated. After the taking of Pondicherry, the islands of Bourbon and Mauritius, with the port of Mahie, on the continent of Asia, were nearly all the possessions that remained to them in that quarter of the world. Nevertheless they contrived to maintain their influence with the native powers, and at length, by means of their emissaries, to excite a powerful combination amongst them, which threatened destruction to the British interest. During the course of the former war, the English East India company had acquired so immense an extent of territory, and seemed still so desirous of grasping at more, that the native princes were become jealous of their greatness, and secretly wished the destruction of their power. Many of them had also private grounds of disgust, arising from the rapacity and unprincipled conduct of several of that company's servants. From some cause of difference a war had broken out between the English company and the Mahrattas, a fierce and warlike nation, and one of the most powerful in Hindostan. The celebrated Hyder Ally Cawn, regent of the Mysore country, was at the same time engaged in a war with the Mahrattas. But in consequence of the intrigues of French agents, means were found to settle the differences between these two powers, and instead of being enemies,

enemies, to unite them as friends. Hyder agreed to join the Mahrattas in the war: Powerful succours were promised to be sent from the French islands of Bourbon and Mauritius: And in the end a confederacy against the English was entered into between the Mahratta states, Hyder Ally Cawn, the soubah of the Decan, and the rajah of Berar, to which most of the lesser powers of Hindostan were prevailed upon to accede. Hyder's country is separated from the territories belonging to the India company by a chain of mountains called the Ghauts. From these mountains Hyder, in the month of June 1780, after making all necessary preparations, descended with an army of an hundred thousand men, who spread themselves like a torrent over the country below. For a considerable time before this invasion, intelligence had been repeatedly conveyed from the frontiers to the presidency of Madras, acquainting them with the hostile disposition manifested by Hyder towards the English, and his preparations for entering the Carnatic. But that board treated with contempt all such intimations, and had taken no sufficient measures for the defence of the establishment against such an attack. Amongst other evils flowing from their shameful indifference and inexcusable negligence, this was not the least, that the company's troops on the coast of Coromandel had not been collected together, but were suffered to remain scattered about the country in different districts and garrisons; from whence it happened that when Hyder made his irruption no sufficient army could immediately be brought into the field to oppose him. When at last the appearance of Hyder's horse, in the neighbourhood of the Mount, convinced the presidency of the truth of their previous intelligence, the troops in Madras and its neighbourhood were assembled; and these, after being joined by the troops from Pondicherry, under colonel Braithwaite, amounted only to fifteen hundred Europeans, and four thousand two hundred sepoys. With this force,

Invasion of the Carnatic by Hyder Ally.

CHAP. XL. 1781. and an artillery of forty-two field-pieces, five cohorns, and four battering cannon, general sir Hector Monro marched from the Mount to Conjeveram, the largest village in the Carnatic, sixty miles distant from Madras, and thirty-five from Arcot, then besieged by the enemy. The march of sir Hector Monro to Conjeveram, as had been foreseen, obliged Hyder Ally to raise the siege of Arcot; and this service being performed, the British general determined to remain in his present situation until he should be joined by colonel Cosby, with a detachment of fifteen hundred sepoys, and some cavalry, then on his march from the Tanjore country, in the south, and by another detachment of three thousand men, including two companies of European infantry, and sixty European artillery-men, with ten field-pieces, under colonel Baillie, coming from the Guntoor Circar in the north. The progress of the last of these officers to the southward had been retarded, partly by the contradictory nature of the orders received during his march, proceeding from the fluctuating and uncertain state of the English councils at Madras, and partly by the overflowing of rivers in his way. However, at length he arrived at Perambaucum, a village within fifteen miles of the main army. Hyder Ally, by means of his emissaries, had exact intelligence of the colonel's motions; and dispatched his son Tippoo Saib, with thirty thousand horse, eight thousand foot, and twelve pieces of artillery, to attack him at Perambaucum, and, if possible, prevent his junction with sir Hector Monro. Numerous as the troops composing this detachment were, compared with the small force under colonel Baillie, the latter, nevertheless, with his usual gallantry, and with great slaughter, repulsed them in various fierce attacks, that lasted for several hours. Still however the enemy hovered round him, with an apparent intention of renewing their attacks whenever there should be a favourable opportunity: And as their numbers seemed to increase, colonel Baillie became doubtful whether

he

he ſhould be able to effect a junction, and acquainted the commander in chief with his apprehenſions. This intelligence reached ſir Hector Monro on the ſixth of September, and, in the evening of the eighth, twelve hundred choſen men under colonel Fletcher were detached to reinforce colonel Baillie. Theſe having moved with great expedition, arrived at Perambaucum at break of day of the ninth, and in the evening of that day the united detachments began their march towards Conjeveram. As ſoon as they were perceived to be in motion, the enemy brought ſome guns to bear upon their left flank, which did conſiderable execution. Theſe guns captain Rumley, with a detachment, was ordered to ſtorm; but being prevented from reaching them by an unfordable water-courſe that intervened, he was obliged to return without effecting his purpoſe. In conſequence of the fire of the enemy, and this unſucceſsful movement, ſome confuſion and diſorder aroſe amongſt the ſepoys; which determined colonel Baillie to halt till the morning. In the mean time Hyder Ally, who received minute information of every thing that paſſed, determined to take advantage of colonel Baillie's embarraſſed ſituation, and in the night decamped from the neighbourhood of Conjeveram, and marched with his army towards Perambaucum. At dawn in the morning colonel Baillie renewed his march, but had not proceeded far when he found himſelf environed on one ſide by Tippoo Saib's army, and on the other by that of his father. Tippoo had already begun to fire upon his left with eight pieces of cannon, and in a ſhort lime ſixteen were opened upon his right from the army of Hyder Ally. The cannonade was briſkly returned by colonel Baillie, and the attacks of the irregular cavalry were ſucceſsfully repulſed for an hour and a half, when, ſome of the tumbrils unfortunately blowing up, the Britiſh guns were ſilenced, partly from a ſcarcity of ammunition, and partly from the number of artillery-men that had fallen. The enemy, obſerving the confuſion

Defeat and diſaſter of a Britiſh detachment under colonel Baillie.

CHAP. XL. 1781.

arising from the blowing up of the tumbrils, now advanced nearer, and seeming in a particular manner to threaten colonel Baillie's rear, he found it necessary to detach for its support captain Ferrier's company of European grenadiers. This movement being made from the front towards the rear, the sepoys, who were unapprised of the cause, and probably conceived it to be a retreat, as soon as they saw the grenadiers in motion, began to follow in great disorder. The grenadiers halted: And every method was taken to restore order, but in vain. The other sepoys, who lay under a heavy cannonade, upon observing the confusion and retreat of their companions, became suddenly panic-struck, and, throwing down their arms, fled to a small coppice-wood at some distance. The Europeans immediately collecting, took possession of a rising ground, where they defended themselves against repeated attacks, whilst the enemy's horse made dreadful havoc amongst the sepoys. It was hoped that the main army, under sir Hector Monro, might still come to their relief: And in the mean time so bravely did this small body of men defend themselves against Hyder's host, that although he advanced, both with his horse and foot, within fifteen yards, he found it impossible to break them. But at last all hopes of succour being at an end, and many having already fallen, the British commander, knowing that it was impossible for such a handful of men to maintain their ground much longer against such a multitude, and willing to save the few that remained, stepped forward with a white handkerchief in his hand, and commanded his men to order their arms, and call for quarter. But this order was no sooner complied with, than the enemy rushed upon them in the most ferocious manner; and numbers were instantly put to the sword. Nor would the carnage have ceased, notwithstanding the surrender, but for the humane interposition of two French officers, Lally and Pimoran, who at last prevailed upon the barbarian Hyder to spare the gallant remains of the

the British detachment. The monster gave orders to stop the further effusion of blood: But could the brave men, who were thus become his prisoners, have foreseen the unexampled miseries they were to endure in the dungeons of the tyrant, during a long captivity, they would have deemed immediate death a happy deliverance from his more than savage brutality.

Hyder, fearful of being attacked by the main army under sir Hector Monro, suddenly retreated, after his victory, to a place called the Round Wells, where he had before been encamped. In fact, when Hyder began his retreat, sir Hector Monro, with his army, was at no great distance from him. The cannonade that happened on the evening of the ninth of September, when the united detachments under Baillie and Fletcher began their march, having been heard at Conjeveram, and reports being brought in, that Hyder's army, which had been encamped in the neighbourhood, was in motion, the British general became apprehensive for the safety of the detachments, and took the resolution of moving that same evening to their assistance. Verbal orders to that effect, it is said, were given; but unfortunately, from some cause or other, the march was delayed until the next morning. When day-light appeared, it was no longer to be doubted that Hyder had decamped; and the cannonade having been heard to commence soon afterwards with redoubled fury, the general immediately gave orders for the army to be put in motion towards Perambaucum. From the mistake of the guide, the army was led by a circuitous route several miles too far to the right, by which some time was lost. When at last it arrived within two miles of the field of action, the firing was observed suddenly to cease; and soon afterwards some wounded sepoys being brought in, that had escaped from the general carnage, related the nature and extent of the misfortune that had happened. Upon receiving this intelligence, the general immediately returned upon his steps to Conjeveram;

veram; and after the heavy cannon had been ſpiked, and ſuch of the baggage and ſtores deſtroyed as could not be eaſily moved, he retreated with the remains of his army to Chingliput, and from thence, in a few days, to the Mount. At Chingliput, the army was joined by colonel Coſby and his detachment, who, although he had to march through a large extent of country, entirely over-run and poſſeſſed by the enemy, had the good fortune to arrive in ſafety, and preſerve his cannon and baggage. By the rapidity of his movements, he in ſome meaſure eluded the deſigns of the enemy; and whenever he was haraſſed by their cavalry, the well-regulated diſpoſition of his march, with the good countenance preſerved by the officers and troops, prevented them from making any ſerious impreſſion.

Ravages committed in the Carnatic by Hyder Ally.

By the retreat of the Britiſh army to the Mount, the whole country was laid open to be ravaged at pleaſure by Hyder and his irregular hoſt. The dominions of the Eaſt India company on the coaſt of Coromandel, which of late were ſo extenſive, might now be ſaid to be confined to Madras, and a few miles round it, and to ſuch forts and garriſons ſcattered about in different parts of the country as were ſtill occupied by the company's troops. To reduce theſe, Hyder now directed his attention. Arcot, the capital of the Nabob's dominions, ſoon fell into his hands, the reduction of it being haſtened by the treachery of ſome of the Nabob's principal ſervants. Not long afterwards Carangooly and Gingee, with many other inferior poſts, were added to the liſt of his conqueſts. And the preſidency of Madras, of late ſo full of ſecurity, now dreaded all the horrors and miſeries attendant upon a ſiege.

They had already applied to the governor-general and ſupreme council of Bengal for aſſiſtance: And to the vigorous meaſures adopted and proſecuted by that board muſt in a great meaſure be attributed the favourable change which not long afterwards took place

in

1781.

in the company's affairs on the coaſt of Coromandel. General ſir Eyre Coote, commander in chief in India, who was then at Calcutta, was requeſted to take upon himſelf the command of the army at Madras; and in order to enable him to carry his plans into execution, independently of the Madras preſidency, who ſeemed deſirous of thwarting all the meaſures of the governor-general and commander in chief, he was furniſhed with fifteen lacks of rupees, over which ſum that board (whoſe diſpoſitions towards the governor-general, and the majority in his council, were well enough known) were not to poſſeſs any control. Sir Eyre Coote was alſo empowered to take a ſeat in the council of Madras; and Mr. Whitehill, the preſident, was ſuſpended. The commander in chief, although then ſixty-three years of age, cheerfully conſented to undertake the arduous charge thus committed to him, of endeavouring to reſtore the proſperity of the company's affairs on the coaſt of Coromandel, and of freeing that country from the ravages of Hyder Ally. He embarked without delay at Calcutta, with three hundred Europeans in battalion, upwards of two hundred artillery-men, five hundred laſcars, ſome pieces of cannon, and a large ſupply of proviſions; whilſt ten battalions of Sepoys, with twenty pieces of cannon, were under orders to march by land from Bengal to the Carnatic. Inſtructions were alſo ſent to general Goddard, who commanded the army acting againſt the Mahrattas, to ſend by ſea to Madras as many troops as he could ſpare. Sir Edward Hughes was ſolicited to block up Hyder's ſea-ports on the Malabar coaſt, and prevent him from receiving ſupplies from the iſlands of Bourbon and Mauritius; and the government of Bombay received orders to make a diverſion on the ſame coaſt in favour of the war carrying on in the Carnatic, and thus alarm Hyder for the ſafety of his own dominions.

The command of the Britiſh army in the preſidency of Madras committed to ſir Eyre Coote.

CHAP. XL. 1781.

Sir Eyre Coote arrived at Madras on the fifth of November, and after surmounting many difficulties and obstacles, which either from the incapacity of the presidency had not been foreseen, or from their negligence were not provided for, took the field in the beginning of the year 1781, with a small but well-appointed army, and an excellent train of artillery. The sieges of Vellore, Wandewash, Parmacoil, and Chingliput, then blocked up by Hyder, were immediately raised; and he, with his whole force, retired to a guarded distance. From this moment the company's affairs on that coast began to wear a more favourable aspect: Some of the forts that had been surprised were in a short time retaken: Hyder's ravages were necessarily confined within narrower limits in consequence of the caution with which he avoided an engagement: And by the British commander's taking the field, the credit of the company's arms, which had been at a low ebb ever since the defeat of colonel Baillie, was restored, and the disaffection of the natives, which had begun to be general, was in a great measure repressed. In the course of the year sir Eyre Coote found means to worst Hyder in several battles; and although the latter still maintained his ground in part of the Carnatic, a large extent of country, which had been over-run, was recovered and freed from his ravages.

Operations of the British fleet in India.

Sir Edward Hughes performed the services expected of him: Hyder's ports on the Malabar coast were not only blocked up, but his shipping destroyed at Calicut and Mangalore, two of his principal arsenals, and his hopes of becoming a maritime power thus nipped in the bud. Towards the close of this year also, the Dutch fort of Negapatam, in the Tanjore country, the garrison of which had been reinforced by two thousand three hundred of Hyder's troops, was taken by a joint operation of the squadron under sir Edward Hughes, and a land force under sir Hector Monro, which the commander in chief

was

was enabled to ſpare, after the favourable change that had taken place in the Carnatic. The immediate conſequence of the fall of Negapatam was the evacuation of all the forts and ſtrong places poſſeſſed by Hyder's troops in the Tanjore country and its borders. Such were the effects of the vigorous meaſures adopted by the governor-general and ſupreme council of Bengal for the relief and aſſiſtance of the Madras government; and ſuch the ſucceſſes that attended the company's troops under the auſpices of their veteran commander ſir Eyre Coote *.

* For a more full and particular account of the military and naval operations in India, at this period, ſee Memoirs of the late War (1778—84) in Aſia: With a Narrative of the Impriſonment and Sufferings of our Officers and Soldiers, by an Officer of Colonel Baillie's Detachment.

CHAP. XLI.

Disaffection to Great Britain of the Southern Colonies—The British Army under Lord Cornwallis joined by a large Reinforcement under General Leslie—Action at the Cowpens, between General Morgan and Colonel Tarleton—Colonel Tarleton defeated—Consequences of Colonel Tarleton's Defeat—The Army under Lord Cornwallis crosses the River Catawba—Lord Cornwallis, joined by the other Division of the Army under Colonel Webster, pursues General Morgan—A Junction formed between the two Divisions of the American Army—General Greene driven out of North Carolina—The Royal Standard erected at Hillsborough—General Greene, again crossing the Dan, re-enters North Carolina—Lord Cornwallis falls back from Hillsborough, and takes a new Position—Effects of this retrograde Movement—Action near Guildford between Lord Cornwallis and General Greene.

CHAP. XLI. 1781.

WE must now return to North America, the grand theatre of the war, where it first began, and where the events of the present year were of such momentous importance as to produce a total change in the future conduct of it, and in effect to place within the grasp of the revolted colonies that independence and sovereignty for which they had been so long contending. From the beginning of the year 1779 the principal efforts of the British arms were directed against the southern colonies, not only as they were deemed the easiest to be reduced, but as, from the nature of their productions, they were the most valuable to the mother-country.

CHAP. XLI.

1781.

Georgia was accordingly recovered in the year 1779, and the province of South Carolina reduced in the year 1780. For ſome months after the taking of Charleſtown, the capital of South Carolina, there was in that province the brighteſt proſpect of returning peace and tranquillity. But too ſoon the ſky became overcaſt; and it was perceived in the ſouthern as it had been already experienced in ſome of the northern colonies, that the inhabitants, after their ſubmiſſion, and even whilſt the Britiſh troops remained amongſt them, did not perform the duties of their allegiance without reluctance, and when left to themſelves, quickly reverted to their old courſes, and joined the ſtandard of revolt. In the tranſactions of laſt year we have endeavoured to aſſign ſome motives for this verſatility of conduct amongſt the inhabitants of South Carolina; but to whatever cauſe their diſaffection was owing, it gave much trouble to earl Cornwallis, and greatly retarded his operations. The efficient army for diſtant ſervice was ſo much weakened by the large detachments left behind for overawing the inhabitants, that a ſingle misfortune was ſometimes ſufficient to render an expedition abortive. In the fall of the preceding year the loſs of major Ferguſon's detachment obliged lord Cornwallis to return from his northern expedition and fall back to Wynneſborough in South Carolina. Still, however, the projected movement into North Carolina was deemed ſo eſſential, that he only waited for a reinforcement to renew it. The expected reinforcement arrived at Charleſtown on the thirteenth of December. It conſiſted of a large detachment of troops under general Leſlie, who, upon landing, received lord Cornwallis's orders to march without delay, and join him with about fifteen hundred men. The general accordingly, after waiting ſome few days to procure horſes and waggons, began his march on the nineteenth of December.

Diſaffection to Great Britain of the ſouthern colonies.

The Britiſh army under lord Cornwallis joined by a large reinforcement under general Leſlie. December.

In the mean time general Greene, who had ſucceeded Gates in the command of the American army, finding it difficult to procure a ſufficient

CHAP. XLI. 1781.

fufficient fupply of provifions in the neighbourhood of Charlotte, as that country had been already exhaufted; and being fenfible that his prefent force was too weak to attempt any direct operation againft lord Cornwallis; refolved to divide it, and by defultory incurfions in different, and nearly oppofite quarters, to alarm and harafs the Britifh out-pofts on the frontiers of South Carolina. By fuch means his troops would be kept in action, and, traverfing different parts of the country, would not only be more eafily fupplied with provifions, but might in their progrefs infufe fome fpirit into the militia, without whofe affiftance and co-operation he faw that he could do nothing effectual. Accordingly the light troops, confifting of three hundred infantry, under colonel Howard, one hundred and feventy rifle-men, under major Triplet, and feventy light dragoons, under lieutenant-colonel Wafhington, were put under the command of general Morgan, who was directed to proceed by the heads of the rivers to the weftern frontiers of South Carolina, and threaten the Britifh poft at Ninety-fix; whilft the reft of the army under general Greene fhould march to the Pedee, and alarm the country in front of Camden.

Towards the end of December earl Cornwallis received information of the divifion of the American army, and foon afterwards an account of the movements of general Morgan, who had paffed both the Catawba and Broad River, and was faid to be rapidly advancing to Ninety-fix. Upon receipt of this intelligence, lieutenant-colonel Tarleton was detached with the light and legion infantry, the fufileers, or feventh regiment, the firft battalion of the feventy-firft regiment, about three hundred and fifty cavalry, two field-pieces, and an adequate detachment of the royal artillery, in all about one thoufand men. He received orders to pafs Broad River for the protection of Ninety-fix, and either to ftrike at Morgan, and pufh him to the utmoft, or at leaft oblige him to leave the country.

Morgan, in his march, had collected about four or five hundred militia, and upon his approach to the district of Ninety-six, was joined by two hundred more, who had fled from the frontiers of Georgia when Augusta was taken possession of by the British troops. Thus the two detachments were nearly equal in point of numbers, but in cavalry, and in the general quality of the troops, Tarleton was greatly superior *.

The British army now proceeded to the north-west, between Broad River and the Catawba. This route, leading to the back country, was chosen, that the army might the more easily be enabled to pass the great rivers in its way at the fords near their source: It also afforded a prospect of cutting off Morgan's retreat, if he should elude Tarleton, or at least of preventing his junction with the army under general Greene: Nor was the British general without hopes, that by following this course he might get between

* Dr. Ramsay, in his History of the Revolution of South Carolina, charges the British with seizing the property of the Americans; and their commissaries and quarter-masters with taking provisions, and all other things wanted by the army, wherever they could be found, charging them, at the same time, to the British government. That peculation was carried on in some departments of the British army, and that many individuals made large fortunes in this way, cannot be denied. But this never took place, in any great extent, in the southern army. And the writer of this, who was commissary to the army under lord Cornwallis, takes the present occasion of repelling the calumniesof Dr. Ramsay, as far as they may relate to himself, and appealing for the innocence and propriety of his conduct to many individuals now living in Carolina, as well as to the gentlemen of the army in which he served. The commissary, during the time when he was at the Congarees, employed in collecting provisions, and settling refugee families on the deserted plantations of the Americans, without being supported by any troops, or covering party, furnished supplies to the army at Wynnesborough and Camden, each post being about forty miles from the Congarees. He had several mills to attend and feed daily, some of which lay six miles apart. The number of persons employed by the commissary in this service was about one hundred and twenty negroes, one serjeant of the 71st regiment, one cooper, and four inspectors or overseers. When the campaign opened in January 1781, there was about fifty thousand weight of meal packed and ready for use. The whole expence, as charged by the commissary to government for this service, guides, expresses, collecting, shelling, grinding, packing, wages, &c. did not amount to one hundred pounds sterling.

Greene's

Greene's army and Virginia, and force him to an action before he was joined by his expected reinforcements. The detachment under general Leslie, which had been purposely halted at Camden, until lord Cornwallis should be ready to march from Wynnesborough, the longer to conceal from the American general the road which the British army meant to take, now received orders to move up the banks of the Catawba, and join the main army on its march. The march both of lord Cornwallis and general Leslie, encumbered as they were with baggage and artillery, was greatly retarded by the swelling of creeks and water-courses. These obstacles Tarleton also experienced; but having the command of light troops, he more easily surmounted them, and probably overtook Morgan something sooner than was expected.

The latter, after retreating over the Pacolet, made a shew of disputing Tarleton's passage by guarding the fords. Tarleton however, on the sixth of January, found means to pass over his detachment within six miles of the enemy's encampment; and Morgan was obliged to make a precipitate retreat, leaving in his camp the provisions that were dressing for his troops half cooked. Tarleton advanced and took possession of the ground that had been left by the enemy only a few hours before.

At three in the morning the march of the British light troops was resumed in pursuit of general Morgan; the baggage being left under a guard composed of a detachment from each corps, with orders not to move till daylight appeared. Tarleton, after a fatiguing march through swamps and broken grounds, at length came in sight of the enemy about eight in the morning: Two of their videttes were soon afterwards taken; and from them information was received that the Americans had halted, and were forming at a place called the Cowpens.

General Morgan, finding himself hard pressed by the British troops, had resolved to hazard an action rather than be overtaken

in

in the ford of the river. With this view he drew up his force in two lines, the militia under colonel Pickens forming the firft line, and the continentals, under colonel Howard, with the Virginia rifle-men, the fecond. Wafhington's dragoons, with fome mounted militia, were drawn up at fome diftance in the rear, as a corps of referve. The ground which he occupied does not appear to have been well chofen: It was an open wood, and confequently liable to be penetrated by the Britifh cavalry: Both his flanks were expofed; and the river, at no great diftance, ran parallel to his rear. In fuch a fituation he gave a manifeft advantage to an enemy with a fuperior body of cavalry; and in cafe of a defeat, the deftruction of his whole detachment was inevitable.

Action at the Cowpens between general Morgan and colonel Tarleton.

Lieutenant-colonel Tarleton, upon receiving the intelligence communicated by the videttes, refolved, without lofs of time, to make an attack upon the Americans. Advancing within two hundred and fifty yards of their firft line, he made a hafty difpofition of his force. The light and legion infantry, and the feventh regiment, were ordered to form in line, a captain, with fifty dragoons, being attached to each of their flanks; and the firft battalion of the feventy-firft regiment, and the reft of the cavalry, were directed to form as a referve, and wait for orders. This difpofition being fettled, Tarleton, relying on the valour of his troops, impatient of delay, and too confident of fuccefs, led on in perfon the firft line to the attack, even before it was fully formed, and whilft major Newmarfh, who commanded the feventh regiment, was pofting his officers: Neither had the referve yet reached the ground which it was to occupy. The firft line of the Americans being compofed of militia, did not long withftand the charge of the Britifh regulars: It gave way in all quarters, and was purfued to the continentals. The latter, undifmayed by the retreat of the militia, maintained their ground with great bravery; and the conflict between them and

CHAP. XLI. 1781.

the Britiſh troops was obſtinate and bloody. Captain Ogilvie, with his troop of dragoons on the right of the Britiſh line, was directed to charge the left flank of the enemy. He cut his way through their line, but being expoſed to a heavy fire, and, at the ſame time, charged by the whole of Waſhington's cavalry, was compelled to retreat in confuſion. The Britiſh reſerve now received orders to move forward; and as ſoon as the line felt the advance of the ſeventy-firſt regiment, the whole again moved on. The continentals, no longer able to ſtand the ſhock, were forced to give way. This was the critical moment of the action, which might have been improved ſo as to ſecure to the Britiſh troops a complete victory. An order, it is ſaid, was diſpatched to the cavalry to charge the enemy when in confuſion; but if ſuch an order was delivered, it was not obeyed; and the infantry, enfeebled by their fatiguing march in the morning, through ſwamps and broken grounds, and by their ſubſequent exertions in the action, were unable to come up with the flying enemy. The critical moment loſt on the one ſide was eagerly ſeized on the other. The American commander, finding that the Britiſh cavalry did not purſue, gave orders to Waſhington to cover with his dragoons the rear of the broken provincials, whilſt he exerted himſelf to the utmoſt to rally them. His endeavours ſucceeded: The continentals were rallied and formed, and now in their turn charged the aſſailants. In diſorder from the purſuit, and unſupported by the cavalry, ſuch of the Britiſh infantry as were fartheſt advanced, receiving this unexpected charge, fell back in confuſion, and communicated a panic to others, which ſoon became general. Waſhington charged with his cavalry; and a total rout enſued. The militia who had fled, ſeeing the fortune of the day changed, returned and joined in the purſuit. The Britiſh infantry were ſoon overtaken, as the ſame cauſes which retarded them in the purſuit, now impeded their flight; and almoſt the whole were either

either killed or taken prifoners. The two field-pieces were alfo taken, but not till the whole of the artillery-men attached to them were either killed or wounded. It was in vain that Tarleton endeavoured to bring his legion cavalry to charge and check the progrefs of the enemy: They ftill ftood aloof, and at length fled in a body through the woods, leaving their commander behind. Fourteen officers, however, remained with him, and about forty men of the feventeenth regiment of dragoons: At the head of thefe he made a defperate charge on the whole of Wafhington's cavalry, and drove them back upon the continentals. But no partial advantage, however brilliant, could now retrieve the fortune of the day: All was already loft; and Tarleton, feeing nothing farther to be done, retreated with the remains of this fmall but brave and faithful band of adherents, to Hamilton's Ford, upon Broad River, in his way to the main army under lord Cornwallis, then at Turkey Creek, about twenty-five miles from the field of action. The only body of Tarleton's infantry that efcaped was the guard left with the baggage, which had not reached the Cowpens at the time of the action: Early intelligence of the defeat being conveyed to the officer who commanded it, by fome friendly Americans, he immediately deftroyed whatever part of the baggage could not be carried off, and mounting his men on the waggon and fpare horfes, retreated to the main army unmolefted. Few of the legion cavalry were miffing: One divifion of them arrived the fame evening in the neighbourhood of the Britifh encampment, with the news of their defeat, and another under Tarleton, who in his way had been joined by fome ftragglers, appeared the next morning. The whole lofs of the Britifh troops, in this unfortunate affair, amounted to at leaft fix hundred men; and of them near one half was either killed or wounded. The lofs of the Americans, according to their report of it, was fo fmall as fcarcely to deferve credit. It amounted to twelve killed, and fixty

Colonel Tarleton defeated.

 wounded.

CHAP. XLI. 1781.

wounded. During the whole period of the war no other action reflected so much dishonour upon the British arms. The British were superior in numbers. Morgan had only five hundred and forty continentals, the rest militia. Tarleton's force composed the light troops of lord Cornwallis's army. Every disaster that befel lord Cornwallis, after Tarleton's most shameful defeat at the Cowpens, may most justly be attributed to the imprudence and unsoldierly conduct of that officer in the action. It was asked, why he did not consult majors M'Arthur and Newmarsh, officers of experience and reputation, who had been in service before Tarleton was born? Colonel Tarleton, in his History of the Southern Campaigns in America, admits that the ground on which Morgan formed had been described with great perspicuity to him. He also admits, that he had obtained a very accurate knowledge of Morgan's situation, and of the ground on which Morgan had drawn up his army. That there was every prospect of success from the animation and alacrity of his troops; that his troops moved in a good line; that his fire was well supported, and produced much slaughter; that the continentals and back woodsmen gave ground, and the British rushed forward; that the ground which Morgan had chosen was disadvantageous for the Americans, and as proper a situation for action as colonel Tarleton could have wished: Under all these advantages in favour of Tarleton, and disadvantages against Morgan, Tarleton is completely defeated and totally routed. Is it possible for the mind to form any other conclusion, than that there was a radical defect, and a want of military knowledge on the part of colonel Tarleton? That he possesses personal bravery inferior to no man, is beyond a doubt; but his talents at the period we are speaking of never exceeded that of a partizan captain of light dragoons, daring in skirmishes. He could defeat an enemy in detail, by continually harassing, and cutting off detached parties.

The

The defeat of his majesty's troops at the Cowpens formed a very principal link in the chain of circumſtances which led to the independence of America. Colonel Tarleton acquired power without any extraordinary degree of merit, and upon moſt occaſions exerciſed it without diſcretion.

Nothing could be more unexpected by lord Cornwallis, than the news of Tarleton's diſcomfiture. If he judged from the events of former actions, where the numbers were not ſo equally balanced, and the diſproportion much more in favour of the Americans, he had reaſon to look for a victory inſtead of defeat. The diſappointment was galling; and the loſs of credit caſt a ſhade over the commencement of the expedition. But another conſequence of the defeat was of a ſtill more ſerious nature: The loſs of the light troops, at all times neceſſary to an army, but on a march through a woody and thinly ſettled country, almoſt indiſpenſable, was not to be repaired.

Conſequences of colonel Tarleton's defeat.

Deeply as his lordſhip was affected with the weight of this misfortune, and greatly as he ſaw his difficulties increaſed by it, he nevertheleſs reſolved to proſecute the original plan of the expedition into North Carolina, as the only means of maintaining the Britiſh intereſt in the ſouthern colonies. The reinforcement under general Leſlie not having yet come up, the eighteenth of January was ſpent in forming a junction with it; and on the nineteenth the army reſumed its march. Some hopes were entertained that Morgan, incumbered as he was with priſoners, might ſtill be overtaken between Broad River and the Catawba. But that active partizan, ſenſible of his danger, quitted the Cowpens immediately after the action, and proceeding to the upper fords on Broad River, paſſed it with his detachment and the priſoners. The wounded, who were unable to travel, were left behind under the protection of a flag of truce. From Broad River Morgan directed his courſe to the Catawba,

tawba, and moved with ſo much celerity that he reached it before the Britiſh army. Yet, ſo cloſely had he been purſued, that the advance of the Britiſh troops arrived at the banks of that river in the evening of the twenty-ninth of January, only two hours after the laſt of Morgan's corps had croſſed. A heavy rain, that fell in the night, ſwelled the river ſo much as to render it impaſſable the next morning; and, as it continued ſo for two days, Morgan had time to make an arrangement for diſincumbering himſelf of the priſoners, and ſending them off under an eſcort of militia, by a different route from that which he propoſed to take. Whilſt the priſoners proceeded on their march, he, with his detachment, remained on the north banks of the Catawba, and, by calling out the militia of the country to aſſiſt him in guarding the fords, prepared to diſpute the paſſage of the Britiſh army.

Previouſly to the arrival of the Britiſh troops on the banks of the Catawba, lord Cornwallis, conſidering that the loſs of his light troops could only be remedied by the activity of the whole army, reſolved to deſtroy all the ſuperfluous baggage. By firſt reducing the ſize and quantity of his own, he ſet an example which was cheerfully followed by all the officers under his command, although by ſo doing they ſuſtained a conſiderable loſs. No waggons were reſerved except thoſe loaded with hoſpital ſtores, ſalt, and ammunition, and four empty ones for the accommodation of the ſick or wounded*. And ſuch was the ardour both of officers and ſoldiers, and their willingneſs to ſubmit to any hardſhip for the promotion of the ſervice; that this arrangement, which deprived them of all future proſpect of ſpirituous liquors, and even hazarded a regular ſupply of proviſions, was acquieſced in without a murmur.

* The remainder of the waggons, baggage, and all the ſtore of flour and rum, were deſtroyed at Ramſour's Mill.

In

CHAP. XLI. 1781.

In the mean time general Greene, upon receiving information of lord Cornwallis's march, and his rapid purſuit of Morgan, left his army upon the Pedee, under the command of general Huger and colonel Williams, with orders to retreat by forced marches to the upper country, in order to form a junction with the light troops wherever it might be practicable, whilſt he, with an eſcort of dragoons, proceeded immediately to that corps, that he might be the better enabled to regulate its movements for facilitating the propoſed junction. After travelling with great expedition, he arrived at Morgan's camp on the laſt day of January.

In the courſe of two days, the river having fallen ſo as to render it fordable, lord Cornwallis determined to attempt a paſſage. That he might perplex the enemy, and draw off their attention from the real object, lieutenant-colonel Webſter, with one diviſion of the army, was detached to a public ford called Beattie's, with orders to cannonade, and make a feint, as if he intended to force a paſſage; whilſt lord Cornwallis, with the other diviſion, marched to a private ford near M'Cowan's, where the paſſage was in reality to be attempted. The diviſion under lord Cornwallis marched from its encampment at one in the morning of the firſt of February, and reached the ford about dawn. The numerous fires ſeen on the oppoſite ſhore quickly convinced the Britiſh commander that this ford, although a private one, had not eſcaped the vigilance of the enemy. General Davidſon, with three hundred militia, had been ſent to guard it only the evening before. Nevertheleſs lord Cornwallis determined to proceed; and the paſſage was gallantly and ſucceſsfully effected by the brigade of guards under general O'Hara. Plunging into the rapid ſtream, in many places reaching above their middle, and near five hundred yards wide, they marched on with the utmoſt ſteadineſs and compoſure; and although expoſed to the fire of the enemy, reſerved their own, according to their orders, until they reached

The army under lord Cornwallis croſſes the river Catawba.

CHAP. XLI. 1781.

reached the opposite bank. The passage of the river was made in the following order: The light-infantry of the guards, led by colonel Hall, first entered the water: They were followed by the grenadiers, and the grenadiers by the battalions, the men marching in platoons to support one another against the rapidity of the stream. When the light-infantry had nearly reached the middle of the river they were challenged by one of the enemy's centinels. The centinel, having challenged thrice, and received no answer, immediately gave the alarm by discharging his musquet; and the enemy's picquets were turned out. No sooner did the guide, who attended the light-infantry to shew them the ford, hear the report of the centinel's musquet, than he turned round and left them. This, which at first seemed to portend much mischief, in the end proved a fortunate incident. Colonel Hall, being forsaken by his guide, and not knowing the true direction of the ford, led the column directly across the river, to the nearest part of the opposite bank. This direction, as it afterwards appeared, carried the British troops considerably above the place where the ford terminated on the other side, and where the enemy's picquets were posted; so that when they delivered their fire, the light-infantry were already so far advanced as to be out of the line of its direction, and it took place angularly upon the rear of the grenadiers, so as to produce no great effect. When general Davidson perceived the direction of the British column, he led his men to that part of the bank which faced it. But by the time of his arrival the light-infantry had overcome all their difficulties: They were getting out of the water and forming, and so soon as they had formed, quickly routed and dispersed general Davidson's militia, killing or wounding about forty of them. General Davidson was the last of the enemy who remained upon the bank, and in mounting his horse to make his escape, received a mortal wound.

In

In effecting this difficult and dangerous passage of the Catawba, in the face of the enemy, the whole loss of the guards amounted only to forty, lieutenant-colonel Hall *, and three privates, being killed, and thirty-six wounded †. The other troops which composed lord Cornwallis's division of the army followed the guards in succession; and, as soon as the whole had landed, lieutenant-colonel Tarleton, with the cavalry, and the twenty-third regiment, was sent in pursuit of the militia. Upon his march, receiving intelligence that the place appointed for their rendezvous was at Tarrant's Tavern, about ten miles distant, he left behind the twenty-third regiment, which took post about five miles from Beattie's Ford, and, for the sake of dispatch, proceeded with the cavalry only. About five hundred of the militia, from different fords, were assembled, when he reached the place of their rendezvous, and appeared not unprepared to receive him. Tarleton, nevertheless, resolved to attack them, and animating his men with a stinging recollection of the action at the Cowpens, made a furious charge upon the enemy, broke through their centre, killed near fifty ‡ upon the spot, and quickly dispersed the whole. The gallantry of the guards in passing the broad river Catawba, in the face of the enemy, and the subsequent rout and dispersion of the militia, first at the ford, and afterwards by Tarleton, at Tarrant's Tavern, made such an impression on the inhabitants,

* Lieutenant-colonel Hall was killed in ascending the bank, after he had crossed the river.

† The following accidents happened to the horses of the general officers in passing the river:—Lord Cornwallis's horse was shot in the water, but did not drop till he reached the shore. General Leslie's horses were carried by the rapidity of the stream some distance down the river, until his groom got upon a rock and held them. Brigadier O'Hara's horse rolled over with him in the water: The brigadier, no doubt, was thoroughly wet from this accident, but received no other injury.

‡ This is Tarleton's account, page 226 of his Campaigns; but a British officer, who rode over the ground not long after the action, relates, that he did not see ten dead bodies of the provincials in the whole.

bitants, that although the country between the Catawba and the Yadkin was deemed the moſt hoſtile part of North Carolina, the army in its progreſs to the laſt of theſe rivers met with no farther moleſtation from the militia.

General Greene had hoped, by guarding the fords with the light troops under Morgan, aſſiſted by the militia, to prevent lord Cornwallis from paſſing, until the other diviſion of the American army, under Huger and Williams, ſhould have time to come up. But the Britiſh general, by forcing a paſſage in the manner already related, quickly put an end to his hopes. The guards ſtationed at the different fords were accordingly withdrawn; and the light troops under Morgan began a precipitate retreat towards the Yadkin.

Lord Cornwallis, joined by the other diviſion of the army under colonel Webſter, purſues general Morgan.

The other diviſion of the Britiſh army, under colonel Webſter, paſſed the Catawba at Beattie's Ford, in the courſe of the day, and at night joined lord Cornwallis's diviſion, about five miles from the ford, on the road to Saliſbury. Early the next morning the Britiſh troops marched in purſuit of Morgan; but the celerity of his movements baffled all their efforts. He reached the trading ford on the Yadkin in the night between the ſecond and third of February, and with the aſſiſtance of all the boats and flats that could be collected, completed the paſſage of his corps, with their baggage, by the following evening, except only a few waggons left under an eſcort of rifle-men. The rifle-men, after a ſlight reſiſtance, fled under cover of the night, and their waggons were of courſe taken.

The American cavalry had paſſed by the ford of the river; but a heavy rain that fell during the day, rendered the river unfordable by the next morning: The ſame rain, by ſwelling the creeks, and increaſing the badneſs of the roads, had alſo retarded general O'Hara on his march; and thus Morgan's detachment, from fortunate incidents, had another hairbreadth eſcape.

All

All the boats and flats having been ſecured by Morgan on the other ſide of the river, the river itſelf being unfordable, and continuing to riſe, and the weather ſtill appearing unſettled, lord Cornwallis determined to march up the weſtern banks of the Yadkin, and paſs by the ſhallow fords near its ſource. All hopes of preventing the junction of the two diviſions of the American army were now at an end; but ſtill another object, not leſs eſſential, remained, which the new line of direction of the march was calculated to favour. This was, to get between the American army and Virginia, to which province it was obvious general Greene meant to retreat, rather than hazard an action with his preſent numbers. As much, therefore, as it was the intereſt of general Greene to ſecure his retreat, and avoid an action, ſo much was it that of the Britiſh commander to intercept him, and compel it, before he was joined by his reinforcements. The lower fords, upon the river that ſeparates North Carolina from Virginia, were repreſented to be impaſſable in the winter ſeaſon, and the ferries to be ſo diſtant that a ſufficient number of flats could not be collected to tranſport the American army in any convenient time. Lord Cornwallis, miſled by this information, directed his march to the upper fords upon the Dan, in order to intercept Greene's retreat, by the only route which at that ſeaſon of the year was repreſented to be practicable.

A junction formed between the two diviſions of the American army.

In the mean time the two diviſions of the American army formed a junction at Guildford Court-houſe. A council of war was held: And by their advice a retreat into Virginia, without hazarding an action, was finally reſolved upon. In order the more eaſily to effect this, a light army was formed of the beſt of the American troops, amounting in the whole to about ſeven hundred men, who were directed to manœuvre in front of the Britiſh line of march, whilſt the reſt of the army, with the baggage, proceeded by the neareſt route to Boyd's Ferry, on the Dan. Orders were ſent for-

 ward

CHAP. XLI. 1781.

ward to prepare every thing necessary for facilitating the passage, whilst general Greene marched on with all possible dispatch. At last he reached the Dan, and so much had lord Cornwallis been misinformed as to the means of passing the river, that the American troops, both the main and the light army, with their baggage, instead of meeting with any difficulty or delay, were passed over with ease, at Boyd's and Irwin's Ferries, in the course of a single day, the fourteenth of February. The light army, which was the last in crossing, was so closely pursued, that scarcely had its rear landed, when the British advance appeared on the opposite banks; and in the last twenty-four hours it is said to have marched forty miles. The hardships suffered by the British troops, for want of their tents and usual baggage, in this long and rapid pursuit, through a wild and unsettled country, were uncommonly great; yet such was their ardour in the service, that they submitted to them without a murmur, from the hope of giving a decisive blow to the American army, before it crossed the Roanoke. And that the latter escaped without suffering any material injury, seems more owing to a train of fortunate incidents, judiciously improved by their commander, than to any want of enterprise or activity in the army that pursued. Yet the operations of lord Cornwallis, during the pursuit, would probably have been more efficacious, had not the unfortunate affair at the Cowpens deprived him of almost the whole of his light troops.

General Greene driven out of North Carolina.

Lord Cornwallis, having thus driven general Greene out of the province of North Carolina, returned by easy marches from the banks of the Dan to Hillsborough, where he erected the king's standard, and invited by proclamation all loyal subjects to repair to it, and take an active part in assisting him to restore order and constitutional government. The loyalists in North Carolina were originally more numerous than in any of the other colonies: But the misfortunes consequent on premature risings had considerably thinned

The royal standard erected at Hillsborough.

thinned them. Some had suffered, others had left the country and joined the king's troops to the southward, and those who remained were become cautious from the recollection of past miscarriages. Their spirits may be said to have been broken by repeated persecutions. Still, however, the zeal of some was not repressed; and, influenced by them, considerable numbers were preparing to assemble, when general Greene, alarmed with the intelligence of their motions, and the presumed effect of lord Cornwallis's proclamation, and being, about the same time, reinforced with six hundred Virginia militia, under general Stevens, took the resolution of again crossing the Dan, and re-entering North Carolina. Even with this addition to his numbers, he had no intention of hazarding an action; but he foresaw that his return into the province would check the rising spirit amongst the loyalists; and he hoped, by means of his light troops, to interrupt their communications with the royal army. Lieutenant-colonel Lee, with his legion, was detached across the river on the twenty-first of February, and the next day general Greene passed it with the rest of the army.

General Greene, again crossing the Dan, re-enters North Carolina.

A number of loyalists being ready to assemble, under a colonel Pyle, upon the branches of Haw River, lieutenant-colonel Tarleton, with the cavalry, and a small body of infantry, was detached towards that part of the country, to give countenance to their rising, and to afford them assistance and protection. The American colonel Lee, having also received intelligence of the proposed insurrection, hastened with his legion towards the same quarter, in order to counteract Tarleton's operations, and, if possible, intercept and crush the loyalists before their junction with the British troops. The loyalists assembled, and on the twenty-fifth of February were proceeding to Tarleton's encampment, unapprehensive of danger, when they were met in a lane by Lee, with his legion. The loyalists, unfortunately mistaking the American cavalry for Tarleton's dragoons,

CHAP. XLI. 1781.

dragoons, allowed themſelves to be ſurrounded before they diſcovered their error. When at laſt it became manifeſt, they called out for quarter; but no quarter was granted; and between two and three hundred of them were inhumanly butchered, while in the act of begging for mercy. Humanity ſhudders at the recital of ſo foul a maſſacre: But cold and unfeeling policy avows it as the moſt effectual means of intimidating the friends of royal government.

Lord Cornwallis falls back from Hillſborough, and takes a new poſition.

The country round Hillſborough being nearly exhauſted of proviſions, and this forward poſition being thought too diſtant, after the return of general Greene's army, for affording effectual protection to the great body of loyaliſts who reſided between Haw and Deep Rivers, lord Cornwallis thought it expedient to retire from Hillſborough, and take a new poſition between theſe rivers, ſo as effectually to cover the country in his rear. This was accordingly done; and the Britiſh army, after paſſing Haw River, encamped on Allamance Creek. The bulk of mankind being guided by external appearances, nothing could be more unfavourable to lord Cornwallis's preſent views than this retrograde movement upon the approach of general Greene's army. If the loyaliſts were before cautious and ſlow, they now became timid to an exceſs, and dreaded taking any active meaſure whatſoever in behalf of the king's government, more eſpecially when they reflected on the diſaſter that had happened to colonel Pyle, whoſe detachment was cut to pieces within little more than a mile of Tarleton's encampment. When lord Cornwallis, therefore, had retired beyond the Haw, he had too much reaſon to complain that he found himſelf amongſt irreſolute friends, and adjoining to inveterate enemies; and that between the two he was ſo deſtitute of information that he had loſt a very favourable opportunity of attacking the American army.

Effects of this retrograde movement.

It has been already ſtated that lord Cornwallis hoiſted the royal ſtandard, and iſſued a proclamation, at Hillſborough. As much has been

been faid upon this fubject, as to lord Cornwallis's leaving Hillfborough before the period ftated in his proclamation had expired, and of the confequent diftrefs of the loyalifts, the author, who had the honour of being commiffary to the army under his lordfhip's command, not wifhing to fhrink from any refponfibility annexed to his fituation, feels it incumbent on him here to ftate a few facts. The author ever believed, and is well founded in his affertion, that one principal caufe of lord Cornwallis's leaving Hillfborough fo foon as he did, was in confequence of a written report being made by the author, as well as from feveral converfations held with lord Cornwallis upon the fubject, ftating the impoffibility of fupporting his majefty's army at Hillfborough. There being few cattle to be had in its neighbourhood, and thofe principally draught oxen, lord Cornwallis had promifed that they fhould not be flaughtered but in cafe of abfolute neceffity; but that neceffity did exift, and compelled the author to direct that feveral of the draught oxen fhould be killed. This meafure, although the effect of neceffity, caufed much murmuring amongft the loyalifts, whofe property thefe cattle were. Moft of the cattle in the neighbourhood of Hillfborough had been confumed by the Americans, who held a poft for a very confiderable time in that town.

During the time the royal army held Hillfborough, the author's cattle-drivers were obliged to go a confiderable diftance from the army for cattle, and even then brought in but a very fcanty fupply. Lord Cornwallis could not have remained as long as he did at Hillfborough had it not been for a quantity of falt-beef, pork, and fome hogs, found in the town. Such was the fituation of the Britifh army, that the author, with a file of men, was obliged to go from houfe to houfe, throughout the town, to take provifions from the inhabitants, many of whom were greatly diftreffed by this meafure, which could be juftified only by extreme neceffity.

As

CHAP. XLI. 1781.

As lord Cornwallis retired, the American army advanced; and general Greene having paſſed the Haw, near its ſource, took poſt between Troubleſome Creek and Reedy Fork; but not thinking himſelf yet ſtrong enough to riſque an action, he changed his poſition every night, in order to avoid the poſſibility of it. The American light troops and militia were poſted upon the branches of Reedy Fork, whilſt general Greene, with the main army, at ſome diſtance, inclined towards Guildford Court-houſe. Whilſt the American army lay in this ſituation, lord Cornwallis, receiving intelligence that their light troops were careleſsly poſted, determined to beat up their quarters, and compel them to retire to a greater diſtance; being at the ſame time in hopes, if general Greene ſhould move to their aſſiſtance, that a favourable opportunity might offer for attacking him to advantage. Accordingly, early in the morning of the ſixth of March, the Britiſh army paſſed Allamance Creek, and marched towards Reedy Fork. Fortunately for the American light troops, they received information of the march of the Britiſh army, whilſt it was yet at ſome diſtance, and haſtily calling in their detachments, retired acroſs Reedy Fork. At Wetzell's Mill, upon that creek, they attempted to make a ſtand, but were quickly diſlodged with conſiderable ſlaughter by the brigade under lieutenant-colonel Webſter. Greene, inſtead of marching to their aſſiſtance, upon receiving intelligence of the advance of the Britiſh army, retreated over the Haw, in order to preſerve his communication with the roads by which he expected his ſupplies and reinforcements. Theſe were now faſt approaching; and in a few days he was joined by another brigade of militia from Virginia under general Lawſon, two from North Carolina, under generals Butler and Eaton, and a conſiderable detachment of regulars raiſed for eighteen months. He had alſo been joined, ſince his laſt return into North Carolina, by the militia from the frontiers under colonels Campbell and

Prefton; fo that his numbers at this time probably exceeded five thoufand men.

General Greene, thus powerfully reinforced, knowing that the time of fervice of the militia would foon expire, determined to avail himfelf of his prefent ftrength by offering battle to lord Cornwallis. Accordingly he again advanced, and, repaffing the Haw, moved forward to Guildford Court-houfe, within twelve miles of the Britifh army, which, fince his laft retreat, had taken a new pofition at the Quakers' Meeting-houfe in the Forks of Deep River.

The near approach of general Greene, and all his other movements, fince he was joined by his reinforcements, indicating an intention of no longer avoiding an action, lord Cornwallis embraced with much fatisfaction the proffered opportunity of giving him battle. On the evening of the fourteenth of March, the baggage was fent off to Bell's Mill, upon Deep River, efcorted by lieutenant-colonel Hamilton, with his own regiment, one hundred infantry of the line, and twenty of Tarleton's cavalry; and, at dawn the next morning, the reft of the army was put in motion towards Guildford Court-houfe. About four miles from Guildford the advanced guards of both armies met, and a fharp conflict enfued, which was well fupported on both fides. Lieutenant-colonel Tarleton commanded the Britifh advance, which confifted of the cavalry, the light-infantry of the guards, and the yagers; that of the Americans was commanded by lieutenant-colonel Lee, and was compofed of his legion, with fome mountaineers and Virginia militia. Lee behaved with great bravery, and maintained his ground with firmnefs, until the appearance of the twenty-third regiment, advancing to fupport Tarleton, obliged the Americans to retire with precipitation. During the fkirmifh general Greene drew up his army on very commanding ground, in order of battle, which confifted of three lines. The two brigades of North Carolina militia, pofted be-

March.

Action near Guildford, between lord Cornwallis and general Greene.

CHAP. XLI. 1781.

hind a fence in the ſkirt of a wood, with open ground in front of their centre, and their two flanks extending into the woods, compoſed his firſt line: The Virginia militia, under Stevens and Lawſon, formed the ſecond line, and were poſted entirely in the wood, about three hundred yards in the rear of the firſt: Two brigades of continental troops formed the third line, and were drawn up chiefly in open ground near Guildford Court-houſe, about four hundred yards in the rear of the Virginia militia. Colonel Waſhington, with the dragoons of the firſt and third regiment, a detachment of continental light-infantry, and a regiment of rifle-men under colonel Lynch, formed a corps of obſervation for the ſecurity of the right flank; and Lee, with his legion, a detachment of light-infantry, and a corps of rifle-men, was appointed to the ſame ſervice on the left.

As ſoon as the head of the Britiſh column appeared in ſight of the firſt line of the Americans, a cannonade was begun from two ſix-pounders, poſted upon the road in their centre, which was immediately anſwered by the royal artillery under lieutenant Macleod; and, whilſt this cannonade continued, the Britiſh commander, with the utmoſt diſpatch, made his diſpoſition for the attack, which was in the following order: The ſeventy-firſt regiment, with the regiment of Boſe, led by general Leſlie, and ſupported by the firſt battalion of the guards, under colonel Norton, formed the right of the Britiſh line; and the twenty-third and thirty-third regiments, led by lieutenant-colonel Webſter, and ſupported by brigadier-general O'Hara, with the grenadiers and ſecond battalion of the guards, formed the left. The light infantry of the guards, with the yagers, poſted on the left of the artillery, and the cavalry in column behind it on the road, formed a corps of obſervation.

This diſpoſition being made, the line received orders to advance, and moved forward with that ſteady and guarded, but firm and determined,

termined, reſolution which diſcipline alone can confer. It has been remarked by an eye-witneſs*, that "the order and coolneſs of "that part of Webſter's brigade which advanced acroſs the open "ground, expoſed to the enemy's fire, could not be ſufficiently "extolled." At the diſtance of one hundred and forty yards they received the enemy's firſt fire, but continued to advance unmoved. When arrived at a nearer and more convenient diſtance, they delivered their own fire, and rapidly charged with their bayonets: The enemy did not wait the ſhock, but retreated behind their ſecond line. In other parts of the line the Britiſh troops behaved with equal gallantry, and were not leſs ſucceſsful. The ſecond line of the enemy made a braver and ſtouter reſiſtance than the firſt. Poſted in the woods, and covering themſelves with trees, they kept up for a conſiderable time a galling fire, which did great execution. At length, however, they were compelled to retreat, and fall back upon the continentals. In this ſevere conflict the whole of the Britiſh infantry were engaged: General Leſlie, from the great extent of the enemy's front, reaching far beyond his right, had been very early obliged to bring forward the firſt battalion of the guards, appointed for his reſerve, and form it into line: And lieutenant-colonel Webſter, finding the left of the thirty-third regiment expoſed to a heavy fire from the right wing of the enemy, which greatly out-flanked him, changed its front to the left; and the ground become vacant by this movement was immediately occupied by general O'Hara, with the grenadiers, and ſecond battalion of the guards. Webſter, moving to the left with the thirty-third regiment, ſupported by the light-infantry of the guards, and the yagers, routed and put to flight the right wing of the enemy, and in his progreſs, after two ſevere ſtruggles, gained the right of the continentals; but the ſuperiority of their numbers, and the weight of

* Lieutenant-colonel Tarleton, p. 273 of his Campaigns.

CHAP. XLI. 1781.

their fire, obliged him, ſeparated as he was from the reſt of the Britiſh line, to re-croſs a ravine, and occupy an advantageous poſition on the oppoſite bank, until he could hear of the progreſs of the king's troops on the right. The Britiſh line, being ſo much extended to the right and left, in order to ſhew a front equal to the enemy, was unavoidably broken into intervals in the purſuit of the firſt and ſecond American lines; ſome parts of it being more advanced than others, in conſequence of the different degrees of reſiſtance that had been met with, or of other impediments ariſing from the thickneſs of the woods, and the inequality of the ground. The whole, however, ſtill moved forward; and the ſecond battalion of the guards, commanded by the honourable lieutenant-colonel Stuart, was the firſt that reached the open ground at Guildford Court-houſe. Impatient to ſignalize themſelves, they immediately attacked a body of continentals, greatly ſuperior in number, that was ſeen formed on the left of the road, routed them and took their cannon, being two ſix-pounders; but, purſuing them with too much ardour and impetuoſity towards the wood in their rear, were thrown into confuſion by a heavy fire received from a body of continentals, who were yet unbroken, and being inſtantly charged by Waſhington's dragoons, were driven back with great ſlaughter, and the loſs of the cannon that had been taken. Lieutenant Macleod, advancing along the road with the royal artillery, had by this time reached the open ground. By a ſpirited and well-directed cannonade he checked the purſuit of the Americans. Fortunately alſo, the ſeventy-firſt regiment, belonging to general Leſlie's diviſion, was ſeen emerging from the woods on the right, and the twenty-third, not long afterwards, made its appearance on the left. To the right and left of theſe regiments, general O'Hara, although ſeverely wounded, rallied with much gallantry and great expedition, the remains of the ſecond battalion of the guards; and the Americans

were

were quickly repulſed and put to flight, with once more the loſs of the two ſix-pounders: Two other ſix-pounders were alſo taken, being all the artillery which they had in the field, and two ammunition waggons. The ſeventy-firſt puſhed forward to an eminence at the Court-houſe, on the left flank of the continentals. Lieutenant-colonel Webſter again advanced acroſs the ravine, defeated the corps that was oppoſed to him, and connected himſelf with the centre of the Britiſh line. The continentals of the American army being now driven from their ground, as well as the militia, a general retreat took place; but it was conducted with order and regularity. The twenty-third and ſeventy-firſt regiments, with part of the cavalry, were at firſt ſent in purſuit of the enemy, but afterwards received orders to return. It is probable that, as the Britiſh commander became more acquainted with all the circumſtances of the action, and the number of the killed and wounded, he found it neceſſary to countermand his orders, and deſiſt from the purſuit. The action being now ended in the centre and on the left of the Britiſh line, a firing was ſtill heard on the right, where general Leſlie, with the firſt battalion of the guards, and the regiment of Boſe, had been greatly impeded in advancing by the exceſſive thickneſs of the woods, which rendered their bayonets of little uſe. The broken corps of the enemy were thereby encouraged to make frequent ſtands, and to throw in an irregular fire; ſo that this part of the Britiſh line was at times warmly engaged in front, flank, and rear, with ſome of the enemy that had been routed in the firſt attack, and with part of the extremity of their left wing, which, by the cloſeneſs of the woods, had been paſſed unſeen.

At one period of the action the firſt battalion of the guards was completely broken. It had ſuffered greatly in aſcending a woody height to attack the ſecond line of the Americans, ſtrongly poſted

upon

upon the top of it, who, availing themſelves of the advantages of their ſituation, retired, as ſoon as they had diſcharged their pieces, behind the brow of the hill, which protected them from the ſhot of the guards, and returned, as ſoon as they had loaded, and were again in readineſs to fire. Notwithſtanding the diſadvantage under which the attack was made, the guards reached the ſummit of the eminence, and put this part of the American line to flight: But no ſooner was it done, than another line of the Americans preſented itſelf to view, extending far beyond the right of the guards, and inclining towards their flank, ſo as almoſt to encompaſs them. The ranks of the guards had been thinned in aſcending the height, and a number of the officers had fallen: Captain Maitland, who at this time received a wound, retired to the rear, and having had his wound dreſſed, returned immediately to join the battalion of guards to which he belonged. Some of the men, too, from ſuperior exertions, had reached the ſummit of the eminence ſooner than others; ſo that the battalion was not in regular order when it received the fire of the third American line. The enemy's fire being repeated and continued, and, from the great extent of their line, being poured in not only on the front but flank of the battalion, completed its confuſion and diſorder, and, notwithſtanding every exertion made by the remaining officers, it was at laſt entirely broken. Fortunately, at this time, the Heſſian regiment of Boſe, commanded by lieutenant-colonel de Buiy, which had hitherto ſuffered but little, was advancing in firm and compact order on the left of the guards, to attack the enemy. Lieutenant-colonel Norton thought the fortunate arrival of the regiment of Boſe preſented a favourable opportunity for forming again his battalion, and requeſted the Heſſian lieutenant-colonel to wheel his regiment to the right, and cover the guards, whilſt their officers endeavoured to rally them. The

The request was immediately and moſt gallantly complied with; and, under the cover of the fire of the Heſſians, the exertions of lieutenant-colonel Norton, and his few remaining officers, were at laſt ſucceſsful in reſtoring order. The battalion, being again formed, inſtantly moved forward to join the Heſſians: The attack was renewed, and the enemy were defeated. But here the labours of this part of the line did not yet ceaſe. No ſooner had the guards and Heſſians defeated the enemy in front, than they found it neceſſary to return and attack another body of them that appeared in the rear; and in this manner were they obliged to traverſe the ſame ground in various directions, before the enemy were completely put to the rout. The firing heard on the right, after the termination of the action in the centre, and on the left, induced lord Cornwallis to detach Tarleton, with part of the cavalry, to gain intelligence of what was doing in that quarter, and to know whether general Leſlie wanted aſſiſtance. But before Tarleton's arrival on the right, the affair was over, and the Britiſh troops were ſtanding with ordered arms; all reſiſtance having ceaſed on the part of the Americans, except from a few hardy rifle-men, who, lurking behind trees, occaſionally fired their pieces, but at ſuch a diſtance as to do no miſchief. Theſe Tarleton, when requeſted, readily undertook to diſperſe with his cavalry, and ruſhing forward under cover of a general volley of muſquetry from the guards and the regiment of Boſe, quickly performed what was expected of him. In this affair Tarleton himſelf received a ſlight wound, but the reſt of his corps returned unhurt. Thus ended the hard-fought action at Guildford Court-houſe.

In this battle the Britiſh troops obtained a victory moſt honourable and glorious to themſelves, but in its conſequences of no real advantage to the cauſe in which they were engaged. They attacked and defeated

CHAP. XLI. 1781.

an army of more than three times their own number*, not taken by surprise, but formed in regular order of battle and ready to engage; an army too, that is allowed on all hands to have been strongly and judiciously posted, on ground chosen with care, and most excellently adapted to the nature of the troops that occupied it. The resistance of the enemy was in proportion to the advantages they possessed; nor did they yield but with extreme reluctance. Even the militia, encouraged by their position, fought with bravery, and greatly weakened the British line before it reached the continentals. The Virginia militia, who composed the second American line, did not quit their ground, it is said, until their commander, seeing them no longer able to withstand the attack of regular troops, and ready to be overpowered, gave orders for a retreat. A victory atchieved under such disadvantages of numbers and ground, was of the most honourable kind, and placed the bravery and discipline of the troops beyond all praise; but the expence at which it was obtained rendered it of no utility. Before the provincials finally retreated, more than one third of all the British troops engaged had fallen. The whole loss, according to the official returns, amounted to five hundred and thirty-two: Of these ninety-three were killed in the action, four hundred and thirteen were wounded, and twenty-six missing. Amongst the killed were the honourable lieutenant-colonel

* By the return of the adjutant of the day it appears that the British troops engaged in the action amounted to 1445. The cavalry are not included in this return, and indeed they were not engaged, except for an instant on the right, after the action in the centre and on the left was over. The Americans were generally supposed to amount to 7000 men; and a letter, found in the pocket of one of their serjeants that was slain, specifies 7000 to be the number of their army: But Gordon, in his History, who appears to have taken theis numbers from official documents, states them to be 1490 continentals, and 2753 militia; in all, 4243 foot soldiers and 200 cavalry. But he seems not to have included the back woodsmen under Campbell and Preston; so that their whole number probably exceeded 7000 men.

Stuart of the guards, lieutenant O'Hara of the royal artillery, brother of the brigadier, lieutenant Robinſon of the twenty-third regiment, enſign Talbot of the thirty-third, and enſign Grant of the ſeventy-firſt; and amongſt the wounded brigadiers-general O'Hara and Howard; lieutenant-colonels Webſter and Tarleton; captains Swanton, Schutz, Maynard, Goodricke, lord Dunglaſs, Maitland, Peter, Wilmouſky, and Eichenbrodht; lieutenants Salvin, Winyard, Schwener, and Graiſe; enſigns Stuart, Kelly, Gore, Hughes, and De Trott; and adjutants Colquhoun and Fox.

The loſs of the Americans in this action has been variouſly eſtimated, and does not appear ever to have been fully aſcertained. If we are to credit their official returns, their whole loſs in killed and wounded, as well of militia as continentals, did not exceed two hundred and fifty men. But, by lord Cornwallis's diſpatches, it appears that between two and three hundred of their dead were found upon the field after the action; and if we proportion their wounded according to the number of the ſlain, their whole loſs in killed and wounded muſt have greatly exceeded that of the Britiſh troops. The number of thoſe who were miſſing, according to their own returns, was confeſſedly great; but as the Britiſh troops took but few priſoners, it is probable that the greateſt part of the miſſing conſiſted of militia, who, eſcaping from the action, fled to their own houſes, and did not afterwards return *.

The

* We ſhall here relate an anecdote reſpecting the late captain Maynard of the guards. He was naturally of a cheerful diſpoſition and great hilarity, and in ſeveral actions, during the courſe of the war, he had ſhewn great gallantry; but a certain preſentiment of his fate on the day of the action at Guildford poſſeſſed his mind, which preſentiment was too fatally realized.—— While the troops were marching on to form the line of battle, he became gloomy, and gave way to deſpondency. Not leſs than two or three different times did he tell colonel Norton, who commanded the battalion, that he felt himſelf very uncomfortable, and did not like the buſineſs at all. Colonel, now the honourable major-general, Norton, endeavoured to laugh him out

CHAP. XLI. 1781.

The wounded of both armies were collected by the Britiſh as expeditiouſly as poſſible after the action: It was, however, a ſervice that required both time and care, as from the nature of the action they lay diſperſed over a great extent of ground. Every aſſiſtance was furniſhed to them, that in the preſent circumſtances of the army could be afforded; but, unfortunately, the army was deſtitute of tents, nor was there a ſufficient number of houſes near the field of battle to receive the wounded. The Britiſh army had marched ſeveral miles on the morning of the day on which they came to action. They had no proviſions of any ſpecies whatever on that day, nor until between three and four in the afternoon of the ſucceeding day, and then but a ſcanty allowance, not exceeding one quarter of a pound of flower, and the ſame quantity of very lean beef. The night of the day on which the action happened was remarkable for its darkneſs, accompanied with rain, which fell in torrents. Near fifty of the wounded, it is ſaid, ſinking under their aggravated miſeries, expired before the morning. The cries of the wounded and dying who remained on the field of action during the night exceed all deſcription. Such a complicated ſcene of horror and diſtreſs, it is hoped, for the ſake of humanity, rarely occurs, even in a military life. Had lord Cornwallis had with him at the action at Guildford Court-houſe, thoſe troops that were loſt by colonel Tarleton at the Cowpens, on the fifteenth of March 1781, it is not extravagant to

out of his melancholy ideas, but in vain; for even after the cannonade began he reiterated the forebodings of what he conceived was to happen. Early in the action he received a wound in the leg; unable to proceed, he requeſted Mr. Wilſon, the adjutant of the guards, to lend him his horſe, that he might ride on with the battalion, and when in the act of mounting, another ſhot went through his lungs, and incapacitated him from proceeding. After being conveyed in a litter to Wilmington, and then lingering a few days, he died of his wounds, greatly regretted.

ſuppoſe

ſuppoſe that the American colonies might have been reunited to the empire of Great Britain. CHAP. XLI. 1781.

Hiſtory, perhaps, does not furniſh an inſtance of a battle gained under all the diſadvantages which the Britiſh troops, aſſiſted by a regiment of Heſſians and ſome yagers, had to contend againſt at Guildford Court-houſe. Nor is there, perhaps, on the records of hiſtory, an inſtance of a battle fought with more determined perſeverance than was ſhewn by the Britiſh troops on that memorable day. The battles of Crecy, of Poictiers, and of Agincourt, the glory of our own country, and the admiration of ages, had in each of them, either from particular local ſituation, or other fortunate and favourable circumſtances, ſomething in a degree to counterbalance the diſparity of numbers: Here time, place, and numbers, all united againſt the Britiſh. The American general had choſen his ground, which was ſtrong, commanding, and advantageous; he had time not only to make his diſpoſition, but to ſend away his baggage, and every incumbrance. His cannon, and his troops, in numbers far exceeding the Britiſh, were drawn out in readineſs to commence the action, when lord Cornwallis approached to attack him.

General Greene, after paſſing Reedy Fork Creek, three miles from the field of action, halted for ſome little time on the other ſide to collect his ſtragglers, and then retreated to the iron works on Troubleſome Creek, about twelve miles farther. When the extent of the Britiſh loſs was fully aſcertained, it became too apparent that lord Cornwallis was not in a condition either to give immediate purſuit, or to follow the blow the day after the action. Added to its other diſtreſſes, the army was almoſt deſtitute of proviſions: Under ſuch circumſtances, although a victory had been gained, a retreat became neceſſary towards that quarter from whence ſupplies could be obtained. About ſeventy of the wounded, not in a con-

CHAP. XLI. 1781.

dition to travel, were left at the Quakers' Meeting-houſe, under the protection of a flag of truce; and on the third day after the action, lord Cornwallis began to retire, by eaſy marches, towards Croſs Creek *.

* Lord Cornwallis was greatly diſappointed in his expectations of being joined by the loyaliſts. Some of them indeed came within the lines, but they remained only a few days.—— I ſhall here relate an anecdote connected with this ſubject, and in itſelf not a little intereſting: The commiſſary, who conſidered it as his duty not only to furniſh proviſions to the army, but alſo to learn the diſpoſition of the inhabitants, fell in about this time with a very ſenſible man, a Quaker, who, being interrogated as to the ſtate of the country, replied, That it was the general wiſh of the people to be reunited to Britain; but that they had been ſo often deceived in promiſes of ſupport, and the Britiſh had ſo frequently relinquiſhed poſts, that the people were now afraid to join the Britiſh army, leſt they ſhould leave the province, in which caſe the reſentment of the revolutioners would be exerciſed with more cruelty; that although the men might eſcape, or go with the army, yet, ſuch was the diabolical conduct of thoſe people, that they would inflict the ſevereſt puniſhment upon their families. "Perhaps," ſaid the Quaker, "thou art not acquainted with the conduct of thy enemies towards thoſe who wiſh "well to the cauſe thou art engaged in. There are ſome who have lived for two, and even "three years in the woods, without daring to go to their houſes; but have been ſecretly ſup- "ported by their families. Others, having walked out of their houſes, under a promiſe of "being ſafe, have proceeded but a few yards before they have been ſhot. Others have "been tied to a tree and ſeverely whipped. I will tell thee of one inſtance of cruelty: A "party ſurrounded the houſe of a loyaliſt; a few entered; the man and his wife were in bed; "the huſband was ſhot dead by the ſide of his wife." The writer of this replied, that thoſe circumſtances were horrid; but under what government could they be ſo happy as when enjoying the privileges of Engliſhmen? "True," ſaid the Quaker, "but the people "have experienced ſuch diſtreſs, that I believe they would ſubmit to any government in the "world to obtain peace." The commiſſary, finding the gentleman to be a very ſenſible, intelligent man, took great pains to find out his character. Upon inquiry, he proved to be a man of the moſt irreproachable manners, and well known to ſome gentlemen of North Carolina, then in our army, and whoſe veracity was undoubted. But a few days after this, the army had a ſtrong proof of the truth of what Mr. ———, who ſtill reſides in North Carolina, and for that reaſon muſt not be mentioned by name, had ſaid. The day before the Britiſh army reached Croſs Creek, a man bent with age joined it; He had ſcarcely the appearance of being human; he wore the ſkin of a racoon for a hat, his beard was ſome inches long, and he was ſo thin, that he looked as if he had made his eſcape from Surgeon's-hall. He wore no ſhirt, his whole dreſs being ſkins of different animals. On the morning after, when this diſtreſſed man came to draw his proviſions, Mr. Brice, the deputy muſter-maſter-general of the provincial forces, and the commiſſary, aſked him ſeveral queſtions. He ſaid, that he had lived

for three years in the woods, under ground; that he had been frequently ſought after by the Americans, and was certain of inſtant death whenever he ſhould be taken; that he ſupported himſelf by what he got in the woods; that acorns ſerved him as bread; that they had, from long uſe, become agreeable to him; that he had a family, ſome of whom, once or twice in a year, came to him in the woods; that his only crime was being a loyaliſt, and having given offence to one of the republican leaders in that part of the country where he uſed to live.

CHAP. XLII.

Proclamation by Lord Cornwallis—The British Army arrives in the Vicinity of Wilmington—General Greene marches against Lord Rawdon at Camden—Embarrassment of Lord Cornwallis—Lord Cornwallis determines to march through North Carolina into Virginia—Lord Rawdon resolves to attack the Camp of General Greene at Hobkirk's Hill—Fort Watson surrenders to the Americans—A Detachment under Colonel Watson joins Lord Rawdon at Camden—Lord Rawdon, after various Efforts to bring General Greene to an Engagement, retires from Camden—and proceeds to Monk's Corner—British Outposts reduced by the Americans—Augusta surrendered to the Americans.

CHAP. XLII. 1781.

PREVIOUSLY to the departure of the army from Wynnesborough, lieutenant-colonel Balfour, who commanded at Charlestown, had been directed to send round by water a competent force to take possession of Wilmington in North Carolina, and occupy it as a post with which lord Cornwallis, in his progress to the northward, might open a communication, for the purpose of obtaining supplies. Major Craig, who was detached on this service, took possession of Wilmington, after a slight resistance from the enemy, about the end of January; and although his force was small, by great labour and perseverance he fortified his post in a short time, so as to secure it against insult, and by some successful excursions into the

the country had made himſelf reſpected. As Wilmington lies near the mouth of Cape Fear River, and the ſettlement of Croſs Creek is upon a branch of the ſame river, about one hundred miles higher up the country, lord Cornwallis hoped, that by marching to the laſt of theſe places, where there was a friendly ſettlement of highlanders, the army would be plentifully furniſhed with proviſions, the ſick and wounded with refreſhments proper for them, and that, by means of the river, a communication might be eaſily opened with major Craig, for obtaining ſuch other ſupplies as the country did not afford, but which the army was now greatly in want of. To theſe conſiderations, another of ſome importance muſt alſo be added, that Croſs Creek was a centrical ſituation for the junction of ſuch friends of government as would be willing to ſtand forth and aſſiſt in ſuppreſſing rebellion; who would have time to make their arrangements for that purpoſe, whilſt the army halted for the recovery of the wounded. Impreſſed with ſuch ſentiments, and ſtill hoping to rouſe the loyaliſts to action, lord Cornwallis, on the ſame day on which he began his march from Guildford Court-houſe, iſſued a proclamation, reciting his victory, calling upon all loyal ſubjects to ſtand forth and aſſiſt in reſtoring order and good government, and promiſing protection in their perſons and properties to all thoſe who had taken part in the revolt (murderers excepted), who ſhould be deſirous of returning to their allegiance, and ſhould actually ſurrender themſelves, with their arms and ammunition, on or before the twentieth of April, with permiſſion to return to their houſes, upon taking a military parole, and a promiſe of ſpeedy reſtoration to all the privileges of legal and conſtitutional government.

Proclamation by lord Cornwallis.

Lord Cornwallis, having iſſued his proclamation, proceeded ſlowly towards Croſs Creek, as well for the convenience of the wounded, as the more eaſy ſubſiſtence of the troops, where he arrived about the

the end of the month. General Greene followed through the fame tract of country as far at Ramfay's Mill, on Deep River: And occafional fkirmifhes happened between the light troops, but nothing of moment between the two armies.

The Britifh army arrives in the vicinity of Wilmington.

Upon the arrival of the Britifh commander at Crofs Creek, he found himfelf difappointed in all his expectations: Provifions were fcarce: Four days forage not to be procured within twenty miles; and the communication expected to be opened between Crofs Creek and Wilmington, by means of the river, was found to be impracticable, the river itfelf being narrow, its banks high, and the inhabitants, on both fides, for a confiderable diftance, inveterately hoftile. Nothing therefore now remained to be done but to proceed with the army to Wilmington, in the vicinity of which it arrived on the feventh of April. The fettlers upon Crofs Creek, although they had undergone a variety of perfecutions in confequence of their previous unfortunate infurrections, ftill retained a warm attachment to their mother-country, and during the fhort ftay of the army amongft them, all the provifions and fpirits that could be collected within a convenient diftance, were readily brought in, and the fick and wounded plentifully fupplied with ufeful and comfortable refrefhments.

During the march of the Britifh army to Wilmington, colonel Webfter of the thirty-third, captains Schutz and Maynard of the guards, and captain Wilmoufki and enfign de Trott of the regiment of Bofe, all of them officers of merit, died of the wounds received at Guildford Court-houfe. The firft is faid to have "united all the virtues of civil life to the gallantry and profeffional knowledge of a foldier *." So amiable and diftin-

* Tarleton, p. 281.

guifhed

guiſhed a character could not fail to be univerſally reſpected, and his death was lamented by the whole army *. CHAP. XLII. 1781.

Lord Cornwallis being under the neceſſity of repairing to a ſea-port town, to obtain neceſſary ſupplies, particularly ſhoes and clothing for the army, was apprehenſive leſt general Greene ſhould return to South Carolina. Accordingly, ſeveral meſſengers were diſpatched to lord Rawdon at Camden, to prepare him for ſuch an event; but unfortunately neither the meſſengers nor their diſpatches ever reached the place of their deſtination.

General Greene marches againſt lord Rawdon at Camden.

Not long after the arrival of earl Cornwallis at Wilmington, he received information that what he apprehended as probable had actually taken place; and that general Greene, upon his return to the upper country, had taken the direct road to Camden, and was marching with the utmoſt expedition to attack lord Rawdon. This intelligence rendered the ſituation of the Britiſh commander more embarraſſing than ever, and left him only a choice of difficulties, none of which were unaccompanied with hazard, nor eaſy to be

* The ſympathetic manner in which lord Cornwallis communicated to the reverend Dr. Webſter, of Edinburgh, the intelligence of his ſon's death, is at once a proof of his lordſhip's goodneſs of heart, his tender ſenſibility, and of the high eſtimation in which he held the deceaſed. The following is a Copy of his Letter on that occaſion:

"Dear Sir, *Wilmington, April 23, 1781.*

"IT gives me great concern to undertake a taſk which is not only a bitter renewal of my own grief, but muſt be a violent ſhock to an affectionate parent.

"You have for your ſupport, the aſſiſtance of religion, good ſenſe, and the experience of the uncertainty of human happineſs. You have for your ſatisfaction, that your ſon fell nobly in the cauſe of his country, honoured and lamented by all his fellow-ſoldiers; that he led a life of honour and virtue, which muſt ſecure him everlaſting happineſs. When the keen ſenſibility of the paſſions begins to ſubſide, theſe conſiderations will give you real comfort.

"That the Almighty may give you fortitude to bear this ſevereſt of trials, is the earneſt wiſh of your companion in affliction, and moſt faithful ſervant,

"CORNWALLIS."

 ſur-

C H A P. XLII. 1781.

Embarraſſment of lord Cornwallis.

ſurmounted. It was undoubtedly his wiſh to afford ſuccour to lord Rawdon; but he knew that it was impoſſible for him, after the progreſs already made by general Greene, to arrive in time. The fate of lord Rawdon and his garriſon muſt be determined long before the Britiſh army could reach Camden; and, ſhould general Greene be ſucceſsful, there was danger that he might have it in his power to hem up his lordſhip while on his march between the great rivers, and, by cutting off his ſubſiſtence, render his arms uſeleſs. On the other hand, if general Greene ſhould be defeated, the return of the Britiſh army would be leſs neceſſary. A meaſure pregnant with ſo much danger in the execution, and promiſing ſo little advantage in the reſult, was not to be haſtily adopted: Yet ſomething was neceſſary to be done. The effective force under his lordſhip, from ſickneſs, deſertion, and the loſs ſuſtained at Guildford Court-houſe, was now reduced to fourteen hundred and thirty-five men, a number which he conſidered as totally inadequate to acting offenſively in North Carolina. To remain where he was would not only be uſeleſs, but, as the heat of ſummer increaſed, endanger the health of the troops. To return to South Carolina by land would be accompanied with the hazards already mentioned *; and to return by water would not only be diſgraceful, but take up much time in waiting for the tranſports, and in the end probably be attended with the loſs of all the cavalry and horſes belonging to the army. Upon ſuch a view of the ſubject, his lordſhip determined to take advantage of general Greene's abſence from North Carolina, to march through that pro-

Lord Cornwallis determines to march through North Carolina into Virginia.

* At this time colonel Tarleton propoſed to lord Cornwallis that he might be permitted to march back through the country to Charleſtown with his cavalry; which propoſition his lordſhip very judiciouſly rejected. Colonel Tarleton, in his publication, has thought proper to cenſure lord Cornwallis for not returning to South Carolina, inſtead of going to Virginia. But olonel Tarleton, throughout his whole Hiſtory, betrays great impatience to get rid of that burden of gratitude which was due to his lordſhip for paſt benefits conferred on him without any extraordinary degree of merit.

vince

vince into Virginia, and join his force to a ſtrong corps that had been acting there from the beginning of the year, firſt under brigadier-general Arnold, and afterwards under major-general Philips, in order to make a diverſion in favour of the Britiſh operations in North Carolina. This movement, it was thought, might have a tendency to draw general Greene back to the northward, and ſeems to have been more readily adopted, as it was the opinion of earl Cornwallis, that vigorous meaſures purſued in Virginia, and the reduction of that province, if practicable, would be the moſt effectual means of ſecuring thoſe poſſeſſions that had been already recovered in the ſouthern colonies, and of ſubjecting ſuch as remained to be ſubdued. Earl Cornwallis, having finally determined to proceed to Virginia, began his march from Wilmington on the twenty-fifth of April, where he had remained juſt eighteen days, to refreſh and refit his army.

Thus we find that the victory at Guildford drew after it ſome, and it will afterwards appear that it was followed by all the conſequences of ſomething nearly allied to a deciſive defeat. He was not joined by the loyaliſts, who were ſtill overawed by the republicans.

We muſt now attend the motions of general Greene, who, in the mean time, had entered South Carolina, and made his appearance before Camden. The amount of the force which he carried with him is very uncertain. The American accounts repreſent it to be nine hundred and thirty continental ſoldiers, and two hundred and fifty-four North Carolina militia; but we are well informed that general Greene had in the action above fifteen hundred continentals, and ſeveral corps of militia. The garriſon at Camden, under lord Rawdon, amounted to ſomething more than eight hundred men. Some well-affected militia, that came from a diſtance to offer their ſervices in this ſeaſon of danger, were neceſſarily, though reluc-

CHAP. XLII. 1781.

tantly, dismissed, on account of a scarcity of provisions; but, by arming every person already in the garrison capable of bearing arms, even musicians and drummers, he mustered an effective force of about nine hundred men. General Greene, whatever his force might be, thought it insufficient for storming the British works, or even regularly investing them. After various changes of position he at length retired to Hobkirk's Hill, about two miles from the British lines, and there encamped, with an intention, it was supposed, of waiting for the junction of colonel Lee with his legion, and Marion with his militia, who were then acting at some distance in the eastern parts of the province. Whilst the American army lay at Hobkirk's Hill, information was brought to Camden that general Greene had detached part of his militia to bring up his heavy baggage and cannon, which, for some cause or other, had been sent off some days before: And as Lee and Marion had not yet joined, lord Rawdon thought this the proper time for an attack, in the absence of the militia, and before the coming up of the cannon. Accordingly, at nine in the morning of the twenty-fifth of April, he marched out with all the force he could muster, and by making a circuit, and keeping close to the edge of a swamp, under cover of the woods, happily gained the left flank of the enemy undiscovered. In that quarter the American camp was the most assailable, because there the ascent of the hill was the easiest; but the impenetrable swamp that covered the approach to it had freed the enemy from all apprehension of an attack on that side. In this fancied state of security, the driving in of their piquets gave them the first alarm of the advance of the British army, which moved on to the attack in the following order: The sixty-third regiment, supported by the volunteers of Ireland, formed the right; the king's American regiment, supported by captain Robertson's detachment, the left; and the New York volunteers the centre of the British line. The South Carolina

Lord Rawdon resolves to attack the camp of general Greene at Hobkirk's Hill.

Carolina regiment and the cavalry were in the rear of the whole, and formed a corps of obſervation.

The enemy, although apparently ſurpriſed, and at firſt in ſome confuſion, formed with great expedition, and met the attack with reſolution and bravery. Their firſt line conſiſted wholly of continental troops, the Virginia brigade being on the right, and the Maryland brigade on the left. Their artillery arrived juſt as the action began, and was poſted in the centre. Their ſecond line was formed entirely of militia. General Greene, after viewing the advance of the Britiſh troops, and the narrow front which they preſented, was ſo confident of ſucceſs, that, with a view of rendering it more complete, and hemming them in on every ſide, he made an alteration in his firſt diſpoſition. The right of the Virginia, and the left of the Maryland brigades, were ordered to take the Britiſh troops in flank, whilſt the remainder of theſe two brigades marched down the hill to attack them in front; and in the mean time lieutenant-colonel Waſhington, with the cavalry, was detached to fall upon their rear. Had theſe ſeveral attacks ſucceeded, undoubtedly nothing but ruin awaited the Britiſh army: But lord Rawdon, diſcovering the enemy's deſign, quickly extended his front, by bringing forward the Iriſh volunteers, and forming them into line. The Americans who deſcended the hill in front, although they fought for ſome time with great bravery, and were well ſupported by a deſtructive fire of grape-ſhot from their cannon, could not long withſtand the impetuoſity of the aſſailants. Being compelled to retire, they were purſued by the Britiſh troops to the top of the hill. Lord Rawdon having gained the ſummit of the eminence, and ſilenced the American cannon, which were immediately drawn off, was enabled to bring the remainder of his force into action, and at length put to rout the whole American army. The continentals ſeveral times rallied and returned to the charge, but were as often broke

and

CHAP. XLII. 1781.

and put to flight. In the mean time Washington with his dragoons, having got into the rear of the British troops, had made a few stragglers prisoners, and exacted paroles from some British officers who lay wounded in the field. When the event of the day turned out different from his expectations, he was fortunate enough to discover it just in time to make good his retreat. Indeed, the Americans were so greatly superior in cavalry, that lord Rawdon, after ordering a pursuit, did not think fit to continue it farther than three miles. General Greene retreated to Rugeley's Mills, about twelve miles off, and there encamped. He was indebted to accident for the safety of his cannon: In the beginning of the retreat they were run down a steep, amongst some brush-wood, which concealed them from the British troops as they passed in the heat of pursuit; and before their return they were carried off by Washington's cavalry. According to accounts said to be taken from lord Rawdon's statement, the Americans lost in this action upwards of five hundred men: Of these about one hundred were made prisoners, and the rest either killed or wounded. But general Greene estimates his loss much lower: He makes it amount only to eighteen killed, one hundred and eight wounded, and one hundred and thirty-six missing; but at the same time admits, not without some degree of inconsistency, that some of the missing were killed, and others wounded. It was a hard-fought action; and the victory was not bloodless on the part of the conquerors: Although thirty-eight only were killed, their whole loss, including the wounded and missing, amounted to two hundred and fifty-eight, a number which, in the present perilous state of the province, could not be well spared. One officer only was amongst the slain; but eleven were wounded.

Had lord Rawdon, instead of marching out to meet the enemy, remained in his works, such was the superiority of Greene, particularly in cavalry, that he must have reduced his lordship, in a short time,

time, to the neceſſity of ſurrendering through want of proviſions. The quick and marked deciſion with which he acted on this, as he had done on former occaſions, formed a very general preſage that he was one day to rank with the great military commanders; though ſo amiable a diſtinction is not to be attained without the happieſt union of courage and genius. A military leader cannot be formed, like many other characters of reſpectability in the ſtate, by mere experience in the common courſe of buſineſs. At the ſame time that he endeavours to control accidents by general maxims and comprehenſive views, he muſt vary his particular meaſures with the varying moment of action. In the midſt of danger, and at a moment's warning, he muſt call to his aid all the reſults of his paſt experience and obſervations; baniſh from his mind every extraneous idea that fancy or caſual aſſociation might ſuggeſt to diſtract his thoughts and miſlead his judgment, and perceive, at a glance, the ſhorteſt and moſt effectual proceſs for attaining his object.

Upon the approach of the American army, a very general ſpirit of revolt ſhewed itſelf amongſt the inhabitants of South Carolina, particularly in the diſtrict of Ninety-ſix, on the weſtern frontier, and on the north-eaſt in that tract of country which lies between the two great rivers Pedee and Santee. Even in Charleſtown itſelf, many of the inhabitants, although awed and reſtrained by the preſence of the garriſon, gave evident ſigns of diſaffection. In the moſt tranquil period of the province, Sumpter, on the north-weſt frontier, and Marion in the north-eaſt, had kept alive the embers of revolt, which, although at different times variouſly agitated, in conſequence of the reſtleſs diſpoſition of thoſe partiſans, were nevertheleſs prevented from gaining ſtrength by the aſcendancy of the Britiſh arms; but they now burſt forth into a flame, as ſoon as intelligence arrived that general Greene had entered the province. To encourage this ſpirit of revolt amongſt the inhabitants, and to make

a di-

CHAP. XLII. 1781.

a diverſion in the north-eaſt part of the province in favour of the attempt upon Camden, general Greene had detached lieutenant-colonel Lee, with his legion, from Deep River, to precede the army, and in conjunction with Marion, to attack ſome of the Britiſh poſts. Lee marched with ſo much expedition, that a junction was formed between him and Marion on the fourteenth of April, and on the fifteenth, in purſuance of their orders, they appeared before Fort Watſon, a Britiſh poſt on the Santee. Fort Watſon is ſituated upon an eminence, about thirty feet above the level of the circumjacent plain. The eminence is an artificial mount, raiſed by the Indians before they were diſpoſſeſſed of the country, and for ſome diſtance round it were no trees to ſhelter the approch of an enemy. The garriſon was without artillery, and ſo were the beſiegers: Neither had the latter intrenching tools to aſſiſt them in making approaches. But the ingenuity of a colonel Maham quickly deviſed a method of reducing the fort, as unexpected as it was efficacious. Under his direction a work upon an unuſual plan was ſpeedily conſtructed which overlooked the fort. Upon the top of this work American rifle-men were poſted, who fired at every one in the garriſon who ventured to make his appearance, and ſeldom miſſed their aim: Preparations being made at the ſame time for ſtorming, the commanding officer made overtures for capitulating upon honourable terms. Theſe were readily granted: And Fort Watſon was ſurrendered on the twenty-third of April. After this exploit, Lee and Marion receiving intelligence that colonel Watſon, with five hundred men, was on his march through that part of the country to reinforce lord Rawdon at Camden, took the reſolution of endeavouring to obſtruct his progreſs. They accordingly ſeized the paſſes upon the different creeks and rivers in his way, and guarded them ſo effectually, that he found himſelf under the neceſſity of returning down the Santee, and paſſing it near its mouth. By this interruption

April.

Fort Watſon ſurrenders to the Americans.

tion much time was loſt, and many hardſhips were encountered in marching through the ſwamps and ſunken grounds: Colonel Watſon, however, perſevered, and proceeding up the ſouth ſide of the Santee, paſſed it again, a little below the confluence of its two great branches, the Congaree and Wateree, and arrived at Camden, with his detachment, on the ſeventh of May.

CHAP. XLII.

1781. May.

A detachment under colonel Watſon joins lord Rawdon at Camden.

The victory at Hobkirk's Hill, like that at Guildford Court-houſe, although moſt honourable and glorious to the officers who commanded, and the troops that were engaged, produced no conſequences beneficial to the Britiſh intereſt. The general diſaffection of the province ſtill continued; the force under general Greene, although diminiſhed, was yet reſpectable; and the American partiſans were more than ever active in making predatory incurſions into various parts of the province, aſſaulting the weakeſt Britiſh poſts, waylaying convoys of proviſion, and interrupting the communication between Camden and Charleſtown. Lord Rawdon, therefore, even in the moment of ſucceſs, ſaw the neceſſity of abandoning Camden, and contracting the Britiſh poſts within a narrower compaſs. But as he was now joined by the reinforcement under Watſon, which replaced the loſs of men ſuſtained in the action, he gallantly reſolved to make one effort more, before he evacuated his poſt, to ſtrike a blow at general Greene, who, after remaining ſome days at Rugeley's Mills to collect his ſtragglers, paſſed the Wateree, and encamped behind Twenty-five Mile Creek. Lord Rawdon had good information of the nature of the ground where Greene was encamped, and thought that by making a circuit, and getting into his rear, an attack might be made with great proſpect of ſucceſs. Accordingly, with this view he marched from Camden in the night ſucceeding the day on which colonel Watſon arrived. But general Greene had by this time decamped

CHAP. XLII. 1781.

from Twenty-five Mile Creek. Having received information of the arrival of Watson's corps, and concluding that lord Rawdon, thus reinforced, would immediately attempt to strike at him, he changed his position for another at a greater distance, much stronger, and more easily defended. Intelligence of this movement being brought to lord Rawdon, while on his march, he proceeded along the direct road to general Greene's new encampment, where he arrived the next day. After driving in his piquets, and examining every point of his situation, he found it too strong to be attempted without suffering such a loss as could not be compensated by a victory. Under such circumstances, his lordship relinquished his design of attacking the American army, and on the same day returned to Camden. On the ninth of May such stores were destroyed as could not be removed, and on the tenth Camden was evacuated; lord Rawdon retiring by easy marches towards Nelson's Ferry, in order to give time to as many of the loyal inhabitants, as chose to accompany him, to carry off their effects and moveable property. The British army completed its passage at Nelson's Ferry, by the evening of the fourteenth, and from thence proceeded to Monk's Corner, for the greater security of Charlestown, the garrison of which, its works being at that time unfinished, was insufficient for its defence. In the mean time the enemy's detachments were too successful in reducing several of the British outposts. Fort Motte, on the Congaree, after a brave defence, was surrendered to Lee and Marion, on the eleventh of May: About the same time, Sumpter possessed himself of Orangeburgh; and on the fifteenth Lee reduced Fort Granby.

Lord Rawdon, after various efforts to bring general Greene to an engagement, retires from Camden; and proceeds to Monk's Corner.

British outposts reduced by the Americans.

General Greene having so far succeeded in his views upon the north and north-east parts of South Carolina, and obliged lord Rawdon to retire to Monk's Corner, now turned his attention to the

the weſtern frontier, and with equal facility hoped to reduce the Britiſh poſts at Auguſta in Georgia, and Ninety-ſix in South Carolina. Orders had been previouſly diſpatched to colonel Pickens to aſſemble the militia of Ninety-ſix; and immediately after Lee's ſucceſs at Fort Granby, he, with his legion, was detached to join Pickens, and lay ſiege to Auguſta, whilſt general Greene, with the main army, marched to inveſt Ninety-ſix. Lee having joined Pickens, their firſt attempt was againſt Fort Golphin, ſituated on the banks of the Savannah, ſome miles below Auguſta, which was ſpeedily reduced by a detachment from Lee's legion. The two commanders now advanced with their whole force againſt Fort Cornwallis, at Auguſta, and began to make regular approaches, and inveſt it in form. At Auguſta lieutenant-colonel Browne ſtill commanded, and prepared to defend it with that ſpirit and reſolution which he had manifeſted on a former occaſion, when beſieged by colonel Clarke. Although the works of the beſiegers were puſhed on with vigour, and their approaches made with judgment, no advantage was for a conſiderable time obtained over the vigilant and brave commander of the garriſon. But at length the ſame mode of attack, the efficacy of which had been tried at Fort Watſon, was here alſo adopted with ſucceſs. Works were conſtructed of a ſufficient height to overlook the fort, from whence rifle-men fired with ſuch unerring aim, that the artillery-men were either killed or driven from their guns; and none of the garriſon could ſhew themſelves without being ſhot down. Neceſſity, therefore, at laſt obliged colonel Browne to capitulate, and the fort, after a gallant defence, was ſurrendered on the fifth of June.

June. Auguſta ſurrendered to the Americans.

CHAP. XLIII.

State of the British Army at Ninety-six—The Siege of Ninety-six raised—Lord Rawdon, having arrived at Ninety-six, pursues General Greene—Lord Rawdon, with Half his Force, marches to the Congaree—Retires to Orangeburgh—Hostilities suspended by the intense Heat of the Season—Lord Rawdon, on account of his Health, embarks for Europe—Action between Colonel Stuart and General Greene, near the Eutaw Springs—Victory in this Action claimed by both Parties.

CHAP. XLIII. 1781.

IN the mean time general Greene had laid siege to Ninety-six. Nintety-six took its name from being that number of miles distant from the town of Kecowee, in the Cherokee country, and, like other villages on the frontiers of the colonies, was originally surrounded with a stockade for the protection of the inhabitants against any sudden assault from the Indians. After it came into the possession of the British troops, in the year 1780, some other works were added, the principal of which, called, from its form, the Star, was on the right of the village. It was planned by lieutenant Haldane of the engineers, aid-du-camp to lord Cornwallis, and consisted of sixteen salient and re-entering angles, with a dry ditch, fraise, and abbatis: But the whole of the works were in an unfinished state at the commencement of the siege.

State of the British garrison at Ninety-six.

When lord Rawdon found himself under the necessity of evacuating Camden, and abandoning the upper country of South Carolina, he was well

well aware of the danger of Ninety-ſix, from the difficulty of ſending ſuccours to ſupport a poſt at ſuch a diſtance: Repeated expreſſes were therefore ſent to lieutenant-colonel Cruger, who commanded the garriſon, directing him to evacuate his poſt, retire to Auguſta, and, after joining his force with that under colonel Browne, and taking the command of the whole, to act according to his diſcretion, and as circumſtances ſhould point out. In caſe theſe ſhould fail, lord Rawdon had alſo taken the precaution of directing lieutenant-colonel Balfour to diſpatch other meſſengers from Charleſtown with the like orders. But ſo univerſal was the diſaffection of the inhabitants of the country, and ſo well had they guarded all the roads and paths leading to Ninety-ſix, that not one of all the meſſengers arrived in ſafety. Lieutenant-colonel Cruger was therefore totally ignorant of the ſituation of the army under lord Rawdon; nor had he any information of the action at Hobkirk's Hill, and the ſubſequent evacuation of Camden, but from an American officer who happened to be made priſoner: But he knew well the diſaffection of the province, and the inveterately hoſtile diſpoſition of the inhabitants around him, and had alſo reaſon to apprehend an attack from the American army. In this ſtate of uncertainty, with reſpect to the poſſibility of obtaining ſuccours, and under ſuch circumſtances of apprehended danger, he thought it incumbent upon him to put his poſt in the beſt poſſible ſtate of defence. The whole garriſon was immediately ſet to work, the officers cheerfully ſharing in the labour with the common ſoldiers; and by their united exertions a bank of earth parapet high was in a ſhort time thrown up round the ſtockade; and the whole ſtrengthened by an abbatis. Block-houſes were alſo erected in the village, traverſes made for the ſecurity of the roops, and caponiers or covered communications between different parts of the works. It has been already obſerved that a regular work called the Star defended the right of the village; and on the

CHAP. XLIII. 1781.

left of it was a valley, through which ran a rivulet that ſupplied the place with water. The county priſon having been fortified, commanded the valley on one ſide, and a ſtockade that was erected on the left covered it on the other. But for the defence of all theſe works there were only three pieces of artillery, and even for theſe a ſcanty and inſufficient ſupply of ammunition. The garriſon itſelf was not numerous: It conſiſted of about one hundred and fifty men of the firſt battalion of Delancey's, and two hundred of the ſecond battalion of New Jerſey volunteers, both of them provincial regiments, and raiſed ſince the commencement of the war. But as they had been conſtantly employed in active ſervice ſince the year 1776, they were at this time, for their number, perhaps equal to any troops. To theſe were added about two hundred loyal militia under a colonel King: And to their honour it is to be related, that although they had the Britiſh commander's permiſſion to quit the garriſon, and, being provided with good horſes, might have effected their retreat either to Charleſtown or Georgia, they nobly diſdained to quit their poſt in the hour of danger, and turning their horſes looſe in the woods, determined to aſſiſt in the defence of the place, and abide the fate of the garriſon. The Britiſh commander was induced to offer this permiſſion both from motives of policy and humanity: He apprehended a ſcarcity of proviſions, if the ſiege ſhould be ſpun out to any length; and from what had happened too often already, he had reaſon to fear, that, ſhould the place ultimately fall, even the ſolemn engagements of a capitulation would not be ſufficient to ſecure to the militia their ſtipulated rights, nor protect them againſt the vengeance of their countrymen.

Such was the ſtate of the garriſon at Ninety-ſix, and in this condition were the works, when the advance of the American army appeared in ſight of it on the twenty-firſt of May. In the evening general Greene encamped his whole army in a wood within cannon-ſhot

ſhot of the village, and in the night, as if he meant to intimidate the garriſon by his boldneſs, two works were thrown up within ſeventy paces of the fortifications. Had he been acting againſt a raw and undiſciplined militia, his temerity might have been excuſable; but both the Britiſh commander and his garriſon had ſeen too much ſervice not to take advantage of ſo raſh a proceeding, and to teach him to his coſt to ſhew them a little more reſpect. By eleven in the morning of the twenty-ſecond of May, a platform was prepared in one of the ſalient angles of the Star, oppoſite to the American works, for receiving the three pieces of artillery, and under cover of an inceſſant cannonade from them, and continued peals of muſquetry from the parapet, a party of only thirty men ſallied from the Star, entered the American works, and put to the bayonet every one they found. Theſe were followed by another party from the loyal militia, who quickly demoliſhed the works, and loaded ſeveral negroes with the intrenching tools of the Americans. Although general Greene put his whole army in motion to ſupport his people in the trenches, the buſineſs was ſo expeditiouſly performed, that both the detachments returned within the fortifications without ſuſtaining any other injury than the loſs of the officer * who gallantly commanded the firſt party that ſallied forth. To the regret of the whole garriſon, he received a wound, of which he died the following night.

In the night of the twenty-third of May, the Americans again broke ground; but at the reſpectful diſtance of four hundred yards, and beyond a ravine. From this point they continued to make regular and guarded approaches; but worked ſo expeditiouſly, that although they were frequently interrupted by ſallies from the garriſon, they had completed their ſecond parallel by the third of June.

* Lieutenant Roney of Delancey's ſecond battalion.

The

CHAP. XLIII. 1781.

The adjutant-general of the American army was now ſent to ſummon the Britiſh commander to ſurrender his poſt. He preſented to the officer who received him, a paper ſigned by himſelf; diſplaying in pompous language the late ſucceſſes of the Americans; declaring that the garriſon had every thing to hope from their generoſity, and to fear from their reſentment; calling upon the commanding officer to ſurrender without delay; and threatening, if he perſiſted in a fruitleſs reſiſtance, to make him perſonally reſponſible for all the conſequences. In anſwer to a paper of ſo extraordinary a nature, not ſigned by general Greene, the Britiſh commander contented himſelf with directing a meſſage to be delivered to the American adjutant-general, importing, that lieutenant-colonel Cruger was determined to defend his poſt to the laſt extremity, and that general Greene's promiſes and threats were alike indifferent to him.

The American batteries were now opened from their ſecond parallel, and a heavy croſs fire commenced, which enfiladed ſeveral of the works. The enemy alſo puſhed on a ſap againſt the Star, and continued to advance their batteries, one of which, conſtructed of gabions, was erected within thirty-five yards of the abbatis, and raiſed forty feet high, ſo as to overlook the works of the garriſon. Riflemen poſted upon the top of it did conſiderable execution, and proved ſo incommodious to thoſe who worked the artillery, that the guns of the Star were neceſſarily unmanned during the day, and uſed only in the night. The garriſon tried to burn the battery by firing heated ſhot, but, from the want of furnaces, did not ſucceed; and the only precaution which they could take againſt this deſtructive fire of the rifle-men, was to crown their parapets with ſand-bags. Loop-holes were however left for the loyal militia to fire through; and with their rifles they alſo did conſiderable execution. An attempt was made by the enemy to ſet fire to the barracks by ſhooting African arrows: But the Britiſh commander fruſtrated their deſign by by directing all the buildings to be unroofed, a meaſure from which both officers and men were expoſed, during the remainder of the ſiege, to all the pernicious effects of the night-air: Nevertheleſs, ſuch was their zeal for the ſervice, and ſuch their confidence in lieutenant-colonel Cruger, that his order was obeyed with the utmoſt alacrity.

The garriſon were now deſtined to have their feelings wounded by an exhibition which they were not prepared to expect. This was the contrivance of lieutenant-colonel Lee. When he joined the American army on the eighth of June, after the reduction of Auguſta, he brought with him the Britiſh priſoners; and either to gratify his vanity, or for ſome other cauſe, hitherto unexplained, marched them paſt Ninety-ſix, in full view of the garriſon, with all the parade of martial muſic, and preceded by a Britiſh ſtandard reverſed. If the intention was to diſcourage the garriſon, it failed entirely of its effect, or rather produced an oppoſite one. Fired with indignation at a ſight ſo unbecoming, they determined to encounter every danger, and endure every hardſhip, rather than fall into the hands of an enemy capable of diſgracing their ſucceſs by ſo wanton an inſult offered to their priſoners.

The American army, ſtrengthened by the junction of the troops who had reduced Auguſta, began to make approaches againſt the ſtockade fort on the left of the village, which kept open the communication with the water. The operations on this ſide were entruſted to lieutenant-colonel Lee, whilſt general Greene continued to direct thoſe againſt the Star. In the night of the ninth of June a ſortie was made by two ſtrong parties of the garriſon. The party to the right entering the enemy's trenches, penetrated to a battery of four guns, which nothing but the want of ſpikes and hammers prevented them from deſtroying. Here they diſcovered the mouth of a mine intended to be carried under a curtain of the Star, and had nearly taken the chief engineer of the Americans, who happened to be viewing it at the time of the fortie. In making his escape he was wounded. The other division upon the left fell in with the covering party of the Americans, put a number of them to the bayonet, and made their commanding officer prisoner. Although lieutenant-colonel Lee broke ground at a respectful distance from the stockade on the left, and made his approaches with great caution, he nevertheless lost a considerable number of men. Chagrined with his losses, and vexed at meeting with so much opposition, he suffered his impatience, on the twelfth of June, to get the better of his discretion. At eleven in the forenoon he directed a serjeant and six men to advance with lighted combustibles, and set fire to the abbatis: The party advanced, and attempted to execute their orders, but not one of them returned. The garrison fired upon them, and the whole fell a sacrifice to the rashness of their commander, who was obliged to solicit a truce to bury the dead. When the cannon arrived from Augusta which this officer had directed to be sent after him, he redoubled his efforts; and by the seventeenth of June the stockade fort was so completely enfiladed by a triangular fire, that, being no longer tenable, it was evacuated in the night, and without loss.

About this time the sufferings of the garrison began to be extreme for want of water. A well had been dug in the Star with great labour, but no water was to be found; nor was any to be procured except from the rivulet on the left, within pistol-shot of the enemy. In the day nothing could be done: But in the night, naked negroes being sent out, whose bodies in the darkness were not distinguishable from the trees that surrounded them, with great hazard to themselves, brought in a scanty supply. That the defence of the place, under such circumstances of distress, could not be much longer protracted, appears obvious enough. But the British commander, even

in

in this extremity, was not discouraged. He placed his confidence in the well-known zeal, activity, and enterprise of lord Rawdon, who he did not doubt would come to his relief the moment he could do it with propriety, and in the mean time, under all his difficulties, he hoped to maintain his post until his arrival. Whilst the British commander was exerting himself to infuse similar sentiments into the garrison, and encouraging them to persevere, an American loyalist, in open day, under the fire of the enemy, having rode through their piquets and reached the village, delivered a verbal message from lord Rawdon, "that he had passed Orangeburgh, and was in "full march to raise the siege." At such a crisis, the prospect of speedy relief dispelled the cloud from every brow: An unusual degree of animation succeeded: Their present distresses were no longer thought of; and the only object that occupied their minds, was the successful defence of the place until the joyful period of lord Rawdon's arrival.

Although that officer, upon receiving intelligence of the siege of Ninety-six, felt the strongest inclination to relieve it, an object of still greater importance, the security of Charlestown in the present disaffected state of the country, demanded his first attention, and obliged him for some time to remain near the sea-coast. Fortunately, however, the arrival of three regiments from Ireland on the third of June, placed the one in a state of safety, and enabled him to march to the relief of the other. On the seventh of June he left Charlestown, taking with him the flank companies of the three newly-arrived regiments, and being joined by the troops from Monk's Corner, proceeded on his march with all the expedition that the heat of the weather, then beginning to be intense, would permit. The route he took inclined a little to the right of the direct road to Ninety-six, and was chosen for the sake of enabling him to get between general Greene and his detachments on the Congaree.

June.

 His

His whole force amounted to near eighteen hundred infantry, and one hundred and fifty cavalry.

General Greene had regular intelligence of lord Rawdon's movements; and finding from his progreſs that it would be impoſſible to reduce Ninety-ſix by regular approaches before his arrival, determined to hazard an aſſault. Although the American works were not entirely finiſhed, they were in a ſtate of great forwardneſs: Their third parallel was completed, and a mine and two trenches had been puſhed on within a few feet of the ditch. In the morning of the eighteenth of June a heavy cannonade was begun from all the American batteries: At noon two parties advanced under cover of the trenches which approached neareſt to the works, and made lodgments in the ditch: Theſe were immediately followed by other parties with hooks to draw down the ſand-bags, and tools to reduce the parapet. The rifle-men in the mean time, poſted on their battery, were ready to take aim at every Britiſh ſoldier that appeared; and the Virginia and Maryland brigades, having manned the lines of the third parallel, fired from them by platoons. The right flank of the enemy was expoſed to the fire of a three-pounder, as well as to that of the block-houſes in the village; and major Greene, who commanded in the Star, with much honour to himſelf, and benefit to the ſervice, from the beginning of the ſiege, had his detachment ready to receive them on the parapet with bayonets and ſpears. As the main body of the American army did not advance beyond the third parallel, and was contented with ſupporting the parties in the ditch by an inceſſant fire from the trenches, the garriſon determined to put a ſpeedy period to the aſſault by an effort of gallantry which confounded the enemy. Two parties of thirty men each, one under captain Campbell of the New Jerſey volunteers, and the other under captain French of Delancey's, iſſued from the ſally-port in the rear of the Star, entered the ditch, and taking

taking oppoſite directions, charged the Americans who had made the lodgment with ſuch impetuoſity, that they drove every thing before them until they met in the oppoſite quarter. The bayonet being the only weapon uſed, the carnage was great: Even the American accounts admit that two-thirds of their people who entered the ditch were either killed or wounded. General Greene, ſeeing it uſeleſs any longer to continue ſo hopeleſs an attempt, called off his troops, and in the evening of the following day finally raiſed the ſiege. His baggage having been previouſly ſent off, his army marched with great expedition, and on the twentieth croſſed the Saluda. The loſs of the enemy, during the ſiege, according to their own accounts, amounted to one hundred and ſixty-ſix men, including one colonel, three captains, and five lieutenants: But as the loſs of the militia, who, it is ſaid, on this occaſion bore the proportion of three to one to the troops in the pay of congreſs, was not included in their returns, their total loſs muſt have been much greater. That of the garriſon amounted to twenty-ſeven killed, and fifty-eight wounded. Lieutenant Roney was the only commiſſioned officer killed; and captains French and Smith of Delancey's, with captain Barbarie and lieutenant Hatton of the New Jerſey volunteers, were amongſt the wounded. On the twenty-firſt of June in the morning lord Rawdon arrived at Ninety-ſix, and when he found that general Greene had retreated acroſs the Saluda, neither the heat of the weather nor the fatigue of the troops, after ſo long a march, prevented his lordſhip from ſetting out in purſuit of him the ſame evening. But ſo rapid was the flight of the Americans, that he ſoon perceived there was little proſpect of overtaking them. Nevertheleſs the purſuit, under many wants, and the rage of a burning ſun, was continued as far as the banks of the Enoree, when his lordſhip, finding it in vain to proceed any farther, returned towards Ninety-ſix. As the poſt of Ninety-ſix was now to be evacuated,

The ſiege of Ninety-ſix raiſed.

Lord Rawdon, having arrived at Ninety-ſix, purſues general Greene.

being

CHAP. XLIII. 1781.

being without the limits to which the Britiſh commanders, from recent circumſtances, had determined to confine their defence, lord Rawdon thought it neceſſary to pay all due attention to the loyal inhabitants who had remained faithful to their engagements. He convened the principal perſons amongſt them, and offered, if they choſe to remain, and would undertake the defence of their diſtrict againſt their own diſaffected inhabitants, to leave a party for their countenance and aſſiſtance, and from time to time to ſend ſuch reinforcements from the Congaree as might be equal to any force that general Greene could ſpare for invading them; but if they were unwilling to remain, he promiſed that care ſhould be taken for the removal of them and their families within the new frontier about to be eſtabliſhed. The inhabitants accepted the laſt of theſe propoſals: And in order effectually to grant that protection which he had promiſed, lord Rawdon left more than half his force with lieutenant-colonel Cruger, to eſcort them when they ſhould be ready to move, whilſt he, with eight hundred infantry, and ſixty cavalry, marched towards the Congaree.

Lord Rawdon, with half his force, marches to the Congaree.

Although general Greene, in his retreat from Ninety-ſix, had paſſed not only the Enoree, but Tyger and Broad Rivers, no ſooner did he hear that lord Rawdon had divided his force, than he returned, with a view of interrupting his lordſhip's operations on the Congaree, where it was ſuppoſed he meant to eſtabliſh a poſt. Lord Rawdon, it is probable, would not have undertaken his march to that part of the country with ſo diminiſhed a force, had he not expected to be met there by a ſtrong corps from Charleſtown, which he had at firſt ordered to take poſt at Orangeburgh, and afterwards to join him upon the Congaree at an appointed time. From ſome cauſe or other, this corps, after it had begun its march, was recalled by orders from Charleſtown; and, unfortunately, the letter from the commanding officer, acquainting lord Rawdon with his recal, and

and the impoffibility of meeting him at the time appointed, was intercepted and carried to general Greene. Upon the receipt of this letter he preffed forward on his march with redoubled expedition, hoping to obtain fome advantage over lord Rawdon, whilft he waited for a reinforcement that was not to join him. Soon after his lordfhip's arrival at the Congaree, one of his foraging parties was furprifed by Lee's legion, and about forty cavalry were made prifoners. The appearance of the enemy's light troops in that quarter of the country, quickly convinced his lordfhip that general Greene's army was at no great diftance; and as he had not been joined by his reinforcement at the appointed time, he thought it neceffary to take meafures for his own fecurity. Accordingly he retired from the Congaree, and marched for Orangeburgh, where he expected to meet the reinforcement from Charleftown. After forcing his paffage at noon day, in the face of the enemy, over a creek, the bridges of which were broken down and its fords guarded by Lee's legion, he without further moleftation arrived at Orangeburgh, and was joined the next day by lieutenant-colonel Stuart, with the third regiment, from Charleftown.

Retires to Orangeburgh.

General Greene, finding that lord Rawdon by his activity and enterprife had extricated himfelf from the danger to which he was expofed, collected all the militia he could, and advanced with his army within five miles of the Britifh encampment, which at the head of his cavalry he reconnoitred in the evening, lord Rawdon giving him no interruption, as he wifhed for nothing more than an attack in his prefent pofition. But the American commander, inftead of preparing for an attack, decamped in the night, and retiring towards the Congaree, had paffed that river before lord Rawdon was apprized of his retreat. It is probable that general Greene's retreat was haftened by intelligence received about this time, that lieutenant-

colonel

CHAP. XLIII. 1781.

colonel Cruger, after evacuating Ninety-ſix, and conducting the loyal inhabitants and their families ſafely within the Britiſh poſts, was advancing to join lord Rawdon with the reſt of the army. Whilſt the main American army retired acroſs the Congaree, Sumpter, Lee, and Marion, with their reſpective corps, were detached by different routes to the lower part of the country, for the purpoſe of haraſſing the Britiſh outpoſts, and waylaying their convoys. They ſucceeded in taking ſome waggons with baggage and ſtores, but failed in an attempt upon the nineteenth regiment at Monk's Corner.

July. Hoſtilities ſuſpended by the intenſe heat of the ſeaſon.

The weather now became ſo intenſely hot, that hoſtilities for ſome time were neceſſarily ſuſpended: General Greene retired with his army to the high hills of Santee, where he was ſoon afterwards joined by the different corps under Lee, Sumpter, and Marion; and lord Rawdon, on account of ill health, availed himſelf, in this interval of inaction, of his leave of abſence obtained ſome time before, and embarked for Europe. At his departure, the command of the Britiſh troops in the field devolved on lieutenant-colonel Stuart of the third regiment, or Buffs.

Lord Rawdon, on account of his health, embarks for Europe.

Although general Greene in the courſe of the preſent year had been driven from South Carolina into Virginia, was afterwards defeated in two general engagements, and finally obliged to raiſe the ſiege of Ninety-ſix, and fly with great precipitation before the Britiſh army; yet, through his own firmneſs and perſeverance, the ſucceſſes of his detachments againſt the Britiſh outpoſts, and the advantages derived from the general diſaffection of the inhabitants to the Britiſh cauſe, he ſucceeded in the main object of the campaign. The Britiſh troops, haraſſed and wearied out with the defence of an extenſive frontier, to which their force was unequal without the aſſiſtance of the inhabitants, were obliged in the end to abandon to him the greateſt part of South Carolina; the limits of their poſſeſſions being

now

now confined within the three great rivers Santee, Congaree, and Edifto; and before the end of the year, as will prefently be feen, their limits were contracted within a much narrower compafs. CHAP. XLIII. 1781.

After the retreat of the Americans from Orangeburgh to the high hills of Santee, the Britifh army under colonel Stuart moved forward to the Congaree, and encamped near the junction of that river with the Wateree. In the mean time general Greene was reinforced by a brigade of continental troops from North Carolina, and intent upon profecuting his plan for the recovery of South Carolina, put his forces in motion as foon as the extreme heat began to abate. On the twenty-fecond of Auguft he marched from the high hills of Santee with an intention to give battle to the Britifh army, and proceeding up the northern banks of the Wateree, croffed it near Camden. From thence he directed his march to Friday's Ferry on the Congaree, where he was joined by general Pickens with the militia of Ninety-fix, and by the South Carolina ftate troops under colonel Henderfon. August.

The Britifh commander, upon receiving intelligence that general Greene was on his march to attack him, fell back with his whole force to Eutaw, about forty miles from the Congaree. This movement was made for the purpofe of meeting a convoy of provifions then on the road from Charleftown, rather than weaken the army whilft an attack was expected, by fending off fo ftrong an efcort as would have been neceffary for fecuring its fafe arrival. General Greene having paffed the Congaree, continued to advance towards Eutaw, but by very flow marches, that he might give time to general Marion to join him with his brigade of militia. This junction was made on the feventh of September about feven miles from Eutaw; and at four in the morning of the following day, general Greene marched with his whole force to make his projected attack. At fix o'clock in the morning came in two deferters from Greene's army

CHAP. XLIII. 1781.

with intelligence that he was on his march to attack the Britiſh army at Eutaw. Unfortunately their report was neither credited nor inquired into; but they themſelves ſent to priſon. A party of four hundred men without arms, with a ſmall guard to cover them, were ſent in ſearch of vegetables in the very road on which the deſerters gave information that general Greene was marching. The event proved that the intelligence given by the deſerters was well founded. The unarmed rooting party and their ſmall guard, making at the leaſt a third part of colonel Stuart's force, fell an eaſy prey to Greene's army; a few ſtraggling horſemen that eſcaped, apprized the Britiſh commander of the enemy's approach, at the ſame time infuſing a degree of panic into all with whom they communicated. The Britiſh were drawn up acroſs the road on the heights near the Eutaw Springs. The flank battalion, commanded by major Majoribanks, covered the right flank of the army, his right being upon a rivulet with an interval of a hundred paces from the water; his left to the road was concealed by a very thick hedge. Two pieces of artillery, with a covering party of infantry, occupied the road. The remainder of the Britiſh force extended to the left of the road, in an oblique direction. The front line of the American army was compoſed of four battalions of militia; the ſecond line, of three brigades of continental troops; colonel Lee, with his legion, covered their right flank, and colonel Henderſon, with the South Carolina ſtate troops, their left: Colonel Waſhington, with his cavalry and the Delaware troops, formed their body of reſerve. Two three-pounders were in front of their line, and two ſix-pounders with the ſecond line. The legion and the ſtate troops formed their advanced guard, and were to retreat on their flanks when the Britiſh ſhould form. The enemy attacked with great impetuoſity; the chief impreſſion ſeemed to be deſigned againſt the artillery on the road, and to turn the left of the Britiſh. The preſſure of the enemy's fire was ſuch as compelled the

Action between colonel Stuart and general Greene near the Eutaw Springs.

third regiment, or Buffs, to give way, the regiment being compofed of new troops. The remains of thofe veteran corps, the fixty-third and fixty-fourth regiments, who had ferved the whole of the war, loft none of their fame in this action. They rufhed with bayonets into the midft of the enemy; nor did they give ground, until over-powered by numbers and fevere flaughter. Various was the fuccefs in the centre and on the right. At this time colonel Wafhington, endeavouring to pafs through the right of the flank corps and the rivulet, led his cavalry with great gallantry to the charge. The flank corps received this charge with great fteadinefs. At the firft fire, colonel Wafhington was wounded and taken prifoner, and feveral of his men fell, which prevented a fimilar attack. The artillery on both fides was feveral times taken and retaken.

At this time the flank battalion, whofe poft had been paffed undif-covered by the main body of the enemy, wheeled round, and coming in the rear of the enemy, threw them into confufion, which being increafed by a fire from the New York volunteers under the com-mand of major Sheridan, who had taken poft in a ftone houfe on the open ground upon the right of the road, decided the action. Inceffant peals of mufquetry from the windows poured deftruction upon the enemy, and effectually ftopped their further progrefs. Although feverely checked, the Americans were not difcouraged, and brought up four fix-pounders to batter the houfe: But the fire of the detachment within continued to be fo well fupported, that the American artillery foon became ufelefs, and moft of the officers and men that were attached to it, were either killed or wounded. In the mean time the left wing of the Britifh army having recovered from its confufion, had again formed the line, and the battle was renewed with great fpirit in that quarter. The conteft was obftinate and bloody; but the Americans were at laft obliged to retire. For want of cavalry, no purfuit could be made; whilft that of the enemy,

 which

CHAP. XLIII. 1781.

which was numerous, covered their retreat. They were obliged to abandon two of the four pieces of cannon that had been brought up againſt the houſe, and they left behind them, according to their own account, one hundred and thirty-nine of their number killed on the field of battle. Their wounded, which may be ſuppoſed to bear the uſual proportion to the killed, were carried off during the action. About ſixty of the enemy were made priſoners, and amongſt them lieutenant-colonel Waſhington, who commanded their reſerve. The whole loſs of the Americans in this action may be eſtimated at more than ſeven hundred * men, including ſixty commiſſioned officers, of whom ſeventeen were killed and forty-three wounded. The loſs of the Britiſh army was alſo very great; it amounted to eighty-five killed, three hundred and fifty-one wounded, and two hundred and fifty-ſeven miſſing; in all, ſix hundred and ninety-three men, including twenty-nine commiſſioned officers, three of whom were killed, ſixteen wounded, and ten miſſing.

Victory in this action claimed by both parties.

The incidents attending this action gave occaſion to both commanders to claim the victory. General Greene founded his pretenſions upon the retreat of the Britiſh line, and its being purſued to the houſe and open ground in the rear; and moſt aſſuredly, for ſome time, the fortune of the day ſeemed to be entirely in favour of the Americans. The Britiſh commander, on the other hand, reſted his claim of victory upon this ground, that although a temporary advantage had been obtained over part of the Britiſh line, which rendered a retreat neceſſary, yet the troops, who had thus retreated,

* The account here given does not agree with the returns publiſhed by congreſs: But that return, as given in Tarleton's Appendix, appears, upon the face of it, to be incorrect. The particulars do not make up the ſum total. The number here eſtimated ſuppoſes the wounded to have borne the uſual proportion to the ſlain. The ſlain being left on the field of battle, their number could not be concealed. Ramſay ſtates, that the loſs of general Marion's brigade of militia is not included in the return publiſhed by congreſs.

afterwards

afterwards formed and renewed the battle with ſo much ſpirit, that the Americans were ultimately obliged to quit the field, and retire to a ſtrong poſition ſeven miles in their rear. This action was nevertheleſs celebrated in America as a great and glorious victory; and in commemoration of it the congreſs voted a Britiſh ſtandard and gold medal to be preſented to general Greene. That it was a bloody, hard-fought action, the loſs on both ſides ſufficiently teſtifies; but that neither party obtained a deciſive advantage over the other, the conduct of both commanders after the action plainly demonſtrates. The Britiſh commander remained upon the ground the night after the action and the following day, without any attempt being made by general Greene to moleſt him; and when he afterwards retired to Monk's Corner for the ſafety and protection of his wounded, the American commander contented himſelf with advancing to the ground left by the Britiſh troops, and ſoon afterwards retreated to his former encampment on the high hills of Santee, placing a large river between him and the Britiſh army. The reaſonable concluſion to be drawn from the conduct of both ſeems to be this, that in the action both armies had ſuffered ſo much, that for ſome time afterwards neither of them was in a ſituation to undertake any thing againſt the other. Indeed this was the laſt action of any conſequence that happened in South Carolina between the king's troops and the Americans: The former, from this time, chiefly confined themſelves to Charleſtown Neck and ſome poſts in its neighbourhood; the ſecurity of that town appearing to be their principal object: And general Greene either was not, or did not think himſelf, in ſufficient force to attempt to reduce it. In this action the Britiſh loſt one field-piece, and took two from the Americans.

CHAP. XLIV.

Operations of the British Army in Virginia under the Command of General Philips—Destruction of American Stores—Death of General Philips—Junction between the Armies under Lord Cornwallis and General Arnold—Charlotteville surprised by Colonel Tarleton—Stratagem practised with Success by Colonel Simcoe on Baron Steuben—Unfavourable Aspect of American Affairs—Apprehension of Sir Henry Clinton for the Safety of New York—Lord Cornwallis crosses James River, and retires to Portsmouth—Evacuates Portsmouth, and concentrates his Force at York and Glocester—Junction of the Forces of Washington and Rochambeau—Naval Operations—The French Fleet under Count de Grasse arrives in the Chesapeak—Partial Action between the Count de Grasse and Admiral Graves—New London taken by General Arnold.

CHAP. XLIV. 1781.

AFTER it had been determined to carry the war into the southern colonies, first a detachment, as has already been mentioned, under general Leslie, and another afterwards under general Arnold, amounting to about sixteen hundred, were sent by the commander in chief from New York into Virginia, for the double purpose of destroying the enemy's stores, and of assisting, by means of a diversion, the operations of lord Cornwallis in the two Carolinas; the first of which services was performed to a very considerable extent. A plan was formed by general Washington for entrapping Arnold, and

and taking him and his whole detachment; which, however, was defeated by the backwardneſs of the French, and the good conduct of the Engliſh admiral.

Operations of the Britiſh army in Virginia under the command of general Philips.

A reinforcement of two thouſand Britiſh troops, under the command of general Philips, arrived ſafely in the Cheſapeak on the twenty-ſixth of March. The general, being of ſuperior rank to Arnold, now aſſumed the command of the whole Britiſh force in Virginia; and although, after viewing the poſt at Portſmouth, he was of opinion that it could not be rendered ſecure, and was alſo too extenſive to be defended by any number of men that could be ſpared from the other exigencies of the ſervice; yet, as the works that had been begun were in a great ſtate of forwardneſs, he continued to employ the troops upon them until they were finiſhed, which happened about the middle of April. The general being then at liberty to purſue other objects, after leaving a garriſon at Portſmouth, embarked the troops, on the eighteenth of April, on board the ſmalleſt veſſels of the fleet, and proceeded up James River. The object in view was, in the firſt place, to diſperſe a body of militia who were ſaid to have aſſembled at Williamſburgh, the former ſeat of government in Virginia, and afterwards to deſtroy ſuch of the enemy's public ſtores, on the ſouth ſide of James River, as had not fallen within the range of general Arnold's expedition. The army, having landed at Burrel's Ferry, was immediately marched to Williamſburgh; but the militia collected there had already fled. They now proceeded, in different diviſions and detachments, to diſtreſs and weaken the enemy as much as poſſible, by deſtroying all the means by which they might be enabled to ſupport the war. If Virginia had been hitherto favoured, it ſeems to have been determined at this time to inflict upon it a more than common portion of vengeance: And, ſo vulnerable is that province, by the joint operation of a land and naval force, that

Deſtruction of American ſtores.

CHAP. XLIV. 1781.

that the Britiſh troops committed the greateſt devaſtations without any ſerious oppoſition, or ſuſtaining any loſs.

General Philips, having proceeded up the river as far as he intended to go, marched his army back to Oſborne's, a village on the banks of James River, and from thence to Bermuda Hundred, oppoſite to City Point, where the fleet was ready to receive him. On the ſecond of May the troops were reimbarked, and the fleet moved ſlowly down the river. As the marquis de la Fayette followed by land with his army, it was thought to have been general Philips's intention, after decoying him to a ſufficient diſtance down the river, to have embraced the firſt favourable breeze of wind, and ſuddenly returning, to have landed above him. By ſuch a manœuvre the marquis de la Fayette would have been ſhut up between York and James River, and to extricate himſelf muſt have riſqued an engagement, or hazarded the loſs of the greateſt part of his force by attempting to paſs either of thoſe rivers in the view of the Britiſh army. But on the ſeventh of May a letter was received from lord Cornwallis, informing the general of his march towards Virginia, and propoſing Peterſburgh as the place where he would wiſh to find the Britiſh army. Upon the receipt of this letter, orders were immediately given for the fleet to move up the river. One diviſion of the army was landed at Brandon, and another proceeded to City Point; and on the ninth both met at Peterſburgh, where they ſurpriſed ſome of the marquis de la Fayette's officers, who had been ſent forward to provide quarters for his army. General Philips at this time lay dangerouſly ill: He had been attacked by a fever ſome few days before, the progreſs of which was ſo rapid, and its ſymptoms ſo malignant, that by the time of the army's arrival at Peterſburgh he was no longer capable of giving orders, and died four days after. By his death the command of the troops devolved again on brigadier-general Arnold.

Death of general Philips.

In

In the mean time lord Cornwallis had arrived at Halifax on the banks of the Roanoke, within ſixty miles of Peterſburgh. In his march from Wilmington to that place he had met with ſcarcely any interruption, a corps of one hundred and eighty cavalry, and ſixty mounted infantry, that preceded the army under the command of lieutenant-colonel Tarleton, being ſufficient to diſperſe any ſmall bodies of militia that were aſſembling in order to obſtruct its progreſs. Colonel Tarleton, in this expedition, was accompanied by that valuable partizan, colonel Hamilton, of the North Carolina regiment; to whom, perhaps, the Britiſh nation owed more than to any other individual loyaliſt in the Britiſh ſervice*.

CHAP. XLIV. 1781.

Junction between the armies under lord Cornwallis and general Arnold.

Lord Cornwallis, having ſent forward Tarleton with the cavalry, and general Arnold having detached Simcoe with the queen's rangers, to take poſſeſſion of the fords on the Nottoway and the Meherrin, the only rivers that intervened, a junction of the two armies took place at Peterſburgh on the twentieth of May. Lord Cornwallis of courſe aſſumed the command of the whole.

It will be remembered, that when the fleet went down James River from Bermuda Hundred, the marquis de la Fayette followed it with his army by land. But as ſoon as it began to return, he marched back with all the diſpatch he could. He rightly judged it to be the intention of general Philips to take poſſeſſion of Peterſburgh, in order to facilitate a junction with earl Cornwallis, and he hoped, by forced marches, to reach that place before him. The expedition with which the Britiſh troops returned, entirely fruſtrated his intention; and upon his arrival at Oſborne's on the ſouth ſide of James River, he found they were already in poſſeſſion of Peterſburgh. Thus foiled in his deſign, he re-croſſed James River, and took a poſition on the north ſide of it, between Richmond and Wilton.

* At Halifax ſome enormities were committed by the Britiſh that were a diſgrace to the name of man.

It

CHAP. XLIV. 1781.

It feems to have been lord Cornwallis's firft object to endeavour to ftrike a blow at the marquis; his next, to deftroy fuch of the enemy's ftores as might be within his reach after the American army had been either defeated or obliged to retire; and laftly, after proceeding to the execution of thefe objects, which probably might be accomplifhed by the time he could hear from New York, to keep himfelf difengaged from any operation that could interfere with the plan that might be devifed by the commander in chief for the further profecution of the campaign. Having fettled his own temporary plan of operations, lord Cornwallis marched from Peterfburgh on the twenty-fourth of May, and croffed James River at Weftover, about thirty miles below Fayette's encampment*. The Britifh army was already greatly fuperior to the continental force in Virginia, and about this time it was confiderably increafed by the arrival of two Britifh regiments, and two battalions of Anfpach troops from New York, fent by the commander in chief (who had not yet received intelligence of lord Cornwallis's arrival) to reinforce general Philips, under an apprehenfion that when the Americans heard of lord Cornwallis's march to the northward, they might make fome attempt to overpower general Philips before a junction of the two armies could be effected. Of this reinforcement the forty-third regiment alone joined the army: The other Britifh regiment, and the two battalions of Anfpach, were fent to ftrengthen the garrifon at Portfmouth.

The force under Fayette being fo much inferior to that which was oppofed to him, he decamped from the neighbourhood of Richmond, as foon as he heard that lord Cornwallis had croffed James River, and retired towards the back-country, inclining his route to

* The channel of the river where the Britifh croffed exceeded two miles. The paffage was effected by fwimming the horfes over a part, and wading through the reft.

the northward, that he might be in readineſs to form a junction with general Wayne, who was on his march through Maryland to reinforce him with eight hundred men of the Penſylvania line. The Britiſh army for ſome time followed the route taken by the marquis de la Fayette, and in this direction proceeded as far as the upper part of Hanover County, deſtroying in their way whatever public ſtores they found. But Fayette's movements were ſo rapid, that lord Cornwallis ſoon found it would be in vain to follow him, and impoſſible to prevent a junction between him and general Wayne: His lordſhip's attention was therefore directed to other objects more attainable, which the intelligence received on his march had preſented to his view.

One of theſe objects was to break up the ſeſſion of the general aſſembly, then met under a guard at Charlotteville, for the purpoſe of voting taxes, draughting the militia, and making an addition to the regular force of the ſtate. The other object was to ſtrike at the baron Steuben, who was ſaid to be at the Point of Fork, on James River, guarding a conſiderable quantity of ſtores, with a ſtrong detachment of troops called eighteen-months men *, and militia. To accompliſh the firſt, Tarleton was detached with one hundred and eighty cavalry of the legion, and ſeventy mounted infantry of the twenty-third regiment, under the command of captain Champagne †: And the execution of the laſt was entruſted to lieutenant-colonel Simcoe, with the queen's rangers, and the ſecond battalion of the ſeventy-firſt regiment, commanded by captain Hutchinſon, the whole

* So called from the time for which they engaged to ſerve.

† The 71ſt regiment was ordered to accompany Tarleton on this ſervice; but upon receiving the order the officers drew up a remonſtrance, and preſented it to lord Cornwallis, ſtating their unwillingneſs to ſerve under Tarleton, from a recollection of his conduct at the Cowpens, where the other battalion of the 71ſt was taken by Morgan. In conſequence of this remonſtrance, the 71ſt regiment was attached to colonel Simcoe.

CHAP. XLIV. 1781.

Charlotteville furprifed by colonel Tarleton.

detachment amounting to five hundred men. Tarleton proceeded to Charlotteville, with great expedition; and on his way overtook twelve waggons loaded with arms and clothing for the ufe of the army in South Carolina, all of which were burnt and deftroyed. The Revanna, a branch of James River, wafhes the foot of the hill on which Charlotteville ftands. Through this river Tarleton charged at the head of his cavalry, and took or difperfed the guards ftationed on the oppofite bank. With the like rapidity he entered the town, and took prifoners feven members of the affembly. The reft made their efcápe. So unexpected was Tarleton's vifit, that the enemy had not time to remove their ftores. A confiderable quantity was found, and the whole deftroyed *. Tarleton, after performing this fervice, proceeded down the Revanna, according to his orders, to co-operate with Simcoe, if he fhould have occafion for his affiftance. The Point of Fork, to which lieutenant-colonel Simcoe was directing his march, is fo called from being the point of land that intervenes at the conflux of the two great branches of James River, the Fluvanna and Revanna. The united ftreams from the point of junction take the name of James River. As the greateft part of his detachment confifted of infantry, his progrefs could not be fo rapid as that of Tarleton; but it was as expeditious as the nature of his detachment would admit: And by the prudent precautions taken for fecuring every perfon met or feen on the road, he effectually concealed his march from the enemy. By fome of his prifoners he found that baron Steuben was apprifed of Tarleton's march, but knew nothing of Simcoe's; and from the fame perfons he learnt that the baron had begun to tranfport his ftores to the fouth

* Stores deftroyed at Charlotteville:—

1000 new firelocks, made at Fredericfburgh.

Upwards of 400 barrels of gunpowder.

Several hogfheads of tobacco, and fome continental clothing.

fide

fide of the Fluvanna, and meant to follow them with his whole detachment. Upon receiving this intelligence, Simcoe preffed forward with ftill greater celerity, hoping at leaft to cut off the baron's rear-guard before it had time to pafs the river. But upon his arrival at the Point of Fork, he found that not only the ftores, but the baron's whole force, had paffed the river, except about thirty perfons then on the bank ready to embark. Thefe were immediately fecured by the cavalry. As both the enemy's ftores and troops were now completely out of Simcoe's reach, a deep and unfordable river intervening, with the boats all fecured on the other fide, he conceived the defign of endeavouring to imprefs the baron with the belief, that the troops now at the Point of Fork were the advance of the Britifh army, hoping, if he was fuccefsful in his endeavours for that purpofe, that the baron, for the fake of moving off with greater expedition, might be induced to leave behind the greateft part of the ftores.

Stratagem practifed with fuccefs by colonel Simcoe, on baron Steuben.

In purfuance of this defign, Simcoe difplayed his force to as great advantage as poffible, upon the heights oppofite to the baron's encampment; and the deception fucceeded beyond his expectation. In the following night the baron moved off, leaving the bank of the river oppofite to the Point of Fork, covered with arms and ftores. In the morning it was apparent that the enemy had fled, and fome fmall canoes being procured, captain Stevenfon, with twenty of the light-infantry, and cornet Wolfey, with four huffars, paffed the river, the huffars carrying with them their faddles. Wolfey was directed, after mounting his huffars on fuch ftraggling horfes as had been left by the enemy, to take poft, at fome diftance from the bank of the river, upon the road by which the enemy retreated; and fhould any of their patroles appear, he was directed to raife a fhout, and make an appearance of purfuing, in order to raife a belief that the Britifh army had paffed the river. This ftep was taken

CHAP. XLIV. 1781.

taken for the ſecurity of captain Stevenſon and his ſmall detachment of light-infantry, who were in the mean time employed in bringing off or deſtroying the ſtores abandoned by the enemy; and it anſwered every purpoſe that was expected from it. In the courſe of the day a patrole of the enemy appeared, which fled with the utmoſt precipitation, upon ſeeing the Britiſh huſſars; and from the report made by this patrole to the baron Steuben, he was induced, though already thirty miles from the Fluvanna, to continue his march twenty miles farther without halting.

In the mean time the marquis de la Fayette, who upon the advance of the Britiſh army had retreated acroſs Rappahannock River, being joined by general Wayne with his detachment, re-croſſed that river, and followed the Britiſh army in its march to Williamſburgh: On the road he was alſo joined by the baron Steuben, with his eighteen-months men, and militia.

Unfavourable aſpect of American affairs.

Although a dawn of proſperity had begun to appear in South Carolina, under the auſpices of Greene, the general ſtate of American affairs ſeemed at this time to be in a ruinous train, and faſt verging towards that period when the conteſt muſt ceaſe, on the part of the congreſs, for want of reſources to maintain it. The bills of credit, by which they had hitherto ſupported the war, now failed them. The depreciation had become ſo immenſe, that they no longer anſwered the purpoſes for which they were iſſued, and, in the courſe of the preſent year, ſunk under their own bulk, and were annihilated in the hands of thoſe that poſſeſſed them. The failure of this medium of commerce multiplied beyond calculation the difficulties under which the congreſs laboured, and had a fatal influence on their ſervice throughout the whole extent of the union. The agents for public departments could no longer make their purchaſes; and warrants of impreſs became neceſſary to force from individuals whatever was wanted for the public ſervice, and the ſupport

ſupport of the army. Even the troops were ready to mutiny in ſeveral places for want of pay and clothing. Although general Waſhington's army was greatly diminiſhed, he found it ſtill too large for the means he had of ſubſiſting it. In a letter written by him on the tenth of May, is the following paſſage:—" From the " poſts of Saratoga to that of Dobb's Ferry, incluſive, I believe " there is not at this moment on hand, one day's ſupply of meat " for the army." And in another letter, dated almoſt two months afterwards, he intimated his fears of being obliged to diſband his army for want of ſubſiſtence. The marine force of the congreſs was not in a better condition than their army: Of all the armed veſſels that had been fitted out by them, two frigates alone remained; the reſt had been all either taken or deſtroyed. The immenſe value of the public property and ſtores deſtroyed in Virginia, darkened the gloomy proſpect, and ſeemed to haſten with rapid ſtrides the æra of public bankruptcy. Nor could they derive any comfort from the commerce carried on by individuals, which was now almoſt annihilated, in conſequence of the captures made by the Britiſh cruizers, and the great loſſes ſuſtained at the taking of St. Euſtatius. The people too, in many of the colonies, were become tired of the war, and ſeemed to languiſh under the long continuance of their diſtreſſes and difficulties.

Some ſignal ſucceſs, ſome atchievement of importance, that ſhould reflect luſtre on the American arms, was therefore neceſſary to reſtore the declining ſtate of their affairs, to rouſe afreſh the ſpirit and energy of the people, and even to enable congreſs to maintain their authority. But no enterpriſe that promiſed ſucceſs could be attempted againſt any of the Britiſh poſts in America, without the co-operation of a French fleet and army. The cougreſs had been already diſappointed in their expectations of ſuch a co-operation for three years ſucceſſively; but as they

had

CHAP. XLIV. 1781.

had renewed their applications on that head, towards the end of the preceding year, and had at the ſame time made the court of France acquainted with the deſperate ſtate of their affairs, which the effect of ſuch a co-operation could alone ſave from ruin; they hoped that the intereſt of that court, as much as its friendſhip, would induce a compliance. Waſhington looked forward with eagerneſs to ſuch an event, as the only thing that could enable them to prolong the conteſt: And, as ſoon as he heard of the arrival of M. de Barras, who was ſent out from France to take the command of the fleet at Rhode Iſland, and brought with him diſpatches for the count de Rochambeau, he haſtened to Connecticut, that he might have a conference with the French general. The count's diſpatches ſeem to have given full ſatisfaction to Waſhington, as at this interview it was agreed between him and the French general, to carry into execution the attempt againſt New York, which they had meditated the preceding year; if their force, when aſſembled, ſhould be found equal to the enterpriſe: But, in all events, it was their determination, upon the arrival of the count de Graſſe, to ſtrike a blow at one or other of the Britiſh poſts, where ſucceſs was moſt reaſonably to be expected. This interview took place on the twenty-firſt of May, and immediately after it, letters were written by Waſhington, requeſting, that the battalions compoſing his army might be filled up to their full complement, and at the ſame time he made a requiſition to the New England ſtates, for ſix thouſand two hundred militia, to be ready to march whenever he ſhould call for them. The expreſs carrying the letters written by Waſhington to congreſs, after this interview with the French general, was intercepted in the Jerſeys; and the letters were carried to ſir Henry Clinton. They diſcloſed the nature of the enterpriſe in agitation, and ſeem to have alarmed him for the ſafety of New York. In conſequence of the information gathered from theſe letters, the commander

Apprehenſions of ſir H. Clinton for the ſafety of New York.

mander in chief made a requisition of part of the troops under lord Cornwallis's command in Virginia, and directed that they should be sent to New York without delay, unless his lordship should at the time be engaged in some important movement that might render it necessary to detain them some time longer; or unless he should be disposed to execute the plan which the commander in chief seems to have had much at heart, of carrying the war to the upper part of the Chesapeak, and upon the Susquehanna, where a number of loyalists had associated for their mutual defence, and were said to be ready to act whenever the king's troops should appear amongst them. At the time of receiving the dispatches containing this requisition, lord Cornwallis was engaged in no important operation: He had returned from his expedition up James River, and was then with his army at Williamsburgh: Neither did he mean to engage in the expedition to the upper part of the Chesapeak, of which he disapproved, without express orders from the commander in chief, which would exempt him from all responsibility, at least for the plan of that expedition. Under these circumstances he prepared, without delay, to comply with the commander in chief's requisition for troops; and as, after their embarkation, he was of opinion that those which remained would not be sufficient to enable him to remain at Williamsburgh, he took the resolution of passing James River, and retiring to Portsmouth. An express was sent off to acquaint the commander in chief with this determination, and with the steps taking for an immediate compliance with his requisition. In the dispatches written on this occasion, which bear date the thirtieth of June, lord Cornwallis takes occasion to mention, that upon viewing York (which had been proposed as a defensive post, proper to be taken for the security of shipping), he was clearly of opinion that it far exceeded his power, consistently with the commander in chief's plans, to make defensive posts there and at Gloucester, both of which

CHAP. XLIV. 1781.

would be neceſſary for the protection of ſhipping; and apparently chagrined with the idea of having his force reduced ſo far as to be obliged to act upon the defenſive in a province where, in his own opinion, the moſt vigorous offenſive operations were neceſſary, he intimated a willingneſs, if the commander in chief approved of it, to return to Charleſtown, and take the command in South Carolina, although in that quarter nothing but mortification and diſappointment was to be expected.

The reſolution of paſſing James River being taken, the army marched from Williamſburgh on the fourth of July, and encamped on a piece of ground that covered a ford into the iſland of James Town; and the ſame evening the queen's rangers paſſed the river. On the fifth the wheel-carriages, and on the ſixth the bat-horſes and baggage, were paſſed over; whilſt the army continued in the ſame encampment. In the mean time the marquis de la Fayette, thinking that the main body of the Britiſh army had already croſſed the river, advanced by forced marches to ſtrike a blow at the rear-guard. Information of his approach was communicated to earl Cornwallis about noon of the ſixth of July, and ſome pains were taken, by ſuffering the piquets to be inſulted and driven in, to confirm him in the belief that only the rear-guard of the Britiſh army remained. About four in the afternoon, ſome of the outpoſts were attacked by rifle-men and militia; but Fayette, with the main body, did not appear till towards ſunſet, when he paſſed a moraſs with nine hundred continentals, ſix hundred militia, and ſome artillery, and began to form in front of the Britiſh encampment. The Britiſh troops were immediately ordered under arms, and advanced to the attack in two lines. On the right, the affair was ſoon over; the Britiſh troops in that quarter being oppoſed only by militia, who were quickly put to flight: But, on the left, lieutenant-colonel Dundas's brigade, conſiſting of the forty-third, ſeventy-ſixth, and eightieth

July.

eightieth regiments, being oppofed by the Penfylvania line, affifted by part of Fayette's continentals, with two pieces of cannon, the action, while it lafted, was fharp and bloody. After a fevere conteft the provincials were routed, and their cannon taken. They fled acrofs the morafs in great confufion; but by the time of their flight it was dark, and to that circumftance alone they owed their fafety: An hour more of day-light would have probably been attended with the ruin of Fayette's whole detachment, as the cavalry were in readinefs to purfue, and the light-infantry and other troops on the right of the Britifh line in excellent condition to fupport them, from having fuftained no lofs in the action. In this action the king's troops had five officers wounded, and about feventy privates killed and wounded. The lofs of the enemy in killed, wounded, and prifoners, amounted to about three hundred. The weight of the action fell upon the feventy-fixth and eightieth regiments, both of them lately raifed; and their firmnefs and intrepidity did them fingular honour: The gallantry and good conduct of lieutenant-colonel Dundas, who commanded them, merited and obtained the higheft commendation. The army having paffed James River, the troops ordered for embarkation were fent forward to Portfmouth, whilft lord Cornwallis followed by eafy marches with the reft.

Lord Cornwallis croffes James River, and retires to Portfmouth.

After the embarkation of the troops, but before the tranfports put to fea, an order arrived from the commander in chief to countermand their failing. He wrote at the fame time to earl Cornwallis, expreffing his furprife that he fhould have taken the refolution of quitting the neck of land at Williamfburgh without confulting him; directing him, if he was ftill there, to remain until further orders; or, if he had left it, to endeavour to repoffefs it, for the purpofe of eftablifhing a defenfive poft for the protection of fhips of the line, which he fuppofed might be found fomewhere within that neck, and probably either at Old Point Comfort on Hampton Road, or York

 Town.

CHAP. XLIV. 1781.

Town on York River: And as the firſt of theſe places was recommended by the admiral, lord Cornwallis was directed to examine it, and, if found eligible, to occupy it either with or without York Town, as ſhould ſeem expedient. For the purpoſe of eſtabliſhing ſuch a poſt as was wanted, his lordſhip was to be at liberty to retain all or any part of the troops ordered for embarkation, that ſhould be found neceſſary: And, in the ſtrongeſt terms, the commander in chief deprecated the idea of quitting the Cheſapeak entirely; on the contrary, he declared, that as ſoon as the ſeaſon for acting in that country returned, he ſhould probably ſend there all the troops he could ſpare from the different poſts under his command: He therefore recommended it to lord Cornwallis, if he had quitted York, to re-occupy it, or at leaſt to hold Old Point Comfort, if it was poſſible to do it, without at the ſame holding York.

Upon the receipt of thoſe diſpatches, lord Cornwallis, who by that time had reached Portſmouth, directed Old Point Comfort to be viewed by the engineers and the officers of the navy. From their report it appeared, that works conſtructed on Old Point Comfort would neither command the entrance into Hampton Road, nor ſecure his majeſty's ſhips when lying at anchor within it: It could therefore be of no uſe as a defenſive ſtation for ſhips: And as Portſmouth was admitted, on all hands, not to be ſuch a poſt as was deſired, from its giving no protection to ſhips of the line, lord Cornwallis was of opinion, that the ſpirit of his inſtructions left him no other option than to fortify York and Glouceſter, the only places that remained capable of affording the requiſite protection to ſhips of that denomination. Meaſures were accordingly taken for ſeizing and fortifying theſe poſts, and for evacuating Portſmouth. Part of the army, in tranſports and boats, proceeded up the Cheſapeak, and took poſſeſſion of them on the firſt of Auguſt; and the evacuation of Portſmouth having been completed on the twentieth, lord Cornwallis's

Auguſt. Evacuates Portſmouth, and concentrates his force at York and Glouceſter.

wallis's whole force on the twenty-fecond was concentered at York and Gloucefter.

In the mean time, general Wafhington had affembled his army at Peek's Kill towards the end of the month of June, and marching from thence to White Plains, was there joined on the fixth of July by the count de Rochambeau with the French troops from Rhode Ifland. In the evening of the twenty-firft, the whole American and part of the French army marched from their encampment towards King's Bridge, and appearing before it early next morning, were drawn up in order of battle, whilft the French and American officers reconnoitred the pofition of the Britifh works. The fame fcene was re-acted in the morning of the twenty-third, and in the afternoon the confederated armies returned to their former encampment. Both the French and American commanders had been for fome time impatiently expecting difpatches from the count de Graffe. At length they arrived about the middle of Auguft, and announced the intention of the count de Graffe to enter the Chefapeak with his fleet about the end of the month, and commence his operations there. They alfo gave intimation, that he could not remain long upon the American coaft.

Junction of the forces of Wafhington and Rochambeau.

If any doubt exifted before, as to the point of attack, it was now removed. Nothing could any-where be done without a covering fleet; and as the count de Graffe had determined to enter the Chefapeak, it was agreed between Wafhington and Rochambeau, that Virginia fhould be the fcene, and an attack upon lord Cornwallis the object, of their joint operations. Letters to this effect were difpatched to meet the count de Graffe on his paffage, and in the mean time meafures were taken to continue fir Henry Clinton in the belief that New York was ftill the object of their enterprife. After feveral movements, and various deceptions practifed to induce this belief, the

CHAP. XLIV. 1781. Naval operations.

the allied army suddenly marched across the Jerseys to Philadelphia, where it arrived on the thirtieth of August.

That the count de Grasse intended to visit the American coast during the hurricane months in the West Indies, was no secret to the commander in chief at New York. He had made this discovery from Washington's intercepted dispatches, and communicated it to earl Cornwallis; and he had also received similar information from the ministry in England. Sir George Rodney, who commanded the British fleet in the West Indies, seems also to have been convinced that such was the count de Grasse's intention, and that the bay of Chesapeak was the place where he might be expected. Advices to this effect were dispatched by him to the commander of the king's fleet on the coast of America, who was also advertised, that at the proper season he might expect to be reinforced by a detachment from the West India fleet, so as to enable him to meet the count de Grasse, and frustrate his intended operations. Sir George Rodney does not appear ever to have entertained the idea, that count de Grasse would proced to North America with his whole fleet; and, indeed, the contrary was rather to be presumed, as it was natural to suppose that part of it must be detached as a convoy for the homeward-bound French trade then collected at Cape François. Upon the approach of the hurricane season, sir Samuel Hood was dispatched to North America with fourteen ships of the line; which, with the fleet then at New York, it was thought would be an overmatch for any force the count de Grasse could bring, even if he should be joined by the fleet from Rhode Island. Sir Samuel Hood made the land to the southward of the Capes of Virginia on the twenty-fifth of August, and having met with none of the British frigates that were stationed to look out for him, proceeded to Sandy Hook, where he arrived on the twenty-eighth. Admiral Graves commanded on the American ſtation, having ſucceeded admiral Arbuthnot as the next ſenior officer, upon his departure for England in the month of July, and was at this time with his fleet, conſiſting of ſeven ſail of the line, in the harbour of New York. Only five of theſe were in readineſs for ſea, the two others being under repair. From the intelligence brought by ſir Samuel Hood, it was conjectured that the count de Graſſe had either by this time arrived, or would ſoon make his appearance on the American coaſt. No time could be ſpared to wait for the ſhips under repair; the five that were in readineſs were ordered out of the harbour to join the ſquadron under ſir Samuel Hood; and admiral Graves, as ſenior officer, taking the command of the whole, ſailed from the Hook on the thirty-firſt of Auguſt. Previouſly to his departure, intelligence had been received, that the French ſquadron under M. de Barras at Rhode Iſland had ſailed on the twenty-fifth; ſo that the moſt ſanguine expectations were entertained that one or other of the French ſquadrons could not fail to be intercepted. But the event turned out very different from thoſe expectations: It was not then known that the count de Graſſe had already arrived in the Cheſapeak, and that the fleet under his immediate command, excluſive of the Rhode Iſland ſquadron, conſiſted of twenty-eight ſhips of the line. The count de Graſſe arrived in the Cheſapeak on the thirtieth of Auguſt, and was immediately joined by an officer from the marquis de la Fayette's army, who had been for ſome time waiting at Cape Henry in expectation of his arrival, to communicate to him the ſtate of things in Virginia, and the poſts occupied by lord Cornwallis's army. In conſequence of the information received from this officer, meaſures were immediately taken for blocking up York River, on the banks of which lord Cornwallis had taken poſt, and for conveying up James River the French land force brought from the Weſt Indies, that it might form a junction with the troops under the marquis de la

The French fleet under count de Graſſe arrives in the Cheſapeak.

CHAP. XLIV. 1781.

la Fayette. In theſe ſervices four of the count de Graſſe's line-of-battle ſhips and ſeveral frigates were employed; and with the reſt he remained at anchor in Lynhaven Bay juſt within the capes.

Partial action between the count de Graſſe and admiral Graves.

In the mean time admiral Graves having examined the entrance of the Delaware by means of his frigates, and finding no enemy to be there, proceeded on to the Capes of Virginia, in ſight of which he arrived on the morning of the fifth of September. His advanced frigates ſpeedily announced by ſignal the appearance of an enemy's fleet at anchor within the capes; and the wind being very fair, the Britiſh fleet entered to offer it battle. As ſoon as the count de Graſſe perceived that the fleet about to enter the bay was the Britiſh fleet, and not the Rhode Iſland ſquadron which he expected, he gave orders for his ſhips to ſlip their cables, and form the line promiſcuouſly as they could get up, with their heads to the eaſtward; that by getting out of the capes he might have more ſea-room, and be able to avail himſelf of his ſuperiority in numbers. The Britiſh fleet having ſtretched in, and its rear being now nearly even with the enemy's van, the admiral made the ſignal for the whole fleet to wear, by which manœuvre it was put upon the ſame tack with the enemy, and lay to windward in a line nearly parallel to them. Both fleets were now ſteering to the eaſtward and getting clear of the capes, the Britiſh fleet bearing down upon the enemy as it advanced. At four in the afternoon a partial action commenced between the van and part of the centre of the two fleets, which continued until night put an end to it. The French van appeared to be conſiderably worſted, as it was obliged to bear away, in order to give an opportunity to the centre to advance to its ſupport: But no ſhip on either ſide was taken. Admiral Graves preſerved the weather-gage during the night, and intended to have renewed the battle next morning, until he found, from the report of the captains, that ſeveral of his ſhips were

were ſo much diſabled, as not to be in a condition to engage until their damages were repaired. Nevertheleſs, the two fleets continued in ſight of each other for five days, and were at ſome times very near. The French, although it was ſeveral times in their option, from having gained the wind, ſhewed no inclination to renew the action; and it was not in the Britiſh admiral's power, from the crippled ſtate of his fleet, to compel them. At length the count de Graſſe, on the tenth, bore away for the Cheſapeak, and the next day anchored within the capes. Upon his arrival he had the ſatisfaction to find that M. de Barras had got into the Cheſapeak in ſafety, whilſt the two fleets were at ſea, bringing with him fourteen tranſports laden with heavy artillery and all ſorts of military ſtores proper for carrying on a ſiege. The loſs of men on board the Britiſh fleet in this action amounted to ninety killed and two hundred and forty-ſix wounded. The whole of the van diviſion under admiral Drake had ſuffered conſiderable damages in their maſts, ſails, and rigging: But the Terrible proved ſo leaky after the action, that on the eleventh it was found neceſſary to abandon her. Her people, proviſions, and ſtores, being taken out, ſhe was ſet on fire, and burnt. The French accounts make their loſs in this action amount to about two hundred and twenty men, including four officers killed and eighteen wounded. Admiral Graves, after reconnoitring the poſition of the French fleet upon their return to the Cheſapeak, and finding that they blocked up the entrance, determined, in purſuance of the advice of a council of war, to return to New York before the equinox, and there uſe every means for putting his ſhips in the beſt poſſible ſtate for ſervice *.

In

* The reader is requeſted to run his eye over the Plan of this action, by which it will appear, that the advantages ariſing from the ſituation of the French were not improved as they might have been; for when the Britiſh fleet arrived, under a very favourable and leading wind, the French fleet was lying promiſcuouſly at anchor; they were obliged to ſlip their cables, and ſeven of

CHAP. XLIV. 1781.

In the mean time the commander in chief at New York, with a view of making a diverſion in Connecticut, and drawing general Waſhington's attention that way, detached brigadier-general Arnold with a conſiderable force to make an attempt upon New London. The troops embarked on this expedition conſiſted of the thirty-eighth, fortieth, and fifty-fourth regiments, the third battalion of New Jerſey volunteers, the loyal Americans, the American legion, ſome refugees, a detachment of yagers, and another of the royal artillery. They paſſed through the Sound in tranſports, and landed in the morning of the ſixth of September, about three miles from New London, in two diviſions, one on each ſide of the harbour. That on the Groton ſide, conſiſting of the fortieth and fifty-fourth regiments, the third battalion of New Jerſey volunteers, with a detachment of yagers and artillery, was commanded by lieutenant-colonel Eyre, and that on the New London ſide, conſiſting of the reſt of the troops, by brigadier-general Arnold. On the New London ſide no great oppoſition was made: A redoubt, from which the enemy had begun a cannonade, was abandoned by them upon the approach of general Arnold with part of his diviſion; and ſoon afterwards Fort Trumbull, that commanded the harbour, was entered by captain Millet at the head of four companies of the thirty-eighth regiment, through a ſhower of grape-ſhot which the enemy diſcharged from their cannon, but without doing much miſchief, only four or five being killed or wounded in the aſſault. General Arnold loſt no time in taking poſſeſſion of New London: He was oppoſed by a ſmall body of the enemy with a field-piece; but they

New London taken by general Arnold.

of them ſtretched acroſs, and ſtood out to ſea from the reſt of their fleet: The remainder was obliged to make ſeveral tacks in working out of the bay. It was very generally ſaid, that had the Britiſh fleet continued its courſe, the wind ſtill being as favourable as it could blow, the ſeven French ſhips ſo advanced muſt have been cut off from the reſt of their fleet. But for ſome reaſon, which has never been explained, the Britiſh admiral hauled his wind. The advance of the Britiſh becoming their rear, the fleet ſtood out to ſea, and were followed by the French. In a ſhort time the action commenced.

were

were ſoon ſo hard preſſed as to be obliged to fly, and leave their piece of artillery behind. On the Groton ſide of the harbour was Fort Griſwold, a regular work of conſiderable ſtrength. It was aſſaulted on three ſides by the fortieth and fifty-fourth regiments, under lieutenant-colonel Eyre, and defended by the enemy with the moſt obſtinate bravery.

At length the gallant efforts of the aſſailants were ſucceſsful; and with fixed bayonets they entered the works through the embraſures, in the face of the enemy, who were armed with long ſpears to oppoſe them. A conſiderable carnage now enſued, until the enemy were driven from the ramparts, and had ceaſed from all farther reſiſtance. The honour obtained by the Britiſh troops in this aſſault was great, but too dearly purchaſed. Two officers, and forty-ſix ſoldiers, were killed, and eight officers, with one hundred and thirty-five ſoldiers, wounded. General Arnold, upon his landing, had been informed that the works at Fort Griſwold were incomplete, and its garriſon inconſiderable: But when he arrived at New London, and, from an eminence, had viewed its great ſtrength, he diſpatched an officer to countermand his orders for an aſſault, who unfortunately reached colonel Eyre a few minutes too late. The fort had refuſed to ſurrender, and the attack was begun. Of the garriſon eighty-five were killed, including colonel Ladyard, their commander; ſixty were wounded, moſt of them mortally, and ſeventy made priſoners. Ten or twelve of the enemy's ſhips were burnt, and among them three or four armed veſſels, and one laden with naval ſtores. The reſt ran up Norwich River in the morning, and made their eſcape. A great number of ſtore-houſes were burnt, that contained an immenſe quantity of European and Weſt India goods. Unluckily they alſo contained ſome gunpowder, unknown to general Arnold, by the exploſion of which the flames were communicated to the dwelling-houſes in the town; and a great part of it was conſumed, notwith-

CHAP. XLIV. 1781.

ftanding every endeavour to ftop the progrefs of the conflagration. Upwards of fifty pieces of cannon, and a great quantity of military ftores found in the different works, were alfo deftroyed *.

* Return of Ordnance, &c. taken in Fort Grifwold and its Dependencies.

In Fort Grifwold: Iron ordnance, mounted on carriages, 1 eighteen-pounder, 14 twelve-pounders, 2 nine-pounders, 1 fix-pounder, 1 four-pounder, 1 three-pounder. Travelling; 1 twelve-pounder, 2 four-pounders. In the Fleche; travelling, 3 four-pounders. On the lower battery, 7 eighteen-pounders, 2 twelve-pounders. Total of iron ordnance, 35.—Mufquets, French, 106.—Pikes, 80.—Round fhot, 1680 eighteen-pounders, 2100 twelve-pounders, 290 nine-pounders, 100 fix-pounders, 200 four-pounders, 40 three-pounders. Grape fhot, 230 eighteen-pounders, 340 twelve-pounders, 75 nine-pounders, 70 fix-pounders, 90 four-pounders, 75 three-pounders.—Cartridges, filled, 12 eighteen-pounders, 23 twelve-pounders, 8 nine-pounders, 4 fix-pounders, 14 four-pounders, 6 three-pounders. Mufquet cartridges 10,000; powder, corned, 150 cwt. fpare carriages, 1 garrifon thirty-two pounder, 1 travelling twelve-pounder, two ammunition waggons, ftores for the laboratory, &c.

Return of Ordnance found and fpiked on the New London fide.

Nine iron eighteen-pounders, mounted at Fort Trumbull, 6 fix-pounders at ditto, 6 twelve, or nine-pounders, mounted at Fort Folly; 2 ditto difmounted; 1 twelve-pounder on the road to New London. Total 24.

In Fort Trumbull, 14 eighteen, and three fix-pounders.

A quantity of ammunition and ftores of different kinds was deftroyed in the magazine at Fort Trumbull, and at the meeting-houfe in New London.

CHAP. XLV.

The Confederate Armies arrive at Williamſburgh in Virginia—Lord Cornwallis vindicated from the Charges of Colonel Tarleton—The Combined Armies encamp before York Town—York Town regularly inveſted—Surrendered to General Waſhington—Efforts of Sir H. Clinton for the Relief of Lord Cornwallis—Recapture of St. Euſtatius—Succeſsful Cruize of Admiral Kempenfelt.

CHAP. XLV. 1781.

ALTHOUGH the damage done to the Americans by this attack upon New London was immenſe, it was not of ſufficient importance to ſtop general Waſhington in his progreſs to Virginia. The enterpriſe in which he was now engaged was of the utmoſt moment. If ſucceſsful, it would have a material influence in ſhortening the duration of the war, and was not therefore to be abandoned for any partial conſideration whatſoever. The combined armies, after paſſing through Philadelphia, marched to the head of Elk River, which falls into the Cheſapeak at its interior extremity. Tranſports from the French fleet were ſent thither to receive them, and by the twenty-fifth of September the whole were landed in the neighbourhood of Williamſburgh, and joined the troops under the marquis de la Fayette and monſieur de St. Simon. General Waſhington, and the count de Rochambeau, with their ſuites, left the army upon its arrival at the head of Elk, and proceeded by land to Williamſburgh, where they arrived on the fourteenth. They immediately repaired on board the Ville de Paris, to wait upon the count de Graſſe; and at

The confederate armies arrive at Williamſburgh in Virginia.

CHAP. XLV. 1781. at this meeting a council of war was held, in which the plan of their future operations was finally fettled and agreed upon.

About this time a party of North Carolina loyalifts, to the number of fix hundred and forty, under the command of Macneil, a colonel of militia, furprifed Hillfborough, furrounded a church where a body of continentals were ftationed, and took about two hundred prifoners, among whom was Mr. Burke, the governor of North Carolina, his council, two colonels, four or five captains, five fubalterns, together with feveral other men of rank; and releafed fixty men that were in gaol on account of their fidelity and attachment to the Britifh government. On their return they were attacked by a body of about three hundred of the enemy, who lay in ambufh near the banks of the Rain Creek. An action took place, in which the loyalifts fuffered the lofs of their colonel Macneil, and captain Doud, killed, and feveral other officers, with twenty privates, wounded; but in which, now under the command of Macdougald, they forced the enemy to leave the field, with the lofs of one colonel and one major killed, and thirty-feven rank and file wounded. The loyalifts then proceeded on their march with governor Burke and the other prifoners, till they arrived, on the feventeenth, at a place called Raft Swamp, where they were joined by a fmall party of friends under colonel Kay. Before their junction with this party they were fo much reduced as fcarcely to be fufficient for guarding the prifoners. They had offered to liberate Burke on his parole; but he would not accept this favour, hoping to be retaken by general Butler, who was marching with his army with all poffible fpeed, down Cape Fear River in purfuit of the loyalifts. Soon afterwards Macdougald with his party arrived at Wilmington, and delivered his prifoners to major Craig, the governor.

Whilft

Whilft that powerful combination between the French and Americans was forming, earl Cornwallis took every opportunity of communicating to the commander in chief at New York the danger of his fituation, in confequence of the French fleet having taken poffeffion of the bay: And from him he received affurances bearing date the fixth of September, that he would join him with four thoufand troops, who were then embarked, as foon as the admiral fhould be of opinion that he might venture. He was alfo informed that admiral Digby was upon the coaft, and daily expected to arrive, with a reinforcement of fhips and troops. In the mean time the troops under his lordfhip were bufily employed in fortifying York, the works at which having been begun later than thofe on the oppofite fide, and being alfo more extenfive, were not in the fame ftate of forwardnefs. It has been fuggefted* that about this period, that is, between the time of the junction of the French reinforcement from the Weft Indies with the marquis de la Fayette, and the arrival of the confederate army from the head of Elk, lord Cornwallis ought to have attacked the former of thefe corps after their junction, and while they lay at Williamfburgh, and that he had a fufficient force to have attempted it with every profpect of fuccefs. But lord Cornwallis's character for enterprife, of which his conduct during all his campaigns in America affords the ftrongeft evidence, forbids even a fufpicion that any opportunity of ftriking a blow at the enemy was loft, which could have been embraced, confiftently with the orders under which he acted, the inftructions he had received, and the intelligence which had been from time to time forwarded to him. It has alfo been faid † that if this meafure was not thought eligible, in that cafe he ought to have abandonnd York Town, and returned with his army to South Carolina. But it ought

Lord Cornwallis vindicated from the charges of colonel Tarleton.

* Tarleton, p. 367, &c. † Tarleton, p. 369.

to

CHAP. XLV. 1781.

to be recollected, that, ſome little time before this, he had been made acquainted with the commander in chief's deſign of commencing ſolid operations in the Cheſapeak, as ſoon as the ſeaſon of the year would permit: And if he had at this time withdrawn his army from Virginia, that plan of operation, which he alſo knew was agreeable to the wiſhes of the Britiſh miniſtry, muſt have been entirely fruſtrated. With this information before him, and with even a conditional aſſurance of relief, he would ſcarcely have been juſtifiable in taking a ſtep that would have been attended with ſuch a conſequence, except under circumſtances of a more preſſing neceſſity than yet exiſted. Beſides this, by his march to Carolina he muſt have abandoned and given up to the enemy, a conſiderable quantity of artillery, the ſhips of war, tranſports, proviſions, ſtores, and hoſpitals, with the ſick and wounded. It ſeems, therefore, under all the circumſtances, that ſuch a ſtep at that time could not have been juſtified: And had he attacked the marquis de la Fayette, previouſly to the arrival of Waſhington and Rochambeau, he muſt have greatly impeded the progreſs of the works at York, by drawing off the troops employed upon them, from whoſe unremitting labour during the month of September, they were in greater forwardneſs by the time the combined army aſſembled at Williamſburgh than could have been expected, although they were not even then nearly finiſhed. The works conſtructing for the defence of York were of two kinds, the one for the immediate defence of the town, and the other a range of redoubts and field-works at ſome diſtance from it, calculated to impede the enemy's approach.

The combined armies encamp before York Town.

In this untoward poſition the Britiſh troops were ſtationed, when the combined army of French and Americans appeared in ſight of York, on the twenty-eighth of September, having marched from Williamſburgh that morning. They encamped that night about two miles from the works, and the next morning were ſeen extend-

 ing

ing themſelves towards the left of the Britiſh army, but at a cautious diſtance. The latter wiſhed to be attacked, but the enemy appeared diſpoſed to proceed with great circumſpection. Nothing material happened on this day, either within or without the lines, until the evening, when an expreſs arrived with diſpatches from the commander in chief at New York, bearing date the twenty-fourth of September. In theſe earl Cornwallis was informed, that at a council held that day, between the general and flag officers, it was agreed that upwards of five thouſand troops ſhould be embarked on board the king's ſhips; that every exertion would be made, both by the army and navy, to relieve him; and that the fleet, conſiſting of twenty-three ſail of the line, might be expected to ſail by the fifth of October: And in a poſtſcript his lordſhip was advertiſed, that admiral Digby, with three more ſhips of the line, had juſt arrived at Sandy Hook. Upon the receipt of theſe diſpatches, lord Cornwallis in the night withdrew his army within the works of the town, in full expectation of being able to hold both the poſts of York and Glouceſter until the promiſed relief arrived, provided it came within any reaſonable time. The works abandoned by the Britiſh troops were occupied the next day by detachments from the combined army: The ſame day the town was regularly inveſted; and in the night the enemy began to break ground, the French making their approaches on the right of it, and the Americans on the left, the extremities of the two armies meeting at a moraſs in front of the centre of the Britiſh works. The ſame day the duke de Lauzun, with his legion, and a body of Virginia militia under general Weedon, took a poſition in front of the other Britiſh poſt at Glouceſter Town, and kept it from that time blockaded. In the night of the ſixth of October the enemy made their firſt parallel at the diſtance of ſix hundred yards from the Britiſh works, and by the afternoon of the ninth, their batteries were completed, which immediately opened

York Town regularly inveſted.

opened upon the town. From this time an inceſſant cannonade was kept up: And the continued diſcharge of ſhot and ſhells from a number of heavy cannon and mortars, in a few days damaged the unfiniſhed works on the left of the town, ſilenced the guns that were mounted on them, and occaſioned the loſs of a great number of men. In the night of the eleventh the enemy, with indefatigable perſeverance, opened their ſecond parallel three hundred yards nearer to the works than the firſt. In the mean time the garriſon did every thing in their power to interrupt them in their work, by opening new embraſures for guns, and keeping up a conſtant fire with all the howitzers and ſmall mortars they could man; and about this time, the loſs of men ſuſtained by the enemy was more conſiderable than at any other period during the ſiege. They were particularly annoyed and impeded in their approaches by two redoubts, advanced about three hundred yards in front of the Britiſh works. Theſe they reſolved to aſſault; and to excite a ſpirit of emulation, the reduction of the one was committed to the French, of the other to the Americans. The attempt was made in the night of the fourteenth, and in both inſtances ſucceeded; and by the unwearied labour of the enemy both redoubts were included in their ſecond parallel before the morning. The Britiſh troops having been weakened by ſickneſs, as well as by the fire of the beſiegers, lord Cornwallis could not venture to make ſo large ſorties as to hope from them much ſucceſs: But at the preſent criſis ſome attempt of that ſort became neceſſary, in order to retard the opening of the enemy's batteries in their ſecond parallel, againſt the fire of which, it was foreſeen that the Britiſh works on the left, already half-ruined, could not ſtand many hours. A ſortie of three hundred and fifty men, under the direction of lieutenant-colonel Abercrombie, was therefore ordered againſt two of the enemy's batteries, that ſeemed in the greateſt ſtate of forwardneſs. A detachment of the guards,

guards, with the eightieth company of grenadiers, under the command of lieutenant-colonel Lake, of the guards, was ordered to attack the one; and a detachment of light-infantry, under the command of major Armſtrong, was to attack the other. The two detachments accordingly ſallied forth a little before day-break of the ſixteenth of October, forced the redoubts that covered the batteries, ſpiked eleven heavy cannon, and after killing or wounding about one hundred of the French troops, who had the guard of this part of the trenches, returned within the lines with very little loſs. But this action, although honourable to the officers and ſoldiers who performed it, yielded little public advantage. The cannon, having been haſtily ſpiked, were ſoon rendered fit for ſervice; and before the evening, the whole battery and parallels appeared to be nearly complete. At this time not a gun could be ſhewn by the garriſon on that ſide of the works attacked by the enemy, and the ſhells were nearly expended; lord Cornwallis was therefore reduced to the neceſſity of either preparing to ſurrender, or attempting to eſcape with the greateſt part of the army; and he determined to attempt the latter, on the Glouceſter ſide of the river, where brigadier de Choisé now commanded, and lay with a ſmall corps at ſome diſtance, in front of the works. It was determined that he ſhould be attacked before break of day by the whole Britiſh force; and the ſucceſs of the attack was not in the leaſt doubted. The horſes taken from him (for he had a conſiderable corps of cavalry) would in part mount the infantry, and the reſt might be ſupplied by others collected on the road. As no baggage was to be carried, his lordſhip intended to have proceeded to the upper country by rapid marches, leaving his future route uncertain, until he came oppoſite to the fords of the great rivers; when he meant to have turned off ſuddenly to the northward, upon a ſuppoſition that the enemy's meaſures would be principally directed to prevent his eſcape to the ſouth-

CHAP. XLV. 1781.

fouthward. After turning to the northward, it was his lordfhip's defign to force his way through Maryland, Penfylvania, and the Jerfeys, and join the commander in chief at New York. Undoubtedly the attempt was beyond calculation hazardous, and the iffue totally precarious; but, if it afforded even a glimpfe of hope, it was preferable to an immediate furrender.

In purfuance of this defign the light-infantry, the greateft part of the guards, and part of the twenty-third regiment, were embarked in boats, and tranfported to the Gloucefter fide of the river before midnight, when a violent ftorm arofe, which not only prevented the boats from returning, but drove them a confiderable diftance down the river. The paffage of the reft of the troops was now become impracticable, and, in the abfence of the boats, thofe that had already croffed could not poffibly return. In this divided ftate of the British force, the enemy's batteries opened at break of day: Fortunately the boats returned foon afterwards, and brought back in the courfe of the forenoon the troops that had been carried over in the night, without much lofs, although the paffage between York and Gloucefter was greatly expofed to the enemy's fire. In the mean time, by the force of the enemy's cannonade, the Britifh works were tumbling into ruin: Not a gun could be fired from them, and only one eight-inch and little more than an hundred cohorn fhells remained. They were in many places affailable already; and if the fame fire continued a few hours longer, it was the opinion of the engineer and principal officers of the army, that it would be madnefs to attempt to maintain them with the prefent garrifon, exhaufted by the fatigue of conftant watching and unremitting duty, and reduced in its numbers by ficknefs even more than by the enemy's fire. Under fuch circumftances his lordfhip, on the feventeenth of October, unwilling to expofe the remains of his gallant army to the danger of an affault, which, from the enemy's numbers and the ruined ſtate of the works, could not fail to be ſucceſsful, made propoſals for a capitulation. The terms were adjuſted in the courſe of the next day, which, though not altogether agreeable to earl Cornwallis's wiſhes or propoſals, were nevertheleſs ſuch as his deſperate ſituation obliged him to accept; and on the nineteenth the poſts of York and Glouceſter were ſurrendered to general Waſhington as commander in chief of the combined army; and the ſhips of war, tranſports, and other veſſels, to the count de Graſſe, as commander of the French fleet. By the articles of capitulation, the garriſon of York and Glouceſter, including the officers of the navy and ſeamen of every denomination, were to ſurrender as priſoners of war to the combined army: The land force to remain priſoners to the United States, and the ſeamen to the moſt chriſtian king. The garriſon was to be allowed the ſame honours which the garriſon of Charleſtown had obtained when it ſurrendered to ſir Henry Clinton. The officers and ſoldiers were permitted to retain their private property; and the officers had liberty to proceed upon parole either to Europe, or any maritime poſt on the continent of America in the poſſeſſion of the Britiſh troops. Although the article for exempting from puniſhment ſuch of the natives or other inhabitants of America as had joined the Britiſh army, and were then at York, was rejected by general Waſhington, the ſame thing was in effect obtained in a different form, by the permiſſion granted to earl Cornwallis to ſend the Bonetta ſloop of war to New York with his diſpatches without being ſearched, and with as many ſoldiers on board as he ſhould think fit, ſo that they were accounted for in any future exchange. By this permiſſion he was tacitly empowered to ſend off ſuch of the inhabitants as were obnoxious to puniſhment; which accordingly was done.

Surrendered to general Waſhington.

By the ſurrender of the poſts of York and Glouceſter the Americans became poſſeſſed of a large train of artillery, many of which

CHAP. XLV. 1781.

which were of brafs, together with a confiderable quantity of arms, ammunition, warlike ftores, and provifions; and to the French were delivered up one frigate, two fhips of war of twenty guns, and a number of tranfports and other veffels. The Charon, of forty-four guns, and another fhip of war, were fet on fire by the enemy's fhells, and deftroyed during the fiege. The combined army confifted of feven thoufand French and nearly the fame number of continental foldiers, and about five thoufand militia. On the day previous to the furrender, the rank and file of the garrifons of York and Gloucefter amounted to five thoufand nine hundred and fifty; but fo great was the number of the fick and wounded, that only four thoufand and feventeen were reported fit for duty.

Efforts of fir Henry Clinton for the relief of lord Cornwallis.

In the mean time fir Henry Clinton had draughted from the garrifon at New York a corps of feven thoufand of his beft troops, with which he propofed to embark on board the king's fhips, and impatiently waited for the moment when the fleet would be ready to fail. He had already informed lord Cornwallis, that it was hoped the fleet would "ftart from New York about the fifth of October;" and afterwards, from the affurances given him by the admiral, that it might pafs the Bar by the twelfth, if the winds permitted, and no unforefeen accident happened: But the fleet did not finally leave Sandy Hook until the nineteenth, the day on which lord Cornwallis furrendered. The commander in chief embarked with the troops, as he had propofed, and the event of the fiege not being then known, both the navy and army put to fea with a determined refolution to make the moft vigorous efforts for the relief of earl Cornwallis, and with confident hopes that thofe efforts would be attended with the moft complete fuccefs. It was, therefore, with extreme mortification, when they arrived off the Capes of Virginia on the twenty-fourth, that they received accounts which led them to fufpect that earl Cornwallis had already capitulated. They however remained

off

off the mouth of the Chesapeak until the twenty-ninth. The intelligence received during this interval was so uniform in its tendency, that no doubt at last remained about the issue of the siege. It was apparent, that the British armament had arrived too late to afford earl Cornwallis the promised relief; and as that relief was the sole object of the expedition, the admiral determined to return to New York. The British fleet at this time consisted of twenty-five ships of the line, two fifty-gun ships, and eight frigates: That of the French amounted to thirty-six sail of the line, besides frigates. Unfortunately, the letter written by earl Cornwallis to the commander in chief, acquainting him with the surrender of the posts of York and Gloucester, and narrating the causes that led to that event, with the motives that influenced his own conduct, produced a difference between them, which terminated in an appeal to the public. Such was the fate of the army; which, if success were the uniform result of merit, would have undoubtedly shared a different fate: If bravery in the field, and patient, and even cheerful, submission to fatigue, inclement skies, and the want not only of the comforts, but sometimes even of the necessaries of life *, have any claim to esteem and admiration. It has been observed, and justly, that in almost all the general actions to the northward, the troops under sir William Howe were superior in number to those under general Washington; but, on the contrary, in every general action to the southward, the enemy greatly outnumbered the British either under lord Cornwallis or lord Rawdon.

The misfortune that happened in Virginia was soon afterwards followed by another in the West Indies, which, although not of equal

* The writer of this narrative relates these things from his own knowledge. The southern army had no provision in the field but what passed through his hands. Their allowance was frequently scanty, and generally bad. The army under lord Cornwallis, in marches and counter-marches, marched above 1500 miles.

3 magnitude,

CHAP. XLV. 1781. Recapture of St. Eustatius.

magnitude, was the cause of much discontent, as it seemed to have arisen from gross negligence or still greater misconduct. This was the recapture of the Dutch island of St. Eustatius by the marquis de Bouillé. The marquis having received minute information, by means of some of the traders, of the state of the island, together with the carelessness of the governor, he determined to attempt the reduction of it by surprise. It has been already noticed, that the island of St. Eustatius might be considered as a natural fortification, with only one safe landing-place, where the town stood, and which was protected by a fort. But at the back of the island were also some small bays, where a landing might be effected in very moderate weather, although at all times accompanied with considerable risk and danger. Of one of these, which had been left unguarded, the marquis de Bouillé had received intelligence; and there he determined to attempt a descent. Having embarked about two thousand men in a number of small vessels, he sailed from Martinique, and took his measures so as to arrive before the place where he proposed to land early in the night. So hazardous was the attempt, that in embarking, many of the boats were dashed to pieces, and a number of soldiers lost; and with all the efforts he could make, not more than four hundred men were landed by an hour before daylight; and as almost the whole of the boats were by this time dashed to pieces, no hopes remained of being able to land the rest. As the troops which had been landed were not equal in number to the garrison, the marquis de Bouillé was sensible that nothing but a bold attempt to take the fort by surprise could possibly succeed. He accordingly put his troops in motion, and marched with the utmost expedition towards the fort, distant about six miles. The way to it was not only difficult, but intersected by a defile where a handful of men might have stopped an army. But in his situation every risk was to be run. His retreat being cut off, nothing but success could possibly save him and his troops

CHAP. XLV. 1781.

troops from destruction or captivity. A discharge of musquetry from the French at a division of the British troops, which was seen exercising in a field at some distance from the fort, gave the first alarm to the garrison. Those who were in quarters immediately hurried to the fort, and so loaded the draw-bridge, that it could not be raised until the enemy arrived, and entered with them. Lieutenant-colonel Cockburn the governor, who had been taking an early ride according to custom, seeing some strange vessels off the island, took the alarm and returned; but the French in the mean time had reached the town, and made him prisoner before he dismounted *.

Thus was the island of St. Eustatius reduced by the marquis de Bouillé on the morning of the twenty-sixth of November, with no other loss than ten soldiers killed and wounded. With the island the conquerors became possessed of a large sum of money, estimated at two millions of livres, being the produce of the late sales of prizes. Whilst St. Eustatius was in the possession of Great Britain, some pains had been taken to fortify it. Sixty-eight pieces of artillery were mounted for its defence, and the garrison consisted of two regiments, mustering six hundred and seventy-seven men. The dependant islands of St. Martin's and Saba were attacked immediately afterwards, and shared the same fate as St. Eustatius.

Successful cruize of admiral Kempenfeldt.

After all these misfortunes, the year 1781 closed with a successful cruize of admiral Kempenfeldt in the European seas. Information had been received in England, that a large convoy of transports with troops, and of store-ships and provision vessels, was getting ready at Brest, and to sail in the month of December, the greatest part of it being destined for the fleet under the count de Grasse, and the

* Lieutenant-colonel Cockburn, a native of Aberdeen, was afterwards tried by a court-martial, and found guilty of culpable neglect in not taking the necessary precautions for the defence of the island, notwithstanding he had received the fullest intelligence of an intended attack.

CHAP. XLV. 1781.

remainder for M. de Suffrein's squadron in the East Indies; and the whole to be convoyed a certain distance by a fleet of ships of war under the command of the count de Guichen. To cruize for and endeavour to intercept this fleet and convoy, admiral Kempenfeldt was dispatched in the beginning of December with twelve ships of the line, a fifty-gun ship, four frigates, and a fire-ship, being all that were then in readiness for sea. On the twelfth of that month he fortunately got sight of them in a hard gale of wind, when the French fleet was much dispersed, and the convoy considerably astern. The admiral determined to profit by the enemy's accidental situation, and by carrying a press of sail to endeavour to cut off their convoy; in which attempt he in part succeeded. A considerable number of prizes were taken, fifteen of which arrived safe in British ports, while some that had struck afterwards escaped in the night. Two or three were said to have been sunk; and many others lost their voyages in consequence of the great dispersion of the convoy that necessarily ensued. In the mean time the count de Guichen was collecting his ships, and forming the line. Towards the evening the British admiral found it necessary to do the same; and, after taking measures for keeping his fleet connected, went upon the same tack with the enemy, intending to engage them in the morning. But when day-light appeared, and he saw the French fleet to leeward, consisting of nineteen ships of the line and two others armed en flute, he did not think it prudent to risk an engagement; and contenting himself with endeavouring to secure the prizes already made, returned with his fleet to Portsmouth. The Agamemnon, however, and the frigate la Prudente, were detached to follow the French fleet, with a view of capturing any of the convoy that might chance to be separated. It does not appear that they met with any success in this design; but on the twenty-fifth of December they made prize of five large ships bound from Bourdeaux to Martinique,

nique, which were deſtined to join the convoy under the count de Guichen. The prizes carried to England had on board near eleven hundred land forces, and between ſix and ſeven hundred ſeamen. They were almoſt all freighted on the French king's account, and were chiefly laden with braſs and iron ordnance, gunpowder, ſmall-arms, flints, bomb-ſhells, cannon-balls, and a vaſt variety of other ordnance and military ſtores. Some of them were laden with cables, ſail-cloth, and cordage; and others with wine, oil, brandy, rum, flour, biſcuit, and ſalted proviſions. From the nature of the lading with which theſe ſhips were freighted, the importance of the capture is very apparent; and fortunately for the ſafety of the Britiſh Weſt India iſlands, the remainder of the French convoy, that eſcaped being taken, was ſo ſhattered and diſabled by ſtormy weather, that only a few of them, accompanied by two ſhips of war, were able to hold on their courſe and join de Graſſe. The reſt put back to repair their damages.

CHAP. XLVI.

Effects of the Capture of Lord Cornwallis's Army—Meeting of Parliament—Siege of Fort St. Philip's in the Island of Minorca—Capitulation of Fort St. Philip's—Reduction of the Island of St. Christopher's—General Carleton appointed Commander in Chief in America instead of Sir Henry Clinton—Naval Engagement between Admiral Rodney and the Count de Grasse—Prosperity of British Affairs in the East Indies—Conduct of the new Administration—Repulse and Discomfiture of the Spaniards and French before Gibraltar—Relief of Gibraltar.

CHAP. XLVI.

1782. Effects of the capture of lord Cornwallis's army.

AFTER ſo many defeats and loſſes to which the arms of congreſs had been ſubjected for ſeveral years paſt, ſo brilliant an event as the capture of a whole army, and at its head a commander who was eſteemed one of the braveſt and moſt enterpriſing of their foes, could not fail to give them the moſt heart-felt ſatisfaction, and was accordingly celebrated with ſuitable rejoicings and every other demonſtration that could ſerve to convey to the people a proper idea of its importance. By ſuch means the authority of congreſs, which had begun to be ſhaken, was again eſtabliſhed; the clamours of thoſe who had become tired of the war, and wiſhed for peace upon almoſt any terms, were ſilenced; the deſponding were re-aſſured; the active and zealous invigorated; and all claſſes, for a time, reconciled to bear their preſent diſtreſſes with patience, in the hope that ſo ſignal an advantage would ſpeedily operate their relief. But greatly as the views

views of congreſs were forwarded by the influence of this event upon the people of the revolted colonies, the benefits thence derived were inconſiderable compared with thoſe that ſprung from the effects produced by it upon the people of Great Britain. The ſums raiſed by parliament for the ſupport of the war, which ſeemed to increaſe every year of its continuance, were already ſo immenſe, that the public burdens impoſed for the payment of the intereſt were nearly inſupportable. The murmurs of the people had been hitherto ſuppreſſed, from the hopes held out of a ſpeedy and ſucceſsful termination of the war; and with the recovery of the revolted colonies, accompanied by the monopoly of their trade, they were taught to expect ſuch an influx of wealth as would ſpeedily compenſate for the preſent extraordinary expenditure. But after the events of the laſt campaign, no one could be found ſo ſanguine as to expect that the revolted colonies could be recovered by force of arms. The experience of nearly ſix years ſerved to ſhow, that although a province might be over-run and ſubdued, it could not be ſecured and preſerved without the concurrence of the inhabitants: And the war waged in the ſouthern colonies for two years paſt, eſtabliſhed the fact beyond contradiction. Although Georgia had been completely reduced, and civil government re-eſtabliſhed: Although all reſiſtance had ceaſed in South Carolina, and a general ſubmiſſion taken place among the inhabitants: Although the Britiſh commanders in thoſe provinces had been uniformly ſucceſsful in all general actions they fought, and had not in a ſingle inſtance been defeated: Yet Charleſtown and Savannah, the two capitals, with a few dependant poſts, were all that at this time remained to Great Britain of thoſe extenſive provinces. Theſe facts naturally led to this inference, that it was madneſs to perſiſt in an expenſive war, in which even ſucceſs failed to produce its natural conſequences. Such were the ſentiments beginning to prevail amongſt the people, when the parliament met

CHAP. XLVI.

1782.

Meeting of parliament.

met on the twenty-feventh of November of the preceding year. In the king's fpeech the loffes in America were neither diffembled nor palliated; but ftated as a ground for requiring the firm fupport of parliament, and a more vigorous, animated, and united exertion of the faculties and refources of the people; whilft his majefty, at the fame time, expreffed his determined refolution to perfevere in the defence of his dominions until fuch a pacification could be made as might confift with the honour of his crown and the permanent intereft and fecurity of his people. An addrefs of thanks being moved for in the ufual form, was violently combated by the oppofition, under an idea, that if they agreed to it, they bound themfelves to fupport his majefty in profecuting the American war; and an amendment of a different tendency was offered by Mr. Fox. But the amendment was rejected, and the addrefs carried in its original form, by a confiderable majority of two hundred and eighteen againft one hundred and twenty-nine. In the courfe of this debate, although the minifters did not feem to be perfectly agreed amongft themfelves, it appeared to be their determination no longer to carry on the war internally in the colonies, but to keep poffeffion of thofe pofts which they at prefent held, and direct their principal efforts againft France, Spain, and Holland.

This difclofure of a change in the mode of conducting the war, although it muft have operated as a relief to the colonies, gave no fatisfaction to the oppofition, who maintained that the general voice of the nation demanded a peace with America; whereas the miniftry ftill avowed the defign of carrying on that war, and had only varied the form. The oppofition now looked forward with eager expectation to the æra of the diffolution of that miniftry which had fo long fuccefsfully withftood their rudeft attacks. The misfortunes of the laft campaign gave them advantages which all the influence and power of the adminiftration were unable to furmount. By this

time

CHAP. XLVI. 1782.

time the American war was generally diſreliſhed amongſt the people; and by the oppoſition it was reprobated, together with the incapacity and miſconduct of miniſters, as the cauſe of all our misfortunes. The proſecution of it, unfortunate as it had been, was ſtill ſuppoſed to be a favourite meaſure with the court. The oppoſition, on the other hand, loudly maintained, that to put an end to it was the only means of ſaving the nation from bankruptcy and ruin: And upon this ground, the ſtrongeſt they could adopt, as being that on which they expected to be ſupported by the nation, they continued to haraſs and diſtreſs adminiſtration by a ſucceſſion of motions in the houſe of commons, until at laſt, on the twenty-ſeventh of February, they ſucceeded in carrying a vote for addreſſing his majeſty to direct his miniſters no longer to wage an offenſive war againſt the revolted colonies, and to aſſure him that they would moſt cheerfully concur in ſuch meaſures as may be found neceſſary to accelerate the bleſſing of returning peace. This victory gained by the oppoſition with a majority of two hundred and thirty-four againſt two hundred and fifteen, was conſidered as a prelude to the diſſolution of the old adminiſtration, which accordingly, about the end of March, gave place to a new one, formed under the auſpices of the marquis of Rockingham. The cabinet, including the marquis as firſt commiſſioner of the treaſury, was compoſed of the earl of Shelburn and Mr. Fox, appointed ſecretaries of ſtate; lord Camden, preſident of the council; the duke of Grafton, privy ſeal; lord John Cavendiſh, chancellor of the exchequer; admiral Keppel, firſt commiſſioner of the admiralty; general Conway, commander in chief of the forces; the duke of Richmond, maſter-general of the ordnance; colonel Barré, treaſurer of the navy; and Mr. Burke, paymaſter-general.

February.

March.

During theſe contentions for power, between the old adminiſtration and thoſe who ſucceeded them, the intelligence that arrived of

CHAP. XLVI. 1782.

new misfortunes and losses sustained abroad in the beginning of the present year, undoubtedly served to hasten the overthrow of the former, and to complete the triumph of the latter. It may be remembered, that in the preceding year a joint expedition having been planned by France and Spain against the island of Minorca, an armament fitted out at Cadiz was landed upon the island on the twentieth of August, which was soon afterwards joined by a considerable body of French troops from Toulon. The duke de Crillon commanded the expedition: He carried with him an immense artillery of one hundred and nine pieces of the heaviest cannon, and thirty-six mortars, for the siege of Fort St. Philip's; and after the junction of the French, his army amounted to sixteen thousand men. General Murray, an officer of undoubted bravery and great experience, commanded at Minorca: The garrison consisted of about two thousand seven hundred men, four hundred of whom were invalids sent from England in the year 1775; but the works of St. Philip's Castle were so numerous and extensive, that the garrison did not amount to half the number which would have been necessary completely to man them. Notwithstanding this weakness, the defence of the place was brave and spirited, and suitable to the high military character of the officer who commanded. For three months after the commencement of the siege, the enemy made scarcely any impression on the works, and did little injury to the garrison; but after they had finished their batteries, and mounted all their guns and mortars; the fire from so tremendous an artillery began to damage the upper works of the castle, and rendered a number of the guns mounted upon them unserviceable. Still, however, the body of the works remained uninjured, and the garrison not much diminished. But, about this time, a most inveterate scurvy began to prevail amongst the troops, which, baffling all medical skill, by the beginning of February had spread so widely, that of the whole garrison

Siege of Fort St. Philip's in the island of Minorca.

rifon only fix hundred and fixty were capable of bearing arms. Under thefe circumftances general Murray was reduced to the neceffity of capitulating. In the articles of capitulation every thing was granted that he required, except the claufe for freeing the garrifon from being prifoners, to which the duke de Crillon was prohibited from confenting by a fpecial inftruction of the king of Spain; but in order to foften the rigour of this inftruction, the troops were allowed to be fent to Great Britain, under the cuftomary condition of not ferving until they were regularly exchanged. The terms of capitulation having been fettled, St. Plilip's Caftle was furrendered on the fifth of February: And thus the ifland of Minorca was reftored to the crown of Spain, after it had been in the poffeffion of Great Britain about feventy-four years. The whole lofs of the garrifon, in killed and wounded, during the fiege, amounted to two hundred and eight: Of thefe fifty-nine were killed, and one hundred and forty-nine wounded.

CHAP. XLVI. 1782. Capitulation of Fort St. Philip's.

Nearly about the fame time the ifland of St. Chriftopher's in the Weft Indies was reduced by the marquis de Bouillé. After the return of the count de Graffe with his fleet from North America, an expedition was planned between him and the marquis de Bouillé againft the ifland of Barbadoes, in confequence of which the latter embarked with eight thoufand troops, and the fleet failed from Martinique on the twenty-eighth of December. By contrary winds it was driven greatly to leeward, and as Barbadoes was to windward of Martinique, and much time would be loft in beating up, the French commanders determined to change the object of the expedition, and proceed againft the ifland of St. Chriftopher's, where the troops were landed on the eleventh of January. Brigadier-general Frafer, a brave old officer who commanded the few Britifh troops that were in the ifland, finding himfelf totally unable to oppofe the landing of the French, took poft with his little garrifon upon Brimftone

Reduction of the ifland of St. Chriftopher's.

CHAP. XLVI. 1782. Hill, where he was joined by governer Shirley with ſome militia of the iſland. The regular force under Fraſer conſiſted of the firſt battalion of the firſt regiment, the two flank companies of the fifteenth, and a detachment of the royal artillery, the whole amounting to ſix hundred men. The militia who joined him with governor Shirley, were about three hundred. Brimſtone Hill, where he took poſt, was a place of great natural ſtrength, from its height and inacceſſibility: Some works had been erected upon the top of it, but in no reſpect ſuitable to the natural ſtrength and importance of the place. The French, having landed, immediately began to inveſt Brimſtone Hill, whilſt the count de Graſſe with his fleet lay at anchor in Baſſe Terre Road, to cover the ſiege. Sir Samuel Hood, who in the abſence of ſir George Rodney commanded the Britiſh fleet in the Weſt Indies, and was then at Barbadoes, having received intelligence of the deſtination of the French armament, ſailed with his fleet for the relief of St. Chriſtopher's, where he arrived in the evening of the twenty-third of January. The next morning at dawn he began to form his line, with a view of bearing down and attacking the French fleet at anchor. His own fleet conſiſted of only twenty-two ſhips of the line: That of the count de Graſſe amounted to thirty-two; but even with this inferiority, relying on the ſuperior ſkill and valour of Britiſh ſeamen, he determined to make a bold attempt for the relief of the iſland. From the circumſtance of two of his ſhips running foul of each other, he was prevented from executing his deſign on that day; and in the mean time he took a French frigate from Martinique, loaded with ordnance ſtores for the ſiege of Brimſtone Hill, the capture of which greatly delayed the enemy in making their approaches. The next morning the Britiſh fleet having formed the line, advanced to the attack. The count de Graſſe, on perceiving their deſign, left his anchorage ground and ſtood out to ſea, with a view of obtaining room to avail

himſelf

himſelf of his ſuperiority in number. Sir Samuel Hood immediately ſaw the advantage to be gained from this movement of the enemy, and ſtill preſerving the appearance of an attack, in order to draw them farther from the land, at laſt puſhed by them with full ſail, and took poſſeſſion of the anchorage which they had quitted. The count de Graſſe attempted to cut off the Britiſh rear; but commodore Affleck, who commanded it, ſupported by his ſeconds, captain Cornwallis and lord Robert Manners, kept up ſo tremendous a fire, that he could make no impreſſion, and, with little loſs to themſelves, greatly covered the other ſhips of the diviſion whilſt getting into their ſtations in the anchorage-ground. Two attacks were made the next day by the count de Graſſe upon the Britiſh fleet at anchor; but in both he was repulſed, and in the laſt with ſo conſiderable loſs, that during the remainder of the ſiege he kept at a diſtance. The loſs of the Britiſh fleet in theſe attacks amounted to ſeventy-two killed, and two hundred and forty-four wounded: That of the French is unknown, but it was ſaid that they ſent a thouſand wounded men to St. Euſtatius. The ſucceſsful manœuvre practiſed by the Britiſh admiral of decoying the count de Graſſe from the road of Baſſe Terre, and occupying it in his ſtead, produced at firſt flattering expectations that the iſland might yet be preſerved. But the great ſuperiority of the French force on ſhore, compared with that of the garriſon, ſoon enabled the marquis de Bouillé to inveſt the fort on Brimſtone Hill ſo cloſely, that all communication between it and the Britiſh fleet was entirely cut off, whilſt, in conſequence of the ſame cauſe, his own communication with the count de Graſſe was open, by means of every other landing-place upon the iſland, except that of Baſſe Terre Road. The French, although expoſed to a vigorous fire from the garriſon, and conſiderably delayed by the capture of one of their ordnance veſſels, and the loſs of another, wrecked upon the rocks, continued to ad-

CHAP. XLVI. 1782.

vance their works and profecute the attack with unremitting induftry, until they had mounted on their different batteries twenty-four large mortars, and twenty-three pieces of heavy cannon. The effect of the fire from fo powerful an artillery acting upon a fpot, the greateft diameter of which was not more than two hundred yards, may be eafily conceived: Early in the fiege, every houfe on the hill was either confumed or torn to pieces by the enemy's bombardment and cannonade: In the latter part of it, almoft all the guns were either difmounted or difabled; and at laft an entire and perfect breach was made on the north-weft fide of the works, which, from the want of intrenching tools, it was impoffible to repair. By this time alfo, from the great defertion of the militia, and the number of the killed and wounded, thofe who remained in the garrifon, fit for duty, did not exceed five hundred men. After all the efforts of courage and perfeverance, governor Shirley and general Frafer were reduced to the neceffity of capitulating. Very liberal terms were obtained both for the inhabitants and the garrifon: And on the twelfth of February, the fort at Brimftone Hill, and the ifland of St. Chriftopher's, with the dependent ifland of Nevis, were furrendered to the marquis de Bouillé. The whole lofs of the Britifh regulars in garrifon at Brimftone Hill during the fiege, amounted to one hundred and feventy-fix; thirty-eight being killed, one hundred and twenty-five wounded, and thirteen miffing. There being no farther occafion for the Britifh fleet to remain in Baffe Terre Road, fir Samuel Hood put to fea in the night of the fourteenth, unperceived by the enemy, and directed his courfe to Barbadoes, where he expected to meet fir George Rodney with a reinforcement of fhips from England. The furrender of Montferrat, as was expected, fucceeded the lofs of St. Chriftopher's and Nevis; a detachment from the French fleet, on its return to Martinique, having appeared before it on the twenty-fecond of February.

From

From the avowed principles and ſentiments of thoſe who held the chief offices in the new adminiſtration, no doubt was entertained that peace with the revolted colonies would be one of the firſt objects of their attention, and that the claim of independence ſet up by the latter, would be no bar to a ſettlement. In the preceding year the American congreſs had granted full powers to five of their agents in Europe to treat of a peace; and with thoſe perſons, or ſome of them, means were found to open an intercourſe early in April: But ſo many previous difficulties were to be cleared away, that ſome time muſt be expected to elapſe before they could enter on the final diſcuſſion of the buſineſs.

General Carleton appointed commander in chief in America inſtead of ſir Henry Clinton.

One of the laſt acts of the former adminiſtration was to appoint general Carleton (now lord Dorcheſter) commander in chief in America in the room of ſir Henry Clinton. He was continued in office by the new adminiſtration; and, in conſequence of the inſtructions he received, a ſort of tacit ceſſation of hoſtilities was obſerved between the two armies in the neighbourhood of New York; neither of them attempting to moleſt the other. In other parts of the world, the war was ſtill to be proſecuted with vigour againſt France, Spain, and Holland. The two former of theſe powers had agreed to renew their attempt this year againſt the iſland of Jamaica: And to fruſtrate their deſigns, ſir George Rodney, ſoon after his arrival in England in the fall of the preceding year, was diſpatched to reſume his command in the Weſt Indies with a reinforcement of twelve ſhips of the line. He ſailed from the Channel in January, and arrived at Barbadoes on the nineteenth of February. In conſequence of the intelligence there received of the attack made on St. Chriſtopher's (the news of its ſurrender not having then arrived), he put to ſea immediately, with an intention of joining ſir Samuel Hood, and attempting its relief. On his paſſage he met the Britiſh fleet returning from St. Chriſtopher's; and as the

CHAP. XLVI. 1782.

the iſland was already ſurrendered, and the count de Graſſe had ſailed for Martinique, he proceeded with the whole fleet to St. Lucie, the moſt convenient ſtation for watching the enemy's motions. For this purpoſe ſome of his frigates were ſtationed ſo as to give him the earlieſt intelligence; whilſt the reſt of the fleet took on board proviſions and water to laſt them for five months. As the ſafety of Jamaica, and indeed of every other Britiſh iſland in the Weſt Indies, depended upon the exertions now to be made to bring the count de Graſſe to action, before he could form a junction with the Spaniſh fleet to leeward, the intervening ſpace of time was probably a period not only of great expectation, but of much anxiety and diſquietude, to the Britiſh admiral.

April.

On the fifth of April intelligence was received, that the French were embarking troops on board their ſhips of war; and on the eighth, at break of day, a ſignal from the Andromache, captain Byron, announced that their fleet was coming out of Fort Royal Bay, and ſtanding to the north-weſt. Sir George Rodney immediately threw out the ſignal for weighing anchor, which was inſtantly obeyed with ſo much alacrity, that the whole Britiſh fleet, conſiſting of thirty-ſix ſhips of the line, was clear of Gros Iſlet Bay before noon, and proceeding with a preſs of ſail in purſuit of the enemy. Before day the next morning the enemy was diſcovered under Dominique; and in this ſituation both fleets were for ſome time becalmed. The enemy got the breeze firſt, and ſtood towards Guadaloupe: The van of the Britiſh fleet, commanded by ſir Samuel Hood, received it next, and ſtood after them with a preſs of ſail; whilſt the centre and rear were ſtill becalmed. Although it was obviouſly the deſign of the count de Graſſe to avoid an engagement, the opportunity which now preſented itſelf of overpowering the Britiſh van, whilſt the centre and rear lay becalmed, was not to be reſiſted: When, therefore, ſir Samuel Hood's diviſion had approached ſo near as to engage, the count de Graſſe bore down upon it with his whole force. At one time, it is ſaid, the Barfleur, Hood's ſhip, had ſeven of the enemy's ſhips firing upon her, and during the greateſt part of the action not leſs than three: And although every ſhip of his diviſion had a ſuperior force to contend with, ſo nobly did they ſupport each other, and with ſuch effect return the enemy's fire, that no advantage could be obtained over them; and, as it afterwards appeared, the enemy in this unequal conflict received more damage than they occaſioned. At length part of the centre got near enough to engage, and take part in the action: But when the breeze reached the rear of the Britiſh fleet, the count de Graſſe withdrew his ſhips from action, and, having the advantage of the wind, kept at ſuch a diſtance as to baffle all the endeavours of the Britiſh commander to renew it. In this action the Royal Oak and Montagu, the two leading ſhips of the van, ſuſtained conſiderable damage, and the ſervice a heavy loſs, in the death of captain Bayne, of the Alfred. Two of the French ſhips were ſo much diſabled as to be obliged to quit the fleet, and take ſhelter in Guadaloupe. The Britiſh fleet lay-to the night after the action to repair their damages, and the next morning made ſail to windward in purſuit of the enemy; but with ſo little effect, that by the morning of the eleventh the French fleet had got ſo far to windward, that ſome of their ſhips were ſcarcely viſible. In the mean time the rear diviſion of the Britiſh fleet, commanded by admiral Drake, had been tranſpoſed to the van, which now became the rear. Fortunately, about noon of the eleventh, one of the enemy's ſhips was ſeen a great way to windward, apparently in a diſabled condition, and repairing her damages: A general chaſe was immediately ordered; and towards evening one of the leading ſhips approached ſo near, that ſhe muſt inevitably have been taken, had not the count de Graſſe, ſeeing her danger, borne down with his whole fleet for her protection.

CHAP. XLVI. 1782.

protection. This movement brought the two fleets so near, that nothing but the approach of night prevented an immediate engagement; which must necessarily happen in the morning, if things were preserved in their present relative state during the night. Such measures were immediately taken by sir George Rodney as he thought would be effectual for that purpose; and when day-light appeared, he had the satisfaction to perceive, that what he had so much desired was on the point of being accomplished; and that it was not in the power of the count de Grasse, if so inclined, to avoid a general engagement. The signal for close action was thrown out; and, about half after seven in the morning, the action was begun by captain Penny in the Marlborough, the leading ship of the British van. The two fleets met on opposite tacks, and there being little wind, the British ships ranged slowly along, and close under the lee of the enemy's line, delivering and continuing a most tremendous fire, which the French received and returned with the utmost firmness. About noon sir George Rodney, in the Formidable, having passed the Ville de Paris, the count de Grasse's ship, and her second, so close as to be almost in contact, and having made a visible impression upon them by a fire so quick and well directed, that it was almost insupportable, stood athwart the enemy's line between the second and third ship astern of the Ville de Paris, followed and nobly supported by the Duke, Namur, and Canada; the rest of his division coming up in succession. The Formidable immediately wore round; and a signal being made for the van division under admiral Drake to tack, the British fleet thus gained the wind, and stood upon the same tack with the enemy. By this bold manœuvre the French line was effectually broke and separated, and the whole thrown into confusion: It decided the fate of the day, although it did not end the action, which continued with unremitting fury till sun-set. The rear of the British fleet being becalmed, did not for some time get into

Naval engagement between admiral Rodney and the count de Grasse.

into action, and when the breeze ſprung up, it was ſo ſmall, that ſir Samuel Hood, in the Barfleur, took an hour and a half to paſs the enemy's line only ſo far as the opening made by the Formidable, keeping up, during all this time, a moſt tremendous, well-connected fire. The French ſhips being crowded with men, the carnage on board their fleet was prodigious: Still however they fought with ſuch obſtinate bravery, as if the fate of their country depended upon the iſſue of the day. Count de Graſſe, with his own and the other ſhips in the centre, withſtood till evening all the efforts of the various ſhips that attacked him. The gallantry of captain Cornwallis of the Canada, a ſeventy-four gun ſhip, was on this occaſion the admiration of the whole fleet: Having fought the Hector, a French ſhip of equal force with his own, until ſhe ſtruck her colours, he left her to be taken poſſeſſion of by a frigate; and, as if emulous to revenge his brother's cauſe, puſhed on to the Ville de Paris, which he engaged for two hours, notwithſtanding the inequality of his force, and left her almoſt a wreck. Still, however, the count de Graſſe refuſed to ſurrender, and ſeemed unwilling to ſtrike to any ſhip without a flag. Towards ſun-ſet ſir Samuel Hood, in the Barfleur, reached the Ville de Paris, and poured in a moſt deſtructive fire. The count de Graſſe bore it for about ten minutes, when he ſtruck his flag, and ſurrendered. At this time, it is ſaid, only three men were left alive and unhurt upon the upper deck, of whom the count de Graſſe was one. Previouſly to the ſurrender of the Ville de Paris, the Hector, as already mentioned, had ſtruck to captain Cornwallis. The Ardent, of ſixty-four guns, taken by d'Orvilliers in the Britiſh Channel, was retaken; the Cæſar and the Glorieux, both of ſeventy-four guns, had alſo ſurrendered, but not till they were reduced to mere wrecks; and the Diadem, another ſeventy-four, had been ſunk by a ſingle broadſide from the Formidable in a generous exertion to ſuccour the Ville de Paris. Night

CHAP. XLVI. 1782. at length putting an end to the engagement, the Britiſh admiral threw out the ſignal for his fleet to bring-to, that he might keep it collected, and ſecure the prizes. But unfortunately the Cæſar, one of them, blew up by accident in the night of the engagement; and a lieutenant and fifty Britiſh ſeamen, with about four hundred priſoners, periſhed by the exploſion. On board the Ville de Paris were found thirty-ſix cheſts of money deſtined for the pay and ſubſiſtence of the troops in the deſigned attack on Jamaica; and it ſeems to have been ſingularly providential, that the whole train of artillery, with the battering cannon and travelling carriages meant for that expedition, were on board the ſhips now taken. The Ville de Paris was the largeſt ſhip in the French king's ſervice: She was a preſent from the city of Paris to Louis the Fifteenth; and no expence was ſpared to render the gift worthy both of the city and the monarch. Her building and fitting for ſea are ſaid to have coſt one hundred and ſeventy-ſix thouſand pounds ſterling.

Sir George Rodney in this engagement happily exemplified the great advantage derived from bringing Britiſh ſhips and ſeamen into cloſe action. The whole loſs of men on board the Britiſh fleet, in the actions of the ninth and twelfth of April, amounted only to two hundred and thirty-ſeven killed, and ſeven hundred and ſixty-ſix wounded: Whereas the loſs of the French, in the ſame actions, was computed at three thouſand ſlain, and more than double that number wounded. That the computation was not exaggerated, appears probable from the known loſs on board particular ſhips: In the Ville de Paris alone were killed upwards of four hundred, and in ſeveral other ſingle ſhips between two and three hundred. And, by the confeſſion of the French themſelves, their ſhips that eſcaped, were ſo ſhattered in the action as to be little leſs than ruined. The Britiſh line conſiſted of thirty-ſix, and the French line only of thirty-two ſhips, after the two diſabled in the action of the ninth had

had left it. But when it is confidered, that fix fhips of Hood's divifion, from the fcantinefs of the wind, never could be brought into action, it will be found that the fuperiority in number of thofe actually engaged, was at leaft on the fide of the French.

The enemy's fhips that efcaped, made off to leeward the night after the action in the beft manner they could, and before morning were entirely out of fight. Four of them ran down to the Dutch ifland of Curaçoa; but the greater part, under Bougainville and Vaudreuil, the fecond and third in command, kept together, and directed their courfe for Cape François. The next morning fir George Rodney, after receiving a report of the ftate of his fleet, attempted to purfue, but was becalmed for three days under Guadaloupe, which greatly favoured the efcape of the enemy. He afterwards, by means of his frigates, examined the French ports to windward, to difcover whether any fhips of their fleet had taken fhelter in them; and being at laft convinced that they were all gone to leeward, he difpatched fir Samuel Hood, whofe divifion had fuffered little in the action, to the weft end of Hifpaniola, in hopes of meeting with fome of their difabled fhips, whilft he himfelf followed with the reft of the fleet to join him off Cape Tiberoon. In the Mona paffage, between Hifpaniola and Porto Rico, fir Samuel Hood got fight of five French fhips, two of them of the line, and three frigates; all of which were taken, except one frigate, that efcaped by a fudden fhift of the wind. Thus the enemy by this action loft in all, eight fhips of the line, and two frigates. Sir George Rodney now proceeded to Jamaica with the prizes, and fuch of the Britifh fhips as were moft difabled, leaving fir Samuel Hood, with twenty-five fail of the line, to keep the fea, and watch the enemy's motions.

In confequence of the defeat of the French fleet, the expedition againft Jamaica was entirely given up; and the action of the twelfth of April may be faid to have terminated the war in the Weft Indies.

 The

CHAP. XLVI. 1782.

The reduction of the inconsiderable British settlement on the Bahama Islands by an armament fitted out at the Havannah, was the only hostile attempt made in that quarter of the world by either of the allied powers after the period of Rodney's victory. The reports carried to the governor of the Havannah of the weak state of the garrison, provoked the attack; and that those reports were not unfounded, seems probable from the facility with which the conquest was made. On the sixth of May, in the evening, the Spanish armament, consisting of three frigates and sixty sail of transports, having on board two thousand five hundred troops, appeared before them: And on the next day, upon the first summons, the governor, after holding two consultations, one with his council and the other with the officers of the garrison, consisting of only one hundred and seventy invalids, and the principal inhabitants of the place, agreed to surrender on terms of capitulation.

May.

Prosperity of British affairs in the East Indies.

Whilst sir George Rodney triumphed over the enemies of Britain in the West; the credit and reputation of her arms were nobly supported in the East, under the auspices of the governor-general of Bengal, Mr. Hastings, and the more immediate direction of sir Edward Hughes by sea, and sir Eyre Coote by land. The latter, under many disadvantages, amongst which a scarcity of provisions for the subsistence of the army was not the least, baffled all the attempts of Hyder Ally to regain that footing in the Carnatic, which he had lost the preceding year: And the former, although he had to contend against M. de Suffrein, one of the ablest officers in the naval service of France, who commanded a very superior force, defeated him in four hard-fought actions within the short space of seven months. But that which served most to advance and secure the British interest in India, was the means that were found to make a peace with the Mahratta States, and detach them from the interest of Hyder Ally. This event took place in the month of May; and, by by one of the articles of the pacification, the contracting parties became bound to compel Hyder Ally to reſtore all the places taken from the India Company ſince the commencement of the war. Thus the Mahrattas were not only detached from the intereſt of Hyder Ally, but proviſionally became bound to act againſt him.

Conduct of the new adminiſtration.

In Europe the principal aim of the new adminiſtration ſeem sto have been to obſtruct, as far as was in their power, the ſailing of the enemy's convoys; to protect the outward and homeward bound Britiſh trade; to prevent the Dutch fleet from forming a junction with that of France and Spain; to relieve the garriſon of Gibraltar, by furniſhing it with the cuſtomary annual ſupplies; and, in general, rather to preſerve things in their preſent ſtate during the conferences for a peace, than incur the riſk of loſs from the deſire of obtaining any poſſible advantage. In the month of April admiral Barrington ſailed on a cruize with twelve ſhips of the line to intercept a convoy ſaid to be then ready to leave Breſt, and on the twentieth fortunately got ſight of it. The convoy conſiſted of eighteen tranſports, having troops on board, and laden with proviſions and ſtores for the uſe of the French fleet in the Eaſt Indies: It ſailed from Breſt under the protection of the Pegaſe and Protecteur, of ſeventy-four guns each, l'Actionaire, of ſixty-four guns, but armed en flute, and a frigate. A general chaſe was immediately ordered by the Britiſh admiral: And, in the courſe of it, the Pegaſe was taken by captain Jarvis in the Foudroyant, l'Actionaire by captain Maitland in the Queen, and eleven or twelve of the tranſports by the other ſhips of the ſquadron. After this ſucceſsful cruize admiral Barrington returned to Portſmouth about the end of the month. Intelligence being received about this time, that the Dutch fleet was ready to ſail from the Texel, lord Howe, with a ſuitable ſquadron, was diſpatched to the coaſt of Holland to watch its motions. The Dutch fleet, inſtead of being only in a ſtate of preparation for coming out, had already ſailed;

CHAP. XLVI. 1782. June.

failed; but, upon receiving intelligence of lord Howe's destination, returned again into port, where it quietly remained during the time of his lordship's cruize, which lasted about a month before he carried his squadron back to Spithead. About the beginning of June the combined fleets of France and Spain, under the command of the count de Guichen and don Louis Cordova, failed from Cadiz; and in its progress to the northward took eighteen ships of a fleet of British merchantmen, bound for Newfoundland and Quebec, chiefly laden with provisions. The rest of the merchantmen, amounting to about ten sail, with the ships of war appointed for their convoy, made their escape. As the combined fleet proceeded to cruize about the mouth of the Channel, great apprehensions began to be entertained for the safety of a homeward-bound Jamaica fleet that had sailed under the convoy of only three ships of the line. The utmost exertions were therefore made to forward the equipment of the Channel fleet, that it might proceed to sea for its protection: But with all that could be done, not more than twenty-two sail of the line were in readiness in the beginning of July. With these lord Howe received orders to put to sea; and he accordingly sailed from St. Helen's on the second of the month. It does not appear that his lordship, during his cruize, either saw the combined fleet, or that for whose protection he sailed: But fortunately the latter got safe into the Channel on the thirtieth of July; and about ten days after, the British fleet returned into port.

Repulse and discomfiture of the Spaniards and French before Gibraltar.

In the mean time the mighty preparations made by the king of Spain, for the reduction of Gibraltar, and the vast expectations formed from them, drew the attention of all Europe towards that fortress. The successive disappointments which the Spaniards had already met with, it would seem, ought to have taught them wisdom, and induced them to abandon the attempt as hopeless; especially as their arms might have been employed in other quarters more

more beneficially to themſelves, and conſequently more injuriouſly to Great Britain: But their obſtinacy and perſeverance ſeemed to increaſe with their diſappointments, and the difficulties which they had to ſurmount. Towards the cloſe of the former year, their advanced works upon the Iſthmus, after being completed at a vaſt expence, were demoliſhed in one night by a ſucceſsful ſortie from the garriſon. The guns and mortars mounted upon the batteries were ſpiked, and the batteries themſelves ſo effectually ſet on fire, that before morning they were nearly conſumed. After this misfortune, the enemy ſeem to have principally relied on an attack by water with floating batteries. The plan of theſe batteries was the contrivance of the chevalier d'Arcon, a French engineer of ſome diſtinction. They were to be of ſuch thickneſs and ſtrength as to be impenetrable by ſhot from the heavieſt cannon, and to be conſtructed of materials calculated to reſiſt the action of fire. From ſhells they were to be protected by a ſloping roof, which by means of a mechanical contrivance might be raiſed or lowered at pleaſure. Thus ſecured, ſuch a ſhort diſtance might be choſen, that the heavy artillery with which they were to be mounted, could not fail in a little time to ruin the works of the garriſon, and render an aſſault practicable. The engineer had the addreſs to repreſent his ſcheme in ſo favourable a point of view, that the moſt flattering hopes of its ſucceſs were entertained, and no expence was ſpared to complete the machines according to his plan. Whilſt they were in a ſtate of preparation, the duke de Crillon, after his ſucceſs at Minorca, was appointed to command the Spaniſh army before Gibraltar: That army was reinforced by twelve thouſand auxiliary French troops; and to add ſplendour to the ſcene, two of the French princes of the blood, the count d'Artois, and the duke de Bourbon, with a number of the firſt nobility, both of France and Spain, repaired to the Spaniſh camp. The battering machines required ſo much time in

CHAP. XLVI. 1782.

preparation that they were not in readineſs before the beginning of September, about which time the combined fleet of France and Spain arrived in the bay. When joined by the ſhips already at Algeſiras, it conſiſted of forty-eight or forty-nine ſhips of the line. The battering machines were ten in number, and were commanded by admiral Don B. Moreno: They were mounted with one hundred and fifty-four pieces of heavy braſs cannon, and had on board upwards of ſix thouſand men, a great proportion of which were artillery-men, thirty-ſix being allotted for the ſervice of each gun. They had alſo on board a number of ſpare guns to replace any that might be damaged in action. To give the utmoſt effect to the attack, it was propoſed that when the battering ſhips ſhould take their ſtation, the Spaniſh gun and mortar boats, of which they had a great number, ſhould place themſelves ſo as to flank the Britiſh batteries on the water, and if poſſible drive the artillery-men from their guns. The combined fleet was to cover and aſſiſt the battering ſhips: And to diſtract the attention of the garriſon, a furious cannonade was to commence from all the batteries on the Iſthmus. An immenſe number of large boats, that had been collected from all the ports in Spain, were alſo to be in readineſs to carry over the bay and land troops in the fortreſs as ſoon as the battering ſhips ſhould produce their expected effect. The plan being arranged, and every thing in readineſs, the battering ſhips got under way about ſeven in the morning of the thirteenth of September, and between nine and ten anchored in a regular line, between the Old and New Mole, at moderate diſtances from each other, and about half a mile from the Britiſh works. Immediately a furious cannonade began, not only from them but from all the enemy's numerous artillery upon the Iſthmus, which was returned by the garriſon with ſhowers of ſhells and red-hot balls towards every quarter from whence the attacks were made. The hills all around were covered with ſpec-

tators

tators to behold a ſcene beyond deſcription grand, awful, and terrific. So fiercely did the garriſon return the enemy's cannonade, that continued torrents of fire and ſmoke ſeemed to iſſue from every quarter of the rock: But the attention of the beſieged was principally fixed on the battering ſhips, which for ſome time appeared to anſwer every expectation that had been formed from them. Neither ſhot or ſhells ſeemed to affect them. At length, about two o'clock, ſmoke was ſeen to iſſue from the upper part of Don Moreno's ſhip: And the people on board were diſcovered uſing fire-engines, and pouring water into the ſhot-holes. Not long afterwards the prince of Naſſau's ſhip, the next in ſize to the admiral's, was obſerved to be in the ſame condition. This ſight, without doubt, animated the garriſon to freſh exertion, and had an oppoſite effect upon the enemy. The other battering ſhips were evidently affected with the ſituation of their admiral and his ſecond, ſo that the fire of the garriſon had gained a viſible ſuperiority before the evening, and it was continued with unremitting fury during the night. About one in the morning the flames burſt forth on board the two ſhips already mentioned, and ſeveral of the others were viſibly on fire. Signals of diſtreſs were now made; and boats were ſent off from the ſhore to their aſſiſtance. Captain Curtis, who commanded the Britiſh naval force at Gibraltar, ſeized this opportunity of completing the deſtruction of thoſe machines, which had created ſo much apprehenſion. He ſtationed his gun-boats ſo as to flank the line of the battering ſhips, and by keeping up a conſtant fire, to cut them off from that aſſiſtance which they had begun to receive from the ſhore. In this dreadful ſituation the battering ſhips remained during the reſt of the night, expoſed to a direct fire from the garriſon, and a raking fire from the gun-boats, cut off from aſſiſtance, and the flames increaſing every inſtant. When day-light appeared, it preſented ſuch a ſcene of diſtreſs, that every hoſtile idea was for a time extinguiſhed,

tinguiſhed, in compaſſion for the miſerable wretches who yet remained on board the enemy's battering ſhips. The fire from the fortreſs ceaſed: And the braveſt exertions were made by captain Curtis and the Britiſh ſeamen, at the riſque of their own lives, to reſcue the Spaniards from the ſurrounding flames. By their intrepid efforts about four hundred of them were ſaved from inevitable deſtruction. Nine of theſe battering machines blew up ſucceſſively in the courſe of the day; and the tenth was burnt by captain Curtis, after he found that ſhe could not be brought off. In this attack by ſea the enemy were ſuppoſed to have loſt about one thouſand five hundred men, including the priſoners and wounded. Thus diſaſtrouſly ended the laſt attempt of the Spaniards for the reduction of Gibraltar.

About the time of this attack lord Howe ſailed from the Britiſh channel with the grand fleet, conſiſting of thirty-four ſhips of the line, to eſcort a number of tranſports carrying troops, and laden with thoſe ſtores and ſupplies which were to enable general Elliott to continue his brave defence. His lordſhip was much delayed on his paſſage by contrary winds; but he at laſt reached the Straits, and entered them on the eleventh of October. That ſame evening part of the tranſports got ſafe to Gibraltar: The reſt, from the ſtrength of the current, were unexpectedly carried paſt it into the Mediterranean. Lord Howe followed with his fleet, and collected them; and by the eighteenth conducted the whole ſafely into the bay, where they diſembarked the troops, and landed their cargoes. Fifteen hundred barrels of gunpowder were alſo ſpared from the fleet, as an additional ſupply to the garriſon. To the honour of his lordſhip it is to be remarked that the whole of this ſervice was ſucceſsfully performed in the face of the combined fleet, which lay in Gibraltar Bay at the time of his arrival. The enemy either depended ſo greatly upon the ſuperiority of their number, or were ſo much

Relief of Gibraltar.

overawed

overawed by their opponent's masterly disposition for defence, that they did not attempt to molest him. The relief of Gibraltar being effected, his lordship on the nineteenth took advantage of an easterly wind to repass the Straits, and enter the Atlantic. The combined fleet followed, and on the twentieth, towards sunset, bore down so far as to commence a distant cannonade, which was held in so much contempt by the British commander, that although three of their number were firing upon his own ship, he did not deign to return a shot. They afterwards made an attempt to cut off some ships in the rear; but were so warmly received as to be obliged to sheer off with loss. In the morning, the combined fleet being a great way to windward, and apparently steering for Cadiz, lord Howe proceeded on his return to England, dispatching on his way eight ships of the line to the West Indies, and six to the coast of Ireland.

During these transactions a partial change had taken place in the British administration. Upon the death of the marquis of Rockingham, about the beginning of July, the earl of Shelburne was appointed first lord of the treasury in his stead. In consequence of this appointment, or from some other cause, Mr. Fox, and several other principal members of administration, resigned their offices, and were succeeded by others, more in the interest of the earl of Shelburne.

Those changes, however, did not affect the negotiations carrying on at Paris for putting an end to the war. Mr. Oswald, a British merchant, and the particular friend of president Laurens, who had been so long confined in the Tower, was appointed to negotiate with the American commissioners; and Mr. Thomas Grenville first, and afterwards Mr. Fitzherbert, were successively deputed to treat with the ministers of the other allied powers. The later events of the present year had all a tendency to bring the powers at war more

CHAP. XLVI. 1782.

nearly upon a level. At the close of the former year, Great Britain seemed nearly overwhelmed by the strength and successes of her numerous foes: But the signal victory obtained by sir George Rodney in the West Indies, with the blow given to the naval force of France in that quarter of the world; the defeat of the Spaniards before Gibraltar, and the successful relief of its garrison, in the view of a superior fleet; and the splendid effects of the British policy and arms in Asia; raised the reputation of the nation to its wonted level amongst the powers of Europe, and gave her additional weight, either for the accomplishment of peace, or the farther prosecution of the war. But the derangement of the finances, both of France and Spain, was the principal cause which disposed those powers to listen to the terms of accommodation.

The internal distresses in every quarter of the revolted colonies, the mutinous disposition of their armies, from the want of all necessary supplies, and the utter inability of the congress to furnish them, were well known to the American commissioners, and strongly prompted them not to let pass the present opportunity of restoring to their country the blessings of peace. The negotiations with those commissioners were therefore first brought to a conclusion: And, on the thirtieth of November, provisional articles of peace were signed by Mr. Oswald on the part of Great Britain, and by Mr. John Adams, Benjamin Franklin, John Jay, and Henry Laurens, on the part of the revolted colonies, now the United States of America, which were not to take effect until peace should be agreed upon between Great Britain and France. By those articles the thirteen united states of America were acknowledged to be free, sovereign, and independent: The limits of their country were ascertained, as far as was practicable, by natural boundaries; and these limits were extended so far to the westward as to contain within them an immense extent of territory, partly unsettled, and partly still inhabited by the Indians, the original proprietors: A right was granted to them to fish on the banks and coasts of Newfoundland, in the Gulph of St. Laurence, and on the coasts, bays, and creeks of all the other British dominions in America, and to cure and dry their fish in any of the unsettled bays, harbours, and creeks of Nova Scotia, Magdalen Islands, and Labrador: It was stipulated that creditors on either side should meet with no lawful impediment in the recovery of their debts: A recommendation was to be made by congress to the legislatures of the different states, to restore the confiscated estates and properties of real British subjects; also of those resident within the British lines in America, who had not borne arms against the United States; and also of persons of any other description, upon their refunding to the present possessors the price *bonâ fide* paid by such possessors at the time of purchasing such estates: It was stipulated, that no future confiscations should be made, nor any prosecutions commenced, for the part taken by any person during the war, nor any future loss be suffered by any one, either in his person, liberty, or property, on that account: It was agreed that prisoners on both sides should be set at liberty, and that the British posts within the United States should be evacuated with all convenient speed: The navigation of the Mississippi to remain free and open to the subjects of both powers. And should any place be taken on either side, before the arrival of these articles in America, such place to be restored without compensation.

The preliminary articles of peace with France, upon which those with America were to take effect, were not signed till the twentieth of January 1783. Those with Spain were executed at the same time. The general ground of those articles was the mutual restitution of all places taken on either side during the war, with some few exceptions. France was to retain Tobago and Senegal; Spain, Minorca and West Florida; and Great Britain to cede East Florida to Spain.

Spain. The Dutch Iſland of St. Euſtatius, and the provinces of Demerara and Iſſequibo, to be reſtored by France to the United Provinces. At the ſame time a ſuſpenſion of hoſtilities with the Dutch was agreed upon, until terms of peace with that nation could be finally adjuſted.

Thus ended the moſt extenſive, difficult, and burdenſome war in which Great Britain was ever engaged *.

THE AMERICAN REVOLUTION is the grandeſt effect of combination that has yet been exhibited to the world: A combination formed by popular repreſentation and the art of printing †. So vaſt a force as was exerted by Great Britain had never been ſent to ſo great a diſtance, nor reſiſted by any power apparently ſo unequal to the conteſt. The military genius of Britain was unimpaired; ſhe

* The foreign debt of America, incurred by the war, amounted to 7,885,085 dollars; the domeſtic debt to 34,115,290 dollars; ſo that taking the dollar at 4s. 6d. ſterling, the foreign and domeſtic debt amounted to 9,450,084 pounds ſterling, the intereſt of which, at 6 per cent. which is the intereſt generally paid in America, amounts to 567,005 pounds. The war is computed to have coſt Great Britain 115,654,914 pounds, and the additional annual burden, in conſequence of that war, 4,557,575 pounds, from January 1775 to the peace in 1783. America is ſaid to have loſt by the ſword and natural deaths in the army and navy, not leſs than 100,000 men. The number of men killed in the Britiſh ſervice, during the war, amounted, by the returns at New York, to 43,633.

By computation the whole territory of the American States contains a million of ſquare miles, in which are 640 millions of acres; of theſe, 51 millions are water, which being deducted, the total amount of acres of land in the United States of America is 589 millions.

† CAPTAIN NEWTE, in his philoſophical and very intereſting Tour in England and Scotland, having delineated Scotland and the North of England as ſhaped by the hand of nature, is led, from the names of places, to ſpeak of the geographical knowledge, and the natural quickneſs in general, of mankind in a ſavage ſtate. On this ſubject he ſays: "In the country of the "Illionois, a chief of the Caſcaſkias conceived the ſublime idea of uniting all Indian nations "and tribes into one grand alliance, offenſive and defenſive. If this had been realized, Dr. "Franklin's confederation of the thirteen States would have cut but a poor figure on the "American continent, and the natural man would have outdone the philoſopher."

rofe with elaftic force under every blow; and feemed capable, by the immenfity of her revenues, of wearying out, by perfeverance, the adverfity of fortune: But wifdom, vigour, and unanimity, were wanting in her public councils. The eloquence of fome legiflators in oppofition to government; the narrow views of minifters at home; and the mifconduct of certain commanders abroad, through a feries of pufillanimity, procraftination, difcord, and folly; brought this country, in fpite of the gallant efforts of the Britifh officers and foldiers by land and fea, the juftice of their caufe, the firmnefs of their fovereign, and the general vows of the people, to a crifis, which has not indeed been followed (fo limited are our profpects into futurity) by all that calamity which was generally apprehended, but which, neverthelefs, although the national character, for fpirit and enterprife, was abundantly fuftained by individuals, cannot be regarded otherwife than as a difgrace to the Britifh: Since it exhibited, in our public conduct, the triumph of party over genuine patriotifm, and a fpirit of peculation and pleafure prevailing in too many inftances, over military difcipline, and a fenfe of military honour. The Britifh minifter did not poffefs that towering genius which is alone fitted, in difficult and turbulent times, to overcome the feditious, and roufe the remifs to their duty. Though a man of fine talents, as well as an amiable difpofition, he was conftitutionally indolent: And, befides this, there was not that degree of cordiality and perfect unanimity that the minifter was led to fuppofe amongft the friends of his majefty's government in America. It is, perhaps, a matter of doubt whether the loyalifts were not, on the whole, too fanguine in their expectations. But it is the nature of men to cherifh the hope of relief with an ardour proportioned to the greatnefs of their misfortunes.

On the whole, the Britifh government did not proceed on any grand fyftem that might control particular circumftances and events;

 but

CHAP. XLVI.

but ſtudied to prolong their own authority by temporary expedients. They courted their adverſaries at home, by a ſhare of power and profit; and the public enemies of the ſtate, by partial conceſſions. But theſe availed much more to the eſtabliſhment of new claims, than all the declarations of parliamentary rights and royal prerogatives with which they were accompanied, did to maintain the rights of eſtabliſhed government: For facts quickly paſs into precedents; while manifeſto is oppoſed to manifeſto, and argument to argument. Had the meaſures adopted by Britain, been adopted in time*, perhaps they would not have been adopted in vain. Their conceſſions, as well as their armaments, were always too late. Earlier conceſſion, or an earlier application of that mighty force which was at the diſpoſal of the commanders in chief in 1777, might perhaps have prevented or quaſhed the revolution.

While the natural ſtrength and ſpirit of Great Britain were embarraſſed and encumbered with the diſadvantages and errors now enumerated, the Americans, in ſpite of a thouſand difficulties and wants, by the energy of liberty, the contrivance of neceſſity, and the great advantages ariſing from the poſſeſſion of the country, ultimately attained their object. The Americans, indeed, were not fired with that enthuſiaſtic ardour, which nations of a warmer temperament, in all ages, have been wont to diſplay in the cauſe of freedom. But they were guided by wiſe councils; they were ſteady and perſevering; and, on all great occaſions, not a little animated by the courage of general Waſhington, who has been proverbially called a Fabius, but in whoſe character courage, in fact, was a feature ſtill more predominant than prudence. The American generals, having the bulk of the people on their ſide, were made acquainted with

* Beſides a mighty navy, Great Britain had a force in America, amounting nearly to 42,000 men, beſides from 25,000 to 30,000 loyaliſts, who were actually enliſted in the ſeveral provincial corps raiſed during the war.

every

every movement of the Britiſh army, and enabled, for the moſt part, to penetrate their deſigns: To obtain intelligence, on which ſo much depends, was to the Britiſh commanders a matter of proportionable difficulty. The Americans had neither money nor credit: But they learned to ſtand in need only of a few things; to be contented with the ſmall allowance that nature requires; to ſuffer, as well as to act. Their councils, animated by liberty, under the moſt diſtreſſing circumſtances, took a grand and high-ſpirited courſe, and they were finally triumphant.

The Revolution of America, though predicted by philoſophy, was generally conſidered as a remote contingency, if not a thing wholly ideal and viſionary. Its immediate cauſes were altogether unforeſeen and improbable. It came as a ſurpriſe upon the world: And men were obliged to conclude, either that the force of Great Britain was ill-directed, or that no invading army, in the preſent enlightened period, can be ſucceſsful, in a country where the people are tolerably united.

I N D E X.

N. B. The Numerals refer to the Volumes, and the Figures to the Pages.

A.

ABERCROMBIE, colonel, killed at Bunker's Hill, i. 128.

Abercrombie, colonel, expedition of, i. 372. His fortie from York, ii. 410.

Adams, Samuel, a leader in the provincial congrefs of Maffachufett's Bay, i. 120. Excepted from the proffered pardon by government, 124.

Allegany mountains, i. 3.

Allen, Ethan, furprifes Ticonderoga, i. 131. And Crown Point, 132.

America. See *Colonies*, *Congrefs*, and the feveral provinces by name.

Americans, fertility of genius of, i. 167. Driven out of Canada, 178. Defeated at Long Ifland, 195. Glorious retreat of, 197. Difheartened by their loffes, 206. Animofities between the northern and fouthern troops, 207. Burn part of New York, 209. Principle of their army, 222. Become defpondent on the fuccefs of the Britifh arms, 225. Of Carolina and Virginia, defeat the Indians, 250. Fleet of, burnt, 305. Difcontents of, on the difappointment at Rhode Ifland, ii. 38. Alliance of, with France, unites and roufes the Britifh, 75. Army of, with that of France, befieges Savannah, 127. Attacks the Britifh lines, 130. Repulfed, 131. Junction of forces under Sumpter, Clarke, and Brannen, 228.

André, major, adventure of, ii. 250. His amiable and refpectable character, 251. General Clinton ftrongly folicits Wafhington in his favour, 252. In vain, *ibid*. His melancholy fate, *ibid*.

Arbuthnot, admiral, fucceeds fir George Collier in North America, ii. 152. Co-operates with fir Henry Clinton at Charleftown, 179.

Arnold, general, propofes to Wafhington to furprife Quebec, i. 138. Difficulties of the enterprife, *ibid*. Difappointed, 139. Summons it to furrender, *ibid*. In great want of artillery, 140. Attacks the city, 141. Wounded, *ibid*. Raifes the fiege, 168. Engaged in the action at Still Water, 336. Diftinguifhes himfelf greatly, 337. Wounded, fighting againft Burgoyne, 341. Difgufted with the American fervice, ii. 247. Caufes of that difguft, 248. Forms a fcheme for delivering up a ftrong poft to the Britifh, 249. Efcapes to New York, 251.

Affemblies, provincial, of America, oppofe the ftamp-act, i. 35. Diffolution of, by the governors, hurtful by diffufing difcontent through the country, 72.

B.

Baillie, colonel. See *Eaft Indies*.

Barrington, admiral, fails with the Britifh fleet againft St. Lucie, ii. 86. Engagement with the French, 97. Wounded, 98.

Boston, riotous opposition to the stamp-act, i. 39. Opposes the board of customs, 59. Riot about the customs, 63. People propose holding a convention, 64. Insult the soldiers, 74. Riot, 75. Meeting at, 82. Petition the governor against the judges, *ibid.* Assembly at, denies the right of parliament to legislate for the colonies, 83. Petition his majesty to remove the governor, 84. Riot about the introduction of tea, 86. People destroy the cargoes of two ships laden with tea, 87. Port shut by an act of parliament, 88. Proceedings in, on hearing of the port-bill, 92. Exhort the other colonies to give up all trade with Britain, 93. Cause of, espoused by the other colonies, 96. Meeting of delegates at, 100. Effects of shutting the port of, 112. Blockade of British troops at, 166. Evacuated by the British, 167. Riot at, between the American and French sailors, ii. 38. See *Massachusett's Bay.*

Britain, government of, resolves to persist in coercive measures, i. 122. People of, generally for the war, 258. Sends commissioners to treat with the Americans, ii. 6. Breaks with France, *ibid.* With Spain, 156. Differences between, and Holland, 257. See *Parliament*, ministers, admirals, generals, and foreign nations by name.

Bunker's Hill, description of, i. 125. Battle of, 126. Errors committed in this action, 129.

Burford, the American colonel, defeated by colonel Tarleton, ii. 193.

Burgoyne, general, appointed commander of the British northern army, i. 318. Employs the savages, 319. Number of his troops, 320. His manifesto, 321. Impolicy of threatening manifestoes, 322. Invests Ticonderoga, *ibid.* And also Mount Independence, *ibid.* Which forts are abandoned by the Americans, 323. The ships of the Americans are destroyed at Skeenesborough, 324. He compels the Americans to abandon their works, *ibid.* Part of his army engages the Americans at Hubberton, 325. Defeats them, *ibid.* Stratagem of the Americans, 326. Blameable for the route he took, 327. Meets with great difficulties at Fort Edward, 330. Sends colonel Baum with a detachment to Bennington, *ibid.* Which is defeated, 333. This defeat owing to Burgoyne's neglecting to send a sufficient number of troops, *ibid.* Colonel St. Leger detached by, invests Fort Stanwix, 334. Obliged to raise the siege, 335. That failure owing to the inadequacy of the force given him by Burgoyne, *ibid.* Opposed by general Gates, who takes the chief command of the Americans, 336. Action at Still Water, 337. Neither party is victorious, *ibid.* The British might have gained a decisive victory, had Burgoyne not burdened himself with more artillery than was necessary, *ibid.* The battle showed that the Americans could fight with courage and conduct on plain ground, *ibid.* Distressed situation of his army, 338. Deserted by the Indians, 339. Retreats to Saratoga, *ibid.* His army nearly surrounded, 340. Bloody battle with the Americans, 341. General Fraser killed, *ibid.* Loss of the British very considerable, *ibid.* Critical situation of the British army, 342. He attempts to draw the Americans to a general engagement, *ibid.* Which they decline, *ibid.* Attempts to retreat to Fort George, 343. Impracticable, *ibid.* Attempts to retreat to Fort Edward, *ibid.* But finds his retreat cut off, *ibid.* Is completely surrounded, 344. Endeavours to force the Americans to fight, *ibid.* Makes overtures to general Gates for a convention, 345. Proposals on both sides, 346—348. Convention ratified, 349. Reflections on this event, 352. The conduct of Burgoyne discussed, 353. Attempts to throw the blame of his miscarriages on sir William Howe, and on lord George Germaine, 355. General cause of his miscarriage, 356. His deportment after his misfortune, 357. Throws himself into opposition, *ibid.*

Burke, the celebrated Edmund. See *Parliament.*

Byron, admiral, sails from Portsmouth with a fleet for North America, ii. 25. Fleet of, dispersed by storms, 46, 47. He arrives at St. Lucie, 91. Sails to St. Christopher's to protect the homeward-bound trade, 92. Returns to St. Lucie, 96. Action with the French, 97. The French admiral avoids a close engagement, 98. French fleet escapes during the night, 99. The loss of the French the greater, 100.

C.

Calder's, sir Henry, services at the reduction of St. Lucie, ii. 87.

Cambridge, in New Hampshire, provincial congress at, i. 113. Hostile designs of, *ibid.* Passes resolutions for preparing arms, *ibid.* American army assembles at, 121.

Camden, lord, applied to by the assembly of Massachusett's Bay to second their petition to the king, i. 60. Dismissed from his office of lord-chancellor, 73.

Campbell, lieutenant-colonel (late sir Archibald), taken

taken prisoner at Boston, i. 168. Mal-treated, *ibid.* Letter of, to sir William Howe, descriptive of the cruelties and indignities he suffered, *ibid.* Expedition of, with Fraser's Highlanders, to destroy the American privateers, ii. 42. Expedition under, against Georgia, 48. Operations and brilliant successes, 66, 67. Masterly movements, by which he compelled the Americans to fight, 70. Defeats them, 71. Reduces Savannah, *ibid.* Praise of him and his troops, 72. Reduces Sunbury, 103. Expedition of, to Augusta in Georgia, 106. Is ordered to retire from Georgia, and return to Savannah, 108.

Canada, act for settlement of, i. 90. People of, addressed by the assembly of Massachusett's Bay, 103. Description of, 130. Act for settlement of, not popular, because deemed arbitrary, *ibid.* See *Carlton*, and other commanders by name.

Carlton, general (now lord Dorchester), unpopular in Canada, because active in framing the act for settlement of, i. 137. Neglects the merchants, cultivating the noblesse only, *ibid.* Almost taken by the Americans, 139. But escaping, arrives at Quebec, *ibid.* Summoned by Montgomery to surrender Quebec, *ibid.* Refuses, *ibid.* Gallant defence of Quebec by, 140. The Americans are forced to raise the siege, 170. Expedition against the Cedars, *ibid.* Which capitulates, 172. He equips an armament against Crown Point and Ticonderoga, 252. Difficulty of the enterprise, 253. Defeats the Americans on the Lakes, 255. Reduces Crown Point, 256. Returns to St. John's, 257. Offended with the appointment of general Burgoyne to the command of the northern army, 318. Much superior to Burgoyne in skill, experience, and knowledge of the country, 319. Resigns his government, *ibid.*

Carlisle, earl of. See *Commissioners*.

Carolina, North and South, originally the same settlement, planted in the reign of Charles II., i. 10. Receives a constitution from Mr. Locke, which, though apparently wise in theory, not reducible to practice, *ibid.* Danger of speculative refinement in legislation, *ibid.* Experience the only sure guide, *ibid.* Proceedings of North Carolina against their governor, Mr. Martin, 151. Who is forced to leave the province, 152. Proceedings of South Carolina against lord William Campbell, their governor, *ibid.* Efforts of the British in North Carolina, 178. Of the Scotch emigrants, *ibid.* Riots between the American French sailors, ii. 19. Many of the inhabitants join the British after the reduction of Charlestown, 192. Again become disaffected to Britain, 198. Many of them found guilty of treachery, 213. For which some are punished, 214.

Chamblée Fort taken, i. 135.

Charlestown, near Boston, description of, i. 125.

——— South Carolina, description of, ii. 111. See *Clinton*, sir Henry.

Christopher's, St. island of, reduced by the marquis de Bouillé, ii. 425.

Climate, greater degrees both of heat and cold in North America than in the same latitudes of Europe, i. 3. Effect of, on the manners of the several provinces, 5, 6.

Clinton, sir Henry, services of, at Bunker's Hill, i. 127. Makes an attempt upon the southern provinces, 183. Issues a proclamation, inviting the Americans to return to their allegiance, *ibid.* Which produces no effect, *ibid.* Makes an attempt against Charlestown, 184. Which proves unsuccessful, 186. Sails for New York, 187. Expedition of, against Rhode Island, 220. Successful, *ibid.* An unwise measure, 221. Expedition of, up the North River, 358. Reduces Forts Montgomery and Clinton, 360. Appointed to succeed sir William Howe as commander in chief, 388. Evacuates Philadelphia, ii. 14. Marches to New York by Sandy Hook, 17. Battle of Freehold Court House, 19. Arrives at New York, 23. Endeavours to make a descent at New London to destroy the American privateers, 39. The unfavourable wind prevents him from landing, *ibid.* Sends several detachments to destroy the American privateers, 41. Attacks Verplank's Neck and Stoney Point on the Hudson River, 140. Reduces them, 141. Expedition of, against Connecticut, 142. Receives a reinforcement, 152. Expedition of, to South Carolina, 176. Fortifications of Charlestown described, 178. Garrison of, 179. Siege of, 181. Reduction of, 185. Great praise of the officers and troops by sir Henry, 187. Address to the people of South Carolina, 190. Departs for New York, 195. Applies to general Washington in behalf of major André, 251. In vain, 252.

Collier, sir George, arrives at Long Island with a reinforcement from England, i. 199. Commands the fleet on the American station, ii. 134. Operations, 136. Expedition of, to destroy the magazines of the Americans, *ibid.* Sails to assist general Maclean at Penobscot, 150.

150. Relieves the garrison, 151. Resigns his command, 152. Succeeded by admiral Arbuthnot, *ibid.*

Colonies naturally seize all opportunities of ascertaining their independence, i. 1.

——, American, had no reason to expect that they could maintain independence against England, but the contrary, i. 1, 2. Geographical description of, 1—3. Divided into northern, middle, and southern, 4. Diversities of manners and inhabitants, and their causes physical and moral, *ibid.* History of the settlement of, 7—9. State of commerce and revenue at the peace 1763, 10—12. See each by name.

Commissioners for peace (earl of Carlisle, governor Johnstone, and Mr. Eden, with the general and admiral for the time being) arrive in America, and enter on their office, ii. 9. Send their secretary (the famous Dr. Adam Ferguson) to state to the congress the terms which they were authorised to offer, 11. To whom a passport is refused by the Americans, *ibid.* Their proposals rejected by the Americans, who will hear of no terms without the previous acknowledgment of their independence, 12. Return to England, 48. Review of their proceedings, 49. Remonstrance of, on the detention of Burgoyne's troops, 57. Manifesto of, 58.

Concord, detachments sent to destroy stores at, by general Gage, i. 116. See *Lexington.*

Congress, general, proposed by the assembly of Massachusett's Bay, ii. 37. Held at New York, 39. Professes loyalty to the king, 41. Affected moderation of their proceedings, *ibid.* Effects of the meeting of, 42. Associations are entered into against the importation of British manufactures, *ibid.* Sowed the seeds of revolution, by uniting the grievances and complaints of the several colonies, 57. Meets at Philadelphia after the passing of the Boston port-bill, 102. Unanimous in reprobating the act, and in denying the right of parliament to tax the colonies, *ibid.* Number of delegates, *ibid.* They fix that each colony should have a vote, 103. Precautions to prevent the whole of their deliberations from transpiring, *ibid.* They publish a declaration of the state of affairs in Massachusett's Bay, *ibid.* Send a letter to general Gage, *ibid.* Issue a declaration of rights and grievances, *ibid.* Ground their claim of rights on the law of nature, on the British constitution, and on their several charters, 104. Petition the king, 105. Address the people of Britain, *ibid.* Recommend the conduct and cause of the Bostonians in an address to the colonies, 106. Address the Canadians, *ibid.* Their address to Canada a very able and hurtful performance, *ibid.* Designs of, on Canada, 130. Send deputies to England to petition the king, 153. They are told that no answer would be given, 154. Proceed to form a constitution for America, 188. New declaration of rights, 189. Of independence, *ibid.* Affect to ground their assertion of independence on the king's refusal to redress their grievances, *ibid.* Vigour of, 228. Wise measures of, for increasing the army, *ibid.* Animating and successful address to the people, 229. Committee of, forms a plan of a constitution for America, 244. Approve of, and transmit the plan to the several states, 248. Pass resolutions inimical to the conciliatory plan of Britain, ii. 9. Refuse to fulfil the terms of Gates's convention with Burgoyne, 7. Manifestly guilty of injustice, 8. Will not admit Dr. Ferguson to lay the British proposals before them, nor listen to any terms, without the previous acknowledgment of their independence, 12. Gross violation of the convention of Saratoga, 58. From considerations of policy averse to a general exchange of prisoners, 2 3.

Connecticut, means of subsistence, and employment of the inhabitants, i. 4. Chiefly occupied in agriculture and pasturage, *ibid.* Planted by Puritans flying from the bigotted tyranny of Laud, 7. Expedition of Clinton against, ii. 142. Great loss to the inhabitants, 144. The people think themselves neglected by Washington and the congress, *ibid.* Murmurs thereupon, *ibid.*

Connelly, Mr. his scheme for attacking the Americans from the back settlements, i. 150. Frustrated, 151.

Coote, sir Eyre. See *East Indies.*

Cornwallis, lord, penetrates into the Jerseys, i. 219. Strikes terror into the Americans, *ibid.* But is restrained by an order from general Howe from taking advantage of their panic, 220. Takes the command of the Jersey army, 236. Endeavours to bring Washington to a battle, who retreats, *ibid.* Marches to the relief of Brunswick, 238. Takes possession of Philadelphia, 295. Commands a strong detachment against South Carolina, ii. 184. Left by Clinton commander in chief there, 195. Administration of, in South Carolina, 196. Wise regulations for the government of the province, 197. Sets out for Camden, 205.
Battle

Battle there with general Gates, 208. Victorious, 209. Conduct as a general universally admired, 211. Marches into North Carolina, 215. A wise measure, but not followed by success in proportion to its wisdom, *ibid.* Obliged to return to South Carolina, 224. Falls sick, *ibid.* Difficulties of the army, 225. Great attachment of the army to their general, *ibid.* Arrives at Wynnesborough, 226. Joined by a large reinforcement under general Leslie, 317. Marches from Wynnesborough, 330. Crosses the river Catawba, 327. Joined by colonel Webster, pursues general Morgan, 330. Drives general Greene from North Carolina, 332. Greene re-enters that province, 333. Lord Cornwallis retires, 334. Battle with general Greene at Guildford, 337. Victorious, 343. But with very considerable loss, 344. Retires towards Cross Creek, 348. Disappointed in his expectations of being joined by the loyalists, *ibid.* Issues a proclamation, inviting the Americans to return to their allegiance, 351. Benevolent and feeling letter to announce the death of colonel Webster to his father at Edinburgh, 353. Sends messengers to lord Rawdon, who are unfortunately intercepted, *ibid.* Embarrassment of, 354. Determines to march through North Carolina into Virginia, 355. Marches from Wilmington, *ibid.* Joined by general Arnold, 385. Endeavours to strike a blow at the marquis de la Fayette, 386. Who decamps and escapes with his army, 387. Part of his troops are sent for by Clinton, 393 Sets off from Williamsburgh, 394. Crosses James River, and retires to Portsmouth, 395. Evacuates Portsmouth, 396. French and American forces join, 397. He concentrates his troops at York and Gloucester, *ibid.* The combined armies, under Washington and Rochambeau, invest York Town, 409. Cornwallis's troops make several sallies, 410, 411. Surrenders to general Washington, 413. Efforts of sir Henry Clinton for the relief of, 414. Effects of the capture of, 420.

Crillon, duke of, commands the Spanish army before Gibraltar, ii. 439.

Crown Point, important situation of, i. 131. Reduced by the Americans, 132. Abandoned by them, 323.

Cunningham, his History of Great Britain, a clear, accurate performance, superior to any in the language for particular and intelligible accounts of military operations, i. 374.

D.

Darby, admiral, succeeds Geary, ii. 264.

Dawson, captain of the Renown of fifty guns, engages with a French ship of eighty-four, ii. 31.

Deane, Silas, American ambassador at Paris, ii. 5.

Delaware, lower counties on, i. 9. Seizure of posts on, unaccountably neglected by general Howe, 238.

D'Estaing, sails with a fleet from Toulon to North America, ii. 25. Comes to anchor off New York, 26. Arrives at Rhode Island, 27. Intends to co-operate with the American general Sullivan, to expel the British from Rhode Island, 28. Frustrated, *ibid.* Is opposed by lord Howe, 29. Offers battle to the British admiral, *ibid.* Who declines fighting on account of the wind, *ibid.* The British admiral appearing at last willing to fight, is separated from him by a storm, 30. His fleet is shattered, 32. Which he refits at Boston, *ibid.* Sails to the West Indies, 47. Attempts to relieve St. Lucie, 87. But is repulsed, 92. Is reinforced by De Grasse, but declines an engagement with the British admiral, *ibid.* On the departure of Byron commences offensive operations, *ibid.* Reduces St. Vincent's, 93. Attacks Grenada, 94. Which surrenders, 95. Battle with the British, 98. Declines a close engagement, though superior in force, 99. Departs for Hispaniola, 102. Sails to North America, 122. Arrives off Georgia, *ibid.* Summons Savannah to surrender, 125. Conduct, precipitate, *ibid.* Attacks the British lines, 130. Repulsed with great loss, 131. Raises the siege, 132. Returns to France, *ibid.*

Digby, admiral, conducts home the Spanish prizes, ii. 257.

Dominica, conquered by the French under the marquis de Bouillé, ii. 84.

Donop, colonel, a German, bravery and conduct of, at Red Bank, i. 302. Wounded, *ibid.*

Dunmore, earl, and governor of Virginia, sends to government a very unfavourable state of the province, 143. Unpopular, makes a conciliatory proposition to the council of Virginia, 144. Rejected, 145. Apprehensive of a design to detain his person, 146. Narrowly escapes being seized, *ibid.* Retires to Norfolk, *ibid.* Issues a proclamation to establish martial law, 147. Emancipates all slaves who should join the British, *ibid.* Attempts to dislodge the enemy from their strong posts, 148. Compelled, with the loyalists, to abandon Norfolk, *ibid.* Joins the army at New York, 149.

E.

Eden, Mr. See *Commissioners for Peace.*

England. See *Britain.*
——, New, physical and moral characters of the people of, i. 5. Carries on a clandestine trade with Spanish America, 15. Displeased with the commercial regulations of Britain, 21. Denies the authority of parliament to levy taxes, 21. Endeavours to excite opposition in the other colonies, 26. Active in opposing parliamentary supremacy, 28. See *Massachusett's Bay*, and the other provinces.
Erskine, sir William, routs a considerable body of Americans, i. 281.

F.

Fergusson, Dr. Adam, appointed secretary to the commissioners for peace, ii. 10. Refused a passport, 11. See *Commissioners for Peace.*
——, major, appointed to command the South Carolina loyalists, ii. 192. Commands a body on the frontiers of North Carolina, 220. His high character as an officer, *ibid.* Attacked and surrounded by a great number of Americans, 222. Intrepid courage and masterly conduct of, *ibid.* Falls, 223.
——, George, governor of Tobago, attacked by the French, ii. 287. Sends an express to Barbadoes, *ibid.* Assistance does not arrive in time, *ibid.* Surrenders the island, 288.
Fleet, English. See *Keppel*, *Pallifer*, *Hood*, *Rodney*, &c.
——, French. See *D'Estaing*, *de Grasse*, &c.
——, Spanish. See *Spain.*
——, Dutch. See *Holland.*
——, Russian. See *Neutrality.*
Florida, East, preparations of the Americans to attack, ii. 105. General Lincoln takes the command of their troops.
——, West, reduction of, ii. 168. Invaded by the Spaniards, 169. Reduced by them, *ibid.* Honourable terms granted to the inhabitants, *ibid.*
Fort Chamblée taken by the American general Montgomery, i. 135.
—— Saint John taken, i. 136.
—— Edward, expedition of colonel St. Leger to, i. 330.
—— Stanwix, invested by St. Leger, 334. Siege of, raised, i. 334.
—— Montgomery reduced by colonel Campbell, i. 360.
—— Clinton, reduced by sir Henry Clinton, i. 360.
Fox, Hon. C. J. made secretary of state, ii. 423. Plan of his administration respecting the war, 437.
France, manifests a disposition hostile to Britain, i. 259. Harbours American privateers, *ibid.* Ships of, accept commissions from the Americans, 260. Carry on depredations against the British trade, *ibid.* Busy in warlike preparations, *ibid.* Treatment of Portugal, the ally of Britain, *ibid.* Enters into commercial and political treaties with the Americans, ii. 5. Acknowledges the independence of America, *ibid.* Notifies the treaties to Britain, 6. Which is considered by Britain as a declaration of war, *ibid.* Fleet of, sails for America, 25. Complains that Britain had commenced hostilities, 77. Fleet of, engages Keppel, 78. Combined fleets of, and of Spain, threaten an invasion of Britain, 162. Appear off Plymouth, 163. An armament from, arrives at Rhode Island, under Rochambeau and Ternay, 245. Chief command of the troops given to Washington, *ibid.* French forces join the Americans against lord Cornwallis, 397. French fleet enters the Chesapeak, 399. Partial action between De Grasse and admiral Graves, 400. The armies of, and of America, arrive at Williamsburgh in Virginia, 405. Encamp before York Town, 408. York and Gloucester invested, 409. British army under lord Cornwallis surrenders, 413. The French, under the marquis de Bouillé, take the Dutch island St. Eustatius from the British, 416. A French and Spanish armament besieges St. Philip's in Minorca, 424. Compels general Murray, the commanding officer, to capitulate, 425. The marquis de Bouillé reduces St. Christopher's, *ibid.* Engagement between De Grasse and sir Samuel Hood, 426. Engagement between De Grasse and admiral Rodney, 432. French completely defeated, 433. See *D'Estaing*, and other French commanders by name.
Franklin, Dr. Benjamin, appointed agent for the province of Massachusett's Bay at the British court, i. 84. Gets into his possession some letters of governor Hutchinson, *ibid.* Transmits the letters to the provincial assembly, *ibid.* Which excites a flame against the governor, *ibid.* Is dismissed from his office of deputy post-master-general for America, 85. Retires to America, 192. Becomes a leading member in the congress, *ibid.* Applied to by lord Howe concerning peace, 193. His answer, *ibid.* Appointed ambassador to the court of France, ii. 5. Principally instrumental in concluding an alliance with that power.
Fraser, general, repulses the Americans at Trois Rivieres, 177. Engages the Americans, 324. Is killed, 325.

G.

Gage, general, notifies to the assemblies of Massachusett's Bay that they must remove to Salem, i. 95. Finds it necessary to order troops to Boston, 98. Fortifies Boston, 100. Receives a letter from the first congress, declaring their rights and grievances, 103. Admonishes the congress of Massachusett's Bay to desist from their unconstitutional proceedings, 108. Proclamation of, prohibiting seditious meetings, *ibid.* Sends a detachment to destroy military stores of the Americans, 116. The detachment driven back to Boston, 118. Is, by the provincial congress of Massachusett's, declared an enemy, 121. Receives a reinforcement from England, 124. Offers the Americans a pardon if they would return to their allegiance, *ibid.* Engagement with the Americans at Bunker's Hill, 126.

Galloway, Mr. an evidence in the inquiry concerning general Howe's conduct, i. 398.

Gaming, of every species, permitted and sanctioned in the British army, i. 309. General bad effects of that vice on the human mind and body, *ibid.* Particular bad effects of, on the army, *ibid.*

Garth, general, takes possession of New Haven in Connecticut, ii. 142.

Gates, general, takes the command of the American army in the north, i. 336. Commands at the battle of Still Water, 337. Declines hazarding a general engagement, 342. Humanity of, to the sick and wounded of the British, *ibid.* Completely surrounds the British army at Saratoga, 343. Orders of, against plundering, 344. Receives proposals from general Burgoyne for a convention, 345. The convention at length, 349. Generous behaviour of, to the unfortunate British, 352. Appointed commander of the southern army, ii. 200. Defeated at Camden, 209. Resigns the command, 233.

Geary, admiral, takes the command of the Channel fleet, ii. 263. Falls in with a fleet of French merchantmen, *ibid.* Resigns, 264.

Germaine, lord George, secretary of state for the American department, accused by Burgoyne of being the cause of his discomfiture, i. 355. Satisfactorily vindicates himself from that charge, *ibid.* Accused by sir W. Howe, 394. Asserts that Howe had power to act according to circumstances and his own discretion, 396.

Gibraltar, repulse and discomfiture of the Spaniards and French before that fortress, ii. 438. Relieved by a fleet under the command of lord Howe, 443.

Grafton, duke of, prime minister, i. 52. Procures an act for duties on articles imported to America, 53. Resigns, 73. But continues on the side of government, *ibid.*

Grant, general, expedition of, to the West Indies, ii. 48. His operations there, 86. Defeats the French, 90.

Greene, general, succeeds Gates in the command of the southern army, ii. 233. Harasses the British outposts in South Carolina, 318. Driven out of North Carolina, 332. Re-enters it, 333. Action with lord Cornwallis near Guildford, 337. Defeated, 343. Marches against lord Rawdon at Camden, 353. Compels Fort Watson to surrender, 360. Encamps at Mill Creek, 361. Besieges Ninety-six, 364. Summons it to surrender, 368. Raises the siege, 373. Pursued by lord Rawdon, *ibid.* Battle between, and colonel Stuart, near the Eutaw Springs, 378. Both parties claim the victory, 380.

Grenville, George, prime minister, measures of, concerning the colonies displeasing to the inhabitants, i. 26. Proposes the stamp-act, 27. Which is strenuously opposed by the parliament, 28. But carried by a great majority, *ibid.* Dismissed from his office, 27. His dismission favourable to the colonies, *ibid.* Causes of his dismission, *ibid.*

Grey, major-general, defeats the American general Wayne, i. 295. Expedition of, to Buzzard's Bay, ii. 39. Destroys the American privateers on the Acushnet River, 40.

H.

Hampshire, New, insurrection in, i. 111.

Hancock, John, riot at Boston concerning a ship belonging to him, i. 63. Made president of the congress of Massachusett's Bay, 108.

Hardy, sir Charles, takes the command of the Channel fleet, ii. 161. Is passed by the combined fleets, 162. His death, 263.

Hastings, Mr. his conduct as governor-general of Bengal, ii. 436.

Heister, de, the Hessian general, routs the Americans at Flat Bush, i. 195.

Henry, Patrick, of Virginia, violent speech of, on the stamp-act, i. 33.

Holland, differences of, with Great-Britain, ii. 257. Carries naval stores to France, 258. The ships of, seized by the British, *ibid.* Suspension of treaties of, with Britain, 262. Commercial treaty between her and America, 272. War between her and Britain, 273. Dutch island of St. Eustatius captured, 280.

Dutch settlements on the Spanish Main taken, 281. Action between the British and Dutch fleets at the Dogger Bank, 296.

Hotham, commodore, his important services on Hudson's River, i. 362. In the Preston, a ship of fifty guns, fights the Tonant, a French ship of eighty, ii. 231. Commands a squadron sent to the West Indies, 232.

Honduras, attack upon, by captain Luttrell, ii. 270.

Howe, general, his conduct at Bunker's Hill, i. 127. Evacuation of Boston, 166. Embarks for Halifax, *ibid.* Censured by many for not going rather to Long Island, 190. Arrives at Sandy Hook, *ibid.* Lands the British troops at Staten Island, 191. Detail of his forces, *ibid.* Is joined by lord Howe with a large reinforcement from Britain, *ibid.* The late arrival of the troops a great injury to the British cause, 192. Empowered, with lord Howe, to treat with the Americans, *ibid.* Opens the campaign, and puts the enemy to flight at Long Island, 195. Declines attacking the American lines, 196. The Americans escape from the island, 197. His orders for pursuit too late, 198. Makes overtures for peace to the Americans, 200. Takes possession of New York, 205. Engages the Americans at White Plains, 212. Censured for dividing his army into small unconnected detachments, 229. Blamed for giving an important command to colonel Rhalle, 234. Disaster at Trenton attributed to that cause, *ibid.* Neglects to fortify the posts on the Delaware, 235. Suffers the Jerseys to be recovered, 239. His conduct contrasted with that of general Washington, 241. Closes the campaign 1776, 243. Opens the campaign 1777, 277. Endeavours to bring Washington to action, 284. Relinquishes the Jerseys, *ibid.* Proceeds to Chesapeak Bay, *ibid.* Action at the Brandywine, 292. Defeats the Americans, 293. But does not improve the victory, *ibid.* Action at German Town, 298. Suffers the Americans to remain undisturbed the whole winter at Valley Forge, 310. General censure of his conduct, 311. Resigns the command of the army, 381. Imputes his resignation to the want of support from administration, *ibid.* That allegation manifestly unfounded, 382. Mischianza, a festival in honour of, 385. Du Portail's letter respecting his conduct, 386. Returns to England, 393. Complains of defamation, *ibid.* Obtains a parliamentary inquiry, 396. Reflections on that inquiry, 398.

——, lord, arrives at Sandy Hook with a fleet from England, i. 190. Empowered, with his brother, to treat with the Americans, 192. Writes to doctor Franklin and general Washington respecting peace, 193. Conference at Staten Island with a committee from congress, 200. Attacks Mud Island, 301. Takes it, 304. Defends the harbour of New York with a small force, ii. 26. Sails to Rhode Island to oppose d'Estaing, 30. The fleets separated by a storm, *ibid.* Resigns the command to admiral Gambier, 33. See *Howe*, general.

Huyne, major-general, services of, at Charlestown, ii. 187.

Hutchinson, governor of Massachusett's Bay, i. 84. Letter of, disgusts the assembly, *ibid.* Petitions for a removal of, from his office, *ibid.*

J.

Jamaica, and other West India islands. See *West Indies*, *Barrington*, *Byron*, and *Rodney*.

Jarvis, captain (now admiral sir J.), captures the Pegase, a French line-of-battle ship, ii. 437.

Jersey, attempt on, by France, ii. 131. Repelled, *ibid.*

——, New, peopled by the Dutch and Swedes, i. 8. Operations there, see *Cornwallis* and *Washington*. For loss of, see *Howe*, general.

Indies, West, clandestine trade of, with the Spanish settlements, beneficial both to these islands and to Britain, i. 14. Distress of, from the war, 258. Expedition of general Grant and commodore Hotham to, ii. 48. Alarm of, on the successes of the French, 102. Quieted by the departure of d'Estaing for Hispaniola, *ibid.* See *Barrington*, *Byron*, and *Rodney*.

——, East, Pondicherry taken by sir Hector Monro and sir Edward Vernon, ii. 82. An armament sets sail for, under general Meadows, 306. Carnatic invaded by Hyder Ally, 307. Defeat and destruction of a detachment under colonel Baillie, 309. Gallant behaviour of the British, and barbarity of Hyder, 310. The Carnatic ravaged by Hyder, 312. The presidency of Madras apply to the governor-general of Bengal for assistance, *ibid.* Vigorous measures of Mr. Hastings and the supreme council for their defence, 313. Sir Eyre Coote takes the command of the army at Madras, *ibid.* General Coote defeats Hyder in several battles, 314. Sir Edward Hughes takes Hyder's seaports, *ibid.* Sir Eyre Coote prevents Hyder Ally from returning to the Carnatic, *ibid.* Sir Edward Hughes defeats Suffrein, the French admiral, in four battles, *ibid.* Hastings detaches the Mahrattas from the interests of Hyder Ally, 437.

Indian ſavages employed by Burgoyne, i. 319. Deſert him, 339.

Johnſtone, governor, one of the commiſſioners for peace. See *Commiſſioners*. Sends private letters to members of congreſs, ii. 50. Obſervations on theſe letters, 54. Withdraws from the commiſſion, *ibid.* Makes prizes of four Dutch Eaſt Indiamen, 305.

Jones, Paul, action between, and a Britiſh convoy, ii. 164. Deſperate courage of, 165.

Judges, American, new regulations concerning, i. 81. Diſguſting to the Americans, 82.

Jury, trial by, claimed by the Americans on the promulgation of the plan for trying certain crimes in England, though committed in America, i. 70.

K.

Keppel, admiral, appointed to the command of the Britiſh fleet in the Channel, ii. 75. Hoſtilities commenced between France and England, 76. Engagement between the Belle Poule, a French, and the Arethuſa, an Engliſh frigate, 77. Engagement between the Engliſh and French fleets, 79. Difference between Keppel and Palliſer, 81. Keppel tried, *ibid.* Honourably acquitted, *ibid.* Rejoicings in London on his acquittal, *ibid.* Receives the thanks of the houſe of commons, *ibid.* Is appointed firſt lord of the admiralty, 423.

Knyphauſen, general, arrives at Long Iſland with a body of Heſſians, i. 212. His ſervices at Fort Waſhington, 217. At Brandywine, 297. His conduct at Freehold Court Houſe, ii. 20. Left commander of the garriſon of New York, 177. His prudent meaſures for the defence of New York, 239.

L.

Lee, the American general, taken priſoner, i. 226. His character and abilities, 227. His conduct at Freehold Court Houſe meritorious, though it met with puniſhment, ii. 20.

Leſlie, major-general, his important ſervices at Charleſtown, ii. 187. Sent by Clinton to cooperate with Cornwallis, 226. Ordered to join him at Wynneſborough, *ibid.* Joins him there, 318. Commands part of the army at the battle of Guildford, 338.

Liberty, too exalted ſpeculative ideas of, lead into moſt fatal conſequences in practice, i. 10.

Lincoln, the American general, commands in the ſouthern colonies, ii. 105. Arrives at Charleſtown, *ibid.* Eſtabliſhes his head-quarters at Puryſburgh near Savannah, 106. Attempts to ſtraiten the Britiſh quarters, 108. Fruſtrated by general Prevoſt, 109. Attacks the Britiſh under colonel Maitland, 117. Repulſed, *ibid.* Is abandoned by a great part of his troops, 119. Retires to Charleſtown, 179. Summoned by Clinton to ſurrender, 180. His firm anſwer, 181. Capitulates, 185.

Locke, the diſtinguiſhed philoſopher, forms a code of laws for Carolina, apparently excellent in theory, but by experience proved ineffectual, i. 10.

Loyaliſts, American, exert themſelves in Virginia, and afterwards retire to Norfolk with lord Dunmore, i. 447. In North Carolina ſet up the king's ſtandard, 178. Join with the Scotch Highland emigrants, 179. Divided in their councils, 180. Proceed to Wilmington, *ibid.* Attack the Americans, 182. Defeated, *ibid.* Thoſe of Jerſey and New York pillaged and inſulted, 242. Conduct of thoſe of Philadelphia on the departure of the congreſs, 230. Stratagem of, 371.

Luttrell, commodore, reduces the Spaniſh fort Omoa, ii. 170.

Lutwych, commodore, deſtroys the American gallies at Skeneſborough, i. 324.

M.

Macartney, lord, governor of Grenada, ſurrenders the iſland, ii. [illegible]

Maclean, colonel, character of, i. 134. His vigorous meaſures to oppoſe the Americans in Canada, *ibid.* Haſtens to the defence of Quebec, 138. Directs the artillery and fortifications, 139.

———, colonel Francis, forms a ſettlement in Penobſcot, ii. 148. Attacked by the Americans, 150. His vigour and conduct diſappoint the attempts of the enemy, 151. Relieved by ſir George Collier, 152.

Maitland, major, expedition of, up the Delaware, i. 376. Deſtroys a great quantity of ſtores and proviſions, and a number of ſhips, *ibid.* Succeeds general Prevoſt in the command at John's Iſland, ii. 116. Attacked by general Lincoln, 117. Whom he repulſes, *ibid.* Marches to the aſſiſtance of general Prevoſt at Savannah, 125. His death and character, 133.

———, captain of the Queen, captures l'Actionaire, a French ſhip of war, ii. 437.

Manners, influence of climate and ſoil on, illuſtrated in the northern, middle, and ſouthern colonies of North America, i. 5—10.

Maryland, firſt ſettlement of, i. 9. Carries on a con-

considerable trade with Lisbon and the Mediterranean, 15. Delegates of, secede from congress when declaring America independent, 189.

Massachusett's Bay, settled by Puritans flying from the persecution of Laud, i. 7. Soon begins to flourish, 8. Pleased with duties imposed by parliament, 21. Assembly denies the right of the British parliament to levy taxes, 22. That denial imputed to the continuance of the republican principles of the first settlers, *ibid.* Proposes assembling a general congress, 36. This proposal generally approved of, 37. Tumults in, on the promulgation of the stamp act, 57, 58. Disagreement between the inhabitants and the governors, *ibid.* Assembly of, enters into a general consideration of grievances, 59. Petition of, to the king, *ibid.* Sends a circular letter to the other colonies, stating grievances, 60. That letter severely condemned by government, but most favourably received by the other colonies, 61. Assembly required to rescind the resolution which produced it, 62. Which they refuse, and are therefore dissolved, *ibid.* The discontents of the people break out into open violence, *ibid.* They form associations for distressing the trade of Britain, 67. Displeased with new regulations about the judges, 81. Assembly denies the right of the British parliament to legislate for them, 83. Apologize afterwards for their violence, 84. Pray for the removal of their governor, *ibid.* The people enter into associations against the importation of tea, 86. The people, by the recommendation of the assembly, enters into resolutions for breaking off all trade with Britain, 97. Violence of the populace, and civil government dissolved, *ibid.* Army and military stores begin to be collected, 100. Delegates of the county of Suffolk meet at Boston, *ibid.* The conduct of the people receives the unqualified approbation of the general congress, 104. Provincial congress held at Salem, 108. Interferes in the regulation of the militia, 109. Provide arms and military stores, *ibid.* Provincial congress meets at Cambridge, 113. Prepares for hostilities, *ibid.* An army raised, 120. See *Boston.*

Mawhood, lieutenant-colonel, expedition under, to assist the loyalists in Jersey, i. 367. Action at Quintin's Bridge, 368. Ingratitude of an American soldier, *ibid.* Action at Hancock's Bridge, 369.

Mathew, major-general, commands at King's Bridge, ii. 235. Sends a detachment under colonel Norton to attack a strong post at Young's House, 236. Publicly thanks the colonel and men for their services, 238. Gazette account of that affair mutilated, 239.

Meadows, general, his gallant and judicious conduct at St. Lucie, ii. 89. Masterly disposition for the defence of his post, 90. Wounded, *ibid.* Sails for the East Indies, 305.

Mississippi, the navigation of that river by the peace to remain free to particular powers, ii. 445.

Moncrieff, captain, his exertions and services as chief engineer at Savannah, ii. 133. His important services as chief engineer at Charlestown, 187. His great abilities and professional character, *ibid.*

Montgomery, the American general, marches to attack Canada, i. 133. Takes Fort Chamblée, 135. St. John's, 136. Montreal, *ibid.* Summons Quebec to surrender, 139. Attempts to storm it, 140. Killed, 142. His character, *ibid.*

Montreal taken by the Americans, i. 130.

N.

Newfoundland, fishery of, suffers by the dispute of Britain with America, ii. 58. St. Pierre and Miquelon, islands near, taken from the French, ii. 83.

Newte, captain Thomas, curious and interesting extract from his Tour in England and Scotland, ii. 446.

New York, trade of, i. 14. General congress held at, 39. Resolutions against the stamp act, 40. (See *Congress.*) Assembly refuses to supply the troops with the articles directed in the new mutiny act, 52. Legislative function of the assembly suspended by act of parliament, 59. But afterwards restored, 67. Preparations to impede the progress of the British, 191. British forces take possession of, 205. Part of it burned by the Americans, 208.

North, lord, made prime minister, i. 73. Introduces a plan for repealing all duties in America, excepting on tea, *ibid.* Increases the demands of the colonists, 79. See *Parliament.*

Norton, colonel. See *Mathews.*

Neutrality, armed, an account of, ii. 259.

O.

Omoa, a Spanish fort, key of the Bay of Honduras, taken by the British, ii. 172. Heroism of a British seaman, *ibid.*

Opposition members support the cause of the Americans,

ricans, i. 69. Their speeches are the means of raising a party at home favourable to the Americans, *ibid.* Defend the conduct of the inhabitants of Massachusett's Bay, 70. Impede the measures of government respecting America, 91. Their forebodings excite the Americans to act as they had foretold, 91. Propose treating with the congress, 159. Support and vindicate general Burgoyne after the disaster of Saratoga, 357. Also general Howe on his return from America, and insist on an inquiry into the conduct of the war, 390.

Oswald, a British merchant, negotiates the peace on the part of Great Britain, ii. 444.

P.

Paper currency of the colonies, an act passed for restraining, i. 18. State of, 19. Observations on paper currency, 24.

Paine, Thomas, powerful effects of his pamphlet called Common Sense in producing the declaration of American independence, i. 190. Writes the Crisis, a severe satire on general Howe's festival, 396.

Pallifer, admiral, commands the rear of the Channel fleet under Keppel, ii. 80. Difference between, and Keppel, 81. Tried and acquitted, *ibid.*

Parker, sir Peter, expedition of, against Rhode Island, i. 220.

——, sir Hyde, commands an armament against Georgia, ii. 48. Success of that expedition, 71. Engages the Dutch fleet near the Dogger Bank, 296.

Parliament, act of, for the suppression of smuggling, i. 12. For imposing duties on certain kind of merchandise in America, 17. Objects of this act, the commerce of the colonies, and revenue of the state, *ibid.* Act for regulating the paper currency of America, 18. These acts occasion great discontents in America, 25. Act for imposing stamp duties, 27. (See *Stamp act.*) Opposed in America as unconstitutional, 40. The right of parliament to levy taxes on the Americans denied by the congress, *ibid.* Act for repealing the stamp act, 45. Accompanied by an act declaring that parliament had a right to legislate for America in every case, *ibid.* Act for providing for the more comfortable subsistence of the troops in America, 51. Act for levying duties on imports into America, 53. Attacked in colonial pamphlets and newspapers, 56. Addresses his Majesty on the disorderly state of Massachusett's Bay, 68. Discontinues all the duties in America, except on tea, 73. Act for exporting tea free of duty, 85. Disgusting to the New Englanders, *ibid.* Act for shutting the port of Boston, 88. Act for changing the constitution of Massachusett's Bay, 89. Act for the better government of Massachusetts, 90. For the settlement of Canada, *ibid.* For prohibiting the most disaffected colonies from trading with any country but Britain, 122. Makes a conciliatory proposition to America, 123. Not accepted, 124. His majesty's speech at the opening of, after commencement of hostilities, 155. Arguments for and against coercive measures, 157, 158. Coercion resolved on, 158. Measures adopted accordingly, 160. Takes the American petition into consideration, 161. Rejects it, 162. Conciliatory bill proposed by Mr. Burke, *ibid.* Rejected, 163. Act for prohibiting all intercourse with America, *ibid.* Conciliatory motion by Mr. Hartley, *ibid.* Rejected, *ibid.* By the duke of Grafton, 164. Rejected, 165. Debates on the proclamation of the Howes, 264, 265. Bill for securing persons accused of high treason, 269. Motion by lord Chatham for addressing the king against the war, 272. Manly speech of the speaker to his majesty respecting the public money, 275. Bills for reconciliation with America, ii. 3.

Patterson, general, services of, at Charlestown, ii. 18.

Penobscot, British settlement in, by general Maclean, and successful defence of, ii. 151.

Pensylvania, planted by Penn with Quakers, i. 9. Assembly of, secedes from congress, 189. See *Philadelphia.*

Penn, William, settles Pensylvania, i. 9.

——, Richard, presents a petition from congress to his majesty, i. 153.

Percy, lord (now duke of Northumberland), sent with a detachment to seize the military stores at Concord, near Boston, i. 116. Annoyed by the Americans, *ibid.* Acquires a high character as an officer, 120. Commands a body at Long Island, 194. Carries the advanced posts of the enemy's camp, 218.

Pitcairne, major, killed at Bunker's Hill, i. 128. His character, *ibid.*

Pitt, William (earl of Chatham), inimical to the system respecting America proposed by government, i. 26. His motion for an address to the throne for peace, 271.

Pigott, major-general, his successful defence of Rhode Island, ii. 35.

Prescot, general, carried off by the Americans, i. 286.

Prevoſt, general, defeats the Americans, ii. 109. Unſucceſsful attempt of, againſt Charleſtown, ii. 2. Departs for Savannah, 116. Beſieged there by the Americans and French, 127. His lines attacked, 130. Repulſes the enemy with great loſs, 132.
Putnam, general, commands a detachment from Connecticut, i. 121. Account of, *ibid.* Makes good his retreat from New York with the American army, i. 207.

R.

Rawdon, lord (earl of Moira), commands a diviſion of the forces at the battle near Camden, ii. 209. Commendation of his vigour and enterpriſe, *ibid.* On the ſickneſs of lord Cornwallis takes the command of the ſouthern army, 224. Difficult march of, in South Carolina, 225. Hardſhips encountered by the troops, *ibid.* Commands the troops in South Carolina, whither Greene alſo marches, 351. Attacks the camp of general Greene at Hobkirk's Hill, 354. Defeats Greene, 356. Maſterly generalſhip of, 358. Returns to Europe, 364.
Rhode Iſland, inſurrection in, i. 111. Attempt upon by Clinton and Parker, 220. Conquered, *ibid.* Attempt of the Americans on, ii. 39.
Rivers, on the eaſtern ſide of North America, navigable to near their ſource, and thus favourable to commerce; but open to naval war, i. 5.
Rockingham party come into adminiſtration, i. 37.
Rodney, admiral (late lord), appointed to command the Britiſh fleet in the Weſt Indies, ii. 299. Convoys the proviſions to the relief of Gibraltar, *ibid.* Revives the naval glory of England, 256. Takes a fleet of Spaniſh merchantmen, *ibid.* Gains a complete victory over the Spaniſh fleet, 257. Relieves Gibraltar, *ibid.* Gains a moſt glorious victory over the French, 432.

S.

Saratoga. See *Burgoyne* and *Gates*.
Savannah, beſieged by the French and American armies, ii. 127. Siege is raiſed, 130.
Simcoe, major, ſtratagem of, i. 374.
Smuggling, prevalent to a very degree in the colonies, i. 12. Regulations to prevent, *ibid.* Produce murmurs among the Americans, 13. Affect branches of fair and lucrative trade, 14, 15.
Spain, favours the Americans, i. 260. Joins the confederacy againſt Britain, ii. 158. Blockade of Gibraltar, 167. Spaniards reduce Weſt Florida, 169. Attack the Britiſh logwood-cutters in the Bay of Honduras, *ibid.* Attack Gibraltar, but are repulſed, 438—442. See *France.*
Stamp-act, oppoſed by a powerful party at home, i. 29. Cauſes of that oppoſition, 32. Not a new ſyſtem, but a continuation of the old, 44. Produces alarms in Britain as well as America, 45. Repeal of, *ibid.* Declaratory act paſſed, *ibid.* Repeal of, cauſes great joy in America, *ibid.* Conſidered as the dawn of independence, *ibid.*
St. Leger, expedition of, i. 330. Inveſts Fort Stanwix, 334. Obliged to raiſe the ſiege, 335.
Sumpter, the American colonel, defeated by Tarleton, ii. 213. Joins Clarke and Brannen, 228.

T.

Taxation. See *Parliament*, *Stamp-act*, &c.
Tarleton, colonel, defeats the American colonel Burford, ii. 193. Surpriſes and defeats the Americans under colonel Sumpter, 212. Repels Marion, the American partizan, 227. Action with the Americans at Blackſtock's Hill, 231. Defeated by general Morgan, 323.
Ticonderoga, capture of, i. 131.

V.

Vaughan, general, commands a detachment of Clinton's army, i. 306. Inveſts Fort Fayette, ii. 192.
Virginia, ſettled in the beginning of James the 1ſt's reign, i. 6. General aſſembly of, oppoſe the ſtamp act, 31. Paſs a reſolution for a faſt on account of the Boſton port-bill, 97. Propoſe an annual congreſs of the citizens, 95. See *Cornwallis*.

W.

Wallace, ſir James, deſtroys the American gallies in Æſopus Creek, i. 366.
Wayne, general, ſurpriſes Stoney Point, ii. 145.
Waſhington, general, ſmallneſs of his army at the opening of the campaign 1776, i. 192. Applies to general Howe for the releaſe of Lee, 227. Surpriſes the Britiſh troops at Trenton, 231. This victory animates the Americans, 233.

Marches into the Jerseys, 235. His judicious retreat, 236. Action with colonel Mawhood, 237. Recovers a great part of the Jerseys, 239. Wisdom and activity of, in the winter campaign, and well-timed proclamation, 291. Distressed situation of his army, 308. Prepares to impede the British in their retreat from Philadelphia, i. 116. Battle of Freehold Court-house, ii. 19. Sends a detachment to encourage the disaffected Carolinians, 199. Distresses of this army. See *Howe*, *Clinton*, and *Cornwallis*.

Webster, lieutenant-colonel, his conduct at the battle of Camden greatly praised, ii. 211. High general character, *ibid.* Death of, see *Cornwallis*.

Y.

York, New, granted by Charles II. to his brother, i. 8. Averse to giving up trade with Britain, 112. Refuses to accede to the resolutions of congress, *ibid.* Local situation of, 205. Taken possession of by the British, *ibid.* British garrison of, in danger from the rigour of the winter, ii. 233.

THE END.

Directions for placing the Plates.

VOL. I.

BATTLE of Bunker's Hill, — to face page 127
Battle of Long Island, or Brooklyn — — 195
Fort Washington, afterwards called Knyphausen — 210
Battle of White Plains — — 214
Camp at Saratoga — — 352
Attack of Fort Clinton — — 362
Fayette's Position, Barren Hill Church, and Matson's Ford 377

VOL. II.

Siege of Savannah — — 132
Siege of Charlestown — — 185
Battle of Camden — — — 210
British Troops crossing the Catawba — 329
Battle at Guildford Court-House, North Carolina — 342
Battle at Hobkirk's Hill, South Carolina — 358
Position of the English and French Fleets immediately previous to the Action of the 5th of September 1781 — 400
Siege of York and Gloucester in Virginia — 412

www.ingramcontent.com/pod-product-compliance
Lightning Source LLC
Chambersburg PA
CBHW051855300426
44117CB00006B/406
* 9 7 8 3 3 3 7 0 1 0 7 8 2 *